THE MOST TRUSTED NAME IN TRAVEL: **FROMMER'S**

FROMMER'S EasyGuide to
LONDON 2019

6th Edition

P9-DCN-064

NOV – – 2018

By Jason Cochran

The neo-Gothic Tower Bridge spans the Thames near the Tower of London.

FROMMER'S STAR RATINGS SYSTEM

Every hotel, restaurant, and attraction listed in this guide has been ranked for quality and value. Here's what the stars mean:

★ Recommended
★★ Highly Recommended
★★★ A must! Don't miss!

AN IMPORTANT NOTE

The world is a dynamic place. Hotels change ownership, restaurants hike their prices, museums alter their opening hours, and buses and trains change their routings. And all of this can occur in the several months after our authors have visited, inspected, and written about these hotels, restaurants, museums, and transportation services. Though we have made valiant efforts to keep all our information fresh and up-to-date, some few changes can inevitably occur in the periods before a revised edition of this guidebook is published. So please bear with us if a tiny number of the details in this book have changed. Please also note that we have no responsibility or liability for any inaccuracy or errors or omissions, or for inconvenience, loss, damage, or expenses suffered by anyone as a result of assertions in this guide.

CONTENTS

**Soldiers guarding
Windsor Castle.**

A LOOK AT LONDON

Throw away any preconceived images you may have of a gray, button-downed, or reserved London. The weather may occasionally be soggy, but London is a Technicolor cornucopia of tantalizing things to do and see. From the eye-popping contemporary art at the Tate Modern to the jumble of upscale shopping arcades near Piccadilly Circus, from the bird's eye views over the Thames from the London Eye to the bursting picnic hampers spread out in the green grass of Regent's Park—London dazzles wherever you look. Whether you explore the city by foot, boat, tube, or bus, expect a bright mixture of architecture, creativity, and culture to meet you around every turn.

Trafalgar Square has always been one of London's great meeting places.

LONDON ATTRACTIONS

The Millennium Bridge, which was the first new pedestrian crossing over the Thames in more than a century, links St Paul's Cathedral to the front door of the Tate Modern. Cross it on one of our walking tours (p. 265).

The iconic Beefeaters lead the guided tours of Tower of London (p. 166).

Centuries of imperial wealth are on display in the vaults of the Crown Jewels at the Tower of London.

Taking a slow spin over the Thames on the London Eye (p. 156).

The popular V&A museum (p. 151) honors the most beautiful decorative objects in the world.

The lion and the chained unicorn of the royal coat of arms of the United Kingdom.

Antiquities from all of recorded time pack the huge British Museum (p. 114), Britain's most popular tourist attraction.

A visit to the Dennis Severs' House (p. 172) feels like traveling through time to 19th-century London.

Tate Modern (p. 158), a superlative contemporary art collection in a rehabbed power plant, is one of London's cultural landmarks.

The Palm House at the Royal Botanic Gardens (p. 183) is one of the most important iron-and-glass Victorian buildings in the world.

The country's greatest artists, writers, and performers are buried or memorialized at Westminster Abbey's Poet's Corner (p. 136).

Tate Britain (p. 134) collects the best of the country's paintings and sculpture—and it's free to visit.

Changing the Guard at Buckingham Palace (p. 130) is a popular photo op.

LONDON LIFE

You can't say you know London if you haven't taken the Tube, the world's first underground railway. Its first segments opened in 1863 and each stop has a unique design.

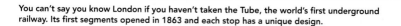

Fortnum & Mason (p. 208) is an opulent department store for gourmet foods, teas, and chocolates—it's literally the Queen's grocery store.

A LOOK AT LONDON | London Life

10 Downing Street, home of the prime minister (p. 260).

Since 1959, the stylish Ronnie Scott's (p. 245) has been London's premier club for such headliners as American trumpeter Christian Scott.

Once disused, the entire southern bank of the Thames is now alive with walkers day and night.

Locals from North London relax in Regent's Park (p. 195) where you'll find the London Zoo, an open-air theater, and vistas from Primrose Hill.

Oxford Street (p. 206) is the king of London shopping streets with major department stores such as Selfridges, John Lewis, and Marks & Spencer.

Covent Garden (p. 35), once a common man's market, is now a central district for boutique shopping, dining, street performances, theater, and pubs.

If you must indulge in the ritual of afternoon tea (and why not?), the Lanesborough Hotel's version is probably London's classiest (p. 89).

The Market Porter (p. 105) pub appeared in the Harry Potter films.

The "Eros" fountain in Piccadilly Circus is a London fixture—but does it really depict Eros? See p. 130.

The Shard (p. 160), the tallest building in Europe, is visible from every quarter of town.

Gourmands flock to Borough Market (p. 94) for local delicacies, fine street food, and elbow-to-elbow grazing.

The weekend market at Portobello Road (p. 226) is touristy but fun.

Hamleys toy store (p. 224) is a classic stop for families.

LONDON DAY TRIPS

The neoclassical Radcliffe Camera library rises above Oxford University in what poet Matthew Arnold called "the City of Dreaming Spires."

Punting on the River Cam is an essential outing for students at the University of Cambridge (p. 300).

The 8th Earl and Countess of Carnarvon still dwell under the sandstone turrets of Highclere Castle (p. 305), better known to television viewers as *Downton Abbey*.

Each year, historians uncover a few more secrets of the prehistoric monument Stonehenge, but we may never unravel all of its mysteries. See p. 304.

The Queen's favorite home, and the modern burial grounds for the royal family, Windsor Castle is easily reached from London by train. See p. 290.

The elegant sweep of the Royal Crescent, a masterpiece of Georgian neoclassical architecture, dates to the 1760s, when Bath (p. 292) was England's most fashionable spa town.

The Fashion Museum of Bath was started with the collection of Doris Langley Moore, a brilliant writer who also costumed Katharine Hepburn in *The African Queen*.

Curators at Hampton Court Palace (p. 182) fill the day with interactive performance by costumed historical characters.

THE BEST OF LONDON

Whether you realize it or not, London shaped your destiny. There's hardly a quarter of the globe that London, as the seat of England's government, hasn't changed. The United States was founded in reaction to London's edicts. Australia was peopled with London's criminals. Modern Canada, South Africa, and New Zealand were cultivated from London. India's course was irrevocably changed by the aspirations of London businessmen, as were the lives of millions of African slaves who were shipped around the world while Londoners lined their pockets with profits. That you bought this book, written in English somewhere other than in England, is evidence of London's reach across time and distance. And its dominion continues to this day: London is the world's most popular destination for foreign tourists.

London is inexhaustible—you could tour it for months and barely get to know it. Few cities support such a variety of people living in remarkable harmony. In 2016, this historically Christian country even elected a Muslim mayor. That diversity makes London like a cut diamond: Approach it from a different angle each day, and it presents an entirely fresh shape and color. From famous stories to high style, London is many things in every moment.

But at this moment, London holds its breath. Two monumental shifts—Britain's exit from its membership in the European Union (Brexit) and the passage of a beloved monarch after a record-breaking reign—will inevitably mold this place into something new, yet no one is confident about how these dual shocks will alter the color of the city and the mood of the nation. London is already an extremely difficult place to live. Locals still pay the highest rate in the world for their public transit, and it's still a brutally expensive city for housing—the average monthly rent for a one-bedroom outside the center of the city is £1,600, but the average salary is only £300 more. Will industry trickle away? Are the high times coming to an end? For now, London waits.

LONDON'S best ATTRACTIONS

- **British Museum** (p. 114): Some of the most astounding treasures of the classical world are housed in one overwhelmingly glorious neoclassical building.
- **British Library** (p. 110): The finest and rarest books on the planet, plus the Magna Carta, are laid open for your eyes.
- **Churchill War Rooms** (p. 131): A time capsule of the tense days of World War II and the most advanced biographical museum in existence.
- **Museum of London** (p. 162): Beside a remnant of a Roman wall, the city's spectacular story is retold with the nonstop dazzle of precious finds.
- **National Gallery** (p. 123): Some 2,000 masterpieces, the cream of every genre, reside at what may be the best fine art collection in the world.
- **Natural History Museum** (p. 148): For kids, it's all about the dinosaurs, but this "cathedral of nature" has major chops as a research facility, too.
- **St Paul's Cathedral** (p. 163): Sir Christopher Wren's masterpiece is the icon of London and a shrine to historic events and people.
- **Tate Modern** (p. 158): Bankside's hymn to the "shock of the new," a former power station, has just completed a milestone expansion.
- **Tower of London** (p. 166): Britain's gruesome underbelly and its glittering Crown Jewels coexist in one sprawling city castle of stone.

The 19th-century Reading Room is the stunning centerpiece of the British Museum's modernized interior courtyard.

Guards and cannons at the Tower of London still protect the legendary Crown Jewels.

- **Victoria & Albert Museum** (p. 151): Always evolving and growing, this is probably the world's finest collection of decorative arts.
- **Westminster Abbey** (p. 136): Be awed by Britain's ancient spiritual heart, where nearly 1,000 years of monarchs have been crowned and many are buried. Last year, the top-level Triforium museum opened for the first time.

LONDON'S essential EXPERIENCES

- **Promenading on South Bank:** In 1957, the Thames was declared "biologically dead." Today, it flows with life. Alongside it, as restaurants, bars, and creative developments continue to pop up, a walk along the South Bank from Westminster Bridge to Tower Bridge has become one of the world's great promenades. The ever-changing perspective from Parliament to the Tower is ceaselessly inspiring.
- **Following in Royal Footsteps:** London is where some of the most famous characters in history played their scenes. Nearly every British monarch since 1066 was crowned in **Westminster Abbey** (p. 136). Henry VIII strutted around **Hampton Court Palace** (p. 182), Charles I lost his head at the **Banqueting House** (p. 140), and Queen Elizabeth II resides at

Buckingham Palace (p. 130) and Windsor Castle (p. 290). And the story continues: The future King George VII and sister Princess Charlotte were diapered in **Kensington Palace** (p. 147).

o **Flying High on the London Eye:** Ride to the top of our generation's contribution to London's beloved landmarks for a far-reaching shot of the cityscape. Time your trip for early evening as the sun starts to sink and the lights come on across the metropolis. See p. 156.

o **Climbing the Dome of St Paul's Cathedral:** Wren's baroque masterpiece stirs emotion in everyone who lays eyes on its lead-coated wooden dome. But it's the climb to the Golden Gallery for a 360° panorama that will stay with you forever. As for Wren, he was forced to

The London Eye on the South Bank is best visited in early evening for spectacular views.

add the balustrade for Queen Anne. "Ladies think nothing well without an edging," he complained. See p. 163.

o **Immersing Yourself in World War II:** More than 70 years later, the Blitz still isn't far from many Londoners' minds. Dig into the power of their resistance at the superlative time capsule of the **Churchill War Rooms** (p. 131), the immersive **Museum of London Docklands** (p. 174), the floating military museum **HMS *Belfast*** (p. 161), and the top-secret code-breaking headquarters of **Bletchley Park** (p. 299).

o **Taking Afternoon Tea:** Look smart at **Brown's,** the **Goring, Fortnum & Mason,** or the **Langham** (p. 88), where the traditional tea ritual carries on as it did in Britain's colonial heyday.

o **Spending an Evening at a West End Theatre:** London is the theatrical capital of the world. The live stages of **Theatreland** around Covent Garden and Soho offer a combination of variety, accessibility, and economy—but the shows of the Fringe are where the future can be found. See p. 230.

LONDON'S best FOOD

o **Tucking into Honest British Ingredients:** After many lost years of too much boiled cabbage and bread, the English have fallen back in love with farm-fresh ingredients. The gastropub movement, epitomized by its still-potent pioneer, the **Eagle** (p. 72), is just the beginning. Delectable

English traditional cooking can be found from the oldest establishments (**Rules,** p. 85) to neighborhood holes in the wall (**Andrew Edmunds,** p. 79; **10 Greek Street,** p. 79).

o **Sinking a Pint in a Traditional Pub:** From Tudor coaching inns to riverside taverns, London's pub culture spans the centuries. Raise a pint where Shakespeare did at **The George** (p. 103), raise one with Sir Ian McKellen at his pub **The Grapes** (p. 104), immerse yourself in an ale at Dr. Samuel Johnson's local **Ye Olde Cheshire Cheese** (p. 108), and drink in a Victorian jewel box of etched glass at the **Princess Louise** (p. 107). Then repeat. See "21 Pubs You'll Love" on p. 101.

o **Mining the Stalls at Borough Market:** The top port of call for foodies is the market under the railway by London Bridge station—not least for the free samples dished out by vendors keen to market their wares. It's gourmet heaven. See p. 94.

o **Enjoying the New English Comfort Food:** London's first Indian restaurant opened in 1810, and Asian food of every origin is now the capital's most popular genre of cuisine. The dozens of curry houses on **Brick Lane** (p. 98) pitch for your business at the curb; or take in a traditional meal under the gold silk wallpaper at Covent Garden's **Punjab Restaurant** (p. 86), opened by an Indian wrestler back in 1947.

o **Chowing Down on Farmhouse Cheese:** England produces hundreds of artisan cheeses. Check out

Rules, London's oldest restaurant, boasts a beautiful stained-glass ceiling.

Curry houses on Brick Lane pitch for your business as you walk by.

the West Country cheddars, red Leicester, and goat cheeses at such cheese-mongers as **Neal's Yard Dairy** (p. 97) or eat a gloppy, gooey plate of raclette at **Kappacasein** (p. 97). But get your fill while you're here: You can't get it back through Customs.

o **Tasting Britain's Fading Traditions:** As young English diners insist on flashier fare, the older ways of cooking become rarer. Whether it's jellied eels in the protected interior of **M. Manze** (p. 97), the deep-fried goodness at the linoleum-lined "chippie" **Fryer's Delight** (p. 76), or the traditional "caff" of the **Regency Café** (p. 93), mid-century Britain is still steaming along—affordably.

LONDON'S best HOTELS

London has some 150,000 hotel rooms—some better than others.

o **Meet the Locals at a Family-Run B&B:** Mom-and-pop inns have taken a hit because of the dominance of corporate hotels. But you can still find some stellar homegrown hospitality where owners put you first, including the Valotis and Cabrals of the **Alhambra Hotel** in St Pancras (p. 37), the Beynons of Bloomsbury's **Jesmond Hotel** (p. 38), and the Callises of **22 York Street** in Marylebone (p. 55).

o **Lose Yourself in a Grande Dame:** The first all-service grand hotel in Europe, the **Langham** (p. 53) was built in 1865, and it's still extending top-flight hospitality to guests with taste—and cash. **Claridge's** (p. 51) and **The Savoy** (p. 41) have attracted royalty and creative misadventures since the mid-1800s. Best of all, you can tour their ground floors without being a guest.

The lobby of Claridge's Hotel is truly grand.

o **Pay Less Than $50:** You may not think it's possible, but with advance planning, you can get a new, impeccably maintained private room in the center of town for only £29 a night. Book way ahead with the British chains **Premier Inn, Travelodge,** or **easyHotel,** or with the imported budget brands **Ibis** and **CitizenM,** and London is yours, cheap. See p. 29.

o **Sleep Where History Happened:** Rather than tear it down, Londoners would rather revitalize it. Be party to the spy stories at **St. Ermin's Hotel** (p. 47), rest under the swoony spires of Gilbert Scott's neo-Gothic **St Pancras Renaissance Hotel** (p. 36), wake up where presses once printed the morning news at **One Aldwych** (p. 41), or relax in the onetime headquarters of the Ministry of Defense at the **Corinthia Hotel London** (p. 54).

- **Enjoy Style for Less:** "Boutique" hotels are encroaching deeper into budget territory than ever before. At the **Nadler** hotels (p. 43 and p. 44), **Z Hotels** (p. 34), and **hub by Premier Inn** (p. 32), you'll surrender some space, but not the chic. Buzzy Dutch boutique **CitizenM** (p. 29) has huge beds and a loopy personality, but a small price.
- **Club It Up:** The new trend is hip new hotels that offer more than beds. Some of them (The Ned, Soho House, Chiltern Firehouse) are too hard for visitors to crack, but there are others. The cool kids meet and mingle at the bar of the **Ham Yard Hotel** (p. 39), and in the member's club of Shoreditch's **The Curtain** (p. 61), built in 2017. Both even have screening rooms.

LONDON'S best FOR FAMILIES

- **Cruising London's Waterways:** In addition to the grand River Thames, London has a working canal system that once kept goods flowing to and from the city's docks. The best value trips are on the **Regent's Canal** (p. 194) and on the **Thames Clipper** passing under Tower Bridge (p. 322).
- **Ride the Tiny Tube:** Climb aboard a segment of the miniature London Post Office Railway, which for 76 years shuttled mail under the capital's streets. It's part of the new and kid-oriented **Postal Museum** (p. 119).
- **Visiting Harry Potter:** Warner Bros.' deep dive into how it designed and made its seven blockbuster films, **The Making of Harry Potter** (p. 184), is one of the country's most popular family attractions, surpassing expectations. Potterheads could happily spend a whole day here.
- **Losing Your Way in the World's Most Famous Hedge Maze:** The green labyrinth at **Hampton Court** twists and turns for almost half a mile. When

It's easy to get lost in the Hampton Court maze.

The *Thames Clipper* passing Tower Bridge offers a great value trip.

you manage to extricate yourself, stroll through centuries of architectural styles at this stunning palace, home of many an English monarch. Don't forget to pick up a kids' activity trail. See p. 182.

o **Going Botanic in Royal Kew:** The **Royal Botanic Gardens,** Kew, house more than 50,000 plants from across the planet, including Arctic and tropical varieties. Youngsters will love the 200m-high (656-ft.) Treetop Walkway, up in the Garden's deciduous canopy. See p. 183.

o **Asking How, Where & Why:** Inside South Kensington's **Science Museum** (p. 150), interactive exhibits keep inquisitive minds occupied. Or pilot a simulated ship at the kid-centric **National Maritime Museum** (p. 178), or learn how to drive a Tube train at the **London Transport Museum** (p. 121).

o **Learn the Panto Lingo:** From November to early January, join one of Britain's most delightful holiday experiences: pantomimes, which are slapstick musical romps through famous stories, usually starring D-list celebrities. Hiss at villains, shout instructions for heroes, and giggle at good-natured drag performers. Try the **Theatre Royal Stratford** (www.stratfordeast. com), the **New Wimbledon** (www.atgtickets.com), the **Hackney Empire** (p. 237), or the **Richmond Theatre** (www.richmondtheatre.net).

- **Seeing Peter Pan in Kensington Gardens:** You'll feel like a character from a Victorian novel as you see Sir George Frampton's beloved 1902 statue of the boy who played the panpipe. There's no better way to admire and enjoy the "green lung"—the largest and most popular open space in a city that holds the record for the most green space for a city of its size. See p. 193.

LONDON'S best FREE & DIRT CHEAP EXPERIENCES

- **Visiting the Great Museums:** London's state museums and galleries—including most of the big names—show off their permanent collections for free. They include the **British Museum, National Gallery, National Portrait Gallery, Tate Britain, Tate Modern, Natural History Museum, Science Museum, V&A,** the two **Museums of London,** and the **British Library.** See chapter 5.

- **Taking in Fresh Air & a City View:** North of the River Thames, **Hampstead Heath** (p. 192) offers miles of woodland trails, historic pubs, and sumptuous mansions. To the south, the flower beds of **Greenwich Park** (p. 192) enjoy a panoramic sweep over the Thames.

- **Dining on the Cheap:** Away from the Michelin-starred hotspots, London is surprisingly well equipped with affordable, tasty places to enjoy a full meal for under £10. Among the best is the West End's most venerable budget pit stop, **Café in the Crypt** at St Martin-in-the-Fields church (p. 82).

- **The King of Libraries:** The **British Library** (p. 110) started as the monarch's private stash but now its doors yawn wide to the public with free exhibitions and priceless manuscripts that must be seen to be believed.

- **Catching a Free Event in the Center of the City:** From the **Lord Mayor's Show** to the **Notting Hill Carnival,** a large number of major public events cost nothing to attend. See "London Calendar of Events" (p. 326).

THE best HISTORIC EXPERIENCES

- **Meeting the Heroes & Villains of History:** Get face-to-face with a rogue's gallery from the past at the **National Portrait Gallery,** where faces seem to watch you across time with a sparkle in their eye. The gang's all here, from a supercilious Henry VIII to a pugnacious Hogarth to a kind-eyed Princess Diana, already fading into a memory. See p. 126.

- **Taking a Tour of Royal London:** From palaces and parks to the royal art collections, history, geography, and culture have been shaped—or owned—by centuries of aristocratic rule. You can see the best of it in a day, including the queen's favorite grocer, **Fortnum & Mason** (p. 208), plus any one of 800 other Royal Warrant holders (p. 216). Roam the very rooms used in daily life by kings and queens at **Buckingham Palace** (p. 130), **Hampton Court Palace** (p. 182), **Kensington Palace** (p. 147), and **Windsor Castle** (p. 290).

The Peter Pan statue in Kensington Gardens makes it easy to imagine this beloved character come to life.

o **Peering into a Time Capsule:** Some museums preserve scenes that were frozen in time. No reconstructions or fakery here: You'll gaze upon authentic World War II military operations at the **Churchill War Rooms** (p. 131); admire the graves of great artists and the location of epic rituals at **Westminster Abbey** (p. 136); explore the secret cloisters of the **Charterhouse** campus (p. 171), founded in 1371 and only opened to tourists in 2017; see the home that made **Charles Darwin** want to stop traveling (p. 185); and marvel at the treasure-crammed townhouse of a 19th-century collector (**Sir John Soane's Museum,** p. 127).

o **Shopping in the Grandest Department Stores of Them All:** And, no, it's not Harrods. **Liberty of London** (p. 210), founded in 1875 and moved to its current half-timbered, mock-Tudor home in 1924, and **Selfridges** (p. 211), both designed and built by Americans, redefined sales methods and played crucial roles in world history.

o **Imagining Domestic Life Through the Ages:** At the **V&A** (p. 151), gape at one of the finest collections of fine historic furniture in the world. But that's a museum—nothing immerses you in the past quite like the brain-bending role-playing of a night visit to **Dennis Severs' House** (p. 172).

SUGGESTED ITINERARIES & NEIGHBORHOODS

Few great modern cities are as multilayered, intricate, and unknowable as London, Western Europe's most populous city (8.7 million in 2017, the highest level since before World War II). Perhaps that's because history was knitted into its layout. London is mostly the haphazard product of blind evolution, which piled up over successive generations to produce a complicated metropolis. One could say that London simply happened.

As recently as the early 1800s, London—and by London, I mean what we now call The City, between St Paul's and the Tower—was a frenzied cluster where many lives, birth to death, were carried out within the same few blocks. The main streets ran south to the river (not east or west, as they do now), the smoke of industry was banished downwind to the east, and kings lived near the Thames for easy transportation. All around The City were dozens of villages, many of which retain their names as modern neighborhoods—and, if you're lucky, a whiff of their original personalities, but not of their original pestilence.

Quickly, London swelled to swallow its current territory. Yet because of ancient echoes, neighborhoods remain surprisingly small—many are just minutes across by foot, and even crucial streets can change names several times. It's still possible to stroll along and sense sudden shifts in energy and character. In many ways, London is still a complex system of hamlets. It's one of the many delights that makes it so surprising. It also means it can take a lifetime to scratch its surface.

Addresses sometimes reflect this improvisation; a building numbered 75 may sit across the street from one numbered 32. Despite this, it's immensely difficult to get lost. The City maintains some 1,200 Legible London map **"Finger Posts"** throughout town. Wherever you are, a map is near.

If you want a hand-held map, forgo the oversimplified one your hotel might offer and don't tax your data plan. The most cherished paper map is the *London A–Z* (www.az.co.uk), first compiled by

London's Neighborhoods

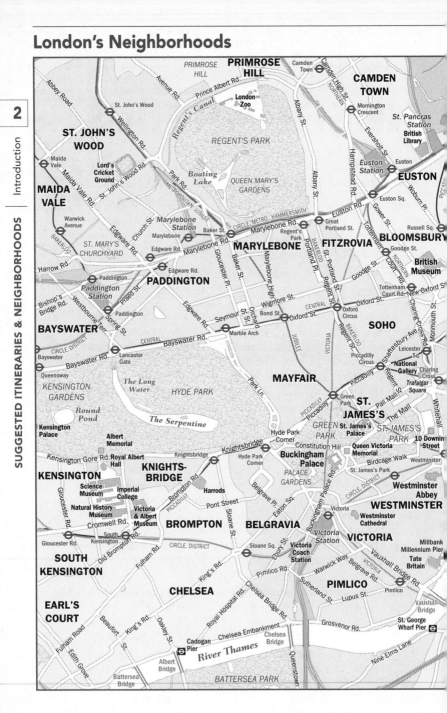

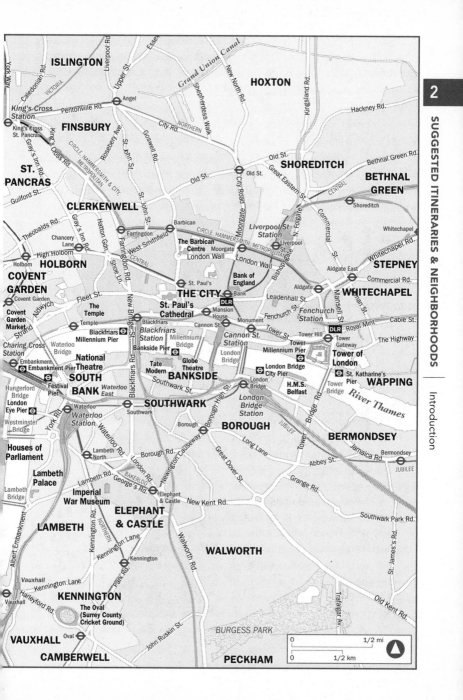

the indefatigable Phyllis Pearsall, who walked every mile of The City for the 1936 debut edition and commanded the resulting cartography empire until her death 60 years later. Its *London Mini A–Z Street Atlas* (£6) fits into a pocket. (Don't buy the app, which drains your smartphone's battery.) Just be sure to call it the "A to Zed" or you'll get a funny look; in England, the last letter in the alphabet is, quite sensibly, pronounced so it doesn't rhyme with eight other letters.

LONDON IN 1 DAY

First of all, what were you thinking? If you're in town on a layover, didn't you know that many airlines will allow you to stick around for a few days at no charge? Never mind. What's done is done. Eat a huge breakfast and make your way to Tower Hill.

---

1 The Tower of London ★★★

Start here (p. 166) because it usually opens an hour earlier (9am) than most attractions. Spend about 2 hours making stops at the **Crown Jewels** and the **White Tower,** and snap that requisite photo of the **Tower Bridge** (p. 166) from the quay. Grab a triangle sandwich (the quintessential London lunch).

Tube it west on the Circle or District lines to Westminster.

2 Westminster Abbey ★★★

Allot a rushed 2 hours to see the effigies of kings and queens (p. 136). Of the **Chapel of Henry VII,** Washington Irving wrote: "Stone seems, by the cunning labor of the chisel, to have been robbed of its weight and density, suspended aloft as if by magic, and the fretted roof achieved with the wonderful minuteness and airy security of a cobweb." Outside, take in the **Houses of Parliament** (p. 132) and **Big Ben's Elizabeth Tower** from across the street. The bell is undergoing its first full restoration since 1859.

Don't miss the Tower of London, even if you're just in The City for a day.

The Chapel of Henry VII was added to Westminster Abbey in the early 1500s.

Walk up Whitehall, passing No. 10 Downing St. (the Walking Tour on p. 253 will guide you).

3 The National Gallery ★★★

At **Trafalgar Square,** a symbolic heart of the city, you can finally see some of the world's most famous paintings in person (p. 123). Park guards also turn a blind eye to tourists climbing alongside those famous bronze couchant lions, each of them 20 feet long. But don't mount them—they're cracking.

From the Strand, head to the back of Charing Cross station and cross the Thames.

4 London Eye ★★

There's time for a revolution on London's favorite contemporary icon and the new focal point of national celebrations (p. 156).

Finish just north of the Gallery, around Leicester Square.

5 West End Show ★★★

Curtains go up around 7:30pm (p. 230). Enjoy an ice cream during interval (intermission)—it's a custom. Afterward, hurry to a **pub** and raise a pint to a city where you've barely scratched the surface (see p. 101 for ideas).

LONDON ON A 2ND DAY

You're going to have to move fast, but you'll be able to see some highlights. Take the Tube to Mansion House, Blackfriars, or St Paul's.

1 St Paul's Cathedral ★★★

As you appreciate the underside of the dome, also appreciate the grave fact that before the 1940s, its flanks were crowded with buildings. Bombings devastated the structures that once hemmed it in.

Cross the Thames on the Millennium Bridge (the Walking Tour on p. 265 will help).

2 Tate Modern ★★★

Here's a museum (p. 158) in a colossal structure with river views that can be more memorable than what's on display inside it—although Rothko's paintings for the Four Seasons restaurant can't fail to put you in a restive mood. If it's summer, catch a matinee at **Shakespeare's Globe** (p. 235), just a few yards east; an afternoon pint across the bridge at the Art Nouveau **Black Friar** (p. 102) will recharge you.

Take the Jubilee line from Southwark to Green Park.

3 Green Park ★★

Walk south through Green Park (p. 191) to behold the front of **Buckingham Palace** (p. 130); if you're here in March, you may be lucky enough

The ornately detailed underside of the dome of St Paul's Cathedral was the work of painter Sir James Thornhill.

to see fields of daffodils in bloom. Return to Piccadilly to browse the classy shops lining it, including **Fortnum & Mason** (p. 208).

Take the Tube's Piccadilly line (notice the century-old tilework) to Russell Square.

4 The British Museum ★★★

You'll spend the afternoon roaming its vast halls (p. 114), but you'll scarcely be able to wrap your brain around the age, rarity, and craftsmanship of what you see. Such aesthetic exertions may induce cravings for cream tea at its Great Court Restaurant or another pint at a Victorian valentine of a pub, the **Princess Louise** (p. 107).

Ancient treasures, such as this statue of Ramses II, fill the British Museum.

Catch Bus 55 toward Oxford Circus. Sit on the top level for the views!

5 Oxford Circus ★★

Wind up the afternoon with a dive into the bustling fitting rooms of the shops on **Oxford Street, Regent Street,** and **Carnaby Street** (p. 205), where you'll find a huge selection of cool clothes at what Londoners call "High Street" prices—meaning they're sane. Maybe get a cocktail at the 1940s-themed **Cahoots** (p. 106) or walk southeast for a few minutes to Frith Street in Soho and have dinner at **Andrew Edmunds** (p. 79), a neighborhood gem with a changing menu that charges prices far below its rank, and afterward, stroll past the lights of **Piccadilly Circus.** If you still have juice left, walk down Haymarket, turn left on Cockspur, and follow it down the Strand to Aldwych.

6 South Bank ★★★

Cross the Waterloo bridge and wander east along the popular promenade of **South Bank.** During the evening, couples stroll, theatres light, cafés buzz, and the water of the Thames glitters in the light reflected from the ancient grey dome of St Paul's. It makes for an unforgettable evening.

LONDON ON A 3RD DAY

Follow the itinerary for 2 days in London, but add in one of The City's South Kensington museums, preferably the **Victoria & Albert** (p. 151), and follow that with a walk through **Hyde Park** (p. 193), possibly to see the **Diana**

A statue of Queen Victoria rules from in front of Kensington Palace.

Memorial Fountain (p. 146) and to tour the public areas of her son's and grandchildren's London home, **Kensington Palace** (p. 147), in adjoining **Kensington Gardens.** Take the Tube or a bus to Westminster and dive into the time capsule of the **Churchill War Rooms** (p. 131). Follow that with a stroll along the South Bank from Westminster to London Bridge, taking your pick among the pubs and restaurants you find along the path.

AN ITINERARY FOR FAMILIES

There's no bad neighborhood to stay in if you've got kids, because London is low-rise and manageable. But make sure they're ready to climb stairs if you're taking the Tube. On paper, some of London's museums sound as if they'd be too dry, but in reality, they bend over backward to cater to children—maybe too much, as it's often at the expense of adult minds. Every major museum, no exceptions, has an on-site cafe for lunch.

Day 1: Double-Deckers & Thames Clippers

Forget expensive open-top tours: Start your day seeing Piccadilly Circus, Trafalgar Square, St Paul's Cathedral, the Tower of London, and much more for the price of bus fare on an antique, double-decker **Routemaster**

bus with an old-style staircase on the end. Take route 15, every 15 min. After visiting the **Tower of London** (p. 166), head to the ferry dock and see The City from the river on a **Thames Clipper** (p. 322). Disembark at **Tate Modern** (p. 158), which comes fully loaded for young exploration with family trails, a learning zone on Level 5, and some very cool video tablets for interpreting the art. Take the Tube to Leicester Square for a **West End musical** (p. 230).

Day 2: Covent Garden & Coram's Fields

Make your way to Covent Garden's **London Transport Museum** (p. 121), where kids can pretend to drive a bus and explore other eye-level exhibits. Then bring your brood on a 15-min. walk north to the **British Museum** (p. 114) and hook them up with crayons and pads, exploration backpacks, and the special object collections tour geared to young minds. If they're the daring types, the mummies never fail to impress. Just east you'll find a city park just for children: The 7-acre **Coram's Fields** (www.coramsfields.org), which was set aside in 1739 for an orphanage at a time when 75 percent of London kids died before the age of 5. Its southern gate is where mothers once abandoned their babies in desperation. Today, no adult may enter without a child, and this once sad spot is now the scene of daily family joy; there's a petting zoo, two playgrounds for all ages, sand pits, and a paddling pool.

Covent Garden offers several family-friendly bars and restaurants.

Day 3: The Brompton Road Museums

Today is devoted to exploration of the Brompton Road museums, a trio of world's-bests for kids: Take the Piccadilly line to South Kensington, where the **V&A** (p. 151) has hundreds of hands-on exhibits for kids (look for the hand symbol on the maps), such as trying on Victorian costumes or donning armor gauntlets. Next door, the plain-speaking signs and robotic dinosaurs of the **Natural History Museum** (p. 148) impress kids as much as the airplanes and space capsules over their heads at the **Science Museum** (p. 150)—both institutions furnish even more kids' trails and activities for free. Go east on the Circle or District Tube lines to Temple, and you're at the dancing water jets (transformed in winter to a

Somerset House has been a meeting place for centuries. In winter, Londoners ice skate here, and in summer, they gather for concerts.

skating rink) of the **Somerset House** courtyard (home of the Courtauld Gallery; p. 121). If the weather doesn't suit that, the **London Eye**'s capsules are safe, climate-controlled, and move imperceptibly—the view will stimulate and inspire kids.

A DISCOVERY WEEKEND

The Frommer's guides are designed to give you a firm introduction to the sights, hotels, and restaurants that speak most to a visitor about what's going on in each destination. But authentic London doesn't begin and end with these pages, and if you dip into neighborhoods where more locals live, your visit will be immeasurably richer.

Day 1: Brixton & Bollywood

When Victoria was queen, families flocked to live near the incandescent lights of Brixton's Electric Avenue, which in 1888 became one of London's first shopping streets lit by electricity. Today, it's a boisterous immigrant community. By day, explore the glazed awnings of its markets, where to inhale the aroma of meat and exotic spices is to walk through a portal to Jamaica, India, or China—and to be reminded that London, like few others, is a truly worldly city. In the evening, experience London's huge South Asian population—Indians are nearly 2 percent of the population, and one of Britain's richest men, Lakshmi Mittal, is Indian-born—by attending a Bollywood film at the **Boleyn Cinema** (www.boleyncinemas.com; Tube: Upton Park), a historic 1938 Art Deco building and the second-largest Bollywood screen in a country that loves the genre.

Day 2: Go Football Mad or Cricket Crazy

London hosts 13 professional football (soccer) teams, more than any other city on Earth. From mid-August to mid-May, catch matches at some of the best Premier League teams: **Chelsea** (www.chelseafc.com), **Arsenal** (London's first club; www.arsenal.com), **Tottenham Hotspur** (www.tottenhamhotspur.com), **Fulham** (www.fulhamfc.com), or **West Ham United** (www.whufc.com), which took up residence in the former Olympic Stadium at Stratford. Filling the gap from April to September, and less likely to pelt you in the skull with a beer bottle, is cricket. Attend "test matches" at Marylebone's **MCC Lord's Cricket Ground** (www.lords.org) or Oval's **Surrey County Cricket Club** (www.kiaoval.com). If you figure out how the game works, fill me in, won't you? It's a little like baseball—and a lot like watching grass grow.

Day 3: Ale, Yorkshire Pudding & Tough Questions

On Sunday afternoons, find a pub with an inviting garden for a traditional **Sunday Roast,** a spread of roasted meats with all the trimmings such as Yorkshire pudding (a popover-like pastry) and gravy, washed down with copious amounts of beer. It's the more leisurely equivalent of brunch: After a long week of working to keep their exorbitantly priced shared

Tottenham Hotspurs are one of five Premier League football teams playing in the London area.

Use the Code

London is chopped into geographic parcels, and you'll see those postcodes on street signs. The heart of The City, in postcode terms, is near the Chancery Lane Tube stop. From there, areas are given a compass direction (N for north, SW for southwest, and so on) and a number (but ignore that, since a number greater than 1 doesn't mean the area is in the boonies). In the very heart of town, addresses get an extra C for "centre," as in WC1, which is where Covent Garden is located. Every address in this book includes its postcode, which corresponds to the neighborhood in which you'll find it. Don't worry—you won't need to memorize these because each listing also includes the nearest Tube stop to help you quickly place locations on a map. Here are some of the most common postcodes:

WC1 Bloomsbury
WC2 Covent Garden, Holborn, Strand
W1 Fitzrovia, Marylebone, Mayfair, Soho
W2 Bayswater
W6 Hammersmith
W8 Kensington
W11 Notting Hill
SW1 Belgravia, St James's, Westminster
SW3 Chelsea
SW5 Earl's Court
SW7 Knightsbridge, South Kensington
SE1 Southwark

SE10 Greenwich
EC1 Clerkenwell
EC2 Bank, Barbican, Liverpool Street
EC3 Tower Hill
EC4 Fleet Street, St Paul's
E1 Spitalfields, Whitechapel
E2 Bethnal Green
E14 Canary Wharf/Isle of Dogs
N1 Islington
NW1 Camden Town
NW3 Hampstead

flats, Londoners hang out until Monday. Some pubs also hold **pub quizzes,** another staple of British life. Form teams and answer trivia for lame prizes, but be warned: Foreigners always fold on the sports and politics questions.

Neighborhoods in Brief

London's neighborhoods were laid out during a period of wagon and foot traffic, when districts were defined in narrower terms than we define them today; indeed, for centuries people often lived complete lives without seeing the other side of town. Ironically, in our times, the Tube has done much to divide these districts from each other. Visitors are likely to hop a train between them and don't often realize how remarkably close together they really are.

Are these the only areas of interest? Not even close. Literally hundreds of fascinating village clusters abound, many with names as cherishable as Ponders End, Tooting, and The Wrythe. And considering that a third of Londoners now belong to an ethnic minority and more than 200 languages are spoken, the flavor of your experience shifts as you go. But visitors are likely to spend time here:

BLOOMSBURY & FITZROVIA

Best for: *Museums, affordable inns, residential streets, universities, and homewares and electronics shops on Tottenham Court Road*
What you won't find: *Evening entertainment, nightclubs*

Bloomsbury's dark-brick, white-sashed residential buildings and leafy squares date mostly from the Georgian period, when the district became the first in a chaotic city to be planned—it was an early version of the modern suburban development. The refined air attracted the intelligentsia nearly from the start, and its two universities are both 19th-century institutions. The British Museum settled here, too. Bloomsbury became a place

Brompton Road in Knightsbridge is the home of the famous Harrods department store.

of remembrance on July 7, 2005; of the 52 who died that day, 26 perished underground on a bombed Piccadilly line train between King's Cross and Russell Square stations, and 13 were killed on a double-decker bus passing above through Tavistock Square. Bloomsbury's cozier sister Fitzrovia, similar in character but devoid of major attractions, lies on the western side of Tottenham Court Road. Famous residents include George Bernard Shaw and Virginia Woolf, who both lived (at different times) at 29 Fitzroy Square.

KING'S CROSS

Best for: *Budget hotels, trains heading north (and south to Paris), alternative/down-and-dirty nightlife, student housing, take-away counters*

What you won't find: *A large restaurant selection, shopping*

A decade ago, the area around King's Cross station was an unsavory tenderloin of porn stores and warehouses. Behind the station, millions of pounds have just transformed once-derelict industrial infrastructure into Granary Square, a canalside center for arts hotspots, restaurants, colleges, and tech HQs. Legend (surely apocryphal) says the Celtic queen Boudicca rests somewhere near Platform 8 of King's Cross. Fans of Harry Potter know that the young wizard boards the Hogwarts Express at the (fictitious) Platform 9¾; the movie versions have shot at Platforms 4 and 5 but used prettier St Pancras station, next door, as a stand-in facade. Change came, as it often has in English history, from France: The Channel Tunnel Rail Link is the starting point for Eurostar train trips to France and beyond.

From Arthur Frommer's *Europe on $5 a Day* (1957)

"All you've heard to the contrary, Londoners are among the warmest people of Europe, and London is a friendly and inviting city. It has charm and a politeness of attitude that belie its big-city status. You'll want to extend your stay. . . . Can you live in London on $5 a day? There's nothing to it."

MARYLEBONE & MAYFAIR

Best for: *Luxe shopping, hotels, restaurants, small museums, strolling, embassies*

What you won't find: *Historic sites, savings*

The middle-class hubbub of Oxford Street west of Regent Street divides high-hat Marylebone from its snobbish southern neighbor, Mayfair. Both play host to upscale shopping and several fascinating, if over-looked, museums, but there the similarities end. World-famous Mayfair, typified by hyperluxe bauble shops and blue-blood heritage (the present queen was born at 17 Bruton St. in a building that is no longer there), has a high opinion of itself as a starchy enclave of wealth, much of it from other countries. Yet Mayfair has less to offer the casual tourist, although it is the city's hot zone for cushy hotels. (The title of the musical *My Fair Lady* is witty wordplay on how its Cockney heroine, Eliza, would have pro-nounced "Mayfair lady.") Marylebone (*Mar-le-bun*), on the other hand, benefits from convenient Tube and bus connections and lively sidewalks crowded with evening cele-brants, particularly around James Street. Also, thanks to a territorial local authority, its main shopping drag (Marylebone High St.) remains one of the last important streets in London that isn't awash with the ubiquitous corporate chain stores. Oxford Street is The City's premier shopping corridor; the west-ern half between Oxford Circus and Marble Arch is the classier end, with marquee department stores such as Selfridges and Marks & Spencer.

SOHO, COVENT GARDEN & CENTRAL WEST END

Best for: *Shopping, restaurants, theater, cinema, nightlife, opera, free art (National Gallery and National Portrait Gallery), star sightings*

What you won't find: *Elbow room, silence*

London's undisputed center of nightlife, restaurants, and theater, the West End seethes with tourists and merry-makers. After work, Old Compton Street and Covent Garden overflow with people catching up with friends; by 7:30pm, the theaters and opera houses are pulsing; by midnight, the action has moved into the nightclubs of Leicester Square and lounges of Soho; and in the wee hours, you might find groups of partiers trawling Gerrard Street, in a teeny Cantonese Chinatown, hunting for snacks. Prim Trafalgar Square, dominated by the peerless National Gallery, has often been called London's focal point. On a sunny day, you'll find few places that exude such well-being.

WESTMINSTER, INCLUDING ST JAMES'S

Best for: *Historic and government sites, river strolls, St James's Park*

What you won't find: *Affordable hotels, a wide choice of restaurants*

Though it's near the West End, this area's energy is more staid. It's a district tourists mostly see by day. South of Trafalgar Square, you'll find regiments of robust government buildings but little in the way of hotels or food. Whitehall's severity doesn't spread far: Just a block east, its impenetrable character gives way to the proud riverside promenade of Victoria Embankment overlooking the London Eye, and just a block west, to the greenery of St James's Park, which is, in effect, the queen's front yard, since Bucking-ham Palace is at the western boundary of this area. North of the park, the tidy streets of St James's are even more exclusive than Mayfair's, if that's possible.

THE CITY

Best for: *Old streets, the Tower of London, St Paul's, financial concerns*

What you won't find: *Nightlife or weekend life, affordable hotels*

Technically, this is the only part of London that's London. Other bits, including the West End, are under the jurisdiction of different local governments, such as Westminster or Camden. The City, as it's called, is where most of London's history happened. It's where Romans cheered gladiators. It's where London Bridge—at least 12 versions—touched shore. It's where the Great Fire raged. And, more recently, it's where the Deutsche Luftwaffe focused many of its noc-turnal bombing raids, which is why you'll find so little evidence of the aforementioned events. Outside of working hours, the main thing you'll see in The City is your own reflection in the facade of corporate fortresses; west of Liverpool Street station, even most of the pubs close on weekends. Although it encompasses such priceless relics as the Tower of London, St Paul's Cathedral, the Tower Bridge, the Bank of England, and the Monument, many of the area's remnants are underfoot—the spider web of lanes and streets dates to the Roman period, with names that hint at their former lives (Walbrook is where the river Walbrook, now hidden underground, flowed down to the Thames; Honey Lane, Bread St., Milk St., and Poultry all once hosted food markets). Buildings have come and gone, but the veins of The City have pumped in situ for thousands of years.

THE SOUTH BANK, SOUTHWARK & BOROUGH

Best for: *Museums, memorable pubs, strolls, gourmet foods and wines*
What you won't find: *Shopping, parks*

During the recent rehabilitation of Southwark (*Suth*-urk) from a crumbling industrial district, its blighted power station became one of the world's greatest museums (the Tate Modern), a master playwright's theater was re-created (the Globe), and a sublime riverfront path replaced the coal lightermen's rotting piers. Now it's where London goes to fall in love with The City. It's a 1-mile riverside stroll between the London Eye and the Tate Modern, and every step is a pleasure. Once-dank railway viaducts are filled with cafes and reasonable restaurants; Western Europe's tallest skyscraper, The Shard, lords over from above; and the nation's dramatic showpiece (the National Theatre) anchors them at South Bank. But it's gratifying to see that some things never change: Borough Market, which attracts gourmet foodies from around the world, is the descendant of a market that fed the denizens of that medieval skyscraper over the water, London Bridge.

VICTORIA & CHELSEA

Best for: *Boutiques, low-cost lodging, town homes, wealthy neighbors*
What you won't find: *Transit options, street life, museums*

Victoria doesn't technically apply to the neighborhood around the eponymous train station—Belgravia (to the west) and Pimlico (south and east) take those honors—but the shorthand stuck. Most of the area, which is residential or uninterestingly workaday, was developed starting in the 1820s in consistent patterns of white stucco-terraced homes. The area around the station, which is being redeveloped in a massive works project, contains two outlier West End theatres, but little else. Just north, you'll face the brick walls of Buckingham Palace Gardens. Chelsea, to its south, has a history of well-heeled bohemianism—Oscar Wilde, James McNeill Whistler, and the Beatles all lived here—although it's known more as one of The City's most exclusive (and some would say insular) communities. A stroll past boutiques and pocket-squared residents on the King's Road, turning ever-more corporate and indistinct, is not the adventure it once was.

KENSINGTON, KNIGHTSBRIDGE

Best for: *Museums, shopping, ultra-luxe boutiques, also-ran hotels*
What you won't find: *Historic sites*

Here, one expensive neighborhood genuflects to another, and barely anyone you meet was born in England. South Kensington and Brompton draw the most visitors to their grand museums; and Knightsbridge is where moneyed foreigners spend and show off—London now has the most billionaires in the world, nearly twice as many as New York or Moscow. They can't legally change most of the facades, so to satisfy their hunger for more space, the big trend among the rich is to burrow downward to build underground rooms—the "pleasure caves" of Kensington. Privilege has long had an address in Kensington—that's a reason those edifying institutions were located here to begin with, away from the grubby paws of the peasants—but it also is home to a core of French expats; you'll find the cafes catering to them on Bute Street. Kensington Palace, at the Gardens' western end, is where Prince William and Kate live when they're in town. When you travel west to Earl's Court, you experience a considerable drop in voltage. It's a frumpy zone deprived of a contingency to the park with undistinguished eats and sleeps; the rise of King's Cross and Shoreditch for younger travelers has reduced it to near-negligible stature. Your parents may have stayed here once, but you shouldn't.

SHOREDITCH, SPITALFIELDS & HOXTON

Best for: *Nightclubs, music, food of all types, galleries, clothing*
What you won't find: *Museums, parks*

If Mayfair is London's champagne, the East End hoods used to be its hangover. For centuries it was an impoverished slum for poor immigrants and shifty souls. Now Spitalfields (*Spit*-all-fields), named for its excellent covered market (p. 227) is being consumed by an unstoppable cancer of soulless, open-plan office buildings from The City. It blends into Shoreditch, big on nightlife and name-dropping, up-and-coming designers. Shopping, restaurants, bars, hipsters—it's all here now. Dalston, young and bohemian, is north of these. East of Spitalfields, in ancient homes that have long housed waves of immigrants (French, then Jewish, now South Asian), you'll find the famed restaurants of Brick Lane (p. 98), the

cafes and dance clubs of the converted Old Truman Brewery, and the art-savvy neighborhood of Whitechapel. Prostitutes are out, £4.50 coffee is in—which may not be an improvement.

GREENWICH

Best for: *Museums, antique and food markets, river views, strolls, boats*
What you won't find: *Hotels, bustle*

Greenwich, on the south bank across from the Canary Wharf developments, retains the tranquility of an untouched village. The town has an illustrious pedigree as a royal getaway (it's got the oldest royal park in London), as a scientific capital, and as one of the world's most crucial command centers. If it all sounds like a living museum, it is: On top of being a UNESCO World Heritage Site (Maritime Greenwich), the village is literally the center of time and space, since it inhabits the exact location of Greenwich Mean Time, and of longitude 0° 0' 0". Set away from Greenwich town there's the colossal O$_2$ dome, The City's iconic concert venue.

Other Popular London Neighborhoods

Mostly because of iffy transit connections (for example, service by a single Tube line that, should it go on the blink, would derail your vacation), this book doesn't focus on these neighborhoods as prime places to stay, but they're still vital parts of town.

BAYSWATER & PADDINGTON

Best for: *Sub-par inns, ethnic food, well-preserved Victorian thoroughfares*
What you won't find: *Attractions, non-chain stores, street life, adorable bears*

Its whitewashed, terraced houses were briefly the most fashionable in The City (Churchill and Dickens were residents), yet today, the sizable transient population of this area deprives it of sustained energy, and its hotels tend to be for immigrant tradesmen. Crowning the muddle is Queensway, a popular shopping street containing Whiteleys, a 1911 department store edifice converted into a mall with fairly unexciting tenants. Although the interior of Paddington station is one of London's most beautiful train hubs (it was built by the architect Isambard Kingdom Brunel in 1838), the facade is obscured by a hotel; *Paddington* (2014)

used Marylebone Station's more atmospheric entrance instead. It's also inconvenient, though Heathrow and Windsor trains go from it.

DOCKLANDS

Best for: *Development, ancient warehouses, super-cheap chain hotels*
What you won't find: *Street life, nightlife*

Most of far east London along the north side of the Thames is ignobly called by a single, sweeping name: Docklands. Captain Cook set off on his explorations from here, and its hand-dug basins teemed with ships bearing goods from around the planet. Docklands made colonial Britain successful—and thus America, Canada, Australia, and South Africa, too. After a fallow generation, East London's hand-dug pools are under constant redevelopment by corporations in stacks of fluorescent-lit office cubes, and the

Olympics settled here in 2012 near the Stratford Tube stop. Away from the river, in salt-of-the-earth neighborhoods like Bethnal Green, Stratford, and West Ham, The City's Pakistani and Indian populations flourish, with marvelous but unglamorous food and shops.

ISLINGTON

Best for: *Antiques, gastropubs, theater, street markets, cafes, strolls*
What you won't find: *Museums, hotels*

Few neighborhoods retain such a healthy balance between feisty bohemianism and groomed prosperity, and almost none retain streetscapes as defiantly mid-20th-century as Chapel Market. Islington's leafy byways are dotted with antiques dealers, hoary pubs with backroom theater spaces, beer gardens, and most pleasingly on a sunny day, pedestrian towpaths overlooking Regent's Canal. Why more tourists don't flood Islington is a mystery—and a blessing—but that hasn't stopped its ascendancy as a choice neighborhood for those with money.

CAMDEN

Best for: *Alternative music, massive clothing markets, junk souvenirs, pubs*
What you won't find: *Elbow room, hotels, upscale restaurants*

London's analogue to San Francisco's Haight-Ashbury District, it was big in the countercultured 1960s and '70s and is still grotty enough for Amy Winehouse to have expired in. The area's shoulder-to-shoulder markets, which hawk touristy hokum, cheap sunglasses, and £5 falafel in the former warehouses and stables serving Regent's Canal, can be pretty awful, and the sort of places where you feel compelled to carry your wallet in your front pocket. Tourists come more out of duty than for any true mission for commerce and they cram the inadequate Tube stop on weekends.

NOTTING HILL

Best for: *Markets, village vibes, restaurants, pubs, tourists, antiques*
What you won't find: *Well-priced shopping, museums, Hugh Grant*

Thanks partly to Hollywood, this westerly nook known to locals for race riots and, in 2017, the horrible Grenfell Tower fire, appears high on many checklists. Its Saturday Portobello Road market, the principal draw, is fiendishly crowded but short on truly wonderful wares. In fact, it's touristy. Like Camden, people go because they think they should. But if you feel compelled, Hugh Grant's blue door from *Notting Hill* (1999) is at 280 Westbourne Park Rd.

WHERE TO STAY

London has always attracted the richest of the rich. The standard for its hotels is among the best in the world—in fact, there are more than 11,000 five-star rooms in the city. And in recent years, those luxury standards have put the squeeze on cheaper properties.

Yes, London's real estate market is diseased—and the affliction is foreign cash. Russian oligarchs, Middle Eastern magnates, and Chinese officials are snapping up real estate—including many buildings that once housed the city's family-run B&B industry—as a place to launder their fortunes. Against that backdrop of extreme wealth, enter Brexit. The banking and investment workers who power London's luxury industry are beginning to decamp for offices on the continent instead. Yet even as London buckled up for a wild ride, rates throughout the U.S. rose by more than 3 percent in 2017. More than ever it behooves you, the visitor, to **check prices for yourself.**

Some ground rules. First, don't get caught up in star ratings. In Britain, a hotel can earn an extra star simply because it will serve you food. In fact, the more stars a place has, the more likely it is to charge for something you don't even use, so focus instead on the location and the price. Second, to save cash, learn to trust smaller hotels that have been carved out of historic buildings, even if that means irregular-size quarters with tiny bathrooms. Third, if you seek the lowest rates possible (usually found only on each place's website), book as far ahead as you can.

London's non-corporate hotels are good about sticking to their posted rates; in fact, every property is required by law to post the *maximum* rate in the lobby. They're also unabashed about charging insanely high prices given any uptick in demand. Beware dates around the London Marathon (Apr), bank holidays, Wimbledon (June or July), New Year's, and summer. Most corporate hotels will grant a discount for nonrefundable bookings, and family-run places tend to cut deals if you stay longer. The cheapest places are still family-run.

Package tours tend to stash tourists in undesirable and inconvenient neighborhoods—Lancaster Gate, Earl's Court, South Kensington, and Paddington—full of lifeless hotels that plod through nights like zombies that crave continental breakfast. The hotels in this chapter strive to keep you out of dead tourist-hotel zones and keep you in the middle of the action. And the hotels that are crazy

London Hotel Price Categories

Hotels are categorized by the lowest en suite (bathroom attached) double rate (suite prices are not included). Many hotels promise the best rate if you book directly. Prices are listed as a guide only; rates may pop higher during highest demand. But with Brexit uncertainty afoot in Britain, rates may actually end up being lower.

Inexpensive	Under £125
Moderate	£126 to £225
Expensive	£226 and up

expensive are often included because there's something worth visiting in them even if you're not staying in one.

Accommodations are subject to a Value Added Tax (VAT) of 20 percent, which you cannot claim back. Happily, almost all small B&Bs include taxes in their rates. More expensive hotels (those around £175 or more) tend to leave taxes off their tariffs, which can result in a nasty surprise at checkout, so it never hurts to ask if the rate "excludes VAT." Absolutely no London hotel charges a "resort fee" or its equivalent; that's a uniquely North American hospitality scam.

THE BUDGET HOTEL CHAINS

We put this section first because it includes a huge number of the best-priced rooms in the best neighborhoods. The chains are all over town. Expect reliable standards, decently sized rooms with private bathroom, and unbeatable lead-in rates for people who pay months ahead of time. Unfortunately, so many people habitually turn to these brands that closer to the dates of stay, prices usually rise far past the point of value. In addition to these names, look into **Motel One** (24–26 Minories, EC3; www.motel-one.com; ✆ **020/7481-6420;** doubles from £99), a stylish and ultra-cheap but cramped German name with a single location in the somewhat inconvenient neighborhood of Tower Hill. For specific locations, look on each chain's website, listed below.

CitizenM ★★★ My favorite affordable London chain is actually Dutch. Their glassy open-plan lobbies lined with shelves of orange-and-white Penguin classic paperbacks (which every self-conscious interior designer in London displays to denote postmodern intellectualism), churn day and night with people sipping fine coffee and telecommuting. Check-in is self-guided by kiosk, and rooms are compact—almost podlike—but arranged with genius. Expect massive platform beds piled with body pillows, curvy unit bathrooms slotted into the space with calculated aplomb, and a bedside tablet that lets you control everything from motorized blinds to the color of the room's mood lighting. There's even a hefty library of free movies (including porn—like I said, it's Dutch). My favorite locations are Bankside (near the Tate Modern) and Tower of London, with rooms and a fab rooftop bar overlooking said eternal fortress.

www.citizenm.com. 3 locations around London. From £125 double. **Amenities:** Free movies; free Wi-Fi.

London-Wide Hotels

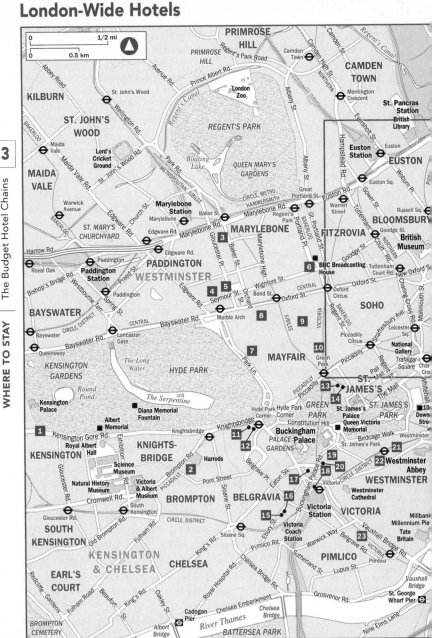

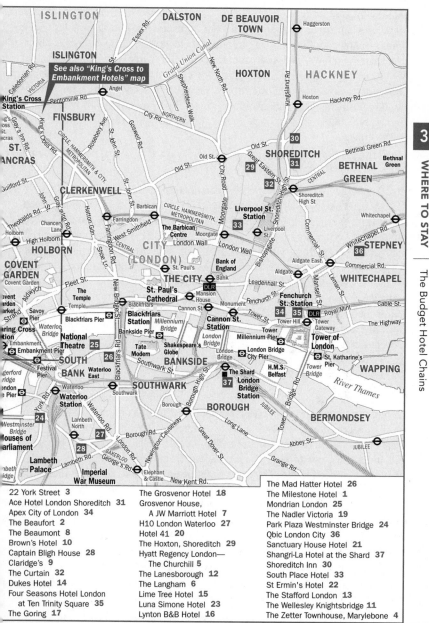

22 York Street **3**
Ace Hotel London Shoreditch **31**
Apex City of London **34**
The Beaufort **2**
The Beaumont **8**
Brown's Hotel **10**
Captain Bligh House **28**
Claridge's **9**
The Curtain **32**
Dukes Hotel **14**
Four Seasons Hotel London
   at Ten Trinity Square **35**
The Goring **17**

The Grosvenor Hotel **18**
Grosvenor House,
   A JW Marriott Hotel **7**
H10 London Waterloo **27**
Hotel 41 **20**
The Hoxton, Shoreditch **29**
Hyatt Regency London—
   The Churchill **5**
The Lanesborough **12**
The Langham **6**
Lime Tree Hotel **15**
Luna Simone Hotel **23**
Lynton B&B Hotel **16**

The Mad Hatter Hotel **26**
The Milestone Hotel **1**
Mondrian London **25**
The Nadler Victoria **19**
Park Plaza Westminster Bridge **24**
Qbic London City **36**
Sanctuary House Hotel **21**
Shangri-La Hotel at the Shard **37**
Shoreditch Inn **30**
South Place Hotel **33**
St Ermin's Hotel **22**
The Stafford London **13**
The Wellesley Knightsbridge **11**
The Zetter Townhouse, Marylebone **4**

easyHotel ★   Prefabricated room units differ only in how little space you're given (the smallest are 6 sq. m/65 sq. ft., space only for a bed and a shallow breath), with rarely an inch of space between mattress and wall. No phone, no hair dryer, no frills at all. Bathrooms are just plastic cubicles combining a shower, toilet, and sink in one wet closet. The cheapest rooms don't even have windows, and you cannot change the thermostat. Want to watch TV? You'll pay £5 for 24 hours. Wi-Fi is £10 a day. I find the no-nonsense atmosphere mercenary and horrid, but some visitors say this is how you do London ultra-cheaply while avoiding hostels. Reservations typically cost £40 for double rooms if you book 6 months ahead, and £80 to £110 if you procrastinate.

www.easyhotel.com. No phone reservations. 5 locations in Central London. Rooms £40–£110. **Amenities:** Wi-Fi £10/day.

hub by Premier Inn ★★   Sleek, cannily designed rooms (just 11.4 sq. m/ 123 sq. ft.) are tight as airlocks, packing in a platform bed for two with storage underneath, a bright and clean-lined shower/toilet module, well-located power outlets and USB charging ports, a fold-down desk, and a lime green chair. The staff won't do much for you, but using an app, you can dim or extinguish the lights, watch TV (all movies are free—the Wi-Fi is mercury-fast, too), or turn on the "do not disturb" light. *Downsides:* You may not get a mobile phone signal and you won't be able to look out a window, but the location is unmatched and there's a cafe for breakfast (under £10). Deservedly, the best rates sell out months in advance—book online only. My favorite location: Covent Garden.

www.hubhotels.co.uk. 7 locations around London. £69–£175 double. **Amenities:** Breakfast (charged); free movies; free Wi-Fi.

Ibis Hotels ★★   This 600-strong French chain by the Accor hotel giant is distinguished by simple but cheerful decor. You'll get a double bed, bathroom with shower, climate control, a 24-hour kitchen, TV, phone, free Wi-Fi, at least one outlet, and a built-in desk. The breakfast charge varies per property (£8 is typical), but food is usually served from 4am, making this a smart choice if you need to catch an early flight or train. The fresh-baked breakfast baguettes are delicious—hey, it's French. There's also **Ibis Styles,** the "all-inclusive" brand that is slightly more upscale and includes breakfast and Wi-Fi, and **Ibis Budget,** a bare-bones, shower-only crash pad once known as Etap or Formule 1; rooms there are ultra-simple (though with style), sleep up to three people, and have free Wi-Fi and TV, but practically nothing else. Check the map before booking, as many of its locations are in outer London.

www.ibishotel.com. No English-reservations hotline. 24+ locations around London. Rooms £101–£238, varying by season and location. **Amenities:** Free Wi-Fi.

Point A Hotels ★   This modern-design import provides everything you need but nothing else: en suite power shower, round-the-clock reception, air-conditioning, but not even a closet—you get hangers. Even windows come at

King's Cross to Embankment Hotels

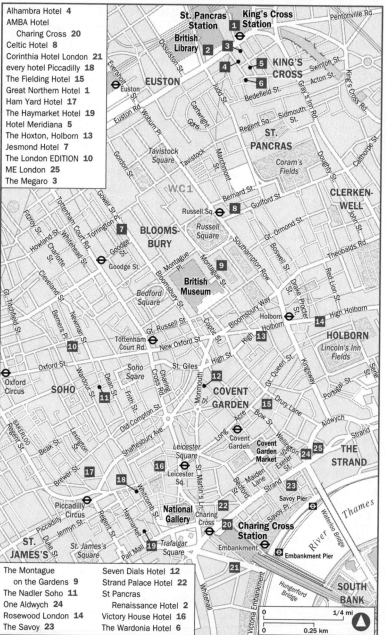

Alhambra Hotel **4**
AMBA Hotel
   Charing Cross **20**
Celtic Hotel **8**
Corinthia Hotel London **21**
every hotel Piccadilly **18**
The Fielding Hotel **15**
Great Northern Hotel **1**
Ham Yard Hotel **17**
The Haymarket Hotel **19**
Hotel Meridiana **5**
The Hoxton, Holborn **13**
Jesmond Hotel **7**
The London EDITION **10**
ME London **25**
The Megaro **3**

The Montague
   on the Gardens **9**
The Nadler Soho **11**
One Aldwych **24**
Rosewood London **14**
The Savoy **23**

Seven Dials Hotel **12**
Strand Palace Hotel **22**
St Pancras
   Renaissance Hotel **2**
Victory House Hotel **16**
The Wardonia Hotel **6**

a price. The a la carte model keeps costs down but isn't a path to luxury, yet the facilities are clean and designed with minimalist zip. Don't write off a windowless room's power to mediate jet lag. Too often, however, rates are around £175, which is too much for this simplicity—around £110 would be more reasonable. My favorite location, for nightlife: Shoreditch.

www.pointahotels.com. No phone. 6 locations in the city. Rooms £35–£125. **Amenities:** Wi-Fi £4 per device per day.

Premier Inn ★★   The largest hotel chain in the country, Premier offers rooms (maximum of two adults) with a king-size bed, bathtub and shower with all-purpose shower gel, tea- and coffee-making facilities, TV, phone, iron, air-conditioning (sometimes), at least three outlets, and a desk. Increasingly, it requires you to check in at a kiosk, eliminating human interaction, but that tells you about the tourist churn that this company is going for. Many locations include a mass-appeal bar/cafe, Thyme. Like airline tickets, prices rise as availability dwindles. Its prices start at £19 nearly a year ahead, but final prices can be poor value, so the key is early booking. Clip £10 off prices by booking ahead with a nonrefundable "Saver" reservation. Some locations are deep in distant suburbs, so consult a map before taking the bait of a low price. My favorite locations: Southwark (Bankside) and County Hall.

www.premierinn.com. ✆ **0845/099-0095.** More than 12 locations around the central city. Rooms £101–£210, depending on season and location. **Amenities:** Bar/cafe; 30 min. free Wi-Fi daily, then £3/per 24 hr.

Travelodge ★   Rates start around £88 for a non-flexible reservation if you book 11 months ahead. That more than makes up for the thin amenities of this economy brand, which has some two dozen properties in Greater London. It's nicer than the American Travelodge brand, which isn't related to it. Expect king-size beds, bathtub and shower, TV (but no phone, hair dryer, or toiletries), paid in-room movies, a wardrobe, at least one power outlet, and a desk. Breakfast, if your property offers it, is £8.50 more (kids 16 and under free). "Family rooms" have a pullout couch for two kids but cost the same as a double. Hotels marked "New Style" have just undergone renovation and are like fresh hotels.

www.travelodge.co.uk. ✆ **08719/848484.** More than 20 locations around the city. Rooms £65–£116, depending on season and location. **Amenities:** Bar/cafe (often); Wi-Fi £3/day.

Z Hotels ★★★   Please say it "Zed," which rhymes with "bed." Now that you've got that down, here's the formula: extremely compact rooms, but lots of room under the duvets; glassy sleek style; and a lobby that's always abuzz with breakfast, coffee, or free daily wine. The formula works because there are design smarts where they count: Shower nozzles swivel the way you need them to, towels are plump and copious, you can control your thermostat. They poured cash into the bedding and the 40-inch TVs but did without closets and drawers. Very cheap rooms may not have windows. Note that if you share a room with a platonic friend, bathrooms are enclosed only by panels of fogged glass. If you try to book too far ahead, they have a nasty trick of charging you £300 for a room. My favorite locations, for convenience: Soho and Piccadilly.

www.thezhotels.com. 8 locations around the city. Rooms £80–£175. **Amenities:** Cafe/ bar; air-conditioning; free evening wine and cheese; free Wi-Fi.

KING'S CROSS & BLOOMSBURY

King's Cross hotels offer small rooms in old buildings, downmarket but respectable, close to six important Tube lines—the chain hotels, listed above, are particularly present here. **Bloomsbury**'s chocolate-colored Georgian brick town houses lie within a 20-min. walk of Soho and Covent Garden, and they're near the Piccadilly Line to Heathrow. To be honest—and let's spill a dirty secret here—these places are better located than some of London's most expensive hotels.

Expensive

Great Northern Hotel ★★ Of all of London's railway terminal hotels, from the outside the Great Northern seems the plainest—and the smallest. Its crescent-shaped building went up quite early, in 1854, and as a consequence it isn't as bombastic as its brethren. Rooms aren't huge, but they have a smart modern edge that includes—daringly for a hotel—cream-colored carpeting. The smallest rooms are called "couchette" because the sled-style queen beds, attached at head and foot to the walls, are said to have been inspired by railway sleepers. (Don't worry—they have much more space for your luggage, although the result is something less than ideal for families.) Etched glass and cute little curved banquettes complete the allusions to trains. High-standard perks pack the other spaces—a good British restaurant, Plum & Spilt Milk (named after a color scheme), is one. *Caveat:* If you're quoted a rate over £300, you can do better elsewhere.

King's Cross St Pancras Station, Pancras Rd., N1. www.gnhlondon.com. ✆ **020/3388-0800.** 91 units. From £230 double. Tube: King's Cross St Pancras. **Amenities:** Restaurant; bar; snack bar; free Wi-Fi.

The Montague on the Gardens ★★ It's not easy these days finding typically British mid-priced hotels that aren't mired in gloomy tour-group dinginess, but the conjoined town houses of the Montague deliver Englishness in demonstration as much as in word. Downstairs, a large staff pays close attention to guest needs, and rooms, always tasteful and richly comfortable, are a mishmash of styles as if in a moneyed home. They're also a mix of sizes, given the age of the buildings, but they're silent, plush, and otherwise appointed with more than you'll need. It's comfortable, dignified, and a homey bolthole for Central London explorations, with the British Museum literally across the road. It's family friendly as well.

15 Montague St., WC1. www.montaguehotel.com. ✆ **020/7858-7731.** 100 units. Rooms £194–£356. Tube: Russell Square. **Amenities:** Restaurant; bar; air-conditioning; free bottled water; free Wi-Fi.

WHAT TO EXPECT AT town house hotels

Unfortunately, the once-famous English B&B is an endangered species, at least in central London. Neighborhoods that were recently dependable for cut-price lodging (Gloucester Place in Maryle-bone, Ebury St. in Victoria, Gower St. in Bloomsbury) are being sold to the ultra-rich, and B&Bs are converting to luxury apartments or selling out. Most desk staff now know London little better than you do.

The ones that survive usually occupy "listed" buildings. What does that mean? It means that it has historical or architectural importance—for example, it's an example of a fine Georgian town house or an original stately Victorian ter-race home. To keep developers from knocking down a gem, "listed" buildings are protected. Changing anything requires permission, down to the color of the paint. American tourists who are unused to London's listed buildings often post huffy online reviews about the very things that define town house hotels, penalizing London inns for being London inns. That hotel is not a dump! It's historic.

Rooms are small by American standards. Interior walls were added to sub-divide the original rooms, but don't blame the current owners. Most subdivision was done after World War II, to fill a housing gap after many of the city's big hotels were destroyed, and now even removing those slapped-up walls requires civic approval, which is nigh impossible. You are unlikely to have a closet, and in some rooms suitcases can be hard to open without using the bed. The largest rooms in such B&Bs usually face the front.

Bathrooms are even smaller. In the old days, guests shared bathrooms. To suit changing tastes, landlords wedged booths containing the staples (toilet, shower, sink) into rooms that weren't designed to have them.

Don't expect an elevator, or "lift." It takes years of begging and a small for-tune to convince the council to permit the installation of an elevator. Assume you'll have to use the stairs. They may be narrower than you're used to. Rooms on higher floors require climbing, but they also receive more light, less noise, and often cost less.

Ceilings get lower as you go higher. Until the 20th century, the floors of fash-ionable town houses served distinct functions. The cellar was for kitchens and coal storage. The ground floor was usu-ally used for living rooms. The first and second floors were reserved for bed-rooms, and the top floor was for servants and for the children's nursery, which accounts for the slightly lower ceilings there.

Not all windows are double glazed. You think you hear traffic now? Imagine when horses and carriages clattered up the cobbles at all hours. If you're a light sleeper, simply ask for a room at the back. Rooms on back stairway landings often don't adjoin other rooms, either, which takes care of more ambient noise.

St Pancras Renaissance Hotel ★★ This Gothic red-brick palace, built in the 1870s as a terminal hotel for a railway line, is one of London's most distinctive buildings; its meticulous 2011 restoration not only rescued a Victorian icon from neglect but also created an enviable property. Premium rooms have an unforgettable view down the ribbed, cast-iron cavern of the train shed, where Eurostar arrives and departs for Paris. There, the epic Cham-bers rooms have 5.5m (18-ft.) ceilings and details such as (now-decorative) fireplaces, arched windows, and substantial wooden doors. Rooms in the new Barlow wing lack those long views and suit corporate hotel tastes—the real show is in the original building. Echoing public spaces are a gilt-and-tile parade of self-important Victorian excess, from the winged Grand Staircase to the lushly carved The Gilbert Scott brasserie (named for the architect; local star Marcus Wareing oversees it) and the old wooden Booking Hall, now a bistro where old English punch cocktails are revived. The building was "too good for its purpose," lamented Scott, whose own son went mad and died in one of the rooms. It's worth a wander even if you're not staying here—management knows it's a jewel, and it welcomes visitors.

Euston Rd., London, NW1. www.stpancrasrenaissance.co.uk. ℂ **020/7841-3540.** 245 units. £250–£440 double. Tube: King's Cross St Pancras. **Amenities:** Restaurant; 2 bars; indoor pool; gym; spa; free Wi-Fi in Chambers rooms, otherwise £15/day.

Moderate

The Megaro ★ This old office building has been tarted up with brassy colors and a cluttered exterior mural, which the neighbors must hate, but inside, the theme is spacious and virtually Scandinavian, with open wood floors, unadorned paneling, smart slide-out makeup desks and workspaces, and fresh tea leaves for your cuppa. Rooms on the main road have killer views of St Pancras and the plaza in front of King's Cross (no. 504, a corner, is the best for that), but if traffic noise irritates you, go for one facing the other way (no. 508, with a small balcony, picturesquely peeks over the pipe chimneys of nearby town houses). If you're traveling with a platonic companion, ask for a room in which your bathroom isn't encased in glass walls; some are, some aren't. It has hiked its prices recently. Don't pay more than £250 for this place.

Belgrove St., WC1. www.hotelmegaro.co.uk. ℂ **020/7843-2222.** 49 units. From £220, save 15% on website. Rates include breakfast. Tube: King's Cross St Pancras. **Amenities:** Restaurant; bar; free Wi-Fi.

Inexpensive

Alhambra Hotel ★★★ The comforting Alhambra is an inn with heart, and a top value in Frommer's ever since *Europe on $5 a Day.* They care. Its proprietors, whose lineage has owned the land for decades and aren't at risk of being elbowed out like so many others, take pride in the business and they keep prices low. Picture simple, small, but dignified rooms squeezed into old spaces, but

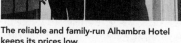

The reliable and family-run Alhambra Hotel keeps its prices low.

always spotless and freshened up with bright bedspreads, inviting royal-blue carpeting, built-in desks with chairs, and flat-screen TVs (but no phones). Bruno Cabral handles the hotel's modern service, such as the addition of free fiber-optic Wi-Fi and in-room safes, rarities for this price point. If you share a bathroom, there are plenty to go around. Guests can use the lobby computer. The same family runs an annex across the street that has the same high standards with rooms sleeping up to four. In winter, it's easy to negotiate rates down by as much as 30 percent.

17–19 Argyle St., WC1. www.alhambrahotel.com. ℂ **020/7837-9575.** 52 units. £87–£118 single, £98–£143 double. Rates include full cooked breakfast. Tube: King's Cross St Pancras. **Amenities:** Lobby computer; free Wi-Fi.

Celtic Hotel ★★

For more than six 6 decades, the eccentric but dedicated Marazzi family, beloved in London's affordable-travel world, have run budget inns where people from around the world mingle. Few other hoteliers put as much heart into making sure guests are acclimated to London by answering questions, obliging special dietary requests, and filling bellies with a cooked breakfast that's so enormous (try the banana yogurt) that lunch might become optional. To keep attracting longtime regulars—there are many, going back more than half a century, because the Marazzis owned the departed St Margaret's Hotel for 56 years—the Celtic, a defiant holdout from the way British hospitality used to be, retains quirky features: Rooms don't have TVs or phones, furniture is endearingly mismatched, and the lounge is a hub for socializing with fellow guests. Add up to £22 if you don't want to share a shower or toilet. You must book directly.

62 Guilford St., WC1. www.celtichotel.com. ℂ **020/7837-6737.** 35 units. From £70 single, from £95 double. Rates include cooked breakfast. Tube: Russell Square. **Amenities:** 2 lounges; free Wi-Fi.

Hotel Meridiana ★

This is what a value hotel should be: not lavish, but you happily get what you pay for. Walls can be thin, rooms truly teeny, and many share bathrooms, but everything is spotless and there's been a recent updating. Heating and hot water are reliable, too, which isn't always the case in buildings of this age, and some rooms have drawers, another relative curiosity. If you just want a dead-cheap place to sleep where you'll have no regrets about hygiene, this no-frills B&B is a decent choice. You're unlikely to get as much value for the price elsewhere.

43–44 Argyle Sq., WC1. www.hotelmeridiana.co.uk. ℂ **020/7713-0144.** 27 units. From £65 single, from £75 double. Continental breakfast £5. Tube: King's Cross St Pancras. **Amenities:** Free Wi-Fi.

Jesmond Hotel ★★★

I have a soft spot for this place near the British Library. I stayed here often when I was just out of college (in room no. 3, a cozy single on the rear landing—still there, still snug). Back then, the Beynon family had a young son, Glyn. Today, Glyn is a grown family man, and he's in charge—and he's doing a proud job of updating the family B&B in a 1780s town house (ask him about its history) far beyond the expectations of its tariff range. He installed new bathrooms with all-new piping, accounting for the larger-than-average showers; he soundproofed the front windows to keep out the roar of Gower Street's traffic. He also converted the former parlor, with its antique (nonworking) fireplace, into room no. 2, a spacious double. It's classic (four units share bathrooms), and in fact, has been a Frommer's selection ever since *Europe on $5 a Day* (when it cost $3.20). Pay for 6 nights from November to February, and you can stay for 7. Don't confuse this place with the Jesmond Dene, a B&B on Argyle Square—it's very good, too, but not as central.

63 Gower St., WC1. www.jesmondhotel.org.uk. © **020/7636-3199.** 15 units. £75–£85 single, £95–£125 double, £150 quad, often a 3-night minimum. Rates include full breakfast. Tube: Goodge St. **Amenities:** Free Wi-Fi.

The Wardonia Hotel ★   For almost half a century in the pages of Frommer's, the Wardonia, in a brown-brick Georgian building, has been suggested for those times when you need a place to be super cheap, no matter the sacrifice: Rooms are wee—like *sooooo* tiny, as if the walls and the bed are in a death match for dominance, recalling the compactor scene in *Star Wars*. Thus warned, you will now be prepared for the impossible value. Very simple in plain brown wainscoting, rooms have bathroom cubbies with showers but not tubs, and you don't get breakfast—all reflected in the crazy low rates, which have barely budged in a decade. The Wardonia is one of London's last "they're charging *how* much?" crash pads.

46–54 Argyle St., WC1. www.wardoniahotel.co.uk. © **020/7837-3944.** 65 units. £50 single, £60 double/twin, £70 triple. Tube: King's Cross St Pancras. **Amenities:** Free Wi-Fi.

SOHO, COVENT GARDEN & WEST END

This is the middle of London. The part of town that offers everything you need outside your door. The area that also offers streets crawling with inebriated 20-year-olds singing drinking shanties in full voice after midnight. You may not care, because staying centrally can save on Tube fare more than it costs in shoe leather. Sunday through Thursday are the cheapest nights here.

Expensive

Ham Yard Hotel ★   Firmdale Hotels is a revered name in London's vanity circles, and the design penchant of its co-owner, Kit Kemp, has made her a style celebrity. Tucked into a mews north of Piccadilly Circus, it's preferred by social butterflies—the huge ground floor bar and four-lane basement bowling alley/cinema complex swarm during the weekend. The hive of activity can put a frenetic spin on a sundowner, but rooms (no two identical, each one seemingly ripped from a design magazine) are buffered from the buzz with soundproofing, plump queen beds, floor-to-ceiling windows, and generous bathrooms of granite and oak with walk-in showers. You're paying for coolness.

1 Ham Yard, W1. www.firmdalehotels.com. ℂ **020/3642-2000**. 91 units. Rooms from £400. Tube: Piccadilly Circus. **Amenities:** Bar/restaurant; fitness center; cinema; bowling alley; rooftop bar; free Wi-Fi.

The Haymarket Hotel ★★ Bubbly colored textures, mismatched but impeccably selected furniture—this Firmdale property is like staying at the country house of a fabulous friend who has made a fortune in coffee-table books. This elegant (but never stuffy) choice takes its cues from nearby St James's, regally situated in a cluster of rehabbed buildings beside the Theatre Royal Haymarket, and it backs up its bright Modern English visuals with five-star features such as a sharp staff, indulgent showers, and an indoor swimming pool. There are no high-end choices closer to the West End action yet serenely removed from its tumult—it's the one property in the Firmdale group not to be routinely mobbed with cocktail-swilling fashion chasers, which makes it a delicious place to land and recharge after a tiring day.

1 Suffolk Pl., SW1. www.firmdalehotels.com. ℂ **020/7470-4000**. 50 units. Rooms from £400. Tube: Piccadilly Circus. **Amenities:** Bar/restaurant; fitness center; basement pool; free Wi-Fi.

ME London ★ The nine-story-tall field of polished black marble in its core atrium is preposterously stylish, and the scene of its 10th-floor rooftop bar, Radio, is ridiculously pretty in both panorama and clientele. An "Aura Manager" hands incoming guests Prosecco and seeks to serve as a concierge, while bedside panels control everything from the temperature to the hue of the mood lighting. For all that folderol, bathrooms are huge, and rooms aren't small, either, even if the windows feel like pointed ship prows poking over the street. This luxury entrant by Spanish group Meliá is not a hotel for Ma and Pa Kettle or little kids—but if you wear your dresses tight and take your pre-clubbing coffee black, the place called ME may suit your preening self-image.

336–337 Strand, WC2. www.melondon hotel.com. ℂ **020/7395-3400**. 157 units. From £285 double. Tube: Temple. **Amenities:** Restaurant; 3 bars; in-room spa treatments; fitness center; free Wi-Fi.

Balcony of a guest room at One Aldwych, which used to be the home of the *Morning Post.*

One Aldwych ★★ The domed 1907 headquarters of the *Morning Post,* imperialist and ultra-conservative, is now home to this high-quality boutique hotel with two restaurants (one of which serves Basque gourmet); a double-tall, sculpture-filled lobby cocktail lounge; and a theatrically lit underground swimming pool where the printing presses were once housed. Rooms are mildly contemporary but frankly, for the price point, need some updates; some sneak a view of the Thames and others admire the Lyceum Theatre. The rooms are no longer quite up-to-date, but you hardly notice because the staff is five-star, usually meeting guests' needs without being asked, and the location feels impossibly considerate, too: steps from Covent Garden and Trafalgar Square, a walk down Strand to St Paul's, and a brief stroll over the Waterloo Bridge to the glories of Southbank. This well-kept secret is a favorite of those in the know.

1 Aldwych, WC2. www.onealdwych.com. ℗ **020/7300-1000.** 105 units. From £400 double. Tube: Covent Garden or Temple. **Amenities:** 2 restaurants; cocktail bar; indoor pool; gym; spa treatments; free Wi-Fi.

Rosewood London ★★★ One of the city's lushest modern hotels is entered through a stone courtyard arch of a gloriously elaborate edifice (constructed with pomp in 1914 as the Pearl Assurance insurance citadel). The foyer is amazingly sheathed in brass, and rooms are so quiet you could hear your champagne bubbles pop. They're also exquisite: Giant 46-inch flatscreen TVs are standard, as is Italian bedding you sink into like a swimming pool. Push a button to bring down your window blinds and sip homemade sloe gin from the minibar. If it weren't for the hard reality of the tariff, it'd be enough to sour you to life on the rest of the planet. There's also a gin bar in the restaurant downstairs, plus a gimmicky bar themed to Scarfe, a cartoonist who is London's modern-day version of Broadway's Al Hirschfeld, but the real find is **The Pie Room** (11am–4pm weekdays), a tucked-away cubby containing the magic of Calum Franklin, a brilliant pastry chef with a cult following.

252 High Holborn, WC1. www.rosewoodhotels.com/london. ℗ **020/7781-8888.** 262 units. Rooms £320–£510. Tube: Holborn. **Amenities:** Restaurant; bar; lounge; fitness center; spa; free Wi-Fi.

The Savoy ★ Few cities can claim hotels as iconic as the Savoy, which merits a visit even if you, like most people, cannot afford to stay there. There may be no more thrilling hotel entrance than the polished gleam of its porte cochere centered around a Lalique fountain. The service puts no foot wrong. Strange, then, that the details pander so—when you pay this much, why can't you have a real painting rather than a print textured to look like canvas? Why are there portraits of Hollywood stars in the famous Thames Foyer? Why is the gimmicky cocktail menu in the sublimely ebony Beaufort Bar designed like a children's book? Still, the Savoy has vibrated with high history, half Edwardian and half Jazz Age, since 1889. The American Bar has been a hushed laboratory for upscale cocktails for a century; its Simpson's in the Strand has been serving roast British dinners since 1828. Corny details can't erase how much happened here: Churchill puffing, Chaplin mugging, Wilde and Bosie dallying, Gilbert and Sullivan pattering in its theater, Monet and Whistler painting the Thames from their windows. A fine honeymooners' selection.

The Strand, WC2. www.fairmont.com/savoy-london. ☏ **888/265-0533** (U.S.), or 020/7836-4343 (London). 268 units. Rooms from £486. Tube: Embankment or Temple. **Amenities:** 3 restaurants; 2 bars; indoor pool; gym; spa; business center; Wi-Fi £10/day.

Moderate

AMBA Hotel Charing Cross ★★★   The railway terminal hotel above Charing Cross Station opened a month after Lincoln's assassination and underwent many lives (and Blitz damage). Now the Charing Cross is an upper-moderate hotel that dips its toes into luxury trimmings (heated bathroom floors, walk-in showers, Nespresso coffee, free minibars that include beer, and so forth) while remaining a supreme value for the cost. The location is spectacular and could command much higher rates: At the nexus of Trafalgar Square, Strand, the Covent Garden area, and the Embankment, you're truly spoiled. Breakfast (crowded; the staff isn't always on top of things) is taken with a view toward St Martin-in-the-Fields, and at night, some 350 LED candles flicker throughout the hallways and up the sweeping central grand staircase. Such echoes of a more genteel age treat you to the grandeur of old London at a good price.

The Strand, WC2. www.amba-hotel.com. ☏ **0800/330-8397.** 239 units. Rooms £173–£368. Tube: Charing Cross or Embankment. **Amenities:** Restaurant; bar; business center; free Wi-Fi.

At the entrance to the Savoy Hotel, guests are greeted by a crystal Lalique fountain.

every hotel Piccadilly ★   Steps from Leicester Square, this hotel shares a concept with other trendy budget brands: Give them comfortable beds and free Wi-Fi, let them check in by kiosk, and then leave them alone. You get a Nespresso coffee machine, a Smart TV, an upper-grade bed, and access to a printer for boarding passes. The stripped-down staff has its drawbacks (if you need someone, you may have to wait), but for what you're saving and the prime spot you're scoring, big deal. Paying £180 is a sweet deal, but to lay down north of £280 would be madness; only the sublime location could validate it.

Coventry St., W1. www.every-hotels.com/Piccadilly. ✆ **0800/330-8395.** 127 units. Rooms from £170. Tube: Leicester Square. **Amenities:** Restaurant; fitness center; free Wi-Fi.

The Fielding Hotel ★   It's nearly impossible to beat the location, just steps from Covent Garden's food and shopping, which is why you overlook the cramped, lift-less quarters at this average family-owned hotel. In this early-19th-century warren of tight staircases and fire doors, the sometimes slightly airless rooms snuggle you with a certain throwaway charisma. It's not top of the line, but it feels like home. Room no. 10 is a double with a sitting area that catches lots of afternoon light, thanks to its corner position and copious windows. Everything's en suite (but mostly shower only), and there are no common areas to speak of. Trivia: Oscar Wilde was convicted of gross indecency in the Bow Street Magistrates' Court next door.

4 Broad Ct., Bow St., WC2. www.thefieldinghotel.co.uk. ✆ **020/7836-8305.** 24 units. £90–£100 single, £140–£180 double. Tube: Covent Garden or Holborn. **Amenities:** Pass to nearby fitness center; free Wi-Fi.

The Hoxton, Holborn ★   It's called Hoxton because that's where this boutique hipster hotel brand began (the original is listed on p. 61). This one is newer (2014), busier, and delightfully it's also a few minutes' walk south of the British Museum, in the middle of it all. There's a restaurant, a bar, and a too-cool-for-school beauty salon. Some find it off-puttingly millennial: The lobby is always packed with Wi-Fi spongers (good luck finding a seat as a paying guest). You get a smallish, winkingly antique-styled room with a double bed, fun throwback touches like wooden desks, vintage-looking music players, a chubby duvet, and an hour's worth of free calls every day. The bathroom is less smart; tiled showers are faux-Victorian but don't have doors. Continental breakfast is delivered in a bag. Every room is a good value—that's the point—but they all have the same amenities no matter the size, so why not go for the cheapest, the 129-sq.-ft. "Shoebox"? Deals tend to be good in advance.

199–206 High Holborn, WC1. www.thehoxton.com. ✆ **020/7661-3000.** 174 units. Rooms £99–£299. Rates include continental breakfast. Tube: Holborn. **Amenities:** 2 restaurants; bar; coffee house; salon; 1 hr. free calls daily; free water and milk; free Wi-Fi.

The Nadler Soho ★★★   The Nadler gets moderate lodging right by providing style without pretension or henpecking guests with fees. Quiet, high-design rooms are compact but nonetheless kitted out with twists such as wide beds, mini-kitchens with a third tap for filtered water, a microwave, big glassy bathrooms with rain showers, plenty of power outlets plus a loaner plug adapter, and flatscreen TVs that let you do everything—read the latest newspapers, listen to a free music library, even stream content. Deluxe rooms, at the top of the middle-rate scale, sleep up to four. There's no restaurant (breakfast can be delivered at any time at prices that aren't marked up), but all of Soho is teeming right outside your door. It was something to sing about when it only charged £140, but success has tempted it to hike prices. It's still a strong, well-run choice in the central West End. Its sister property in Victoria (10 Palace St., SW1; ✆ **020/3697-3697**; £164–£260; Tube: Victoria) does the exact same "affordable luxury" thing within steps of Buckingham Palace, where there's less nightlife, and for a lot less. The Kensington branch lacks pizzazz.

10 Carlisle St., W1. www.nadlerhotels.com. ✆ **020/3697-3697**. 78 units. Rooms £224–£332. Tube: Tottenham Court Rd. or Piccadilly Circus. **Amenities:** 30 min. free national calls daily; free Wi-Fi.

Strand Palace Hotel ★ It was once the sort of desultory pillow mill favored by shuffling package tours and lost weekends, but this year, Frommer's declares it's finally worth a look in. That's because this dowager has finally gotten wise to its stellar location—right across from the Savoy, beside Covent Garden—by renovating the 1980s right out of the walls and returning it to the land of the living. Rooms are getting sophisticated new looks—the "cosy" ones are wee, windows could be larger, but beds are great and everything is a good value while the hotel's reputation is being rehabilitated. And, for the first time since its 1908 construction, rooms now have air-conditioning. Floor-by-floor renovations are rolling until 2020; to get a good room, ask for "deluxe" or "superior."

372 Strand, WC2. www.strandpalacehotel.co.uk. ✆ **020/7379-4737**. 785 units. Rooms £90–£250. Tube: Charing Cross or Temple. **Amenities:** 2 restaurants; 2 bars; business center; fitness center; free national calls; free minibar (deluxe rooms); free Wi-Fi.

Victory House Hotel ★★★ The location is beyond perfect: behind a gorgeous 1898 French Renaissance facade on the north side of Leicester Square—it gets noisy at night outside, but doubled panes keep the clatter to a soothing murmur. Lobby and rooms alike are small but nonetheless higher-end and magnetic. The monochrome palette is a nod to the Square's decades of classic movie premieres, the bathrooms a higher grade than most with Bigelow toiletries and heated towel bars, the beds large even if the ceilings are low, and the perks pleasing (like snacks and soft drinks you can raid for free and free local calls via a handheld device that can also guide you around town). Its snug comfort makes it hard to leave, but at least when you do, you never have far to go to be in the middle of it all.

14 Leicester Place, WC2. www.victoryhouselondon.com. ✆ **020/3909-4100**. 86 units. Rooms from £175. Tube: Leicester Square. **Amenities:** Bistro; access to nearby gym; handheld device with free local calls; free Wi-Fi.

SIX TRICKS FOR saving

To save money on guesthouses and inns, obey six simple rules:

1. **Off-season is cheaper.** Many big hotels have two seasons: April through September vs. October through March (excluding holidays). Prices will be 10 to 25 percent cheaper in winter. Interestingly, very few family-owned B&Bs and inns bother with this system, pricing uniformly.

2. **Stay longer.** I haven't found a family-run hotel that wasn't willing to lower prices for anyone staying more than 5 or 6 nights.

3. **The days matter.** Any given hotel tends to be cheaper at one time of week over another: weekends in business zones like the City, weekdays in touristy Soho.

4. **Go mom-and-pop.** Their rates usually include taxes, but big hotels' rates don't.

5. **Book directly.** The chains now tend to give the best rates if you do that. (That said, in Frommer's' tests, Booking.com and HotelsCombined compare well to competitors, and Booking.com tends to include tax in its quotes, which helps.)

6. **Last-minute deals are rare but do exist.** Routes for looking into deals within a week of travel are Hotwire.com, Priceline.com, and the app Hotel Tonight.

Inexpensive

Seven Dials Hotel ★   There are almost no truly budget hotels in the West End, so hoteliers get away with merely functional facilities. Here, everything is little: the stairway, the rooms, the charm. And correspondingly, the rates. There's usually barely enough storage space, a TV mounted on an armature, a basic writing desk, teeny clean bathrooms, and firm beds, albeit ones covered with dowdy bedspreads. Forget the lack of a lift and all the ways it's average and slipping year by year. Its footing on Monmouth Street, steps from a rainbow of pubs, boutiques, and food clustering around Covent Garden, is without comparison. Dump your bags and go play, because the price is fair.

7 Monmouth St., WC2. www.sevendialshotel.com. ℂ **020/7681-0791.** 18 units. £90–£100 single, £85–£120 double, sometimes there's a 3-night min. Rates include buffet breakfast. Tube: Covent Garden. **Amenities:** Free Wi-Fi.

KENSINGTON, VICTORIA & KNIGHTSBRIDGE

You might have heard West London was a major tourist zone, but things have changed. After affordable prospects developed in King's Cross and Southwark, it now makes less sense to put up with the Tube ride required to stay here, and for most tourists, South Ken and Victoria have all but slipped off the radar, although many package tours take advantage of the slipping rates by placing group bookings here. Some well-established old guard names are still going strong, though.

Expensive

The Beaufort ★★ Quiet as a dropped pin, this tidy, well-run hotel down a dead-end residential street just west of Harrods (your neighbors: the 1%) distinguishes itself by offering more services than the standard: free afternoon tea with homemade scones, free cocktails by evening. Rooms—most of which are tucked away in a tortuous maze of corridors resulting from the combination of several town houses—are spacious for London, tastefully and conservatively decorated with delicate wallpaper and big cushy beds, finely equipped, and a value compared to others of the same price. It's fairly good with options for families. The museums of South Kensington are a 5-min. walk away, as is Hyde Park.

33 Beaufort Gardens, SW3. www.thebeaufort.co.uk. ℂ **020/7584-5252.** 29 units. From £255 double. Tube: Knightsbridge. **Amenities:** Free cocktails; free afternoon tea; free Wi-Fi.

The Goring ★★ Only one five-star hotel has the Royal Warrant from the queen for Hospitality Services. Only one has been run by the same family since 1910. Only one hosted Kate Middleton, the wife of a future king and mother of another, in her final night as a single girl before she walked down the aisle of Westminster Abbey. This is the Goring, classic but not self-importantly so, assiduously appropriate in style and rich in expensive fabrics,

The Silk Room at the Goring offers classic luxury.

down to the Gainsborough silk on the walls, yet still goofy enough to put a stuffed sheep in every room. The fleet of doormen wears bowler hats, and the signature canary-yellow china at its hotly pursued afternoon tea (4-month wait; p. 88) is made just for the hotel. The effect is something like an English country house, especially as you look out oversized windows at its blooming garden. When you're here, there's no mistaking you're steeping in London culture.

Beeston Place, SW1. www.thegoring.com. © **020/7396-9000.** 69 units. Rooms £323–£840. Tube: Victoria. **Amenities:** Restaurant; bar; gym access; free Wi-Fi.

Hotel 41 ★★ A secret romantic nest only steps from Buckingham Palace, Hotel 41 is a hushed hideaway on the top floor of its moderately priced cousin, The Rubens. You take a tiny private lift and tread a snug network of creaking corridors to reach its heart, a two-level, galleried conservatory bedecked like something to make Henry Higgins purr: mahogany shelves, inviting seating, sculptural busts and an oversized globe, and a yawning skylight to let the light in. There, staff makes the rounds, quietly addressing guests by name and filling glasses with champagne and plates with an endless flow of scones and hors d'oeuvres. People forget to go outside and see London. The rooms are equally individualized and top-flight: done nearly entirely in black-and-white and lacking nothing. There's no on-site restaurant or spa, and some rooms have no view to speak of—the focus is on intimacy, service, and discretion. The duplex Conservatory Suite, with a skylight over the bed, is popular with newlyweds and other nuzzlers.

41 Buckingham Palace Rd, SW1. www.41hotel.com. © **020/7300-0041.** 30 units. Rooms £377–£540. Tube: Victoria. **Amenities:** Bar; free snacks; access to nearby gym; free Wi-Fi.

The Milestone Hotel ★★★ The Milestone steeps itself in all things Anglophilic. First is the location on the southern edge of Kensington Gardens—upper-floor rooms have a view of Kensington Palace itself. The hotel is actually three town houses that have been combined, so each room is distinct in size and shape, and the furnishings—antique paintings, rich rugs, enormous beds, fat couches—make you feel like you're staying in a rich relation's country mansion rather than a citified hotel. You're awash in thoughtful amenities, from a welcome cocktail in the glass conservatory to a small bag of prunes and another of handmade hard candy waiting bedside at night. Staff, from the top-hatted doormen to the butler that attends to higher-level rooms, is alert yet unfussy. High tea in the plush lounge is a treat here as well.

1 Kensington Ct., W8. www.milestonehotel.com. © **020/7917-1000.** 63 units. Rooms from £292. Tube: High St. Kensington. **Amenities:** Restaurant; tea room; welcome beverage; bar; conservatory; fitness center; spa, indoor resistance swimming pool; room service; free bottled water; free Wi-Fi.

St. Ermin's Hotel ★★ A decade ago, it was a package-tourist misery locals nicknamed "St. Vermin's." But with a new owner, much investment, and a hookup to Marriott's points system, glory has been restored to this

A hotel since 1899, the handsome St. Ermin's was once a headquarters for British spy efforts.

handsome 1889 Queen Anne structure, a hotel since 1899. The lobby's latticed riot of plasterwork and sweeping Art Nouveau stairs is enough to make a tourist drop one's baggage to rhapsodize about the London-ness of it all, but the history is just as rich: The premises were long used as a headquarters for British spy efforts—Ian Fleming, the creator of James Bond, worked here. Room sizes vary wildly, from puny to palatial, so you may need the guidance of a live person to get the right one, but they're all quiet and well-appointed—not five-star but solidly four. Children are emphatically welcomed (family rooms are available), and there's an agreeably pubby bar on premises; the Tube is on the same block and Westminster Abbey a 5-min. stroll east. The buffet breakfast is weak, but that can always be improved—precious Old World British vibrations such as these are to be protected and patronized.

2 Caxton St., SW1. www.sterminshotel.co.uk. ☎ **020/7222-7888.** 331 units. Rooms £227–£459. Tube: St James's Park. **Amenities:** 2 restaurants; bar; fitness center; free Wi-Fi.

Moderate

The Grosvenor Hotel ★ May we pause to celebrate the resplendent creation that was the English train station terminal hotel? The Grosvenor ("Grove-nor") opened in 1862 with a 1910 extension—it was the first hotel in town to install a lift—and although it's no longer at the top of the hospitality food chain, its wide corridors and sweeping staircases can still make you feel like you're the central character in a romantic novel, but affordably. The one-time first class railway lounge is now Réunion, a dusky cocktail bar overlooking the concourse of Victoria Station (some rear rooms can hear platform announcements). While the common spaces are Victorian, the high-ceilinged rooms strike a modern tone: striped fabrics, metal- and earth-tone velour upholsteries, and air-conditioning. Avoid the "Wing Building" rooms, which are too far from the lobby and too small, with bad views. For more space, simply upgrade to an Executive.

101 Buckingham Palace Rd., W1. www.guoman.com/grosvenor. © **020/7523-5055.** 345 units. Around £150 single, £199 double, £268 Executive. Cheaper Sat–Sun. Tube: Victoria. **Amenities:** 2 restaurants; tea room; cocktail lounge; room service; fitness center; executive club; free Wi-Fi.

Lime Tree Hotel ★★   Matt and Charlotte Goodsall brightened a once-frumpy guesthouse into a place that feels as current as it is friendly. The conjoined brick town houses are historic, so no lift is permitted, but everything is updated with slate-and-white paint, fresh curtains, and touches such as bedside reading lights. If you have a first-floor room on the front, you'll have a small balcony over busy Ebury Street; in the quieter back, you'll overlook the cute flower garden. Only three rooms have their own bathrooms; the rest share. A basement room is larger than the others but has no view. The Lime Tree is popular so the owners have no need to discount for longer stays.

135–137 Ebury St., London SW1. www.limetreehotel.co.uk. © **020/7730-8191.** 25 units. £140–£180 single, £180–£230 double. Rates include full breakfast. Children 4 and under not permitted. Tube: Victoria or Sloane Square. **Amenities:** Free Wi-Fi.

Sanctuary House Hotel ★   Once, many pubs ran nondescript inns as sidelines. The pub here, where you take breakfast, is a truly typical Fuller's location (there are hundreds of them), but the hotel upstairs is a creaking, well-tended reward unto itself for value and charm, and the staff is unusually responsive for such a small property. The look plays up its Victorian origins with faux-antique telephones and plenty of handsome wood trim, but the modernized bathrooms and soft beds betray the fact that it's the beneficiary of some recent renovations by intelligent hoteliers. Even more miraculously, it's so near Big Ben that you can hear the bell peal (or you could, at least, if it wasn't being restored). You'll find a similarly oh-so-London pub hotel experience at its sister, **The Mad Hatter Hotel** (www.madhatterhotel.co.uk; © **020/7401-9222;** Tube: Blackfriars or Southwark), a block off the Thames near the Tate Modern. But that one is less recommended for 2019 because of ongoing area construction.

33 Tothill St., SW1. www.sanctuaryhousehotel.co.uk. © **020/7799-4044.** 34 units. From £193 double including breakfast, cheaper Sat–Sun. Tube: St James's Park or Westminster. **Amenities:** Air-conditioning; free Wi-Fi.

Inexpensive

Luna Simone Hotel ★   Because this prototypical town house budget B&B began as two hotels that were conjoined in the 1990s, you'll sometimes see it called the Luna & Simone. A protected building with old metalwork on the banisters and oddly sized guest rooms, it has kept up by way of inexpensive furniture and basic amenities, but it's the thoughtful service that attracts many return guests. Eat quickly—the simple English breakfast ends early, at 9am. There's no lift or air-conditioning, but also no sharing of bathrooms. Cheap and cheerful, the way London used to do it—the owners have been at it since 1970.

47–49 Belgrave Rd., SW1. www.lunasimonehotel.com. ⒸⓅ **020/7834-5897.** From £95 single, £135–£159 double. Rates include breakfast. Tube: Victoria or Pimlico. **Amenities:** Free Wi-Fi.

Lynton B&B Hotel ★ Like a place you might find with a time machine, the Lynton, close to Victoria Station, is the kind of prototypical family-run crash pad London has mostly stamped out. Brothers Mark and Simon Connor took it over from their nan, who ran it since the mid-1960s (it's been a guest-house since after World War II, but a century ago was the home of a local horse doctor). The Gentrification Fairy has not yet pummeled the Lynton with her merciless wand—it's pleasingly dog-eared, and the Connors, some of the last London-bred B&B proprietors left on Ebury Street, care deeply about their family tradition and dispense opinion at the slightest encouragement. Expect quarters that are sufficient but hardly deluxe, for those who'd rather spend money on other things. There's no lift—the council won't allow one.

113 Ebury St., SW1. www.lyntonhotel.co.uk. ⒸⓅ **020/7730-4032.** 13 units. £70 single, £80–£115 double, depending on shared or en suite bathroom. Rates include breakfast. Tube: Victoria. **Amenities:** Free Wi-Fi.

SHOULD I pack IT?

- Although all hotels include towels and linens, at family-run places you'll find for the most part that travelers are expected to bring their own washcloths.
- Many beds have duvets but not top sheets. It's just a European style; locals would probably explain that the duvet cover *is* the top sheet.
- You may find that your bed is made each day, but your sheets aren't changed. This, too, is normal, and it saves on water, electricity, and detergent. If you want them changed, simply request it.
- In the budget category, nearly all rooms have TVs these days, but not cable, so expect only four or five broadcast (or "terrestrial") channels.

- Ask for a loaner hair dryer or curling iron because your non-British one probably can't handle the voltage. New non-British hair curlers fare better, although they may get hotter than they do back home.
- Not every small hotel stocks irons, sometimes for safety reasons.
- Family-run B&Bs can't afford a porter, but rare is the place that doesn't have at least one strong person to help with your baggage. But you must ask.
- Cheaper places don't have air-conditioning because before climate change, London didn't get that hot. That's changing fast.

MARYLEBONE & MAYFAIR

For visitors who want a balance of central location and private residential vibe, Marylebone's the place. A 10-min. walk takes you to the "smart" end of Oxford Street and Mayfair to the south, or the wide-open fields of Regent's Park to the north.

Expensive

The Beaumont ★★★ The proprietors call this relative newcomer "American-style," but you might peg it for Art Deco; after all, its 1926 facade was once the garage of Selfridges' department store, the halls and lifts are full of glossy shots of bygone stars, and its bar and restaurant—serving duck egg hash at breakfast—strongly evoke a 1930s Los Angeles grill, like a Mayfair version of Hollywood's Musso & Frank. Or maybe they mean that it's friendly, not stuffy—after all, the top-hatted doormen welcome you by name whenever you return, such as from Selfridges itself, steps away. Either way, it's a five-star hotel that benefits from the fact its guts were custom-built a few years ago, meaning rooms could be customized to be cutting-edge (free streaming movies, free minibar, heated bathroom floors). It's a top-quality luxury stay in a modestly sized hotel, but without the affected snottiness of some London properties. The Beaumont is most noted for Antony Gormley's geometric sculpture of a brooding man perched on one of its outcroppings—inside is an arty wooden suite that's favored by society spenders. You're more likely to love a "Classic" room facing the courtyard or a "Superior" facing the quiet street and a pocket park.

8 Balderton St., W1. www.thebeaumont.com. © **020/7499-1001.** 73 units. Rooms from £370. Tube: Bond St. **Amenities:** Restaurant; bar; fitness center with hammam; free local shuttle car; free local calls; free movies; free Wi-Fi.

Claridge's ★★★ The red brick Claridge's is the quintessential luxury Mayfair hotel, proudly proclaiming taste in discretion as administered through glittering Deco accents. The building dates to 1894 (when Gilbert & Sullivan's producer rebuilt it), but modern amenities are installed among the gilded plasterwork and (non-working) fireplaces—neither floorboards nor exacting staff dare grumble. From the bathrooms (heated floors, high-tech toilet/bidets) to cavernous wardrobes and plump beds as wide as some studio apartments, there's not much to complain about. Its main lift is the last in Central London to be operated by hand—there's a sofa inside should you tire during your five-level journey to the top floor—and its clubby cocktail bars and Fera restaurant are favored by modern-day fashion icons (your Von Furstenbergs, your Jaggers, your Eltons) who detest the starched exclusivity that can make the Ritz such a drag. Pedigreed unconventionality has always been a theme: In 1945, Winston Churchill declared suite 212 temporarily Yugoslavian territory so baby Prince Alexander II could claim to be born on home soil. Don't miss the lobby Christmas tree, designed each year by a new design luminary (in 2017, it was Karl Lagerfeld).

Brook St., W1. www.claridges.co.uk. © **020/7629-8860.** 203 units. Rooms from £420. Tube: Bond St. **Amenities:** Restaurant; 2 bars; spa; fitness center; business center; free Wi-Fi.

Dukes Hotel ★★ In St James's, a neighborhood not wanting for luxury boltholes, Dukes sets itself apart for coziness and clubby service. It's virtually hidden near Green Park in a tight lane beside Spencer House (p. 134)—so no views—which makes this 1908 classic feel like it exists in a world of its own. Beds are big and soft, bathrooms have those fancy mechanized Asian toilets, hallways wind and creak the way you'd want them to. Make a table reservation for the deservedly popular bar—Ian Fleming, creator of James Bond, is often said to have been a regular, so tourists flock to it. Potables are freshly mixed on a wooden trolley at your table, but do not order your martini "shaken, not stirred"—Bond's recipe is widely considered to be a way to ruin the vodka. Drinks in there are £21 (but skimp on nothing), but the rooms upstairs are much more affordable than they ought to be. To think that Premier Inn sometimes charges the same price (before VAT) as this pocket miracle—it boggles the mind, so let this be our secret.

35 St James's Place, SW1. www.dukeshotel.com. © **020/7491-4840.** 90 units. Rooms from £260–£345. Tube: Green Park. **Amenities:** Restaurant; bar; fitness center; morning newspaper; free Wi-Fi.

The Lanesborough ★★★ I sneezed at the Lanesborough. Moments later, my butler—everyone has one here—flew to my side bearing a silver tray of hot tea, fresh-cut ginger on a porcelain plate, and acacia honey. And so it should be at one of the finest hotels in which I hope you will ever be so lucky to stay, where guest needs are meticulously anticipated and fresh-cut blooms are delivered to your bathroom counter the moment your back is turned. A recent £80-million renovation tore out every fixture and fully recrafted the interior with gilt, made-to-measure finery—like a mansion of Wedgwood china, Corinthian leather, and canopy king beds. It's an English pastiche for the super-wealthy, but a pitch-perfect one, and honeymoon nirvana. At the Lanesborough, intense formality dwells discreetly with new tech: TVs repose

behind false paintings in gilt frames. Downstairs, near two portraits that, though unremarked, are actually originals by Sir Joshua Reynolds, money-eyed regulars sip glasses of port dating as far back as 1778 and smoke £4,000 cigars in what many consider the world's best-stocked cigar lounge. Should the tariff at London's most expensive hotel understandably be out of your reach, at least stop by for the exquisite Afternoon Tea (p. 89) in its magnificent Regency-style restaurant, Céleste.

A sitting area in a guest room at the posh Lanesborough Hotel.

Hyde Park Corner, SW1. www.lanesborough. com. © **020/7259-5599.** 93 units. Rooms from £645 including VAT. Tube: Hyde Park Corner. **Amenities:** Restaurant; bar; cigar lounge; fitness center; complimentary chauffeured car; free landline calls to U.S., Canada, and Europe; free Wi-Fi.

The Langham ★★   The Langham has two claims to fame: It was the first grande dame hotel, in 1865, and it popularized afternoon tea. A lot has changed since then—for a while it was even occupied by the BBC. It was fully rebuilt in the early 1990s, so although you'll see a scant few Victorian touches, rooms are sized to modern standards while the huge three-building complex (the Regent Tower is the most secluded and has great views down Regent Street) maintains that luxurious grande dame feel. Americans have always felt at home here, partly because it's not off-puttingly fussy while being comfortable. The Wigmore, its on-site pub, serves meals with piquant flavors, and its cocktail bar, Artesian, puts a playful twist on serious mixology. If you can, spring for a Club Level access, where you can get all three meals and free cocktails. It's a few short blocks from Oxford Street's best shopping.

1c Portland Place, Regent St., W1. www.langhamhotels.com. © **020/7636-1000.** 380 units. Rooms £380–£500. Tube: Oxford Circus. **Amenities:** 3 restaurants; 2 bars; indoor pool; spa; fitness center; business center; free Wi-Fi.

The Stafford London ★   When it opened in 1912, the intimate Stafford appealed to Americans on a European spree; it even named its yacht-clubby bar The American Bar. Today, renovated to business-class standards (its Mews outbuilding is a particular romantic zone, but all areas are quiet and have super-soft beds), this rambling hideaway down a cul-de-sac in St James's, a

The Stafford London adds modern British decor to a Victorian hideaway on a St. James cul-de-sac.

AND BEAR IN mind

London attracts the world's most spendy visitors, so it has one of the world's biggest supplies of luxury hotels. The choices below are comfortable indeed, and if they were £200 cheaper they'd be more prominently featured—but in recent years, their prices have exceeded their weight class. The unpredictability of Brexit may wreak havoc on their price points, though. If that happens, get in quick.

Brown's Hotel The rambling Brown's, in Mayfair, has history in every creak: The first-ever phone call was placed from its ground floor. While staying here, Agatha Christie devised murders, Rudyard Kipling finished *The Jungle Book*, and Stephen King started *Misery*. But modernization beat the sense of tradition out of it, which disappoints those expecting more authenticity. In a crowded field, it's just all right. 30 Albemarle St., W1. www.brownshotel.com. ℰ **020/7493-6020.** £485–£580 double. Tube: Green Park.

Corinthia Hotel London This 1885 building near the river was first the Hôtel Métropole and then the Ministry of Defence, but today it's a celebrity magnet, and perhaps managers have let this go to their heads—it charges 50 percent over its equals. You'll find a top jazz bar, one of the city's best spas, commodious quarters, and frequent stars. Whitehall

Place, SW1. www.corinthia.com/london. ℰ **020/7930-8181.** Rooms from £600. Tube: Charing Cross.

The London EDITION This impudent lifestyle brand now has 11 worldwide locations, all tipped to the proclivities of the wealthy hipster—faux fur sculpturally strewn on your bed, prefab wood panel decor slumming it like a 1970s basement rumpus room, staff hired as much for the cornflower blue of their eyes as their credentials. Its Berners Tavern, festooned with artwork like a continental salon, is well worth a visit, as is its immensely cool bar, Punch Room. 10 Berners St., W1. www.editionhotels.com. ℰ **020/7781-0000.** £350–£662 double. Tube: Tottenham Court Road.

The Wellesley Knightsbridge The Hyde Park Corner ticket hall of the early Piccadilly Line once lay behind its iconic 1906 facade of arched oxblood-red tiles, although everything behind it has been exquisitely rebuilt for your comfort and, it must be said, your ego. Your 24-hour butler is just a button's push away, and there's a Rolls Royce to take you within 1.5 miles—but no gym, and just setting foot in its record-breaking cigar lounge costs £25. 11 Knightsbridge, SW1. www.thewellesley.co.uk. ℰ **020/7235-3535.** £425–£560 double. Tube: Oxford Circus.

short passageway from Green Park, is still popular with Americans, so it doesn't succumb to the arrogance rife in London's top-tier hotels. Having a subterranean wine cellar that's some 400 years old, which consequently empowers it to be the only hotel in London to retain its own Master Sommelier (only 249 people have ever attained that designation), goes a long way toward attracting a discerning, but not snobby, clientele. 16–18 St James's Place, SW1. www.thestaffordlondon.com. ℰ **020/7493-0111.** 127 units. Rooms from £344. Tube: Green Park. **Amenities:** Restaurant; bar; fitness center; free Wi-Fi.

The Zetter Townhouse, Marylebone ★★★   In nearly every way, it plays the part of the curious abode of an eccentric "wicked uncle" who collects oddities and likes to drink—each room has its own quirky character of antique mismatched furniture, hand-hung wallpaper, vintage glass slides embedded in bathroom walls, and expensive punchbowl-set glassware. Yet the essence of this spot near Hyde Park and Oxford Street is fully modern, down to strong showers. Downstairs, the dusky, parlor-style lounge bar (Seymour's Parlour) keeps pouring coffees and well-made cocktails deep into the night. This is detailed luxury living with a frisky point of view, and it's a winkingly Londonish one at that; instead of a door hanger, you use a bowler hat painted with messages for the housekeeper ("NOT NOW"). There's another location in Clerkenwell, but this area has more going for it. *Tip:* The Studio Suite has a four-poster that could rival the Great Bed of Ware in the V&A, but the basement room has the least charm.

29–30 Seymour St., W1. www.thezettertownhouse.com/marylebone. ℂ **020/7324-4544.** 24 units. Rooms from £220. Tube: Marble Arch. **Amenities:** Bar/restaurant; free Wi-Fi.

Moderate

22 York Street ★★   You might wonder at first if you have knocked on the door of a private home of some bohemian doctor or lawyer. Inside, Michael and Liz Callis (not always there; they have staff) are going for a farmhouse feel, with warm wooden floorboards, plenty of antiques and oriental rugs, and large bathrooms, almost all of which have tub/shower combinations.

The kitchen and dining table at 22 York Street provide a homey feel to guests.

Guests are let loose to treat the five-level (no lift) premises as their own, which includes plenty of tea, coffee, and biscuits. Adding to the homey feel, breakfasts are served in the kitchen at a communal country table where you meet your fellow guests. Although they're not explicitly banned, kids may not feel comfortable here. The top floor gets hot in the summer.

22 York St., W1. www.22yorkstreet.co.uk. ℰ **020/7224-2990.** 10 units. From £95 single, from £150 double, £180 triple. Rates include continental breakfast. Tube: Baker St. **Amenities:** Free Wi-Fi.

Grosvenor House, A JW Marriott Hotel ★
I include this for those with Marriott points to burn. It's a big 1920s edifice with corporate-hotel fallibility (oversubscribed service, overcrowded lifts, and a rammed executive lounge), but rooms are decently sized. The position in far western Mayfair grants some rooms winning park views, but it also means there aren't many shops and restaurants out the door and the Tube is a 10-min. walk in any direction. If you don't have your heart set on charm, it's passable.

86–90 Park Lane, W1. www.marriott.com. ℰ **020/7499-6363.** 217 units. Rooms £232–£316. Tube: Marble Arch. **Amenities:** Bar/restaurant; fitness center; slow Wi-Fi free, fast Wi-Fi £5/day.

Hyatt Regency London—The Churchill ★★
A strong choice for those with Hyatt membership considerations, it's a 2-min. walk from the back door of Selfridges' department store, and many rooms recently received smart

FINDING HOTELS online

If you contact the hotel directly, you'll usually not only get the lowest price, but you'll also have the power of negotiation.

Another danger of making a reservation through a third-party site: There are heaps of lousy budget options in London, particularly around Paddington and Earl's Court, that post misleading images, and it's easy to wind up in a seedy one. This is why you trust a book like Frommer's—we have been to every single place we recommend.

Most of the popular online travel agents have acquired each other to the point where the inventory doesn't change much between them. **Expedia** ate **Travelocity, Hotwire,** and **Orbitz. Hotels.com** ate **Venere. Priceline** ate **Agoda.com** (but the latter delivers better results). **Trivago** sometimes comes through. Some major chains have

teamed up to create **RoomKey.com,** which collects discounted rates from only their holdings. And **Tingo.com** refunds the difference if a hotel price drops after you book. Remember that a deal on an expensive hotel may not be a steal; as luxury hotels add star levels, they also add extra charges beyond the rate.

HotelsCombined.com, Kayak.com, and **Mobissimo.com** are "aggregator" sites that scan dozens of sites for deals and pull results together. If you hit them, you don't feel pressured to hit Expedia and the like, because they include them in the search.

Last-minute deals: They're also best on the hotel's own site. **Lastminute. co.uk** is one of the most popular U.K. booking sites, but its rates don't always represent savings, though the app **Hotel Tonight** sometimes bears slightly reduced fruit.

renovations with completely fresh bathrooms (robot toilets!) and truly well-selected art. Ten years ago, this circa-1970 building was a bit tired, but Hyatt has put the property on its front burner with millions of pounds in investment. Now it offers everything a five-star should, like all-night room service, and even if the location is a little off the main, it's still near the Tube, unquestionably comfortable, and run with snap for such a large place.

30 Portman Square, W1. http://londonchurchill.regency.hyatt.com. ✆ **020/7486-5800.** 440 units. Rooms £264–£431. Tube: Marble Arch. **Amenities:** 2 restaurants; bar; fitness center; tennis and jogging track in adjoining square; free Wi-Fi.

THE SOUTH BANK & SOUTHWARK

From medieval times until about 15 years ago, "respectable" Londoners wanted nothing to do with this once-industrial area. They all wish they'd bought property now. It's a terrific place to dwell in good weather, when it comes alive with walkers, booksellers, pub-goers, and playgoers. Furthermore, moderate hotels are proliferating: Brands such as Hilton, Holiday Inn, and Mercure are all along Southwark Road now. Don't forget the excellent CitizenM (p. 29).

Expensive

Shangri-La Hotel at the Shard ★★ Staying here, on the 36th to 52nd floors of a glass-sheathed skyscraper, means that your room will be encased with floor-to-ceiling windows overlooking the city. You're a bird singing in a gleaming cage. When you take a bath (in your marble-coated washroom with heated floors), you may feel as if you're flying over the Tower of London, and when you swim in the horizon pool in the sky above St Paul's, the vista is so surreal that you may wonder if it's all a dream. Such glassy nirvana comes with Zen interiors to match: clean-lined, simple, and inflected by the Asian culture from which the Shangri-La brand hails (for example, in-room amenities might be stored in a bento-style box). Rates are sky-high, but literally so are the rooms, and a non-stop view is worth a little extra, don't you think?

31 St Thomas St., SE1. www.shangri-la.com/london/shangrila. ✆ **020/7234-8000.** 202 units. King rooms from £400. Tube: London Bridge. **Amenities:** Restaurant; bar; indoor pool; fitness center; in-room Nespresso coffee and tea; free Wi-Fi.

Moderate

Mondrian London ★ Not quite central, alienating at times, the Mondrian is still special in some ways because the vistas from its Thames-front units have no competition; book one and you'll feel like you're on a ship at water—which happens to be the theme here, coppery nautical motifs and all. There are plenty of self-aware embellishments (a basement cinema, yoga in the rooftop Rumpus Room bar, the Dandelyan bar serving excessively bespoke no-ice cocktails for a nip less than £20 each), but although the Mondrian esteems itself in its ironic stylings, it's in fact at its best when you use it to simply welcome the skyline into your bedroom—the restaurant opens to the river, the famous riverfront path literally runs beside it. If you had to take a room that doesn't face the water, I wouldn't bother. Despite its hipster preening, it's decent for families, too, since so many room types interconnect.

20 Upper Ground, SE1. www.morganshotelgroup.com. © **020/3747-1000.** 359 units. Rooms from £215. Tube: Waterloo or Southwark. **Amenities:** Restaurant; 3 bars; spa; fitness center; free Wi-Fi (slow), fast Wi-Fi £7–£10/day.

Park Plaza Westminster Bridge London ★ This glassy mega-hotel looks like a carburetor on a curb, but you won't believe the view from the "Iconic View" rooms: straight down Westminster Bridge at the Houses of Parliament and Big Ben's tower, like a floor-to-ceiling fantasy. Otherwise it's a well-greased business-class formula that feels more like a convention center, and the cheapest "Internal Facing" atrium-view rooms (scrutinize the room description) are starved of natural light. Still, that means less-desirable rooms are discounted in low season. Studio rooms have microwaves, fridges, and pullout beds, and there's a dark and soothing indoor pool. And that location!

200 Westminster Bridge Rd., London SE1. www.parkplaza.com/westminster. © **0800/092-7671,** 800/777-1700 in U.S. 1,019 units. £152–£404 double, "Iconic View" starting at £250. 3-night minimum in some periods. Tube: Waterloo or Westminster. **Amenities:** 2 restaurants; bar; indoor pool; fitness center; spa; free Wi-Fi.

Inexpensive

Captain Bligh House ★★★ For a delicious taste of local London life without venturing far from the center of town, the Bligh—where Captain

---

HOW TO GET YOUR HOTEL FOR free

What if I told you that you could spend 6 nights in London, airfare and hotel included, for $899 in winter and $1,099 in summer? It's called an **air-hotel package,** and it can cost about the same as airfare alone—except it *also* comes with hotel, breakfast, and often a tour or two thrown in. How do they do it? Contracted rates and bulk buying.

The lowest prices are from eastern American cities such as New York and Boston, but for a few dozen dollars more, you can leave from just about any other American city. You can also often extend the return by as much as a month without having to buy more hotel nights through them. The catch is this: Many of the least expensive hotel options are pillow mills that have seen better days. For a little more peace of mind, upgrade to a slightly more expensive property.

The king of affordable air-hotel deals is **Go-Today.com** (www.go-today.com; © **800/227-3235**), which usually offers 4- and 6-night packages to London, sometimes paired with other European destinations, including local flights between the cities (as low as $800 for 6 nights). Others: **Virgin Vacations** (www.virgin-vacations.com; © **888/937-8474**) and **Gate 1 Travel** (www.gate1travel.com; © **800/682-3333**). Scrutinize the airline-run sales like **British Airways Holidays** (www.baholidays.com; © **877/428-2228**), because those rates may not always be the cheapest.

William Bligh lived after that sordid mutiny affair—is a transporting choice. Artists Gayna and Simon approach their teeny guesthouse, built in the 1780s (before the invention of the lift), as a quiet home away from home: Units have little kitchens for cooking up market ingredients, but you also get a starter pack of breakfast supplies. Although the Imperial War Museum (p. 156) is across the street, it's not a neighborhood crawling with tourists, so you'll kick back at the local pub and jump the many bus lines that go past. The value is over-the-top.

100 Lambeth Rd., SE1. www.captainblighhouse.co.uk. © **020/7928-2735.** 5 units. £90–£125 double. Tube: Lambeth North. **Amenities:** In-room kitchen; free Wi-Fi.

H10 London Waterloo ★★★ The sole London branch of a popular and well-run Spanish brand, the H10 is a recently built tower, so rooms are nicely sized and modern, with art that actually speaks of good taste, with a bonus of having a healthy floor-to-ceiling window that lets London in. Its flatiron shape means everyone gets lots of light, plus there's a fantastic 8th-floor terrace bar with London Eye views. The blocks nearby are slightly sleepy, but there's much choice within a 5-min. walk in most directions. It sells out frequently because it's worth it.

284–302 Waterloo Road, SE1. www.h10hotels.com. © **020/7928-4062.** 177 units. From £125 double. Tube: Waterloo, Lambeth North, or Southwark. **Amenities:** Restaurant; 3 bars; spa; free Wi-Fi.

THE CITY & EAST LONDON

Not long ago, the City went to sleep at 7pm. Now, with Shoreditch and Spitalfields rapidly being developed, there are more reasons for creative types to linger by night. Some of London's prime party zones, straight and gay, are near hotels where rates bottom out on weekends. The Liverpool Street station area lacks character, but north of it, things ooze it. Just be wary of going *too* far east in East London: There are corporate choices in the Canary Wharf district and temptingly cheap rooms by the ExCeL convention center in the Docklands region, but they're intended for conference-goers, and from there it will take you 45 minutes to reach Piccadilly Circus by the Tube and DLR. If sightseeing is your aim, make Shoreditch your eastern cutoff.

Expensive

Four Seasons Hotel London at Ten Trinity Square ★★ This luxury newcomer (2017) is ideal for sinking deep into your bed and vanishing into the sanctum of your room—most don't have views, after all, despite the seminal location overlooking the Tower of London, so when you're here, you feel indulgently removed from the City. Your personal space, bathroom included, is massive because this used to be a civil office building (the conversion created such a maze that even you will have a hard time finding your door), clad in the finest materials and swaddled with softness because, after all, this is the Four Seasons. Add to that the prestigious La Dame de Pic, a highly rated experimental French restaurant, and you've got a super-luxe escape that's so removed from tourist clatter—the neighborhood virtually shuts down after dark and on weekends—that it creates its own world. For that reason, and for that Four Seasons-level tariff, this is a good honeymoon choice.

10 Trinity Square, EC3. www.fourseasons.com/tentrinity. © **020/3297-9200.** 100 units. Rooms from £500. Tube: Tower Hill. **Amenities:** 2 restaurants; cocktail bar; spa; fitness center; free kids' amenities; indoor pool; free Wi-Fi.

South Place Hotel ★★★ Plugged-in, stylish, and sexy: That's the City crowd this hotel goes for, and you'll feel that way, too. Rooms are much larger than the London usual, every inch was run through the design filter (those push-button blackout blinds!), and much of the art was commissioned by celebrated contemporary artists. Rooms, charcoal-grey with wool carpets, are large (especially the showers) and hushed, and you'll find plenty of outlets, AV connections, and a huge bed you can flop around in. The two restaurants and several bars lure lively professionals who work in the area. On Sundays, there's no food to be found for blocks, but the scenes of Old Street and Shoreditch are 10-min. walks away.

3 South Place, EC2. www.southplacehotel.com. © **020/3503-0000.** 80 units. From £199–£500 double. Tube: Moorgate or Liverpool Street. **Amenities:** 2 restaurants; 3 bars; guests' lounge; gym; spa; business center; free in-room movies; free Wi-Fi.

Moderate

Ace Hotel London Shoreditch ★★ If you've grown up enough to have some money, but not enough to demand much of hotel staff, the Ace can plug you in to Shoreditch Cool. A stay here isn't about service but about style, since the Ace's agreeable pretentions have become a "lifestyle brand" for the fashionably impressionable. Area freelancers tap away on laptops all day at the lobby workbenches and well-dressed revelers thump away in its basement club. It's just a converted mid-level business hotel (so if you pay in the £300s, you'll feel ripped off), but rooms might be considered cushy if you're a hipster (check the room-width built-in window sofas) and styled with self-knowing false irreverence (instead of drawers, you use plastic crates, as if you were still in kindergarten, your bedspread is denim, and there's a guitar—an Ace signature). It's too much of a scene, perhaps, but fun.

100 Shoreditch High St., E1. www.acehotel.com/london. © **020/7613-9800.** 97 units. £170–£370 double. Tube: Shoreditch High Street or Liverpool Street. **Amenities:** Restaurant; rooftop bar; basement club; gym; free Wi-Fi.

Apex City of London ★★★ An excellent contemporary boutique brand from Scotland that appeals to high standards for space and style, Apex is a friendly and peaceful urban retreat that actually looks like its website's pictures. You'll find it literally steps from the Tower of London, and a few rooms glimpse the Tower Bridge—along with the balcony, worth the upgrade of £15–£30. It's handsomely designed in hardwood and walnut, with bathrooms larger than many B&Bs' guest rooms, including walk-in power showers. The only downside is the City is deader than Old Marley in the off hours, which is why it can be a steal on weekends. The **Apex London Wall,** just as good but often even cheaper, is on the side streets north of handy Bank station, and the **Apex Temple Court,** off Fleet Street, is also tops (and closer to the West End).

No. 1 Seething Lane, EC3. www.apexhotels.co.uk. ✆ **020/7702-2020.** 179 units. £150–£377 double, best prices Sat–Sun. Tube: Tower Hill. **Amenities:** Restaurant; bar; gym; free local calls; free Wi-Fi.

The Curtain ★★★   In 2017, Michael Achenbaum, behind Manhattan's Gansevoort Hotels, brought downtown New York style to Spitalfields. This purpose-built, loft-looking building is riven with nooks and crannies to cram cool things in—a cellar spa and cinema, an outpost of Marcus Sammuelsson's Red Rooster Harlem (an American comfort food joint that books fantastic musical acts), a rooftop pool deck with a fab City view (where you take breakfast), and a "member's club" (Billy's Bar) with a separate entrance that you, as a guest, may imbibe in. Rooms, too, do things London doesn't usually do—exposed warehouse-style brick, floor-to-ceiling windows, showers that convert into steam rooms. It's simply really well-done, quite fun, spacious and modern, and until the area catches onto what's here, it's cheaper than it should be (future rates will likely start in the mid-£200s). The rapidly changing neighborhood, as if it needs saying, is where the cool kids are these days.

45 Curtain Rd., EC2. https://thecurtain.com. ✆ **020/3146-4545.** 120 units. £188–£280 double. Tube: Liverpool Street or Shoreditch High Street. **Amenities:** 2 restaurants; rooftop pool; spa; fitness center; access to co-working space; member's club; free Wi-Fi.

Inexpensive

The Hoxton, Shoreditch ★★   The advent of "the Hox" changed the way London thought of budget lodging: Chintz and linoleum went out, to be replaced by good-looking staff versed in local hotspots and compact rooms that pack in more style and cleverness than the low price would allow. You sleep on a platform bed under exposed brick walls and among set pieces like Union Jack pillows and steamer trunks for chests of drawers. You bathe under a rain shower in a futuristic cylinder. Your continental breakfast is delivered each morning via a bag you hang on the door, which can make you feel like a monkey at the zoo, and there's free water and milk for your little fridge and an hour of free telephone calls a day, even if you call internationally. Downstairs there's a grill, a bar, and coffee and free Wi-Fi flowing at all hours, make it as much a gathering place for disaffected millennials as it is a way station for travelers. Book as far ahead as possible to keep the price down.

1 Austin St., E2. www.hoxtonhotels.com. ✆ **020/7550-1000.** 208 units. Rooms £69–£359. Tube: Aldgate or Tower Hill. **Amenities:** Restaurant; 1 hr. free calls; free Wi-Fi.

Qbic London City ★★   From a tiny affordable design hotel brand in Holland, Qbic is a wacky antidote to the formula budget hotels. Everything you need—bed, outlets, bathroom with a rain shower, TV—is part of a prefabricated bed/bathroom structure that dominates the center of the room. The cheapest rooms, called "Smart," don't have a window—did you need one? It's not a capsule hotel, just one that came up with a multipurpose hospitality unit with plenty of room to walk around and stash your suitcase. Your lamp is made out of petrified garden hose, your clothing rack a strange ladder/planter of some sort—it's just fun. There are free coffee and tea machines on every floor and a preposterously funky lobby where organic continental breakfast is served. You'll be within walking distance to Spitalfields/Shoreditch (15 min.) and the Tower of London (15 min.). As a bonus, the staff gives good advice on local culture.

42 Adler St., E1. http://london.qbichotels.com. ℃ **020/3021-3300.** 171 units. Rooms £80–£202. Tube: Aldgate East. **Amenities:** Lounge; free coffee; free Wi-Fi.

Shoreditch Inn ★★   Budget hotels are few and far between in this part of London, which now values cachet above saving cash, but here you find a modern value-priced hotel that won't frighten you. Encumbered by none of the lifestyle-obsessed frills that its preening neighbors obsess over, it's simply clean and recently refit with the little touches that distinguish it as a standout of its price class: double-glazed windows (to muffle Shoreditch revelry), quality toiletries, roomy quarters, and enough selection at breakfast, even if said breakfast is taken in the basement. That it's in the middle of the action and front rooms that overlook a church from 1740 have me wondering when the dream will end and the owners will put the price out of reach. They could ask for more.

1 Austin St., E2. www.shoreditchinn.com. ℃ **020/3327-3910.** 14 units. £112–£168 double. Rates include continental breakfast. Tube: Bethnal Green. **Amenities:** Free Wi-Fi.

RENT A ROOM

Airbnb is old hat in England: Hosted accommodations were long one of its essential travel realities. Partly because of the post-Blitz housing crunch, Londoners have long considered it normal to make a few pounds by welcoming strangers into their homes. One potential hidden advantage of this sort of stay comes if you've got a car—for example, if you're stopping in London during a drive round the island. Staying with a family in Zone 3 or 4 may enable you to park your car cheaply. What's included? At the minimum, a bed and breakfast. Everything else depends, since homestays are as unique as the hosts themselves. Airbnb has, however, revolutionized what tourists demand. Increasingly, they prefer renting their own flats, so the old B&B agencies are quickly dying out. Here are a few brokers that should still be able to pair you with suitable options:

- **At Home in London** (www.athomeinlondon.co.uk; ℃ **020/8748-2701**). Operating since 1986. Properties in West London, near the Tube: mid-£80s (central London) to £30 a night (Zones 2 & 3).

- **Happy Homes** (www.happy-homes.com; ℃ **020/7352-5121**). Operating since 1989. Specializes in homestays in southwest London, about a 25-min.

commute to the West End: £20 to £40, plus a one-time fee of £45 to £65 per room.

○ **London Bed and Breakfast Agency** (www.londonbb.com; ☏ **01474/708-701**). Specializes in finding trustworthy hosts for single female travelers: between £70 and £120 in Zones 1 to 3.

RENT A FLAT

If you don't want to rent a room in a home, rent a whole flat. When you arrive, you'll often find a folder that schools you in the best local shops and restaurants, and you may encounter neighbors keeping an eye on the place and on your welfare (at one property I know of, the owner herself pops round and pretends to be a helpful neighbor), which is an advantage if you want to learn more city secrets. Many properties have minimum stays of 5 to 7 nights. Renters such as **Airbnb.com, FlipKey.com, HomeAway.com** and **Housetrip.com** (owned by the same company), and **VRBO.com** can charge as much as nice hotels. Those become a value when you've got a group. If you want a layer of protection, British-based **FG Properties** (www.fgproperties.com; ☏ **020/3865-0596**) meets the hosts who list units on its database, which itself populates to Airbnb and HomeAway, and serves as a responsible intermediary for customers.

Because London apartments are in such high demand, there is little incentive for owners to upgrade facilities, so it's easy to rent a stinker. For higher-quality results, we recommend booking through a London rental specialist—one who has vetted the unit and has a relationship with its owner. Our favorite, for its interesting span of 60-odd homes from mid-range to fantasy, is **Coach House Rentals** (www.chslondon.com/london; ☏ **020/8355-3192**), run by the passionate Harley Nott, who furnishes concierge services and responds 24 hours a day. It shines brightest in West London and Westminster. Large, well-appointed units go from around £115 to £300 a night—for places that sleep up to 10 people. Discounts kick in after 6 nights.

The highly recommended **New York Habitat** (www.nyhabitat.com; ☏ **212/255-8018** in U.S.) represents hundreds of flats and has a licensed, U.S.-based office. Units for two range £80 to £250, but they come larger.

London Perfect (www.londonperfect.com; ☏ **888/520-2087** in U.S.) has class and its flats, many of which feel like living spreads from lifestyle magazines, are extremely well-maintained; owners who allow fittings to get dated are cut from the roster. Someone meets you at the property when you arrive for the first time. Prices start around $200 a night for studios and one-bedrooms sleeping up to 4 people, largely in tony neighborhoods like South Kensington and Chelsea. There's usually a 7-night minimum.

Set up in 1995, **Outlet 4 Holidays** (www.outlet4holidays.com; ☏ **07974/729-099**) has flats better located for tourists than perhaps any other firm. Locations are around Soho's cafe-and-club scene, smack in the West End. The norm is £150 a night, but there are extra fees for checking in outside of business hours or anytime on Sunday. Should trouble arise, its representative is in Soho, so you won't have far to go for assistance.

A high-end renter, **One Fine Stay** (www.onefinestay.com; ℂ **7826/529-286** in the U.K., **855/553-4954** in the U.S.) shoots its flats as if it's photographing a fashion spread, which tells you something about its target market. Central London digs are over £200 a night, with impeccable design and service to match.

Citadines (www.citadines.com; ℂ **011-33-141-05-79-05**) runs corporate-style hotel rooms fitted like little apartments, and it has five locations city-wide. In order of centrality: Trafalgar Square, The Cavendish, Holborn, South Kensington, and Barbican (cheapest, from £87).

HOME EXCHANGES

You'd be surprised how many Londoners are dying to visit your own stomping grounds, and if you make contact with the right people, you can swap homes (sometimes simultaneously). It sounds strange, but nothing tends to get stolen because swappers often become good friends. Not just that, but neighbors will often pop by to check up on you, so you have a built-in source of insider advice.

So which club should you choose? Here are the biggies, in alphabetical order:

HomeExchange.com (ℂ **888/609-4660**): This slick service claims 65,000-plus listings in 150 nations. This is important because the more members, the more potential swaps. Results can be broken down by interest. It costs $150 a year for Americans to list.

Homelink.org (ℂ **800/638-3841**): Popular with British and Australian travelers (with reps in 27 countries) since 1953, this service costs $95 per year.

Intervac (www.intervacus.com; ℂ **866/884-7567**): Intervac has been around for 6 decades and its claim to fame is that some 80 percent of its listings are international (30,000 families are represented), which means (as it puts it), "you compete with fewer Americans for overseas properties." Access to all listings is $99 a year, but you can take a limited 20-day trial for free.

Additional exchange sites include **SabbaticalHomes.com,** catering to academics; and **HomeAroundtheWorld.com,** for gays and lesbians (£45 for a year). Or you could roll the dice with a website like **CouchSurfing.com,** on which folks (generally younger) offer spare space to visitors. That's free, but there is no vetting system, so consider the risks before taking an offer.

CHEAP COLLEGE ROOMS

Staying in a college room in holiday periods is an ideal budget saver for visitors of any age. Reservations are accepted starting in spring. At all of them, expect a wood-frame bed with linen, a desk, a dresser, an in-room sink, the possibility of an equipped kitchen (although it might be shared), an en suite bathroom (usually), laundry facilities, breakfast (often at a reasonable charge), Wi-Fi, and phones in the room or in the hall.

London School of Economics (www.lsevacations.co.uk; ☏ **020/3437-0050**): Check these out first. Its eight properties are in terrific condition, with the dignity that you'd expect of a school that trains the world's power players in business. Rooms rent cheaply (£46–£150) for July, August, and the first chunk of September. A few rooms may be available at Christmas or Easter, too.

Some single "private accommodation" rooms at **City University London** (www.city.ac.uk/accommodation; ☏ **020/7040-7040**) are available from early July to early September. Prices are around £210 a week.

University College London (www.ucl.ac.uk/residences; ☏ **020/7529-8975**, or ☏ 020/7387-4537): Its dorms, clustering in Bloomsbury, are less prestigious than LSE's, but they aren't depressing. From late June to September, 10 residences are available at £38 to £59, but only five properties have private bathrooms.

King's College (www.kingsvenues.com; ☏ **020/7848-1700**): As of 2018, six halls are available for short rental from late June through mid-September. Kitchens but no utensils, no air-conditioning. They rent for around £45 to £65.

International Students House (229 Great Portland St., W1; www.ish.org.uk; ☏ **020/7631-8300;** Tube: Great Portland St.): Part dorm, part subdued hostel, in two buildings. Rates are £54 single, £40 twin, £32 quad (cheaper if booked by mid-May), including continental breakfast. Bathrooms are shared, female-only rooms are available, and some rooms are co-ed but partitioned. Other academic choices are more private.

WHERE TO DINE

4

I n 1957, Arthur Frommer visited London for his seminal *Europe on $5 a Day*. His report was gloomy: "With great despair, this book recommends that you . . . save your money for the better meals available in France and Italy. Cooking is a lost art in Great Britain; your meat pie with cabbage will turn out just as tasteless for 40¢ in a chain restaurant as it will for $2 in a posh hotel." The report today is happily quite different: Bon appétit!

As it turns out, good English cooking wasn't a lost art at all. True, there are still plenty of places you'll find a crappy meal, but cabbage is no longer the national affliction, as it was in the days of rationing. Now that London swarms with people from across the world, you'll find nearly every style of cuisine—ask any Londoner for their favorite restaurant and it's bound to be a foreign food. In the past 40 years, British consumption of sugar, potatoes, and flour have halved. Countless restaurants now serve ingredients fresh from the farm. Even most of the major museums (listed starting on p. 110) run cafes that, surprisingly, more than pull their weight. The high-quality dining boom has been so explosive that recently, some of the weaker chains have seen business all but die out.

London's greenie culture thrives, and virtually every menu will have plenty of dishes for **vegetarians** to eat. The situation for **vegans** isn't quite as obvious, but cooks here are well-educated, so most kitchens understand **vegan** dietary requirements. The news is just as good for people with **food allergies:** A majority of potentially irritating ingredients are marked when you buy pre-made food at the major shops.

Do not rely on Google, Yelp, or Apple Maps to find places. Online inventory is often incomplete, opening hours are often way off, and the results favor chains, so you'll miss a lot of good things. You can sometimes find some meal deals on **OpenTable.co.uk** and **SquareMeal.co.uk.** A late-night dining culture is not universal here, so don't be surprised if a kitchen closes by 9:30 or 10pm (check ahead if you intend to eat late).

There are plenty of flashy places where tourists can't get a table or the party dies when the star chef moves on. But each place in this book is enduring, will welcome out-of-towners, and was chosen to say something about London of the moment—you'll taste what it's like to eat like a Londoner today.

Price categories are based on a typical main course.

- **Expensive** £20 and up
- **Moderate** £10 to £19
- **Inexpensive** under £10

Most restaurants expect you to give up your table after 90 minutes to 2 hours. Always check the bill to see if service is included. If it is, you don't have to tip. If not, 10 to 15 percent is customary.

BLOOMSBURY, FITZROVIA & KING'S CROSS

These areas north of the central tourist district are more residential and consequently less of a scene than other parts of town can be, but now that the hip developments around Granary Square, north of King's Cross, are coming online, the scenesters are beginning to follow.

Moderate

Bill's ★★ INTERNATIONAL   A 5-min. walk from the British Museum and handy for many uses—big breakfasts, lunches, dinner, tea with scones and clotted cream, feeding kids, or downing cheap cocktails. In few other London establishments will you find mac-and-cheese, burgers, pecan pie, and Caesar salad on the same menu. It's a lifesaver when you're in need of drama-free, family-friendly grub served briskly, which is why you'll be glad to hear there are also locations near Piccadilly Circus (36–44 Brewer St., W1), off the Long Acre shopping street (St Martin's Courtyard, WC2), in Southwark (Victor Wharf, Clink St., SE1) and not far south of Buckingham Palace (6 Cathedral Walk, SW1). The afternoon tea is around £11 and not half bad, plus there's free Wi-Fi.

42 Kingsway, WC2. www.bills-website. co.uk. ⓒ **020/2742-2981.** Main courses £9–£13. Mon–Sat 8am–11pm; Sun 9am–10:30pm. Tube: Holborn.

Caravan ★★ INTERNATIONAL The development of the 67-acre post-industrial void north of King's Cross station just remade a canalside gasworks ghetto into London's new Silicon Alley, ruled by fresh facilities for YouTube and a certain monolithic search engine that starts with G. Caravan, in the old Granary building, led the way for all. So industrial-feeling

Enjoy a macchiato from Caravan.

London-Wide Restaurants

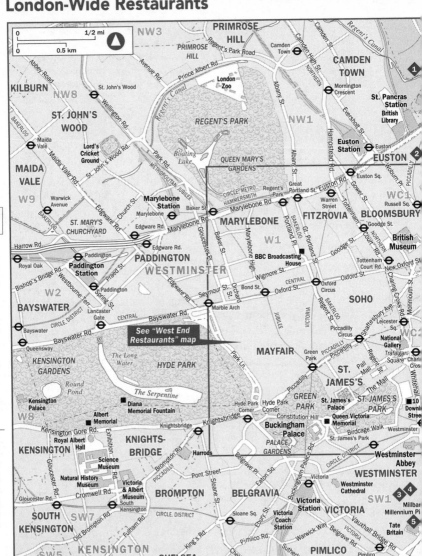

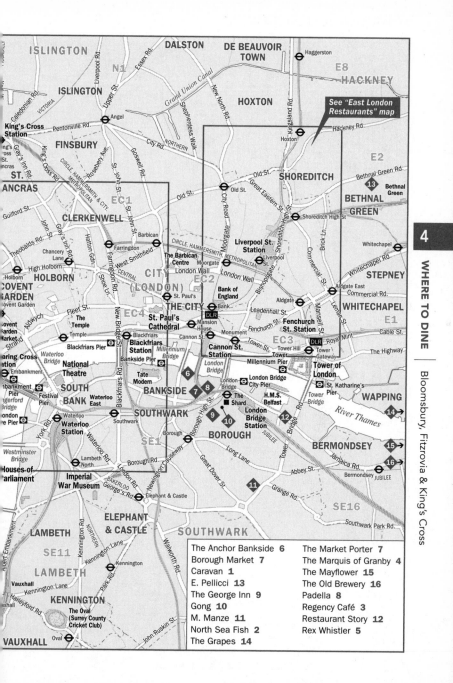

The Anchor Bankside **6**
Borough Market **7**
Caravan **1**
E. Pellicci **13**
The George Inn **9**
Gong **10**
M. Manze **11**
North Sea Fish **2**
The Grapes **14**

The Market Porter **7**
The Marquis of Granby **4**
The Mayflower **15**
The Old Brewery **16**
Padella **8**
Regency Café **3**
Restaurant Story **12**
Rex Whistler **5**

West End Restaurants

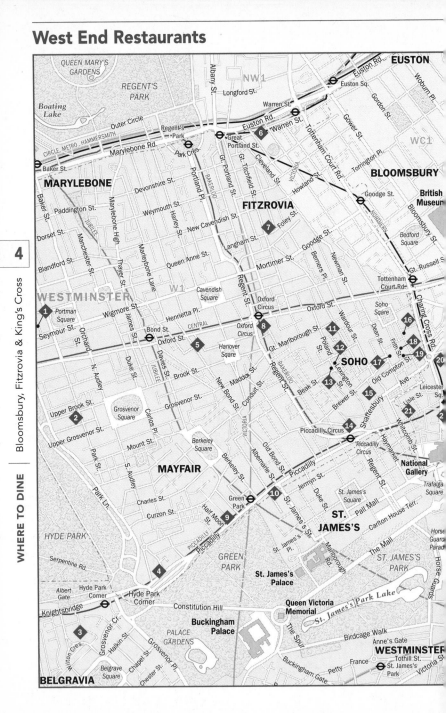

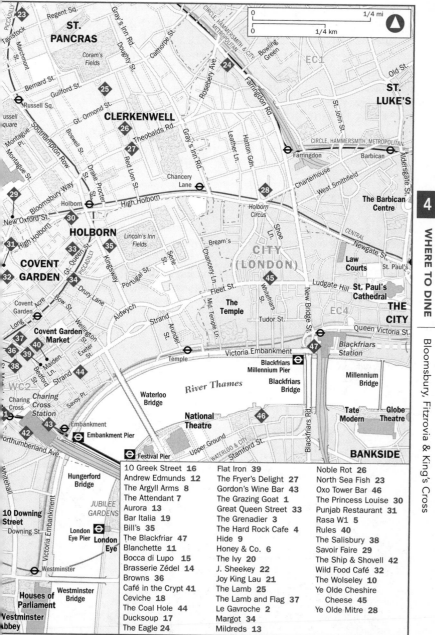

ST. PANCRAS

Regent Sq.

Coram's Fields

CLERKENWELL

Theobalds Rd.

EC1

Bowling Green

ST. LUKE'S

CIRCLE, HAMMERSMITH, METROPOLITAN

Farringdon

Barbican

Charterhouse

West Smithfield

The Barbican Centre

HOLBORN

Lincoln's Inn Fields

COVENT GARDEN

Covent Garden Market

WC2

Holborn Circus

CITY (LONDON)

Fleet St.

The Temple

Tudor St.

Law Courts

St. Paul's

St. Paul's Cathedral

EC4

Queen Victoria St.

THE CITY

Blackfriars Station

Charing Cross Station

River Thames

Waterloo Bridge

National Theatre

Blackfriars Millennium Pier

Blackfriars Bridge

Millennium Bridge

Tate Modern

Globe Theatre

Embankment Pier

Festival Pier

BANKSIDE

Hungerford Bridge

JUBILEE GARDENS

10 Downing Street

London Eye Pier   London Eye

Westminster

Houses of Parliament

Westminster Bridge

Westminster Abbey

10 Greek Street **16**	Flat Iron **39**	Noble Rot **26**
Andrew Edmunds **12**	The Fryer's Delight **27**	North Sea Fish **23**
The Argyll Arms **8**	Gordon's Wine Bar **43**	Oxo Tower Bar **46**
The Attendant **7**	The Grazing Goat **1**	The Princess Louise **30**
Aurora **13**	Great Queen Street **33**	Punjab Restaurant **31**
Bar Italia **19**	The Grenadier **3**	Rasa W1 **5**
Bill's **35**	The Hard Rock Cafe **4**	Rules **40**
The Blackfriar **47**	Hide **9**	The Salisbury **38**
Blanchette **11**	Honey & Co. **6**	Savoir Faire **29**
Bocca di Lupo **15**	The Ivy **20**	The Ship & Shovell **42**
Brasserie Zédel **14**	J. Sheekey **22**	Wild Food Café **32**
Browns **36**	Joy King Lau **21**	The Wolseley **10**
Café in the Crypt **41**	The Lamb **25**	Ye Olde Cheshire
Ceviche **18**	The Lamb and Flag **37**	Cheese **45**
The Coal Hole **44**	Le Gavroche **2**	Ye Olde Mitre **28**
Ducksoup **17**	Margot **34**	
The Eagle **24**	Mildreds **13**	

(long blond-wood tables, canvaslike sheets for window shades, plain metal racks for bar shelves) that it feels like it could be converted to a ceramics shop overnight, Caravan is always busy but glows with *joie de vivre* on days when its front patio is open. The place roasts its own coffee, bakes its own goods—the jalapeno cornbread is moist and kicky—and pushes its tapas-size dishes into fun flavor realms like coconut lime chicken salad, salt beef terrine, and bulgur-and-halloumi fritters. After dinner, kick back in its front yard in an amphitheater overlooking the Regent's Canal. Another, newer location is found a few streets behind the Tate Modern (30 Great Guilford St., SE1; ℂ **020/7101-1190;** Tube: Southwark or London Bridge).

1 Granary Sq., off Goods Way, N1. www.caravanrestaurants.co.uk. ℂ **020/7101-7661.** Small plates £5–£7; pizzas £7–£9. Mon–Fri 8am–10:30pm; Sat 10am–10:30pm; Sun 10am–4pm. Reservations recommended (but not accepted Sat–Sun daytime). Tube: King's Cross St Pancras.

The Eagle ★★ TRADITIONAL BRITISH   By now, the trend is so widespread that the term *gastropub* is meaningless, but foodies note: That trend began here in 1991 (or so most agree), in Clerkenwell, a then-ungentrified area between Bloomsbury and Islington. So old are this place's roots that it actually makes a cameo in the nursery rhyme "Pop Goes the Weasel": "Up and down the City Road/In and out of the Eagle/That's the way the money goes/Pop goes the weasel." You'll be happy for your money to go here. Behind

The Eagle gastropub.

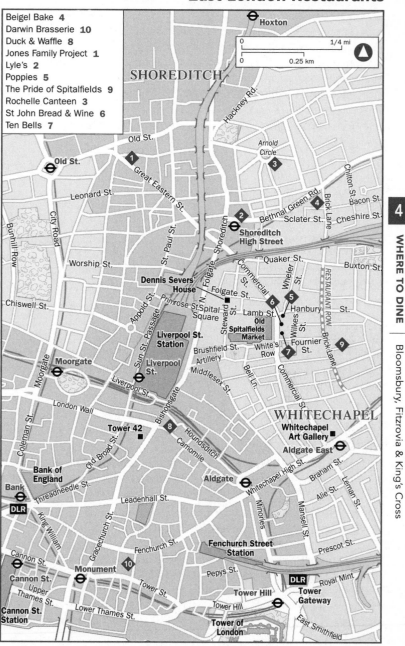

East London Restaurants

Beigel Bake **4**
Darwin Brasserie **10**
Duck & Waffle **8**
Jones Family Project **1**
Lyle's **2**
Poppies **5**
The Pride of Spitalfields **9**
Rochelle Canteen **3**
St John Bread & Wine **6**
Ten Bells **7**

0   1/4 mi
0   0.25 km

Hoxton

SHOREDITCH

Old St.

Great Eastern St.

Arnold Circle

Old St.

Leonard St.

City Road

Bunhill Row

Worship St.

Hackney Rd.

Chilton St.

Bacon St.

Brick Lane

Bethnal Green Rd.

Sclater St.

Cheshire St.

Shoreditch High Street

St. Paul St.

Shoreditch

Folgate

Quaker St.

Buxton St.

Chiswell St.

Appold St.

Sun St. Passage

Dennis Severs' House

Primrose St

Folgate St.

Spital Square

N. Steward St.

Wheler St.

RESTAURANT ROW

Hanbury St.

Wilkes St.

Lamb St.

Old Spitalfields Market

Commercial St.

Fournier St.

Brick Lane

Liverpool St. Station

Liverpool St.

Brushfield St.

White's Row

Moorgate

Moorgate

Liverpool St.

Artillery

Middlesex St.

Bell Ln.

London Wall

Bishopsgate

WHITECHAPEL

Coleman St.

Old Broad St.

Tower 42

Houndsditch

Camomile

Whitechapel Art Gallery

Aldgate East

Bank of England

Threadneedle St.

Leadenhall St.

Aldgate

Whitechapel High St.

Braham St.

Alie St.

Leman St.

Bank

DLR

King William

Gracechurch St.

Fenchurch St.

Minories

Mansell St.

Fenchurch Street Station

Prescot St.

Cannon St.

Monument

Pepys St.

DLR

Royal Mint

Cannon St.

Upper Thames St.

Tower St.

Tower Hill

Tower Gateway

Cannon St. Station

Lower Thames St.

Tower Hill

East Smithfield

Tower of London

4

WHERE TO DINE | Bloomsbury, Fitzrovia & King's Cross

73

the bar of a bare-to-the-wood corner saloon, rebuilt in 1901, the sometimes-surly staff prepares a changing selection of about a dozen flavorful dishes a day, from the likes of pork loin salad to pan-roasted sole to the house specialty, the insidiously spicy Bife Ana steak sandwich dripping with marinated garlic and onion. Tables are shared (it's bad for groups), menu by blackboard only (preview today's on Instagram: @eaglefarringdon), furniture reassuringly shabby and mismatched. Order at the bar and relax with a beer, because here, the food's the thing, and it arrives on its own schedule, not much pop about it.

159 Farringdon Rd., EC1. www.theeaglefarringdon.co.uk. ✆ **020/7837-1353.** Main courses £10–£22. Mon–Sat noon–11pm; Sun noon–5pm. Tube: Farringdon.

Honey & Co. ★★ MIDDLE EASTERN   It's packed for good reasons. First, the food brilliantly adapts Middle Eastern dishes to London palates. Spectacular lamb shawarma is tender as brisket and spiked with pomegranate and mint, and is served in a little pot with hot and soft pita. Chicken dumplings come in a broth that smells like love. The "strawberry spliff" dessert proves that berries, phyllo, mint, and olive oil go well together. The other reason this place, which is near the southern tip of Regent's Park, is packed is it's knee-knockingly tiny: 20 table seats and 4 in the window, so make a reservation or miss out on this assured, sometimes revelatory, meal.

25a Warren St., W1. www.honeyandco.co.uk. ✆ **020/7388-6175.** Main courses £8–£15. Mon–Fri 8am–10:30pm; Sat 9:30am–10:30pm. Tube: Warren St. or Great Portland St.

Noble Rot ★★ BRITISH   East of the British Museum and 2 blocks from the Charles Dickens Museum, behind an old storefront amid the transporting upscale boutiques of Lamb's Conduit Street, spend a languid meal sampling spectacularly well-chosen wines, cheeses, and sublimely fine slices of Spanish hams. There are also a few changing British-drawn dishes like gnocchi with wild garlic, baked Scottish cod, and Middlewhite pork chops. It's perplexing how such simplicity can yield such a delightful few hours and make you wish you lived like this every day.

15 Lamb's Conduit St., WC1. www.noblerot.co.uk. ✆ **020/7242-8963.** Plates £9–£29. Mon–Sat noon–2:30pm and 6–9:30pm. Reservations strongly suggested for dinner. Tube: Russell Square.

North Sea Fish ★★ SEAFOOD   Don't expect a linoleum-lined chippie, but a classy fish market-cum-restaurant, hidden on a lost-in-time side street. Every hotel manager within a walkable radius recommends it. Portions are huge, and there's always a selection of fresh fish (sole, salmon, halibut, and so on). If you need a healthier option, you can also get your fish grilled. Try the terrific homemade tartar sauce, or, for fans of little fishies, sample grilled sardines with salad. Here, take-away is about half the price of sitting down.

7–8 Leigh St., WC1. www.northseafishrestaurant.co.uk. ✆ **020/7387-5892.** Main courses £12–£20. Mon–Sat noon–2:30pm and 5–10pm; Sun 5–9:30pm. Tube: King's Cross St Pancras or Russell Square.

Noble Rot serves well-chosen wines and cheeses, east of the British Museum.

Savoir Faire ★★★ FRENCH After braving the rummage sale of mediocre gastronomic clip joints around the British Museum, patrons are known to smugly proclaim this their "discovery"—omitting the reality that it's been presenting what it correctly terms "affordable gourmet" since 1995. How could anyone have ignored this traveler's gift, where nothing is processed and everything is made-to-order? Meals are more than reliable; in this area, they're miracles on plates. Baguette sandwiches and burgers are under £9, but upgrade: Lunch prix-fixe is £16 (dinner £26) and might include ample portions of nimbly executed dishes like red-wine-braised duck legs, bouillabaisse, tequila-lime chicken, or beef daube so tender you wonder if they've got Julia Child's ghost back there.

42 New Oxford St., WC1. www.savoir.co.uk. ℗ **020/7436-0707.** Main courses £5–£15; 2-course set menu £16–£25. Daily noon–4pm and 5–10:30pm. Tube: Holborn or Tottenham Court Rd.

Inexpensive

The Attendant ★ CAFE A unique one for the coffee culture fans. They only serve light meals here, but they roast their own beans and the setting is worth a detour: a gourmet coffee/loose-leaf tea cafe in an underground men's toilet in Fitzrovia. The facilities had been abandoned for 50 years; the

If you're watching your money, bear in mind these cultural differences:

Avoid eating in: By law, restaurants must charge you a higher tax rate if you eat on premises, so the take-away menu is always cheaper.

Avoid over-tipping: Credit card slips may have a line for a tip, even if the tip was already built in (if it is, it'll be about 12.5 percent and the description may be as subtle as "discretion"). Only tip (10–20 percent) if the menu says "service not included" or similar.

Avoid soda: It can cost more than £2.50, no refill, or even more now that the government taxes beverages with more than 50g of sugar per liter. Many brands

reformulated with chemicals to avoid paying it, but Coke refused, so it costs more.

Avoid rice dishes: It's customary to pay £2 to £3 for a side dish of plain rice, even if you think it should come with what you ordered.

Avoid water: Well, avoid it bottled. If you just order "water," waiters may bring expensive bottled water, so if you want it for free, specify "tap water."

Avoid cocktails: Mixed drinks can cost a dizzying £9 to £12, and because pours are standardized, they're usually of the same middling strength. If you do drink, stick to beer (£3–£4 a pint) or wine (around £5 a glass).

conversion was so artful you might not realize it at first: Eight elaborate Doulton & Co. Victorian porcelain urinals are now individual coffee-sipping bays, and an overhead water tank became an unexpected planter. If you're hungry, try the sea salt caramel brownies or bacon on sourdough with tarragon butter. The coffee's so good, Attendant has added more locations, but those lack the charm of being in a loo.

27a Foley St. at Great Titchfield St., W1. www.the-attendant.com. ☎ **020/7580-3413.** Sandwiches and baked goods £3–£5. Mon–Fri 7:30am–5:30pm; Sat 9am–5:30pm; Sun 10am–5:30pm. Tube: Oxford Circus or Goodge St.

The Fryer's Delight ★★ TRADITIONAL BRITISH/TAKE-AWAY In this age, no one would dare name their joint something as hydrogenated as The Fryer's Delight. Fortunately, this joint is not of this age. It's a true old-world chippy, where the fry fat is from beef drippings, chips come in paper wrappings, the wooden booths and checkered floor date to the lean postwar years, and the men behind the counter are almost callously gruff. Prices are anachronistic, too: Nothing's more expensive than £7. Order yours with mushy peas. It's a 10-min. walk east of the British Museum; look for the logo of a codfish tipping his bowler hat (seriously). If you like fish and chips more upscale, try **Bonnie Gull** in Fitzrovia (21 Foley St., W1; www.bonniegullsea foodshack.com; ☎ **020/7436-0921;** £15 at dinner) or **Golden Union** in Soho (38 Poland St., W1; www.goldenunion.co.uk; ☎ **020/7434-1933;** £12).

19 Theobald's Rd., WC1. ☎ **020/7405-4114.** Main courses £5–£6. Mon–Sat noon–10pm. Tube: Holborn or Chancery Lane.

SOHO & LEICESTER SQUARE

Visitors spend much of their time around here, the dining and entertainment hub of London. So a miasma of dining also-rans, from junky steam-table buffets to overpriced bistros, sponge off tourists. Soho's southern fringe hosts a meager some 80 eating establishments in the neon-tinted 2-block section between Leicester Square and Shaftesbury Avenue. I don't think many of them are distinguished enough to single out. Many of them use MSG, too, despite public health currents.

Expensive

Bocca di Lupo ★ ITALIAN Stripped-down Italian expertly conceived and delivered like tapas: This simple, classy conceit—and its chipper buzz, and that long, alluring bar in front of the open kitchen—have made it a mainstay in Soho for over a decade. The menu might be printed twice a day to keep up with the availability of fresh ingredients (or with the adventurous ideas: squirrel ravioli has been known to make appearances, while sea bream carpaccio and cream of langoustine and red prawn risotto appear more reliably). If one of them fails to impress, you didn't pay much for it, so it's easy and fun to try another. The rich concepts hail from around Italy, and the region of origin is marked, like wine, to help guide your palate. The wine list, too, isn't ignored. It's among the best in town for this price.

12 Archer St., W1. www.boccadilupo.com. ℂ **020/7734-2223.** Small plates £6–£13; large plates £13–£22. Mon–Sat noon–3pm and 5–11pm; Sun noon–3:30pm and 5–9:30pm. Reservations strongly recommended. Tube: Piccadilly Circus.

The Ivy restaurant offers a mix of new fare and classics.

The Ivy ★ TRADITIONAL BRITISH A West End tent-pole for 101 years, from Coward to Cumberbatch, this is where London thespians pretend to slum it, lifting hamburgers alongside cognac beneath its iconic wood paneling and harlequin mullioned windows. "The Ivy is like a safari park in which the rare and exotic creatures are nurtured," wrote the *Guardian.* At its sumptuous flat-iron bar—you can drink at it, but you're required to eat something, too—spotting celebrities, should there be any (try after 9pm), is made all the more subtle. The menu of Ivy classics (lobster macaroni, shepherd's pie) has been embellished with Asian-ish notions (barbecued squid salad, Togarashi popcorn rock shrimp),

LONDON food chains I RECOMMEND

London, like so many other cities, is experiencing an economic shift that squeezes out mom-and-pop establishments in favor of better-heeled chains; you'll see these mid-priced, kid-friendly names on storefronts wherever you go. They're delicious and most are English-owned, so rely on them as well:

- **Busaba Eathai:** Peppy noodles and Asian dishes at communal tables.
- **Carluccio's:** New York–style Italian. Tile walls, pasta, fish, meats, coffees.
- **Franco Manca:** Well-priced pizza on soft sourdough crust.
- **Giraffe:** Every kind of comfort food, extremely family-friendly, can get noisy.
- **Leon:** Free-trade, organic alternative to fast food includes "hot boxes"

of Moroccan meatballs, halloumi wraps, and "superfood" salads.

- **M&S Simply Food:** Marks & Spencer's (p. 211) stand-alone shops for sandwiches, hit-or-miss ready-made dishes, and well-selected inexpensive wines.
- **Pizza Express:** Artisan-style pie. No one pays full price; see www.pizza-express.com/latest-offers for consistent discounts such as 25 percent off.
- **Simit Sarayi:** Turkish coffee, stuffed buns, sandwiches on seeded bread.
- **Wagamama:** Hearty noodle bowls eaten at shared long tables.
- **Wahaca:** Substantial Mexican done well with British-grown ingredients.

Wagamama serves patrons at shared tables.

which only increases the bohemian affect. From the glass jug on the bar, order a "100 Year Legacy," which is a never-ending cocktail—a Martinez, an archaic variation of a Manhattan made with gin—dispensed from a communal spout and added to as time goes on. It's an experiment that only began in

2017, but if anyplace has the wherewithal to nurture an eccentric quirk into long tradition, it's The Ivy.

1–5 West St., WC1. www.the-ivy.co.uk. (ℰ) **020/7836-4751.** Main courses £15–£20. Set menu (Mon–Thurs 2:30–6pm and all day Sun) 2 courses £24, 3 courses £28. Mon–Wed noon–11:30pm; Thurs–Sat noon–midnight; Sun noon–10:30pm. Reservations recommended. Tube: Leicester Square or Covent Garden.

Moderate

10 Greek Street ★★★ CONTEMPORARY EUROPEAN   Sometimes, restaurants get it so right—from friendly and knowledgeable staff to unfussy surroundings (chalkboard, mirrors) to pure, clean, well-made food—that you wonder why they can't all be this way. The menu, all choices a top value for the money, changes but the impeccable standards don't: Frequent standouts include whole lemon sole with samphire (an edible coastal plant) and artichokes, Brecon lamb, Gloucester Old Spot pork, elderflower sorbet, a continuous trickle of fresh-baked breads, and an affordable wine list chosen with as much care as the fish and meat cuts. If there's a downside, it's that they only take reservations for lunch (noon–2:30pm), which means you risk missing out on dinner if you don't come early. Or just sit at the tiny bar.

10 Greek St., W1. www.10greekstreet.com. (ℰ) **0209/7734-4677.** Main courses £12–£19. Mon–Tues noon–2:30pm and 5:30–10:15pm; Wed–Sat noon–2:30pm and 5:30–10:45pm; Sun noon–9pm. Tube: Tottenham Court Rd.

Andrew Edmunds ★★★ BRITISH   The relaxed, town house–style storefront, a study in natural woods and candle-lit purity, has been going for 30 years, enduring most likely because it hasn't caved to Soho trendiness and its stupendous wine list is priced fairly. Chairs don't match, staff isn't in uniform, and the menu is hand-scribbled daily with a haste that belies the effort the chef puts into sourcing farmhouse meats and preparing seasonal ingredients. Expect choices along the lines of skate wing with cauliflower and capers, free-range Aylesbury duck breast, and artichoke spaghetti with wild garlic and almond pesto, plus the occasional nose-to-tail adventure. Superb dessert cheeses are selected from area farms. It's very London.

46 Lexington St., W1. www.andrewedmunds.com. (ℰ) **020/7437-5708.** Main courses £13–£23. Mon–Fri noon–3:30pm and 5:30–10:45pm; Sat 12:30–3:30pm and 5:30–10:45pm; Sun 1–4pm and 6–10:30pm. Reservations essential; dinner accepted a month ahead, lunch accepted 3 weeks ahead. Tube: Piccadilly Circus or Oxford Circus.

Blanchette ★ FRENCH   Divinely assembled tasting plates, which change with seasons, focus on ingredients: things like grilled flavor-rich beef *onglet* (hanger steak) with snails or mushrooms, grilled asparagus with aged Comté cheese, hot bread delivered in a brown paper bag with soft butter spread with a wooden paddle. The food may be crafted, but there's no fussiness in the welcome nor in the funky-pop soundtrack. The look is much like a casually urbanized French farmhouse of rough wood and exposed brick; a long bar under caged light bulbs is ideal for tasting charcuterie and cheese and

The dining room at Brasserie Zédel features gilt and marble.

sipping wine and cocktails. The pre-theater menu brings three courses for under £20.

9 D'Arblay St., W1. www.blanchettesoho.co.uk. ⓒ **020/7439-8100.** Small plates £3–£8; larger plates £10–£15. Mon–Sat noon–11pm; Sun noon–8:45pm. Tube: Oxford Circus.

Brasserie Zédel ★★★ FRENCH   When you enter via its grand staircase, you feel like Toulouse-Lautrec in search of tonight's muse: The gilt-and-marble cellar dining room, awash in *fin-de-siècle* statements like platter mirrors and vested waiters, is a perfect piece of Paris off Piccadilly. This is not a crusty holdover but a pitch-perfect recreation out of what was once the Regent Palace Hotel, which in 1915 was the largest hotel in Europe. Menu choices are as authentic as Pernod, pastis, oysters, quiche Lorraine, and sublimely seasoned steak tartare (often, the first thing I order upon returning to town). The adjoining **Bar Américain,** a 1930s Art Deco treasure by an architect survivor of the *Lusitania,* does indulgently uptight cocktails and champagne, while its 80-seat cabaret, **Le Crazy Coqs/Live at Zédel** is an elegant venue that does matinees and evening shows (£15–£35, no drink minimum). This bit of the Continental high life is not nearly as expensive as it looks, and its Gallic poise only adds to the deliciousness.

20 Sherwood St., W1. www.brasseriezedel.com. ⓒ **020/7734-4888.** Main courses £13–£15; 2 courses £10; 3 courses £13. Mon–Sat 11:30am–midnight; Sun 11:30am–11pm. Tube: Piccadilly Circus.

Ceviche ★★★ PERUVIAN   This is my firm favorite in Soho. Owner Martin Morales quit his job at Disney's European music division to pursue his true passion: food. Now he is a TV personality, a cookbook author, and runs this hopping, cheerful Peruvian hangout that pours the best pisco sour in town. Flavors are indescribably punchy, citrusy, and unrepeatable anywhere else you've eaten. Favorite small plates include the *don ceviche* sea bass made with *limo chili* tiger's milk, and the succulent *anticucho* skewers of beef heart marinated in *panca chili* marinade. Once your tongue tastes its first vibrant zip, you'll feel compelled to come back. They now give diners a spoon to lap up leftover tiger's milk—probably because I kept asking. A second, spacious location is just north of the Old Street Tube stop (2 Baldwin St., EC1), while the owner's similar **Andina** is in Shoreditch (1 Redchurch St., E2; www.andinalondon.com; ℭ **020/7920-6499;** Tube: Shoreditch High St. or Liverpool St.).

17 Frith St., W1. www.cevicheuk.com. ℭ **020/7292-2040.** Small plates £7–£14. Mon–Sat noon–11:30pm; Sun noon–10:15pm); hot kitchen closed Mon–Thurs 3-5pm. Reservations suggested. Tube: Piccadilly Circus or Tottenham Court Rd.

Ducksoup ★★ INTERNATIONAL   The sort of invisible hidey-hole you have to be told about, Ducksoup feels like "your" spot. Indeed, when you first open its old door, the first thing you see is a stack of LPs and a record player, the sole sound system, that might be playing Grace Jones' "Nightclubbing" or Toots & the Maytals' "Funky Kingston." The metal grille on the windows and life-beaten walls make it look like a greasy cafe that would sling a fry-up at you, but instead, there's a funky wine list and solid, whole-food selections, which change daily, such as grilled artichoke with lemon and capers, rabbit pappardelle, and chargrilled bream. The room feels like a London that went out with Thatcher, but dishes sit solidly within London's 21st-century gustatory passions.

41 Dean St., W1. www.ducksoupsoho.co.uk. ℭ **020/7287-4599.** Main courses £8–£18. Mon–Sat noon–10:30pm, Sun noon–5pm; bar open later. Tube: Tottenham Court Rd.

Mildreds ★ VEGETARIAN   Packed since 1988, it's where vegetarians with palates go. The menu is ever-changing but always assembled with more care than the usual beans and tofu: Sri Lankan sweet potato and lime cashew curry, wood-roasted mushroom and ale pie, and green falafel with sour cherry and pistachio rice are three samples from its international menu. Big bowls and plates, appetizing presentation, and a vibe like home have secured Mildreds a following even among carnivores—it even had a pretty cookbook published. Save room for the peanut butter chocolate brownie—you won't believe it's gluten-free. Monday through Friday, it also does a take-away salad bar lunch.

45 Lexington St., W1. www.mildreds.co.uk. ℭ **020/7494-1634.** Main courses £9–£12. Mon–Sat noon–11pm. No reservations. Tube: Tottenham Court Rd.

Inexpensive

Bar Italia ★★ COFFEE/ITALIAN   Italians settled Soho in the 1940s, and before they decamped for the suburbs, they installed a set of mod, gleaming coffee bars and cafes. This straggler from 1946 is a haunt of slumming celebrities and artists, yet modest enough for the rest of us. While this institution is busy all day—making simple sandwiches, delivering pastries—it swells with revelers after midnight. Even Rome doesn't have bars that steam, press, and shuffle coffee across such defiantly worn 1950s linoleum with such gusto. "Like everything in this city that Londoners really enjoy, it reminds us of being abroad," quipped the *Guardian.* Whatever; it practically leaks hipness.

22 Frith St., W1. www.baritaliasoho.co.uk. ☏ **020/7437-4520.** Coffee £3–£4; pizza £10–£11; panini £7. Mon–Sat 6:30am–4:30am; Sun 6:30am–2am. Tube: Leicester Square.

Café in the Crypt ★ INTERNATIONAL   Super-central and unquestionably memorable, it's the tastiest graveyard in town! Under the sanctuary of the historic St Martin-in-the-Fields church at Trafalgar Square, atop the gravestones of 18th-century Londoners, one of the West End's sharpest bargains is served. The menu at this dependable 200-seat cafeteria changes monthly, but the large portions always include a few hot meat main dishes, a vegetarian choice, soups, salads topped with meats, and sweet apple crumble with custard; there's also fish and chips on Friday. The church keeps the draft beer and the wine (even by the bottle) flowing, and afternoon tea is but £10—so is Sunday roast. It's fun, delicious, central, and a budget savior.

Trafalgar Sq., WC2. www.smitf.org. ☏ **020/7766-1158.** Main courses £7–£10. Mon–Tues 8am–8pm; Wed 8am–10:30pm (with 8pm jazz for ticket holders only after 6:30pm); Thurs–Sat 8am–9pm; Sun 11am–6pm. Tube: Charing Cross.

Gordon's Wine Bar ★★★ INTERNATIONAL   The atmosphere is matchless at London's most vaunted and vaulted casual wine bar. It was established in 1890 (when Rudyard Kipling lived upstairs) and, thank goodness, hasn't been refurbished since—look in the front window and you'll see untouched champagne bottles intentionally left to grow furry with dust. These tight, candle-lit cellars beneath Villiers Street are wallpapered with important newspaper front pages from the mid-20th century—the Crystal Palace blaze, the death of King George VI—and the wood barrels behind the bar are filled with port on tap (a *schooner* is small, a *beaker* is larger). Everything is suffused in a mustardy ochre from more than 42,000 past evenings of indoor tobacco smoke (no longer legal). Music is not played—not that you could hear it over the din of conversation. Pick a bottle of wine (it's affordable) from one of the binders and they'll give you the glasses, and for a light meal, select from a marble table of English and French cheeses or a steam table of hot food. In good weather, the event expands outside along Embankment Gardens with casual alfresco fare such as barbecue and sweet potato fries. (The stone arch was built around 1625 as a palace gate on the Thames, but its mansion is long gone and the river moved 46m/150 ft. south.) Come down in mid-afternoon, well before offices let out, or you won't secure seating.

47 Villiers St., WC2. www.gordonswinebar.com. ℂ **020/7930-1408.** Set meals £13; cheese plates £8–£18. Mon–Sat 11am–11pm; Sun noon–10pm. No reservations. Tube: Charing Cross or Embankment.

Joy King Lau ★ DIM SUM   For the tipsy Soho revelers in Chinatown, there's this long-termer with multiple levels, perpetually packed on weekends and bank holidays. Decor? Tired. Service? Robotic. Food quality? Swings between crapshoot and rapture. Customers who aren't used to the brisk attitude of servers in a Chinese food hall like this may feel rebuffed, but there's something invigorating about joining the carnival and slurping down whatever they place in front of you. Sticking to the dim sum menu from noon to 5pm (and not springing for the Cantonese set menu) satisfies most people.

3 Leicester St., WC2. www.joykinglau.com. ℂ **020/7437-1132.** Main courses £8–£19. Mon–Sat noon–11:30pm; Sun noon–10:30pm. Tube: Leicester Square.

COVENT GARDEN

The area was once more interesting, but CAPCO, which governs the leases, has adopted a policy of squeezing out oddballs in favor of imported brands such as Shake Shack, Le Pain Quotidien, Apple, and Balthazar. The food within the market is tourist-priced, but if you simply must eat there, head to the lower level where you'll find £6 *tartines* (open sandwiches) at **Chez Antoinette** and good cheese at the **Crusting Pipe** wine bar.

Expensive

J. Sheekey ★★ SEAFOOD   Smartly turned-out waiters prep you with so many strange fish-eating utensils that your place setting starts to look like a workstation at Santa's workshop. Such presentational flourishes are appropriate to theaterland, where this has been a bistro-style classic for years, and although prices aren't generous, portions and quality are. The least expensive main dish, fish pie, is fortunately its trademark, but there are plenty of other choices, from shrimp-and-scallop burgers to a delectable lemon sole, plus a changing slate of game and meats for the fish-averse. Despite all the fuss, children are welcomed.

28–35 St. Martin's Ct., WC2. www.j-sheekey.co.uk. ☏ **020/7240-2565.** Main courses £18–£44. Weekend lunch set menu: 3 courses £29. Mon–Sat noon–3pm and 5pm–midnight; Sun noon–3pm and 5:30–10:30pm. Reservations recommended. Tube: Leicester Square.

Margot ★★ ITALIAN Perfect house-made pasta, carefully sourced meats, attentive service that aims high but never condescends, and a contemporary, bright dining room filled with bespoke furniture—in Mayfair, a tourist like you wouldn't get in, but in Covent Garden, it's a convivial and civilized place to dine and discreetly people-watch through great glass windows. Even though the house olive oil is dispensed—liberally—from silver coffee pots, it looks more buttoned-down than it actually is. To whisper romantic secrets over your meal, ask to be seated in the smart, club-like basement room. Intentionally tailored for West End evenings, it serves food late, has some 350 wine choices, and two cocktail bars.

45 Great Queen St., WC2. www.margotrestaurant.com. ☏ **020/3409-4777.** Main courses £18–£32. Mon–Fri noon–3pm and 5:30pm–midnight (last food orders at 11pm); Sat noon–3pm and 5:30–10:45pm; Sun noon–3pm and 5:30–9:45pm). Reservations recommended. Tube: Holborn.

A classic Dover sole is expertly deboned tableside at J. Sheekey.

Rules ★★ TRADITIONAL BRITISH   For a high-end kitchen that takes British cuisine seriously, go with an icon. Rules is London's oldest restaurant (est. 1798), and its patrons have included Graham Greene, Charles Dickens, Evelyn Waugh, and Edward VII, who regularly dined here with his paramour Lillie Langtry. (The management is less than discreet about it; the nook they used is named for him.) Being a major stop on the tourist trail has gone slightly to its head and it's steeped in its own hype; beer comes in a "silver tankard," for example, and the landmarked rooms are an overdressed Georgian yard sale of yellowing etchings, antlers, and rich red fabrics. But what's on the table is indisputably high-class: English-reared meat like haunch of venison, whole roast squab or grouse (it serves 18,000 game birds annually), and cocktails like that famous one made of tonic, juniper, and quinine. Its nearest rival, **Simpsons-in-the-Strand** at the Savoy hotel (p. 41) has been going since 1828.

35 Maiden Lane, WC1. www.rules.co.uk. ✆ **020/7836-5314.** Main courses £22–£35. Mon–Sat noon–11:45pm; Sun noon–10:45pm. Dress code: smart casual. Tube: Covent Garden.

Moderate

Browns ★ TRADITIONAL BRITISH   In London, there's a Browns for fashion, and a Brown's Hotel, but Browns the spacious brasserie is the Browns you can afford. Installed in the former Westminster County Courts, this high-quality, Brighton-based English chain serves updated English food and imported beer. The globe lanterns, enormous mirrors, and staff buttoned into crisp white oxford shirts impart the sense of a Gilded Age chophouse. Expect lots of indulgently hearty dishes such as lobster risotto, steak and Guinness pie, fish and chips, or a nice fat burger with Irish cheddar. A sense of tradition—starchy, but the kind that's welcoming to tourists—is the main product here.

82–84 St. Martins Lane, WC2. www.browns-restaurants.com. ✆ **020/7497-5050.** Main courses £11–£19; Sunday roast £13–£17; 2-course pre-theatre meal £15, Mon–Sat 4–7pm. Mon–Thurs 8am–10:30pm; Fri 8am–11pm); Sat 10am–11pm; Sun 10am–10:30pm. Tube: Leicester Square.

Flat Iron ★★★ STEAK   For a mere £10, you get an absolutely perfect 200g steak or steakburger, a cup of salad, a serving of beef-dripping popcorn, and on the way out the door, a cone of caramel ice cream topped with shavings from a block of dark chocolate. No wonder there's a queue at peak hours. The menu is focused—no chicken, no pork, and sorry, vegetarians—plus good cocktails and well-suited side dishes. Specializing makes the cooking expert and the juicy meat is over-the-top delicious. The beef comes from a herd of cows in Yorkshire "cared for by third-generation beef farmer Charles Ashbridge," and each week, 7 tons of it are served at Flat Iron's several locations (others include 9 Denmark St., off Tottenham Court Rd., and 17 Beak St., off

Carnaby St.). This version by Covent Garden is the best for killing time before your table is ready.

17/18 Henrietta St., WC2. www.flatironsteak.co.uk. No phone. Mains £10. Mon–Sat noon–midnight; Sun noon–11pm). No reservations. Tube: Covent Garden or Leicester Square.

Great Queen Street ★★★ TRADITIONAL BRITISH   Here, the people behind the seminal **Eagle** (p. 72) present the essence of gastropub cuisine in the more convenient environs of Covent Garden and with showier meats. There's a pub feel with scuffed wood floors, burgundy walls, and sconces capped with fringed mini-shades. The slow-cooked dishes are clean and reassuringly ingredient-proud. Offerings (they change) may include Old Spot (a breed of pig) pork chops with sticky shallots, Hereford beef, or griddled quail with celery salt. One menu regular is lamb's shoulder cooked for 7 hours and accompanied by *gratin dauphinoise* (potatoes in crème fraîche)—that one feeds four, which hints at the social atmosphere encouraged here. The Cellar Bar (open until midnight Tues–Sat) serves the cold dishes from the same menu.

32 Green Queen St., WC2. www.greatqueenstreetrestaurant.co.uk. ℭ **020/7242-0622.** Main courses £16–£34. Mon–Sat noon–2:30pm and 5:30–10:30pm; Sun noon–3:30pm. Tube: Covent Garden or Holborn.

Wild Food Café ★★ VEGAN   Upstairs in the Granola Triangle of Neal's Yard, above the excellent homeopathic dispensary Neal's Yard Remedies, this popular and packed place serves plant-based fare that's truly flavorful at prices Covent Garden left behind: olive and shiitake burgers, pine-nut quinoa with horseradish tahini, and raw chocolate as a component in some very impressive desserts. At peak mealtimes, there may be a bunch-up at the door (no reservations). Don't be daunted; wait for a communal seat whether it's at the bar or at a table. It's some of the best vegan food you'll find in the city, even if its crunchy self-image as a "well-being oasis" is a little too earnest.

First Floor, 14 Neal's Yard, WC2. www.wildfoodcafe.com. ℭ **020/7419-2014.** Main courses £6–£15. Summer daily 11:30am–11pm; rest of year Mon 11am–4pm, Tues–Thurs 11:30am–8pm, Fri–Sat 11:30am–9pm, Sun 11:30am–6pm. Tube: Covent Garden.

Inexpensive

Punjab Restaurant ★★★ INDIAN   Ignore that it looks like every other hack kitchen sponging off the Covent Garden tourist trade—this place predates the recent curry trend, which is why it survived the crest of the popularity wave. Punjab has been cooking since 1947, when it was opened by Gurbachan Singh Maan, a wrestler, and moved to this location in 1951 to serve the bureaucrats of the India High Commission during a tumultuous political period. Now, his fourth generation runs it with striking professionalism. It proclaims itself the oldest North Indian restaurant in the U.K., and staff have worked here for decades. Cooking is light on the oil and *ghee* (clarified butter). Meats and tandoori (the oven was installed in 1962) are well marinated, and so they arrive tender. The menu is cheeky, too: "If you have any erotic activities planned for after you leave us, perhaps you should resist this sensational garlic *naan*." Reserve ahead on weekends.

80 Neal St., WC2. www.punjab.co.uk. © **020/7836-9787.** Main courses £8–£13, sometimes a £15 per person minimum. Mon–Sat noon–11pm; Sun noon–10pm. Tube: Covent Garden.

MAYFAIR & MARYLEBONE

It's hard to find a dining establishment in these high-toned hoods that isn't overpriced, swooning with self-importance, and wooing a clientele that's better-connected than you are. The "in" spots seem to change with the tides, but you may rely on—and be welcomed by—these stalwarts.

Expensive

Hide ★★★ CONTEMPORARY   In 2017, one of the city's most celebrated chefs, Ollie Dabbous, abruptly pulled the plug on his 34-seat eponymous restaurant so he could debut this—three levels in a sparse Scandinavian style, with plenty of space to throw money at ideas and allow diners to absorb the ministrations of his staff of 200, including 15 sommeliers. The wine list from Hedonism, one of the city's most comprehensive wine stores, is one of the largest in the world (more than 6,000 bottles—you will splash out in more

Hide on Piccadilly serves artful cuisine on three levels and has an impressive and large wine list.

STEEPED IN TRADITION: afternoon tea

Afternoon tea is an overpriced tourist's pursuit, to be sure, but that doesn't mean it's not delightful to pass the time by pretending to be fancy. Arrive hungry and you'll be served a never-ending banquet of scones, clotted cream, pastry, light sandwiches, and a bottomless brewed torrent. Dress up, if you please, and be discreet about photos. Hundreds of places throw teas, but these are among the most transporting, legendary, or best-located. Most places will add champagne for £5 to £20 more.

Brown's Hotel This Mayfair institution, open since 1837, offers exacting execution and a handsome paneled room but is not overly snooty. It veers trendy: "Tea-Tox" is its lower-fat, lower-carb version. www.roccofortehotels.com.
℗ **020/7518-4155.** Noon–6:30pm; £55. Tube: Green Park. Also see p. 54.

Fortnum & Mason The venerable department store on Piccadilly has sold tea for 3 centuries, so naturally in its Diamond Jubilee Tea Salon, nibbling off duck-egg-blue china and serenaded by grand piano, you choose from 150 tea types, many of which are supplied to the other hotels on this list. The crowd can be touristy. www.fortnumandmason.com.
℗ **020/7734-8040.** £45. Tube: Green Park. Also see p. 208.

The Goring Near Buckingham Palace, it serves on its own bespoke canary-yellow china in your choice of the blood-red lounge, the airy conservatory, or the garden. Book at least 3 months ahead, but sit as long as you want once you're there. www.thegoring.com.
℗ **020/7396-9000.** 3–4pm; from £49. Tube: Victoria. Also see p. 46.

Tea at Brown's Hotel is a Mayfair institution.

ways than one). Choose the street-level, a la carte Hide Ground, serving all three meals, afternoon tea, and baked creations; or Hide Above, overlooking Green Park, for fine-dining tasting menus; Hide Below is the bar and wine cellar (try the martini made with birch sap instead of ice). Any choice will wow, with dishes weaving acid and richness to deliver amazements that always belie the deceptively plain menu descriptions. This is what happens when a talent is given full license to play—you get a menu full of headliners. Charred asparagus in meadowsweet and hay buttermilk with praline; 7-year aged Simmenthal beef tartare with nasturtium, tobacco, and molasses; miso-glazed goose or turbot in verbena and a sauce made of its own bones; a saffron-indulged bouillabaisse that has caused many a grizzled food critic to exalt like the Pythia channeling Apollo. Don't expect any dish to loiter on the menu for long, because Dabbous has built the perfect personal theme park for

Great Court Restaurant, The British Museum Enjoy more sensibly priced scones under the courtyard's central glass canopy. It's a gorgeous but casual setting you're sure to visit anyway. www.britishmuseum.org. ℂ **020/7323-8990.** 3–5:30pm; £20. Tube: Russell Square. Also see p. 114.

Houses of Parliament Take tea overlooking the Thames in the modern Terrace Pavilion rooms behind the House of Commons. www.parliament.uk/visiting. ℂ **020/7219-4114.** Generally 2 and 3:45pm on a scattered schedule; £29 plus price of tour. Tube: Westminster. Also see p. 132.

The Lanesborough Dazzling in every way, from the delicacy of the pastry to the airy Regency frills of the conservatory glass overhead, for cozy class this Knightsbridge hotel institution defeats The Ritz by a strong scone's throw, I'd say. www.lanesborough.com. ℂ **020/7259-5599.** Mon–Fri 2:30–4:30pm, Sat–Sun 3–4:30pm; £39. Tube: Hyde Park Corner. Also see p. 52.

The Langham The first London hotel to initiate the custom (in 1865) is still top quality, but it's also one of the most commercial, having branded itself with a Wedgewood partnership. This Oxford Circus tradition is particularly popular with Asian tourists. www.palm-court.co.uk. ℂ **020/7636-1000.** 5 seatings 12:15–5:30pm; £55. Tube: Oxford Circus. Also see p. 53.

The Milestone The antiqued, library-like Park Lounge overlooking Kensington Gardens is your stop if you're near Kensington Palace. It doles out 11,000 doggy boxes a year for guests who can't finish—a courtesy that's uncommon at teas. www.milestonehotel.com. ℂ **020/7917-1000.** 3 seatings 1–5pm; from £50. Tube: High St. Kensington. Also see p. 47.

The Ritz The only way most of us can afford the formal gilding, mirrors, and boisterous floral arrangements of the Ritz, at 150 Piccadilly, is to submit to the machinelike attentions of the servile waiters in its Palm Court (1906), who process 400 people daily during hours the gentry would find unseemly for tea. It's fancy but not cuddly. No jeans or sneakers, with jacket and tie required for men. Book 6 to 8 weeks ahead. www.theritzlondon.com. ℂ **020/7300-2345.** 5 seatings 11:30am–7:30pm; £57 adults, £35 children. Tube: Green Park.

inventing new thrills. He's thought of everything, down to the phone chargers in the tables and the lighting, which (for real) intentionally eliminates shadows so you can properly Instagram your dinner, because once the mastery of the cooking is complete, each plating yields a second work of art. Make reservations as far ahead as you can.

85 Piccadilly, W1. www.85piccadilly.co.uk. ℂ **020/3146-8666.** Main courses £18–£32. Tasting menus from £100, wine pairings from £65. Mon–Fri 7:30am–midnight; Sat 9am–midnight; Sun 9am–11:45pm. Last food orders at 11pm. Reservations required. Tube: Green Park.

Le Gavroche ★★★ FRENCH There are always newcomers in Mayfair hoping to capture the vanity crowd, and trendy styles with fresh young chefs rise and burn out, but Le Gavroche remains the top choice for classical French cuisine. Its leader, Michel Roux, Jr., is the son of the chef who founded the restaurant in 1967. The famous cheese soufflé is still there after all these years. Also on the menu: lobster with lemongrass and coconut-infused *jus,* roast suckling pig, and roast Goosnargh duck, plus desserts including apricot and Cointreau soufflé. The cheese board is exemplary. It's all beautifully presented and served with style. The wine list is a masterclass in top French wines, and is kind to the purse as well on lesser-known varieties. It all takes place in a comfortable, conventional basement dining room that may be too old-fashioned for some, but is endearingly classic to those who have cherished this place for a half century.

43 Upper Brook St., W1. www.le-gavroche.co.uk. ℂ **020/7408-0881.** Main courses £35–£60; set lunch £66; tasting menu £150 (without wine). Tues–Fri noon–2pm and 6–10pm; Sat 6–10pm. Reservations required. Tube: Marble Arch.

The Wolseley ★★★ CONTEMPORARY EUROPEAN "No Flash or Intrusive Photography please," chastises diners in a footnote on the menu. That's because this opulent bistro in the Grand European style, posing with every polished surface to appear like something Renoir would want to paint, is home base for celebrities and power lunchers. Built as a luxury car dealership for a doomed manufacturer, then used as a bank, a decade ago it became a caviar-scooping, oyster-shucking, tea-pouring hotspot, convincing nearly everyone who sips its pea-and-lettuce soup that it's always been this way. Waiters are unattainably attractive and look down their noses as they gingerly place salad Niçoise and Swiss soufflé, enacting the calculated Continental crispness we crave.

160 Piccadilly, W1. www.thewolseley.com. ℂ **020/7499-6996.** Main courses £13–£30; sandwiches £15. Mon–Fri 7am–midnight; Sat 8am–midnight; Sun 8am–11pm. Tube: Green Park.

Moderate

The Grazing Goat ★ BRITISH A block north of Oxford Street, this farmhouse-style gastropub (light wood, bare tables, a bar presiding over the conversations, strong but casual service) attracts a varied crowd for wine or a locally brewed pint, quality house-cured meats, and classic British proteins such as rotisserie beef, venison, chicken, fish and chips, and the title character served with a raisin mustard *jus.* The all-day Sunday Roast (beef, pork, or lamb) with all the trimmings is swishier than what a pub serves, but a tonic for feet run weary by shopping at nearby Selfridges. ***Hidden gem alert:*** It also has

The Grazing Goat attracts a varied crowd.

food halls OF FAME

Inspired by the markets and food trucks of the United States, London has welcomed a multi-course banquet of gourmet gatherings that function like foodie markets for fresh, ready-to-eat creations. Some of the best:

Borough Market The king of foodie meccas; the one all the others wish they were. See p. 94. Tube: London Bridge.

Camden Markets The downmarket choice—mostly cheap and simple—but bountiful. Star attraction: The Cheese Wheel, where hand-rolled tagliatelle is tossed in a bowl made of a huge truckle of melting parmesan. See p. 226. Tube: Camden Town.

Eataly It's the Italian eater's paradise that itself is devouring the world. London finally gets its own in 2020 at 135 Bishopsgate, in the City. Tube: Liverpool St.

Maltby Street Market Purveying gorgeous flavors such as "bad brownies" oozing salted caramel, egg-shaped waffles, and "African volcano" hot sauce. Partly outdoors amid the railway vaults south of the Tower Bridge. Maltby St., SE1. www.maltby.st. ℰ **020/7394-8061.**

Sat 9am–4pm; Sun 11am–4pm. Tube: London Bridge or Bermondsey.

Market Hall Victoria Another late 2018 opening: some 14 restaurants, 3 bars, and seating for 300 in an Edwardian Baroque shopping arcade opposite the station vacated by a nightclub. Terminus Place. www.markethalls.co.uk. Tube: Victoria.

Market Hall West End In late 2018, a onetime BHS department store was announced, planning with more than 35 bars, restaurants, food stalls, and a demonstration kitchen, making it the U.K.'s largest food hall. 252–258 Oxford St. www.markethalls.co.uk. Tube: Oxford Circus.

Mercato Metropolitano Dedicated to small producers and emerging chefs, not flashy chains, this former factory space has been popular since its 2016 opening. Fresh-baked woodfire pizzas, racks of cheeses, and a filling overuse of the term *artisan*. 42 Newington Causeway, SE1, www.mercatometropolitano. co.uk. ℰ **020/7403-0930.** Mon–Fri 8am–11pm; Sat 11am–11pm; Sun 11am–10pm. Tube: Elephant & Castle.

eight country-house-inspired B&B rooms, each with a king bed and free Wi-Fi (from £210).

6 New Quebec St., W1. www.thegrazinggoat.co.uk. ℰ **020/7724-7243.** Main courses £11–£22. Mon–Sat noon–10pm; Sun noon–9:30pm, kitchen closes 1 hr. prior, bar closes 1 hr. later. Tube: Marble Arch.

The Hard Rock Cafe ★ AMERICAN You'll find one in every city from Key West to Kuwait. Its burgers (though excellent) nudge £20, it's cramped, and much of the so-called memorabilia consists of instruments played once and tossed aside. But this Hard Rock was the world's first, opened in 1971, so there is a grudging authenticity. And you don't have to eat here to take a free tour of its cellar museum, The Vault (until 10:30pm), packed with historic guitars.

150 Old Park Lane, W1. www.hardrock.com. ℰ **020/7514-1700.** Main courses £12–£17. Mon–Thurs 11:30am–12:30am; Fri 11:30am–1am; Sat 11am–1am; Sun 11:30am–10:30pm. Reservations recommended. Tube: Hyde Park Corner.

Rasa W1 ★ INDIAN   Oxford Street is for corporate stores and predictable chain food—you can do better. This kicky Indian alternative, which shines a light on the fun flavors of southwest India, lies off a quiet side street just southeast of the Bond Street station. It may be casual like a standard Indian joint (pinkish walls, tablecloths too nice for its price point), but even everyday items are pumped up—what's just "coconut rice" on the menu is in fact blended with cashews, a leading crop of Kerala. It also does sublime mango *lassi*, with the hint of lime, and if you're on the go, grab a box lunch for £6. And imagine this: mangoes and green bananas cooked in yogurt with green chilis, ginger, and fresh curry leaves. That's the sweet-and-sour *moru kachiathu,* and it's a menu highlight.

6 Dering St., W1. www.rasarestaurants.com. ✆ **020/7629-1346.** Main courses £11–£16. Mon–Sat noon–3pm and 6–11pm; Sun 1–3pm and 6–9pm. Tube: Bond St. or Oxford Circus.

4 KENSINGTON & WESTMINSTER

South Kensington near the museums is a particular quandary; the museums offer insultingly overpriced food services while most nearby establishments would not be a culinary credit to most cities. If you must eat in South Ken, scout around the cafes at Exhibition Road around the Tube stop; look into **Orsini** (8A Thurloe Place; www.orsinicaffe.co.uk; ✆ **020/7581-5553**), serving competent Italian; frenetic local tapas chain **Casa Brindisa** (7–9 Exhibition Rd., SW7; www.brindisakitchens.com; ✆ **020/7590-0008**); or **Franco Manca** (91 Old Brompton Rd.; www.francomanca.co.uk; ✆ **020/7584-9713**), a local brand that does pizza on sourdough crust. Otherwise, the pickings are ripe with the usual chains.

Expensive

Rex Whistler ★★ BRITISH   Should one find oneself in a parlor conversation about dining history, one could validly submit that the Rex Whistler, opened in 1927 within the Tate Britain, began the trend of fine dining inside great museum institutions. Back then it was a bit of a lark, encircled by Whistler's whimsical mural *The Expedition in Pursuit of Rare Meats,* in which a food-finding expedition travels on bicycle through lands populated by unicorns and truffle dogs, but in years since, the restaurant has garnered serious appreciation for its rich wine list—the sommelier will even consult with you before you arrive. Today's luncheon menu champions British seasonal produce, from Scottish salmon to Yorkshire mutton to succulent guinea fowl.

Tate Britain, Millbank, SW1. www.tate.org.uk. ✆ **020/7887-8825.** 2-course meals from £30; 3-course meals from £36. Daily noon–3pm; frequent evening openings to coincide with popular exhibitions. Reservations essential. Tube: Pimlico.

Inexpensive

Regency Café ★★★ TRADITIONAL BRITISH   The mid-20th-century "caff" diner, once a staple of London life, is rapidly being swept into Formica heaven by trendy bistros. Among the few holdouts still doling out classic English breakfasts all day is the 1940s Regency, a discount-Deco requiem to a lost age in yellowed white tiles and bolted-down plastic chairs. This isn't a gustatory treasure (the fryer is in heavy use, white bread heaped high, sausage a food group); it's an anthropological one. Big-value food including £2.60 burgers or homemade meat pie is prepared with lightning speed, and your order is jarringly bellowed so that you can come fetch it. For another marvelous "caff," see E. Pellicci (p. 101).

17–19 Regency St., SW1. www.regencycafe.co.uk. ℂ **020/7821-6596.** Main courses £2.60–£7. Mon–Fri 7am–2:30pm and 4–7:15pm; Sat 7am–noon. Tube: Pimlico or Westminster.

THE SOUTH BANK & THAMES

For a casual street food meal, head behind the South Bank Centre for the South Bank Market, a collection of changing food stalls cooking up curries, duck confit burgers, sausages, and other cheap and ready-to-eats. It runs Friday through Sunday, starting around noon and wrapping up by about 8pm.

Expensive

Restaurant Story ★★ MODERN BRITISH   This event restaurant has been celebrated for its creativity as much as its skill; in 2018, it closed temporarily for a total refit, including the menu, but before the change, it went like this: The moment you sat, your server lit a white taper as you pulled your menu from the leaves of *Sketches by Boz* by Charles Dickens, who lived nearby in his penniless youth. By the time a fusillade of about six *amuse-bouche* "snacks" hit you (paper-thin cod skin studded with emulsified cod roe, a sweet black eel mousse "Storeo"), your candle had melted, you were told that the wax was actually beef fat, and you were handed a leather pouch of fresh-baked bread to sop up the rich drippings. More unfurled: scallop carpaccio with cucumber balls rolled in dill ash; Jensen's gin (Sellers loves gin) and apple consommé topped with garlic blossoms; and "Three Bears" porridge—one sweet, one salty, one just right. The dramatic and whimsical flourishes are by hot talent Tom Sellers, who earned a Michelin star for his narrative-as-meal concept. His new prix-fixe menu, promises a fully bespoke menu catered to you and often prepared tableside. The price is extreme, but the experience is like none other, and a high-wire act few other chefs would be capable of.

199 Tooley St., SE1. www.restaurantstory.co.uk. ℂ **020/7183-2117.** Lunch: 5 courses £50 or 8 courses £100; Dinner: 10 courses £125, 12 courses £145. Mon 6:30–11pm; Tues-Sat noon–5pm and 6:30–11pm; in Dec, also Sun 6–11pm. Reservations essential. Tube: London Bridge or Bermondsey.

Borough Market combines Victorian commercial hubbub with farm-fresh flavors.

Moderate

Padella ★★★ ITALIAN   Eaters go wild for its succulent and savory pasta dishes—there's always a line curling out the front door into this one-room fishbowl alongside Borough Market. I wouldn't tell you about it if it wasn't worth the wait. Once you're in, you mount a stool at a counter (facing the cooks is best, but it'll be too busy for you to be choosy) and get busy delighting yourself from a brief list of small-plate superstars like creamy gnocchi with nutmeg butter, *pici cacio e pepe* (cheese-and-pepper pici noodles), and pappardelle with a ragu of 8-hour Dexter beef shin from Ireland, plus a few tap wines and beers. Padella has been toying with an app-based system to hold your place in line; check its site to see if it has successfully implemented one.

6 Southwark St., SE1. www.padella.co. No public phone. Main courses £5–£9. Mon–Sat noon–3:45pm and 5–10pm; Sun noon–3:45pm and 5–9pm. Tube: London Bridge.

Inexpensive

Borough Market ★★★ INTERNATIONAL   Countless visitors cite it as a highlight of their London vacations. This popular complex combines Victorian commercial hubbub with glorious, farm-fresh flavors, rendered as finger food for visitors. If there's any country that has farming down, it's England,

and this market is its showplace. About a dozen greenmarket vendors sell their country meats, cheeses, and vegetables beneath its metal-and-glass canopy all week long, but the market really blooms Thursday through Saturday, when more than 100 additional vendors unpack and the awe-inspiring scene hits its swing. The least crowded time is Thursday between 11am and noon; Saturdays are plain nuts. It's best to pay with cash—most dishes are around £6 to £8—and you'll eat standing up. Buy a flute of Prosecco from one of the vendors selling it and feel your palate lighten. Some don't-miss stops (you'll find more of your own):

o Under the Victorian glass canopy of Three Crown Square, **Le Marché du Quartier** (www.marketquarter.com) does duck confit sandwiches.

o Sample never-exported cheeses like melt-in-your-mouth **Bath soft cheese** (www.parkfarm.co.uk) or aromatic unpasteurized **Gorwydd Caerphilly** (www.trethowansdairy.co.uk).

o **Shellseekers,** the fishmonger in the center, is known for hand-dived Devon scallop, served in its own shell and topped with a bacon and sprout stir-fry; a bathtub-big pot of paella bubbles at its neighbor **Bomba.**

o The **Green Market,** along the fence by the cathedral, is a carnival of individual stalls serving various international dishes. **Roast Hog** (www.roast hog.com) slices pig off a turning spit; **Greedy Goat** scoops lactose-free goat milk ice cream (rhubarb custard, "Billi Vanilli").

THE world COMES TO LONDON

Those fortunate enough to have traveled broadly know how sadly rare it is to find places where people of wildly different colors, religions, and nationalities can live together in relative harmony. London, though, like New York City, Toronto, or Sydney, is certifiably multi-ethnic, with some 300 languages and 45 distinct ethnic communities. (By 2030, it's predicted, half the city's population will be foreign-born.) It's a fine opportunity for some culinary world travels of your own. Here are the Tube or rail stops for some of the major concentrations:

Bangladesh: Bethnal Green, Whitechapel

Caribbean: Brixton, Willesden Junction

Egypt: Shepherd's Bush

Ghana, Nigeria, Congo, West Africa: Seven Sisters, Hackney Central, or Hackney Downs (National Rail)

India, especially northern: Southall (National Rail)

Ireland: Kilburn

Kenya: Barking

Kurdistan: Manor House

Lebanon: Shepherd's Bush

Nigeria: Peckham Rye (National Rail)

Persia: Edgware Road

Poland: Hammersmith, Ealing Broadway

Somalia: Streatham (National Rail)

Sri Lanka and South India: Tooting (National Rail)

Syria: Shepherd's Bush

Turkey: Dalston Kingsland and Stoke Newington (National Rail)

Vietnam: Hackney Central or Hackney Downs (National Rail), Old Street

TALL orders

London's skyscrapers are sprouting like bamboo, and with them, dining aeries. Taste buds are too sophisticated to tolerate a top-floor restaurant with bottom-feeder grub—these places compete with terrific cuisine that's a pleasure to eat. Only the prices could be considered unpleasant. Reservations are suggested for all of them.

Darwin Brasserie   *The scene:* The atrium atop the "Walkie-Talkie" is like an upscale mini-mall of evening pursuits, including thump-thump-thump beats at Sky Pod bar and a seafood place, Fenchurch. Our choice, Darwin, has an honest menu (Cornish lamb, Scottish rib-eye, fish and chips) on an elevated floor where some of the horizon may be obscured by the tower's drooping-eyelid roofline, but it's still spectacular. (Soak in the panorama from elsewhere in the atrium after dinner.) *The view:* the Tower of London, the Thames, the Shard, and beyond. Sky Garden, 36th Floor, 20 Fenchurch St., EC3. www.skygarden.london/Darwin. *©* **0333/772-0020.** Dinner main courses £17–£26. Breakfast Mon–Fri 7–10am; Sat 8–9:30am. Lunch Mon–Fri 11:30am–4:30pm; Sat–Sun 11:30am–3:30pm. Dinner Mon–Sat 5:30–10:30pm; Sun 5:30–10pm. Tube: Monument or Bank.

Duck & Waffle   *The scene:* All day and night—yes, it's 24 hours, and doubles as a skilled *cocktailerie*—it cycles through shared-plate menus that lean toward richness. *The view:* It's a little inland from the Thames, so the nearest views are of the Gherkin and the City. 40th Floor, 110 Bishopsgate, EC2. www.duckandwaffle.com. *©* **020/3640-7310.** Sharing plates £9–13. Tube: Liverpool St.

Gong   *The scene:* Take cocktails, small bites, and sashimi on the 52nd floor of the Shard in this tight little bar, and London's highest, atop the Shangri-La Hotel (p. 57). *The view:* sweeping eastern panorama from Southwark, including London Bridge Station, the Tower of London, and Tower Bridge. 35th floor, The Shard, 32 London Bridge St., SE1. www.gong-shangri-la.com. *©* **020/7234-8208.** Dinner main courses £23–£38. Mon–Sat noon–1am; Sun noon–midnight. Tube: London Bridge.

Oxo Tower Bar   *The scene:* Behold, a gratitude-inducing panorama over the Thames from an Art Deco landmark which, like Tate Modern, was once a power station. The associated restaurant is a favorite for celebrating special occasions. *The view:* St Paul's and the City from Southbank. 22 Barge House St., SE1. www.oxotowerrestaurant.com. *©* **020/7803-3888.** Lunch £17. Mon–Thurs 11am–11pm; Fri–Sat 11am–midnight; Sun noon–10:30pm. Tube: Blackfriars or Waterloo.

o Artisan cacao in drink and food at **Rabot 1745** on Bedale Street.

o **Roast** (www.roast-restaurant.com), which runs an expensive restaurant upstairs, has a stall for rich meats such as roast pork belly with crackling, or Bramley applesauce and beef with horseradish cream.

o At **Maria's Market Café,** the second-generation proprietor slaves over a stove making fresh *bubble* (a mushy version of home fries) for vendors and visitors alike.

o The **Brindisa Grill** booth (www.brindisa.com), facing Stoney Street, feeds a steady line of punters its grilled chorizo sandwich with oil-drizzled pequillo peppers from Spain.

○ Outside on Stoney and Park streets, by the well-stocked **Market Porter** pub (p. 105) and casual sit-down restaurant **Elliot's,** are more finds: **Kappacasein** dairy from Bermondsey (www.kappacasein.com), which melts great wheels of Ogleshield cheese into decadent *raclette* or a goopy grilled cheese sandwich; **Monmouth Coffee Company** (www.monmmouthcoffee.com), for 40 years one of London's most revered roasters, which sends tasters around to world to monitor the single-source growers of its beans; and **Neal's Yard Dairy** (www.nealsyarddairy.co.uk), the gold standard for English cheese, tended by clerks in caps and aprons.

It's all food you can only enjoy in London. You may locate all or none of these delicacies among the clamor; this overstimulation of the senses is an individual game. This was the setting of a shocking terrorist knife attack in June 2017 that began on London Bridge and ended when the three assailants were shot dead in front of the **Wheatsheaf** pub. You will not find any reminders of that dark night, and workers prefer not to be asked about it (several of them were injured or killed). In London, the market goes on, as it has for centuries on this very spot. There has been one on this very spot since the 1100s. Welcome to its story.

8 Southwark St., SE1. www.boroughmarket.org.uk. ℂ **020/7407-1002.** Mon–Wed 10am–3pm; Thurs 11am–5pm; Fri noon–6pm; Sat 8am–5pm. Tube: London Bridge.

M. Manze offers Cockney classics like meat pies and jellied eels.

M. Manze ★★ TRADITIONAL BRITISH If you're truly fearless, brave the classic East End dishes of jellied or stewed eels. But if not, there's still a reason to come here: a jewel box of a shop, serving since 1891, with green glazed Victorian tile and wooden benches, which is in such rare condition it's protected by the government. In fact, when it was awarded its historic plaque, no one could figure out how to mount it to the wall without breaking preservation laws. Manze also does meat or vegetarian pastry pies—which to be fair, most customers prefer—as it has done since the days when it fed dockworkers and laborers. The parsley-made "liquor" sauce doesn't really taste like much, but the gravy and mash taste like nostalgia itself.

87 Tower Bridge Rd., SE1. www.manze.co.uk. ℂ **020/7407-2985.** Main courses £3–£6. Mon 11am–2pm; Tues–Thurs 10:30am–2pm; Fri 10am–2:30pm; Sat 10am–2:45pm. Tube: Borough.

Brick Lane, named for its medieval status as a source for bricks, was once a Jewish area but has become so strongly identified with immigrants from the Indian subcontinent that its name has transcended geography to become a shorthand term for England's South Asian population. In the span of just a few blocks, most of which have signage in both English and Bengali, lines of Indian restaurants jockey for business. No discerning Londoner would claim that any serve the city's best Indian cuisine, and most of them are in fact run by Bangladeshi or Pakistani entrepreneurs catering to a milder English notion of northern curries. (If you want something more modernized, try **Gunpowder** [www.gunpowderlondon.com], a block west on Commercial Road at White's Row.) But it's nonetheless a fun place to leverage competition and sit down for a bargain meal in a happening hood. Bring your own wine, though, since most are run by Muslims who don't sell alcohol. By day, the connecting Dray Walk is a short block of sophisticated boutiques and laid-back cafes. On weekends, it hosts blocks upon blocks of markets for vintage clothes, books, food, and art—Sundays are good for hours of browsing and noshing (www.bricklanemarket.com).

4

EAST END & DOCKLANDS

Much of the city's most exciting cooking for a fun night out has migrated to Shoreditch and Spitalfields, leaving Mayfair to cater to the expense-account gourmets and Soho to feed the beery hordes.

Expensive

Lyle's ★★ BRITISH   The kind of place where chefs like to eat, where the dishes appear simple and fluid and yet require authority to accomplish, Lyle's has a short, changing New British-meets-Nordic menu, but it runs deep with inventiveness and delicacy: lemon sole with buttermilk and sea aster (a salt marsh plant), raw beef with mussels that's actually chopped beef with shellfish emulsion, soured cream with chocolate as a dessert. Dishes are neatly creative, but flavors remain clean, even if the blank loft space in which they're served is a bit factory-like. If things are busy, you can always sit at the bar.

Tea Building, 56 Shoreditch High St., E1. www.lyleslondon.com. © **020/3011-5911.** Main courses £9–£24; 3-course set dinner £59; bar menu £4–£16. Mon–Fri 8am–11pm; Sat noon–11pm. Reservations recommended. Tube: Shoreditch High St. or Liverpool St.

Moderate

Jones Family Project ★★ BRITISH   If you love beef, the way JFP's Josper grill can almost mystically seal in the flavors of its Yorkshire Longhorn could blow your mind, but then again, the burger topped with oxtail-stock mayo might also do it. It's not just about beef, though; fish, duck, and pork (that's cut like beef) are also knowingly prepared in generous portions—most proteins come from The Ginger Pig, a network of principled farmers. Sides such as truffled mac-and-cheese and tomato salad underscore the traditional cuisine goals, but the friendly, groovily 1970s downstairs dining space makes a convivial hideaway, good for conversation and stretching out when you're in Shoreditch. It's an especially good stop on Sunday afternoons for its weekly roast, and the upstairs bar is open until midnight Monday to Saturday.

78 Great Eastern St., EC2. www.jonesfamilyproject.co.uk. (€) **020/7739-1740.** Main courses £15–£28. Mon–Sat 11am–midnight; Sun noon–6pm (Sun food until 4:30pm). Tube: Old St.

Poppies ★★ SEAFOOD Big crispy portions flopping on big oval plates eaten with a big knife and fork to big 1950s sock-hop music: The franchise-ready Poppies does for British fish and chips what peppy jukebox diners have done for mid-20th-century American food. Amusingly, it wraps its chips in custom-printed newspaper since it's now illegal to use the chemical-laden real thing. For all its plastic theatricality, it hews to authenticity: The chief dish, cooked to order, is sustainably caught and sourced from third-generation fishmonger T. Bush at Billingsgate Market. For those whose palates swerve differently, there's also chicken, the chance to try jellied eels, and Minghella ice cream hailing from the Isle of Wight. There's a Soho location (55 Old Compton St., W1; (€) **020/7734-4845;** same hours) for strolling the West End with chips.

6–8 Hanbury St., E1. www.poppiesfishandchips.co.uk. (€) **020/7247-0892.** Main courses £9–£17. Mon–Thurs 11am–11pm; Fri–Sat 11am–11:30pm; Sun 11am–10:30pm. Tube: Shoreditch High St. or Liverpool St.

Rochelle Canteen ★★ BRITISH A sublime secret is hidden away, discovered only if you ring a doorbell beside a green door in a brick wall. You'll pass through the grassy yard of an 1880s school, and in the old bike shed, join a daytime garden party. The changing menu is rigorously British and fresh, yet without flourish: green pea soup, roast sirloin, leek and wigmore tart, fish and chips, loose-leaf tea. Your companions will be high-functioning artists, designers, and professionals, many of whom now lease space in the former school, plus the occasional kid, if they behave as well as a Victorian child. In fine weather, it's easier to find a seat because dining spills outdoors, the better to enjoy jugs of rhubarb and ginger fizz.

Rochelle School, Arnold Circus, E2. www.rochelleschool.org. (€) **020/7729-5677.** Main courses £13–£15. Mon–Wed 9am–2:30pm (spring–summer to 3:30pm); Thurs–Fri 9am–2:30pm (spring–summer to 3:30pm) and 6–10pm; Sat 6–10pm; closing changes seasonally. Reservations suggested. Tube: Shoreditch High St.

St John Bread & Wine ★★ TRADITIONAL BRITISH Hand-in-hand with the gastropub trend is "nose-to-tail" eating. That's a polite way to say you'll be eating various animal body parts, resulting in tastes that were commonplace to agrarian English forefathers (heart, cockscomb, marrow, whole pigeon) but are new to most North American tongues. I personally hate it, but it's always on the foodie dream lists. Most places charge, um, an arm and a leg for it, but you can sample it at this lower-priced offshoot of the influential St John restaurant (still running in Smithfield), which in the 1990s brought back British cooking in a big way. Walls are simple white, chairs are plain wood, and the kitchen staff is serious about food, no matter its form. Experience dishes like cold lamb with chicory and anchovy, smoked sprat (sardines) with horseradish, and laver bread (made with seaweed) with oats and bacon. A meal here can be an adventure (ever eaten dandelion?).

94–96 Commercial St., E1. www.stjohngroup.uk.com. © **020/7251-0848.** Main courses £7–£10 before 6pm, around £15 after 6pm. Mon–Fri 8am–4pm and 6–10pm; Sat 8:30am–11pm; Sun 8:30am–10pm. Reservations recommended. Tube: Aldgate East or Shoreditch High St.

Inexpensive

Beigel Bake ★★ BAKERY   The city's most famous bakery, Jewish or otherwise, never closes but there's often a line. The queue moves quickly here even if time doesn't—signs still post an area code that hasn't been active since 2000. The patronage is a microcosm of London, ranging from bikers to hipsters to arrogant yuppies to the homeless. Its beigels (*bi*-gulls) are not as puffy or as salty as the New York "bagel" variety, and they even come filled for under £2—the same price, astonishingly, as a half-dozen plain ones. Its pastries are gorgeous, too: The chocolate fudge brownie, less than £1, could be nursed for hours. Watching the clerks slice juicy chunks of pink salt beef in the window, then slather it onto a beigel with nostril-clearing mustard from a

SAVE BREAD WITH sandwiches

You'll go all day without crossing paths with a bobby or a Cockney, but you can't walk a block in London without passing a sandwich shop. The cheapest ones are what I call the **triangle sandwiches,** which are ready-made, sliced diagonally, and sealed into triangular containers. They are made fresh every day by the million, cost less than £5, and can rescue both time and money during your busy touring schedule.

A few ubiquitous chains in the triangle sandwich trade:

○ **Eat** (www.eat.co.uk): Its quality is ahead of Pret, with a good selection of organics, wraps, and whole grains.

○ **Gregg's** (www.greggs.co.uk): Its sandwiches are average in every way, but it also does pies and hot meat rolls.

○ **Marks & Spencer** (www.marksandspencer.com): Lots of cheap stuff, well done, and around dinnertime, markdowns up to 50 percent.

○ **Pret A Manger** (www.pret.com): Right behind Eat in clever flavors, with gourmet fixings in snazzy combinations.

crusty jar, is an attraction unto itself. Londoners complain it's gotten touristy, but what tourist trap serves tea for just 60p, I ask you?

159 Brick Lane, E1. www.beigelbake.com. ℗ **020/7729-0616.** Daily 24 hr. Tube: Shoreditch High St.

E. Pellicci ★★★ TRADITIONAL BRITISH   London's tradition of mid-20th-century diners, or "caffs," is quickly being gentrified into nostalgia, but this fry-up on deeply authentic and unflashy Bethnal Green Road has been run by the affable Nevio family since 1900. Some of them were born upstairs, and the matriarch of the family has commanded the kitchen since 1961. The Deco interior, a greasy spoon fantasia of sunburst icons, chrome, and primrose, was carved by a regular in 1946 and is now protected by law. You'll be boisterously welcomed with open arms—Mama, cooking Italian specialties such as cannelloni, may wave to you from the kitchen—and you'll spend a happy meal sharing a table with locals ("Where are you from?" "Looks like rain tomorrow"), sipping the best cuppa 70p tea you ever had. As proof of your acceptance by the regulars, after you're done you may be sent out with a parting gift of homemade cake. There's no more iconic "caff" in town, certainly none happier.

332 Bethnal Green Rd., E2. www.epellicci.com. ℗ **020/7739-4873.** Main courses £2–£8. Mon–Sat 7am–4pm. Tube: Shoreditch High St. or Bethnal Green.

21 PUBS YOU'LL LOVE

Pubs are the beating heart of British life, as they have been for centuries. Your neighborhood hangout is called your "local," but many of the oldest premises have been so well-loved (or so well-bombed) that their original features are gone. Most are now company-owned, depressingly standardized, and modern-looking—how many British pubs have stripped out ceilings and carpeting to expose ductwork and wood in a feeble attempt to look modern? The following pubs, however, all centrally located, should do you right. All of them serve food of some kind (burgers, meat pies, and the like) for at least part of the day; you usually order at the bar, where you receive a numbered tag for your table so that servers can find you.

Pubs commonly charge around £5 for a pint of the favored serving size—about 20 American ounces—and the ABV percentage tends to be strong. Guinness is Irish (and takes about 2 minutes to pour properly). A good cask ale is a specialty you must try while you're in England. Cask ale is not refrigerated because it's stored in the cellar, where the temperature is right for the fermentation process to continue until the drink hits your glass. Cask ale is drawn using stiff hand-pumped taps, and it only stays fresh for a short time, like bread or pastry—so don't be surprised if the beer you select has already run out. To find pubs that persevere in the dying art of pouring old-fashioned cask ales, visit the **Campaign for Real Ale** (www.camra.org.uk). Mixed drinks are also served, but mixers are charged extra and don't expect a generous pour because measures are standardized. They'll have bottled beer and cider, too. When the bell is rung, it's last call—as early as 11pm—and the landlord *will* turf you out.

The Anchor Bankside ★★ This Thameside patio in sight of St Paul's dome is perhaps the most agreeable (and popular) spot in London at which to sit with a fresh-pulled pint. There's been a tavern here at least since the 1500s, when Londoners ferried to Southwark for bear baiting, gardens, brothels, and Shakespeare (the playwright surely would have known the place). Diarist and royal confidant Samuel Pepys is said to have watched London burn to the ground from the safety of this shore in 1666. The industrial Anchor brewery that subsumed it for 200 years was cleared away in the 1980s, and a spacious (but always crowded) riverside terrace was added. Beer snobs kvetch that it's become a tourist draw, but that's all right with me; pubs have always been hangouts for the common man. Few pubs so perfectly meld abundant history with an enviable location.

34 Park St., SE1. www.greeneking-pubs.co.uk. ⓒ **020/7407-1577.** Mon–Wed 11am–11pm; Thurs–Sun 11am–11:30pm; Sun noon–10:30pm; food served until 10pm (Mon–Sat), 9:30pm (Sun). Tube: London Bridge.

The Argyll Arms ★★ Having a beer in here can feel like drinking in a bejeweled red velvet box, thanks to the acid-etched glass screens that subdivide the busy bar into dignified drinking areas. Originally installed in 1895 to prevent brawls between the working and middle classes (at a time when even subway rides were segregated), the screens somehow survived the 20th century. Drinks are £1 more than they should be, but it's one of the prettiest pubs in London, and its location southeast of Oxford Circus makes it an easy stop.

18 Argyll St., W1. www.nicholsonspubs.co.uk. ⓒ **020/7734-6117.** Mon–Thurs 10am–11:30pm; Fri–Sat 10am–midnight; Sun 10am–11pm. Tube: Oxford Circus.

The Blackfriar ★★★ Deservedly protected by landmark status, this 1904 Art Nouveau masterpiece (also spelled the Black Friar) is as jolly as the fat friars that bedeck it in bronze, wood, and glass. A short walk from St Paul's, it was once snuggled down a few dark alleys, but neighboring demolitions liberated it; now it's blessed with a noisy outdoor patio and walls of windows bathed in afternoon sunshine from over the Thames. The back saloon was designed for the upper classes, hence its exceptionally overbaked interior in marble and bronze; the undulating front bar, where pop music plays and pub crawls frequently pass through, is extraordinarily well-stocked with a range of cask ales and cider. Pricey food is shuttled from the upstairs kitchen via a hand-cranked dumbwaiter.

174 Queen Victoria St., EC4. www.nicholsonspubs.co.uk. ⓒ **020/7236-5474.** Mon–Fri 10am–11pm; Sat 9am–11pm; Sun noon–10:30pm. Tube: Blackfriars.

The jolly Blackfriar is a 1904 Art Nouveau masterpiece, well-stocked with a range of cask ales and cider.

The Coal Hole ★ A onetime haunt of actor Edmund Kean, who drank himself to an early curtain, was rebuilt in 1904 in the Arts and Crafts style and is still a hangout for performers at the adjoining Savoy Theatre. Use the entrance in back, by the stage door, to access the clubbier lower level. The antique street lamp on the Strand is a vestige of an experimental gaslight piping system that burned off sewage gases before the farty stink could overcome citizens. Bottoms up!

91–92 Strand, WC2. www.nicholsonspubs.co.uk/thecoalholestrandlondon. ℂ **020/ 7379-9883.** Sun–Wed 10am–11pm; Thurs 10am–11:30pm; Fri–Sat 10am–midnight. Tube: Charing Cross or Embankment.

The George Inn ★★★ Unquestionably one of the most important ancient pubs still standing, the George traces its lineage to at least 1542, when a map of Southwark first depicted it; the Tabard Inn, where Chaucer's pilgrims gathered in *Canterbury Tales,* was then a few doors south (it's gone now). Shakespeare knew it (check out Pete Brown's 2012 book *Shakespeare's Local*), and Dickens memorialized it in *Little Dorrit.* The oldest section, a galleried wood-and-brick longhouse, dates to 1677, built after a horrific fire swept the district.

It later functioned as an 18th-century transit hub, its courtyard encircled with a tavern, a hotel, stables, wagon repair bays, and warehouses; the rise of a railway nearly destroyed it, and only one side of the complex survives. (The National Trust now protects it.) Sip ale in the low-ceilinged timber-and-plaster chambers, or sit in the cobbled courtyard, in the Shard's shadow, and soak up the fading echoes of history.

75–77 Borough High St., SE1. www.greeneking-pubs.co.uk. *℗* **020/7407-2056.** Mon–Thurs 11am–11:30pm; Fri–Sat 11am–midnight; Sun noon–10:30pm; food until 10pm (Mon–Sat), 9pm (Sun). Tube: London Bridge.

The Grapes ★★ It's in every way a classic pub, cherishable in that inimitable English way—Victorian wooden bar with stools, red carpeting, worn plank floors, a blissful lack of clanging "fruit machines." But then again, that tiny back porch with a smashing riverfront panorama of a bend in the Thames all but waves a magic wand over it. If you find it all preposterously winsome, you wouldn't be alone—it's ridiculously narrow and jams at peak hours, but come at noon and it's a dream. Charles Dickens, who partied here, wrote about it in *Our Mutual Friend*, and the wizardly Ian McKellen loved it so much (he lives nearby so it's been his local for decades) that when it came up for sale, he and his ex-boyfriend teamed up to buy it and preserve it. Sir Ian is known to pull pints and host Monday's quiz night when he's not performing somewhere. The prize is £50 in drinking money, which you'll find delightful to spend here.

76 Narrow St., E14. www.thegrapes.co.uk. *℗* **020/7987-4396.** Daily noon–11:30pm; food served until 9:30pm. Tube: Limehouse DLR or Westferry DLR.

The Grenadier ★★★ They say this was the Duke of Wellington's local bar and the unofficial clubhouse for his regiment, hence the battlefield artifacts on display; they also say someone was beaten to death here for cheating at cards, hence the routine ghost sightings. This tiny plank-floored, currency-festooned pub/restaurant, pretty as a picture in a cobbled mews, comes off like a boozer in some upcountry village, with only 15 places at its pewter-topped island bar. Once a haunt for servants of the surrounding townhouses, clientele these days skews toward an international mix of students and businessmen. The pub is also said to be known for its Bloody Marys (I think they're overrated). To find it, head down Grosvenor Crescent from Hyde Park Corner station, hang a hard right just before Belgrave Square onto Wilton Crescent, and take your first right onto Wilton Row.

18 Wilton Row, SW1. www.greeneking-pubs.co.uk. *℗* **020/7235-3074.** Mon–Sat 11am–11:30pm; Sun noon–11:30pm; food served until 9:30pm. Tube: Hyde Park Corner.

The Lamb ★ Quiet, not too touristy, this east Bloomsbury choice (where Ted Hughes took Sylvia Plath on their early dates) is representative of a neighborhood local that still has some prime Victoriana from the old days. Check out the rare sunburst etched-glass snob screens obscuring the bar, built so you don't have to look the help in the eye. Or put 50p in the polyphon in the corner—that's a musical metal disc that works like a music box and was the gramophone of a century ago. The carpet is a tired tartan, the walls lined with sepia photographs of long-forgotten stage actresses, and the cask beers are out-of-the-ordinary enough to intrigue.

94 Lambs Conduit St., WC1. www.thelamblondon.com. © **020/7405-0713.** Mon–Wed 11am–11pm; Thurs–Sun 11am–midnight; Sun noon–10:30pm; food served noon–9:30pm. Tube: Russell Square.

The Lamb and Flag ★★ Too tiny and thronged after work to supply much respite, it is nonetheless the epitome of a city pub, tucked down an atmospheric brick alley and blessed with an original fireplace. It has been known throughout its 380 years as both the Coopers Arms and the Bucket of Blood (the latter because it hosted illegal prizefights in the early 1800s), and its building is said to be Tudor in origin. No one can prove it, since it was heavily rebuilt in the 1890s. You'll find it on a lane just east of the intersection of Floral and Garrick streets, near Covent Garden. But you probably won't find a place to sit unless you start drinking after lunch, which the regular drinkers on its memorial wall surely did.

33 Rose St., WC2. www.lambandflagcoventgarden.co.uk. © **020/7497-9504.** Mon–Sat 11am–11pm; Sun noon–10:30pm; food served until 9pm. Tube: Covent Garden or Leicester Square.

The Market Porter ★ Facing the gastronomic mayhem of Borough Market, this lovely old timber-beamed boozer is a fine place to drink in any time of the week. In fact, more times than most pubs, because its location earned a special license to open at 6am when vendors are working. Sundays and off-hours are pleasant for sitting by a double-sided fire drinking one of its nine traditional ales (choices change) or eating upstairs—ingredients all come from the market. It can also act: It appeared as the Third Hand Book Emporium in the third Harry Potter film.

9 Stoney St., SE1. www.themarketporter.co.uk. © **020/7407-2495.** Mon–Fri 6–8:30am and 11am–11pm; Sat noon–11pm; Sun noon–10:30pm; food served until 1 hr. before closing (until 5pm Sun). Tube: London Bridge.

The Marquis of Granby ★ Amusingly, some pubs near the Houses of Parliament are equipped with a "division bell," which rings—rather like a fire alarm—to warn socializing MPs they have only 8 minutes to scurry back to vote. Other pubs with division bells—St Stephens Tavern on Bridge Street across from Big Ben, the Red Lion on Whitehall—are cloyingly touristy, but not The Marquis. A single-room pub with bare floorboards and high wood walls, it's a hangout for government types and prides itself on real hand-pumped ale.

41 Romney St., SW1. www.nicholsonspubs.co.uk. © **020/7227-0941.** Mon–Fri 11am–11pm; Sat noon–9pm. Tube: Westminster or Pimlico.

The Mayflower ★   The story goes that in 1620, local resident and sea captain Christopher Jones was recruited by some dissenters, who boarded his ship the *Mayflower* alongside this pub (then it was the Shippe; the current building is from the 1700s) to set sail to Southampton and thence to the New World. It's hard to imagine, and otherwise it's a fairly traditional pub (oak beams, wood paneling) with real ales and a fire. The tiny backyard on the Thames is a worthy place to raise a pint and survey your personal slice of the river on a summer day. Would the Pilgrims have called that a sin? Surely, but you're more fun than they were.

117 Rotherhithe St., SW16. www.themayflowerrotherhithe.com. ℂ **020/7237-4088.** Mon–Sat 11am–11pm (food served until 10pm); Sun noon–10:30pm (food served until 9pm). Tube: Rotherhithe.

The Old Brewery ★★   In 2010, a new microbrewery named Meantime took up residence in Sir Christopher Wren's palatial Old Royal Naval College (a stately UNESCO World Heritage site where the Paris scenes in 2012's *Les Misérables* were shot), which sits on the Thames in outlying Greenwich. It occupied the very brewery building that once furnished Napoleonic War veterans with their three daily pints. Now, the Old Brewery, run by respected British beermaker Young's, serves drinks on a large outdoor patio, and seasonal English fare inside. The beer selection isn't as rewarding as it once was, but on a sunny day, there are few places more dreamy for a pint in Maritime Greenwich (p. 176).

The Pepys Building, Old Royal Naval College, SE10. www.oldbrewerygreenwich.com. ℂ **020/3437-2222.** Mon–Sat 10am–11pm; Sun 10am–10:30pm; food served until 10pm. Tube: Cutty Sark DLR.

ADVENTURES IN cocktails

London has fallen in love with bars that are as densely themed as Disney rides. Like **The Bletchley** (www.thebletchley.co.uk), a World War II codebreaker-themed joint where you have to solve the clues to get your quaff. Or **The Cauldron** (www.thecauldron.io)**,** an ostensibly Harry Potter–themed potions laboratory where guests don robes, wave wands, mix smoking drinks, and conjure beer from a tap in a magical tree. Both were blockbuster pop-ups in 2018; check if they're back. Or head to the permanent **Cahoots** (13 Kingly Court, W1.

www.cahoots-london.com. ℂ **020/7352-6200.** Tube: Oxford Circus), a cocktail bar themed to the London Underground. In the 1940s. Probably during the Blitz. It's amusingly detailed (the menu is a newspaper, announcements in the toilets), sometimes there's live swing music, and tourists love it despite the premium prices. Book ahead, and if possible, get a seat in the Tube carriage. Don't be a snob—you can order a basic G&T at your hotel bar. The point is to have fun. Cheers.

The Pride of Spitalfields ★★ Lovingly shabby, with a tired floral carpet and weary red upholstered banquettes, the backstreet boozer east of Brick Lane is the embodiment of a homey pub pulling pleasing pints. The upright piano is rarely played (recorded classic punk is preferred), the sewage system is finicky, the beer bottles are dusty, but the goings-on are lively and neighborly. Unlike in some neighborhood joints, they understand tourists, so if you're friendly, you'll have fun. In the afternoon, you can get cheap salt beef for a few pounds. Jack the Ripper suspect James Hardiman, a "cats meats vendor," drank here when it was called the Romford Arms; today, however, a cat runs the place—the entitled rescue house cat, Lenny. He's the only pretentious one here.

3 Heneage St., E1. ℂ **020/7247-8933.** Mon–Tues and Thurs–Sat 11am–midnight; Wed 11am–11pm; Sun noon–10:30pm. Tube: Aldgate East.

The Princess Louise ★★★ This Victorian fantasia just south of the British Museum is worth a visit even if you don't drink. Its lost-in-time feeling begins with the proud signage, a traditional marquee of gold lettering on black. The 1891 interior has been miraculously maintained in mint condition: Morris & Son etched glass, mirrors, mahogany privacy screens, cast-iron bar, Corinthian columns, Simpson & Son mosaic tile floor—even the men's room marble urinals are legally protected from alteration. There's no music, no TVs, and all of the libations are by the resolutely old-fashioned Samuel Smith, which has been brewing since 1758 in Yorkshire and still draws its water from its original well.

208 High Holborn, WC1. www.princesslouisepub.co.uk. ℂ **020/7405-8816.** Mon–Fri noon–11pm; Sat noon–11pm; Sun noon–6:45pm; food served Mon–Thurs noon–2:30pm and 6–8:30pm, Fri noon–2:30pm. Tube: Holborn.

The Salisbury ★ The Covent Garden/Leicester Square location is unbeatable, and the ornate exterior and interior are unmistakably Victorian—ostentatious, just-how-drunk-was-the-designer Victorian, to be precise. Thrill to the Grecian urns in the brilliant-cut glass, the pressed-copper tables, and the nymphs entwined in the bronze lamps. Long a haunt of the city's theatrical community, it's now a suitable pit stop for any West End exploration. It does burgers and fish and chips, too, albeit by the corporate recipes of the Taylor Walker pub company. Theater fans should check out the cellar, which is papered with posters, many of them rare, from 1980s and '90s shows.

90 St Martin's Lane, WC2. www.greeneking-pubs.co.uk. ℂ **020/7836-5863.** Mon–Thurs 11am–11pm; Fri–Sat 11am–midnight; Sun 11am–10:30pm; food served until 10pm. Tube: Leicester Square.

The Ship & Shovell ★★ One of the most endearing configurations for any pub you'll ever see, it's cleft in two by an alley trod by commuters on their way to Charing Cross. On the north, there's a traditional Victorian-style space, and on the south, a cozier room with a languidly sloping floor and private snugs. A cellar links the halves. The bewigged tubby chap on the swinging sign is Admiral Cloudesley Shovell who, in 1707, wrecked his ship and drowned 800 sailors, which certainly gives the interior's nautical theme an ignoble context. It's special for another reason, too, being one of the few pubs in town to pour Dorset ales from Hall & Woodhouse, a family brewer dating to 1777.

1–2 Craven Passage, WC2. www.shipandshovell.co.uk. ℂ **020/8391-1311.** Mon–Sat 11am–11pm; food served Mon–Fri noon–3:30pm, Sat noon–4pm. Tube: Charing Cross or Embankment.

The Ten Bells ★   It's said that Annie Chapman, one of Jack the Ripper's victims, downed her last beer at this Spitalfields boozer, while another, Mary Kelly, picked up her clients outside; for an icky period in the 1970s, the pub capitalized on infamy by being renamed for their slayer. These days, the toilets are a bigger threat to health and safety than Jack the Ripper ever was. The pub's Victorian tilework has been restored, and now it's a busy waterhole where the clientele is young, the furniture casually mismatched, and the partying ever more intense as the evening advances. Nicholas Hawksmoor's Christ Church, which towers next door, silently observes the latest mortals at play.

84 Commercial St., E1. www.tenbells.com. ℂ **020/7247-7532.** Sun–Wed noon–midnight; Thurs–Sat noon–1am. Tube: Liverpool St.

Ye Olde Cheshire Cheese ★★★   Just the sort of rambling, low-ceilinged tavern you imagine London is full of (and was, once), it was built behind Fleet Street in the wake of the Great Fire in 1666; steady log fires and regularly strewn sawdust make it smell like it's still burning. In later generations, it played regular host to Dr. Samuel Johnson (who lived behind on Gough Square), Charles Dickens (who refers to it in *A Tale of Two Cities*), Yeats, Wilde, and Thackeray. You can get pretty well thackered yourself today: There are six drinking rooms, but the cozy front bar—of pallid light, candles in the fireplace, and antique paintings of dead fish—is the most magical. Observe the stuffed carcass of Polly the Parrot, enshrined above the bar since 1926: Her "adept use of profanity would have put any golfer to shame," according to her obituary in the *New York American*. *Note:* Don't confuse this place with the Victorian-era Cheshire Cheese pub at Temple.

Wine Office Ct., off 145 Fleet St. ℂ **020/7353-6170.** Mon–Sat 11am–11pm. Tube: Blackfriars, Temple, or Chancery Lane.

Ye Olde Mitre ★★★   Suspended in a hidden courtyard and seemingly between centuries, this enchanter—no televisions, no music—was once part of a great palace mentioned by Shakespeare in *Richards II* and *III*. The medieval St Etheldreda's Chapel, its surviving place of worship, stands outside. This extremely tiny pub (established in 1546 but built in its present form in 1772) has two entrances that feed either side of the bar. The one on the left grants you access to "the Closet," a fine example of a semiprivate sitting area called a "snug"; the one on the right brings you face-to-face with a glass case containing a blackened stump said to be part of a cherry-tree maypole that Elizabeth I danced around. (Yeah, right, drink another one.) Suck down a house specialty: pickled or Scotch eggs. To find the pub, look for a little alley among the jewelry stores on Hatton Garden, between 8 and 9 Hatton Garden.

1 Ely Ct., off Ely Place, EC1. www.yeoldemitreholborn.co.uk. © **020/7405-4751.** Mon–Fri 11am–11pm. Tube: Farringdon or Chancery Lane.

EXPLORING LONDON

E ngland has been a top dog for 500 years, and London is where it keeps its bark. Many of the world's finest treasures came here during the Empire and never left. Most cities store their best goodies in one or two top museums. In London, riches are everywhere. The major attractions could by themselves occupy months of contemplation. But the sheer abundance of history and wealth—layer upon layer of it—means that London boasts dozens of exciting smaller sights, too. You could spend a lifetime seeing it all, so you'd better get started.

Sightseeing discounts, such as 2-for-1s, are sometimes offered at **LastMinute.com** (click on the Experiences tab). The heavily promoted **London Pass** (www.londonpass.com) gets you into a bevy of attractions and a Golden Tours sightseeing bus for a fixed price (such as £69 a day or £94 for 2 days), but is unlikely to pay off in the small amount of time you're given to use it. Only the version that lasts 6 days (£154 adult, £114 child) would potentially pay off, but still only *marginally* and only if you barely pause to eat.

Historic Royal Palaces operates the Banqueting House (p. 140), Hampton Court (p. 182), Kensington Palace (p. 147), Kew Palace (p. 186), and the Tower of London (p. 166). An annual membership pass will possibly save you money if you plan to see several of them; do the math (www.hrp.org.uk; ✆ **020/3166-6000;** £52 one adult, £80 two adults, £74 for one adult plus up to six children, £105 two adults plus up to six children).

BLOOMSBURY, FITZROVIA & KING'S CROSS

The British Library ★★★ MUSEUM One of the planet's most precious collections of books, maps, and manuscripts, the British Library holds approximately 150 million items and adds 3 million each year, so when it puts the cream (about 200 items) on display, you will be positively astounded. The **Treasures of the British Library,** at the Sir John Ritblat Gallery, displays these in a cool, climate-controlled suite of black cases and rich purple

Children's prices generally apply to those 15 and under. To qualify for a **senior discount,** usually you must be 60 or older. **Students** require ID for discounts. Some places offer **Family Tickets** with discounts for up to three kids with adults. Museums may post prices that include a voluntary **"gift aid"** donation; British citizens get tax back for it but you don't, so no one will mind if you ask to have it removed.

In addition to closing on public holidays and on December 25 and 26 (Boxing Day), some heritage properties open only in the summer.

carpeting. It ought to be mobbed, but isn't. The trove changes whenever something needs to take out of direct light:

TOP DON'T-MISS EXHIBITS AT THE BRITISH LIBRARY

o Two of the four known copies of the **Magna Carta,** 800 years old in 2015

o The **Gutenberg Bible** from 1455

o The Beatles' first lyric doodles: "A Hard Day's Night" on Julian Lennon's first birthday card (with a choo-choo on it) and "Michelle"

o The **Diamond Sutra,** the oldest known printed book, which was found in a Chinese cave in 1907 and was probably made by woodblock nearly 600 years before Europeans developed similar technology

o The *Codex Sinaiticus,* one of the two oldest Christian Bibles (the Pope has the other) and illuminated manuscripts from Buddhism, Jainism, and Islam

o Milton's contract for *Paradise Lost* (he ended up getting paid just £10)

o A letter from Elizabeth I to James VI of Scotland warning him not to open diplomatic relations with Spain

o **Captain Scott's diary** of his failed North Pole exploration, found on his body

o Michelangelo's letter to his nephew telling him he had finished *The Martyrdom of St. Peter,* and pages from **Leonardo da Vinci's notebook,** in mirror writing

o Works in the hand of Mozart, Handel (his *Messiah*), Oscar Wilde, P. G. Wodehouse, Mary Shelley, Bela Bartók, and more

o An 11th-century copy of *Beowulf* on vellum, in Old English; it's the only surviving manuscript, written when Ethelred the Unready was king.

Entrance gate to the British Library.

London-Wide Attractions

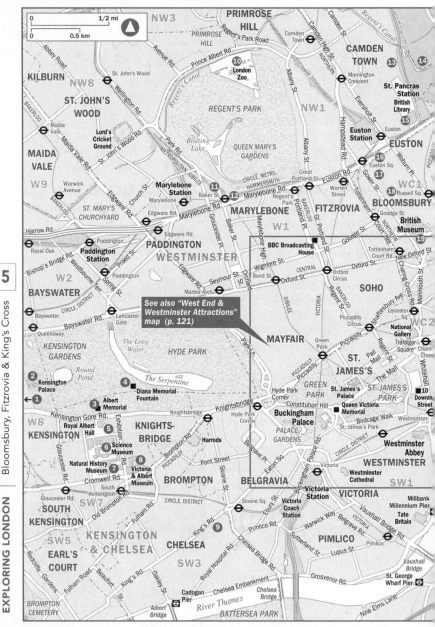

See also "West End & Westminster Attractions" map (p. 121)

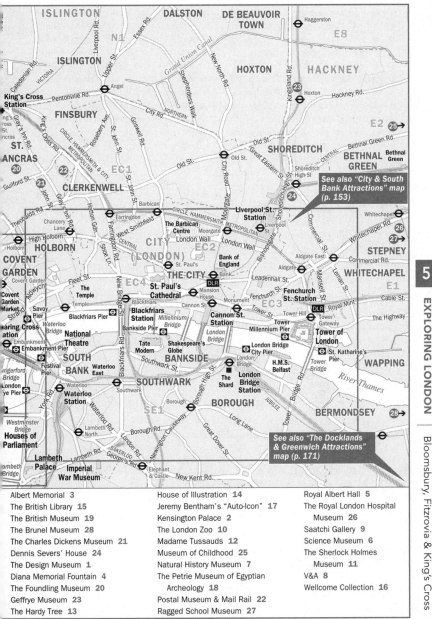

See also "City & South
Bank Attractions" map
(p. 153)

See also "The Docklands
& Greenwich Attractions"
map (p. 171)

Many of London's biggest museums are free to enter, but there's a catch: To make up the cash they miss out on, they find lots of other revenue streams. Many institutions charge £1–£2 for **maps** (to get around that, take a digital photograph of the posted floor plan in the lobby and use that as a guide). They also charge £12 or more for the most interesting **temporary exhibitions;** the most popular ones sell out ahead, so do some advance planning. Many will also loan out their star works to other institutions for money, so a marquee work named in this guide may be temporarily on vacation. Fortunately, the new British funding model also gives museums an incentive to operate superlative shops, publish wonderful keepsake guidebooks, and run gorgeous **cafes** that even attract people off the street— you'll never go hungry at the major attractions.

The King's Library, some 85,000 tomes assembled by King George III, floats in a glassed-in central tower and forms the core of the collection, like Thomas Jefferson's library does for Washington's Library of Congress— which means that the King who lost America and a principal engineer of that loss provided the seeds for their respective nations' libraries. The hall contains the **Philatelic Exhibition,** 500 drawers containing thousands of rare stamps.

You can't handle books unless you're a scholar, but the Library encourages anyone to hang out in its public spaces. In addition to the Treasures, the Library presents about 150 annual talks featuring celebrities and historians and some strong temporary exhibitions (about £12; check www.bl.uk/whats-on), including ones on Gothic horror, punk, and comic books. Twice a day, you can book an £8 tour of the facilities, although for all the hype over its architecture, the men's and women's washrooms are on opposite sides of the building and the whole place is riddled with little staircases.

96 Euston Rd., NW1. www.bl.uk. © **01937/546-546.** Free admission. Mon and Fri 9:30am–6pm; Tues–Thurs 9:30am–8pm; Sat 9:30am–5pm; Sun 11am–5pm. Tube: King's Cross St Pancras.

The British Museum ★★★ MUSEUM   Founded in 1753 and first opened in 1759 in a converted mansion, the British Museum is as much a monument to great craftsmanship as it is to the piracy carried out by 18th- and 19th-century Englishmen who, on their trips abroad, plundered whatever goodies they could find and then told the bereft that the thievery was for their own good. Yet the exquisite taste of these English patriarchs is unquestionable, and now the British Museum may be the museum to beat all the rest. In fact, it's the top attraction in the country—5.9 million people a year now. Put on your walking shoes because it's not the king of museums for nothing.

Because museum staff will do nothing beyond ensuring you aren't stealing or misbehaving (even the Info Desk just reads off the website), it's imperative that you do advance research and learn the background of the things you see. Check the schedule of daily talks and exhibitions either online or by the pillar

British Museum

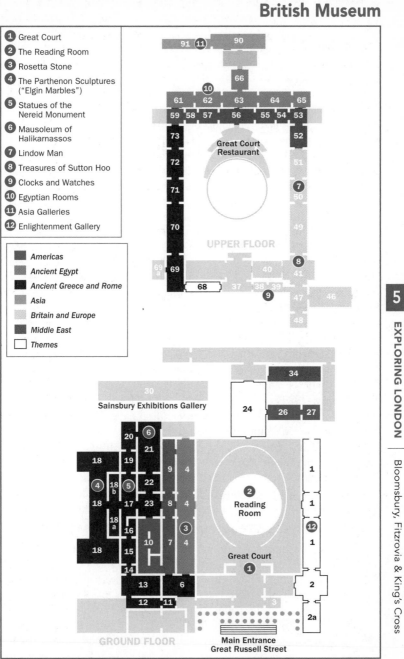

1 Great Court
2 The Reading Room
3 Rosetta Stone
4 The Parthenon Sculptures ("Elgin Marbles")
5 Statues of the Nereid Monument
6 Mausoleum of Halikarnassos
7 Lindow Man
8 Treasures of Sutton Hoo
9 Clocks and Watches
10 Egyptian Rooms
11 Asia Galleries
12 Enlightenment Gallery

- Americas
- Ancient Egypt
- Ancient Greece and Rome
- Asia
- Britain and Europe
- Middle East
- Themes

UPPER FLOOR

Great Court Restaurant

Sainsbury Exhibitions Gallery

Reading Room

Great Court

GROUND FLOOR

Main Entrance
Great Russell Street

to the right as you enter the Great Court. These include a bevy of freebies: 15 daily **Eye-Openers,** focused on particular rooms; 45-min. **Lunchtime Talks** with guest curators (Tues–Fri 1:15pm); 20-min. **Spotlight tours** about major holdings on Friday evenings; and **Hands On,** which allow you to touch some things (11am–4pm). The website also has some suggested **"object trails"** for what to look for if you have limited time—useful because the staff rarely knows about anything except crowd control.

This museum is so full that it risks being relentless or dull if you don't have context, and unfortunately, curators don't give you much to go by. They want you to buy things instead. Books from its gift shop may help. Consider renting a handheld audio/video tablet (£7, both adult and kids' versions) that spotlights 200 of the best objects. From 10:30am to 3pm on weekends, borrow free kids' backpacks that include discovery trails. **Maps** range from £2 to £6 depending on the level of guiding information you want, and even those are paltry, so for a free and better one, print floor plans from the website.

Dominating the glass-roofed **Great Court** like a drum in a box, the cream-and-gold round **Reading Room,** completed in 1857, was once part of the British Library containing King George III's exemplary book collection. Patrons had to apply for tickets, and they included Lenin and Karl Marx, who developed their political theories here; other habitués included Bram Stoker, Sir Arthur Conan Doyle, and Virginia Woolf, who wrote upon entering "one stood under the vast dome, as if one were a thought in the huge bald forehead which is so splendidly encircled by a band of famous names." The **Great Court Restaurant** above the Reading Room serves full afternoon tea from 3pm for just £20—a bargain (reserve online or at ✆ **020/7323-8990**). The Reading Room is closed to the public, but don't miss the paneled King's Library rooms (1827), now known as the **Enlightenment Gallery** and brimming with cabinets of curiosities retrieved from the ends of the Earth by the likes of Captain Cook himself.

Other holdings are grouped in numbered rooms by geography, with an emphasis on the Greek and Roman Empires, Europe, and Britain. Given the rarity and beauty of this massive collection, it feels perverse to call anything a highlight, but these are some that the museum itself names as standouts (check locations because exhibits are currently being shifted around).

TOP DON'T-MISS EXHIBITS AT THE BRITISH MUSEUM

o The museum's most famous, and most controversial, possessions are the so-called **Elgin Marbles,** gingerly referred to as the **Sculptures of the Parthenon** (rooms 18 and 19) to disguise imperialist provenance. These slab sculptures (called friezes and Metopes), plus some life-size weathered statuary, once lined the pediment of the famous Parthenon atop Athens' Acropolis. After being defaced (literally—the faces were hacked off) in the 500s by invading vandals (okay, not the East Germanic Vandal tribes— these guys were Persian), the sculptures suffered further indignities in a 1687 gunpowder explosion before being sawed off and carted away by Lord Elgin. They're laid out in the gallery in the approximate position in which they appeared on the Parthenon, only facing inward so you can admire them. Greece begs ceaselessly for their return, but the British have argued that they're better cared for in London. The smog-burnt portions left behind in Athens, despite their glossy new galleries, make a muddy issue of conservation and politics even murkier.

o Fragments of **sculptures from the Mausoleum at Halikarnassos,** one of the lost Seven Wonders of the Ancient World, loom in room 21. They're colossal in the original sense—one horse's head measures 2.1m (7 ft.) long.

o The pivotal **Rosetta Stone** (196 B.C.), in room 4, is what helped linguists crack hieroglyphics, and its importance to anthropology can't be exaggerated. Napoleon's soldiers found it in Egypt in 1799, but the British nabbed it in 1801. Consider it his first Waterloo. At the back of the ground floor, in room 24, find the giant **Hoa Hakananai'a.** It was plucked from Easter Island in 1868 and stood outside, under the portico, for nearly 80 years before being brought indoors. So much for the "we take care of things better" argument.

o The grisly array of **Egyptian Mummies** in rooms 62, 63, and 64 petrifies living children, and on your visit these galleries will be thronged as usual. In addition to the wizened corpses, there are painted coffins; the hair and lung of the scribe Sutimose, dating to 1100 B.C.; and scarabs galore. In room 64, check out the body from 3400 B.C., found in a fetal position without a coffin, which was preserved by dry sand. Beside it is another one, 400 years younger, that rotted to soil because it was laid to rest in a basket.

o Kids stare moon-eyed at crumpled, leather-faced **Lindow Man** in room 50; he was discovered, throat slit, in a Cheshire bog nearly 2,000 years after his brutal demise. Preserved down to his hair and fingernails, he looks like he could spring to life and pound the glass of his case. Nearby (room 49) is the **Mildenhall Treasure,** a hoard of new-looking silver Roman tableware unearthed by Gordon Butcher, a Suffolk farmer, as he plowed fields in 1942; the saga of how he was cheated of his fortune was chronicled by writer Roald Dahl. (Yes, pillage is something of an underlying theme in this place.) The **Lewis Chessmen** (room 40), cartoonish and made from walrus ivory, are whimsical favorites.

o The **oldest known map** in the world, by the Babylonians, was carved on a clay tablet in the 6th century B.C. and now resides in room 55.

o Room 70, on Level 3, contains many remarkable holdings: the bronze **head of Roman Emperor Augustus,** found in the Sudan and unsettlingly lifelike (it still has its eyeballs of glass and stone); the **Portland Vase,** a black, cameo-glass jug that would be very difficult to make even today; beside that, the historically important **Warren Cup,** a 1st-century silver chalice graphically depicting homosexual sex in relief; and a 3rd-century Roman **crocodile-skin suit of armor.**

Great Russell St., WC1. www.thebritishmuseum.org. © **020/7323-8299.** Free admission. Sat–Thurs 10am–5:30pm; Fri 10am–8:30pm. Tube: Tottenham Court Rd. or Holborn or Russell Square.

5

EXPLORING LONDON

Bloomsbury, Fitzrovia & King's Cross

JEREMY BENTHAM'S "auto icon"

England's own Ben Franklin, **Jeremy Bentham** (1748–1832) was a philosopher, a progressive, a subversive, a prison reformer, a supporter of suffrage and the decriminalization of homosexuality, an educator, and a pen pal of U.S. President James Madison. Bentham worked to enable equal access to courts and schools, and he coined the words *international* and *maximize*—he codified *codification* itself.

He was so ahead of his time that he refuses to stay in the past: His will stipulated eternal access to his corpse—the gift that keeps on giving, really. Starting years before his death, he purportedly carried around a pair of glass eyes that were intended for his future "Auto Icon" (auto = self, icon = image), which would represent him forever. After he expired, his body was dissected for students. In 1850, a colleague dressed his remains and Bentham's severed head was placed between his own feet. There his remains remain, in a lobby at University College London. His skeleton is under his original clothing and gloves. Unfortunately, his noggin was clumsily preserved and kids kept swiping it (in 1975, some hooligans held it for a £10 ransom), so today, it's stashed in the vaults, staring blankly with those long-pocketed blue eyeballs. You can see the real head on an electronic display. "Some visitors find it disturbing to look at," warns the caption after you're already recoiling at the sight of the leathery thing. His new lifelike, doughy face sagely observes the current scholarly crop at UCL from beneath a straw hat. You'll find this freak show on the east side of Gower Street between University Street and Grafton Way, opposite the red-brick Cruciform Building. Go in the gates, veer right, and enter the door marked South Cloisters. Then hang a right and head for the stone lions (Tube: Euston Square).

Other Bloomsbury Area Attractions

The Charles Dickens Museum ★ MUSEUM   Although Dickens moved around a lot, his last remaining London home, which he rented for £80 a year when he was 30, is now his testament. A museum since 1925, and restored to a period look in 2012 (when the attic and kitchen were opened for the first time), these four floors don't exude many Dickensian vibes; after all, he departed in 1839 after staying less than 2 years. It could be anyone's humble home. Still, his celebrity got a kick-start while he lived here: *Oliver Twist* and *Nicholas Nickleby,* arguably his biggest hits, were written while he was in residence. As you inspect his desk, his razor, and bars from a prison where his spendthrift dad was locked up, an unpleasant realization sets in: Charles Dickens was a brilliant storyteller, one of the most gifted in the history of the English language, but also a jerk. Tough on his kids and unfaithfully cruel to his wife, his other great talent seems to have been for ego.

48 Doughty St., WC1. www.dickensmuseum.com. ℰ **020/7405-2127.** Admission £9.50 adults, £7.50 seniors and students, £4.50 children 6–16. Tues–Sun 10am–5pm; last admission 1 hr. before closing. Tube: Chancery Lane or Russell Square.

The Foundling Museum ★★ MUSEUM   Small but devastating, it tracks the history of the Foundling Hospital, which took in thousands of orphans between 1739 and 1953. This was a period in which kids were treated like rubbish: For example, in 1802 a law was passed limiting the time children could work in mills—to 12 hours a day. By that measure, the benefactors were actually helping kids by locking them in this borderline prison—the kids were treated poorly to discourage mothers from giving them up. Don't miss the heartbreaking cases of tokens that mothers left at the doorstep with their babies. These tiny objects, into which a lifetime of hopes was imbued, never made it to their children lest they compromise anonymity. Also take the time to listen to the oral histories by some of the last kids to be raised by the Hospital; at the time of recording, they were elderly but still obviously quite shaken. Upstairs is the exquisitely rococo Court Room (1745) and a modest but respectable collection of 18th-century English works (Hogarth, Reynolds, Millais), which, because this was an institution that attracted positioned benefactors, was one of the first permanent art exhibitions in the world. Today, the museum also brings in temporary exhibitions exploring the relationship between adult artists and children. The composer Handel loved the Hospital: He wrote his *Messiah* as a benefit for the facility in 1754 (a score is on display). The former exercise grounds, now called Coram's Fields, are still the domain of the child; adults are not permitted to enter without a kid in tow. Perhaps not at all coincidentally, J. M. Barrie's original *Peter Pan* play had 8 Grenville Street (demolished 1938), across Brunswick Square, as the Darling home, where the orphan Peter Pan flew into the nursery in search of his shadow.

40 Brunswick Sq., WC1. www.foundlingmuseum.org.uk. ✆ **020/7841-3600.** Admission £10 adults, £7.50 seniors and students, free for children 15 and under; higher posted prices include a "voluntary donation". Tues–Sat 10am–5pm; Sun 11am–5pm. Tube: Russell Square.

The Petrie Museum of Egyptian Archeology ★★ MUSEUM   Britain made a lot of mistakes when it comes to Egypt, and not just with Suez. Almost as soon as "explorers" could break into ancient tombs, they would lose track of thousands of things they discovered or leave poor information about how they found it. Since the 1800s, University College London has worked to properly collect, identify, and date more than 80,000 artifacts; roaming its treasure-crammed cases, some of which are stocked with items that still stump scholars, can be awe-inspiring. From the cotton Tarkhan dress last worn 5,000 years ago to Roman funerary portraits painted in beeswax, the things one finds in these stacks could blow a mind.

Malet Place, University College London, WC1. www.ucl.ac.uk/culture/petrie-museum. ✆ **020/7679-2884.** Free admission. Tues–Sat 1–5pm. Tube: Goodge St.

Postal Museum & Mail Rail ★★ MUSEUM   In an industrial patch of Central London no tourist usually wanders into, you can now find two new, well-done attractions in one, and both are perfect for kids. The first holds exhibits about the social history of mail delivery in the country, from origins

(Henry VIII was once the only guy allowed to get mail) to antique vehicles to old "pillar" post boxes to Arnold Machin's sculptures of the young Queen Elizabeth II photographed to make stamps. There are lots of things for kids to press and bang, including a pneumatic tube that sends messages whizzing in an overhead tube across the hall, and there's a mail-themed play space, which costs a little extra. But the most memorable aspect of a visit will be a 20-min. loop on the Mail Rail, a little-seen 22-mile underground line that from 1927 to 2003 was used to deliver millions of letters a year. A short portion (with recorded narration and a plastic dome over the carriages, which are as tiny as the train in the kiddie section of a carnival, so please refrain from being tall) now carries curious tourists on a 1-mile looping journey 70 feet below the streets. (Claustrophobes can see what riders do by getting an Exhibitions Only ticket and watching what they missed on screens near the boarding platform.)

15–20 Phoenix Place, WC1. www.postalmuseum.org. 📞 **0300/0300-700.** Full admission £15.50 adults, £14 seniors and students, £9.50 kids age 1–15; exhibition only £10 adult, £8 seniors and students, free kids age 1–15; higher posted prices include a "voluntary donation." Daily 10am–5pm. Tube: Farringdon or Chancery Lane.

Wellcome Collection ★★ MUSEUM   Once upon a time, there was a very strange Midwestern pharmacist named Henry Wellcome. Henry got very wealthy and developed a taste for hoarding medical oddities, such as Napoleon's toothbrush, hair from George III, oil paintings of childbirth, and Japanese sex toys. When he died, he bequeathed a flashy museum for them, which now makes for a highly amusing hour's visit. Besides the permanent collection, there's always an offbeat temporary exhibit or two, pertaining to the human body and its uses—recent ones were on sex research and corpse forensics. It's always one of the most compelling museums in town, and its sizable shop is one of the more intellectual.

183 Euston Rd., NW1. www.wellcomecollection.org. 📞 **020/7611-2222.** Free admission. Tues–Wed and Fri–Sat 10am–6pm; Thurs 10am–10pm; Sun 11am–6pm. Tube: Euston Square, Warren St., or Euston.

The Hardy Tree

In 1866, as laborers dug their way through his churchyard to create the new St Pancras Station, the Vicar of St Pancras noticed with horror that they were tossing aside thighbones and skulls. His cemetery contained the remains of Mary Wollstonecraft, J.C. Bach, Sir John Soane, and Ben Franklin's son, the last colonial governor of New Jersey, so the Vicar assigned a young architecture student named Thomas with the unenviable task of overseeing the relocation of some 8,000 bodies. As he worked, Thomas carefully arranged their discarded headstones around a tree. The tree survives, and today its trunk grows around the markers. Now it is called the Hardy Tree—you see, young Thomas, who created this eerie living monument, was about to become the famous novelist Thomas Hardy. (St Pancras Old Church, Pancras Rd., NW1; www.posp.co.uk; 📞 **020/7424-0724;** Tube: King's Cross St Pancras.)

SOHO, COVENT GARDEN & WEST END

The Courtauld Institute of Art Gallery ★★★ MUSEUM   Art historians consider it one of the most prestigious collections on Earth, but alas, you cannot visit this year. It's undergoing a £50-million renovation until 2020. **Somerset House** (www.somersethouse.org.uk), its home, was once a naval complex and later was where Londoners came to settle taxes. Now it's a favorite hangout. The courtyard, beneath which lie the foundations of a Tudor palace, has a grove of 55 ground-level fountains that delight small children, and it's the scene of both popular summer concerts and a winter ice rink. Free 30-min. tours go Tuesday, Thursday, and Saturday from the information desk in the Seamen's Hall; check ahead for timings since they may change if something else big is going on. Also look for changing exhibitions (either free or £10 adults, £8 seniors/students depending on what's on). The Victoria Embankment terrace overlooking the Thames (from across the street) can be enjoyed for free.

Somerset House, Strand, WC2. www.courtauld.ac.uk. ☏ **020/7848-2526.** Closed until 2020. Tube: Temple.

London Transport Museum ★★ MUSEUM   Try to imagine London without its wheeled icons: the red double-decker bus, the black taxi, and the

London Transport Museum.

West End & Westminster Attractions

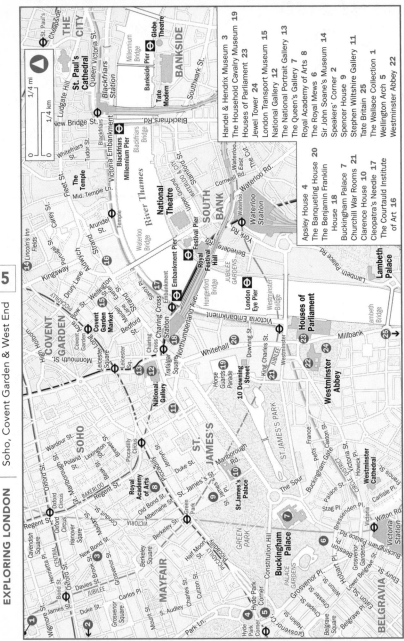

Apsley House 4
The Banqueting House 20
The Benjamin Franklin House 18
Buckingham Palace 7
Churchill War Rooms 21
Clarence House 10
Cleopatra's Needle 17
The Courtauld Institute of Art 16

Handel & Hendrix Museum 3
The Household Cavalry Museum 19
Houses of Parliament 23
Jewel Tower 24
London Transport Museum 15
National Gallery 12
The National Portrait Gallery 13
The Queen's Gallery 7
Royal Academy of Arts 8
The Royal Mews 6
Sir John Soane's Museum 14
Speakers' Corner 2
Spencer House 9
Stephen Wiltshire Gallery 11
Tate Britain 25
The Wallace Collection 1
Wellington Arch 5
Westminster Abbey 22

Tube, which are the best of their kind in the world and a draw for visitors. In Covent Garden's soaring cast-iron-and-glass 1871 flower-selling hall (Eliza Doolittle would have bought her flowers here), the vehicles' development and evolution are traced with excellent technology (lots of ambient sounds and video displays, although some are getting grubby or outdated) and detail (there are even fake horse apples beneath the antique carriages). You can board a fleet of intact landmark vehicles, such as Number 23, a steam locomotive that powered the Underground in its most unpleasant days ("a form of mild torture," wrote the *Times* then); also on display are plenty of the system's famous Edwardian and Art Deco posters, many of which are art unto themselves. Designers will appreciate the background on Johnston, the distinctive typeface created in 1916 for the Underground by Frank Pick, which could now be considered London's unofficial font. Along the way, you'll learn a great deal about shifts in London life; you may even feel a twinge of embarrassment about the state of your own town's public transportation. It's a must for fans of London history and a good place to entertain children—but if you're childless, you'll need patience. The gift shop, which doesn't require a ticket, is exemplary.

Covent Garden, WC2. www.ltmuseum.co.uk. © **020/7565-7299.** Admission £17.50 adults, £15 seniors and students, free for children 17 and under. Sat–Thurs 10am–6pm; Fri 11am–6pm; last admission 45 min. before closing. Tube: Covent Garden.

National Gallery ★★★ MUSEUM   When the bells of St Martin-in-the-Fields peal each morning at 10am, the doors promptly open on one of the world's greatest artistic fireworks shows—each famous picture follows an equally famous picture. Few museums can compete with the strongest, widest collection of paintings in the world—one of every important style is on display, and it's almost always the best in that genre. There are 2,300 Western European works, which is plenty to divert you for as long as you can manage. Almost six million visitors are drawn here every year, although most of them just wander around without getting properly close to the brushwork. Be different.

This stupendous museum is unfortunately marred by lazy presentation; it's very difficult to find the works you want to see. The map (£1) is a poor value since it omits major works. Directional signs lack room numbers, and the staff cares mostly about controlling visitors, not edifying them. It's almost like they want you to wander confused and unenriched. (To find a specific painting, track down a staffer wearing a lime green shirt—there's usually one in the Trafalgar Square lobby.) Mostly, they tell you to use your smartphone to look things up on the museum's website, using the museum's Wi-Fi, which may not work. (You can recharge your phone in the downstairs Espresso Bar if you have a cord.)

Posted signs are awfully straight-laced. Comprehensive audio tours covering 1,200 of the works are £4 and leaflets guide you to a subset of them in themed varieties (Impressionists, technique, etc.). A $2 app catalogs more than 1,500 paintings—if there's a symbol by the work, you can look it up on the app—and a free version supplies 183 highlights. The website has some touring trail suggestions, but your visit would be best illuminated by some expert input. Check the info desk for events, such as the **10-Minute Talks** about a single work (Mon–Fri 4pm); 45-min. **Lunchtime Talks** (1pm) about a specific work or artist; storytelling for kids; or the few hour-long tours (check the schedule online). Permanent displays are supplemented by temporary exhibitions, one free and one paid (£8–£18). The Gallery schedules most family activities for Sundays. The two restaurants are top-quality but overpriced, and besides, the view from the restaurant at the National Portrait Gallery next door (see below) is better. But don't miss the superlative gift shops, which will print you a color-matched custom copy of any of the 1,200 works or even mail a framed version home.

Galleries imperceptibly surge through time in a clockwise arrangement. The best course is to start in the Sainsbury Wing (the first wing upon your entrance from Pall Mall East), which will order viewings more or less chronologically.

TOP DON'T-MISS EXHIBITS AT THE NATIONAL GALLERY

o Piero della Francesca, one of the most sought-after Renaissance painters, is represented by *The Baptism of Christ* (1450s, room 66 in the Sainsbury Wing). With its then-advanced use of light and foreshortening, its faces verge on bemusement, and the dove, representing the Holy Spirit, seems to fly straight at viewers.

o After Sandro Botticelli fell under the spell of the hardline reformer Savonarola, he burned many of his finest paintings in the Bonfire of the Vanities and changed to an inferior style, so his best works are rare. *Venus and Mars* (1485, room 58 in the Sainsbury Wing), depicting the lovers reclining, is one of them.

o Michelangelo's *The Entombment* (ca. 1500, room 21) is unfinished but powerful. The feminine figure in the red gown is now thought to be St John, but it's hard to know for sure, since the artist favored strong masculine traits.

o Kids love Holbein's *The Ambassadors* (1533, room 4), full of symbolic riddles that refer to the guy on the left, and famous for a stretched image of a skull that can only be viewed in proper perspective from the side. Get close; the fine brushwork extends even to the feathers on the shoes.

o Nearby is Hans Holbein the Younger's oil-on-oak portrait of *Christina of Denmark, Duchess of Milan* (1538, room 4), painted for King Henry VIII when he was wife-shopping. She declined to marry him, and as a happy consequence, survived to 1590.

o Kids also love Quinten Massys' grotesque, porcine *An Old Woman* (*"The Ugly Duchess"*; 1513, room 5), thought to be a satire on ladies who try to look younger than they are, but possibly a woman suffering from a disease.

National Gallery Highlights

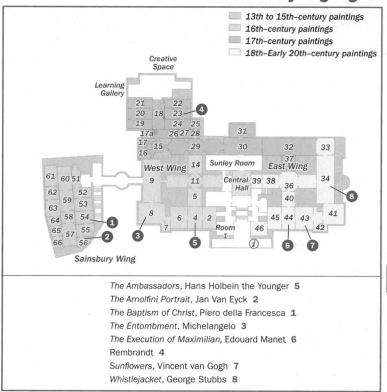

13th to 15th-century paintings
16th-century paintings
17th-century paintings
18th-Early 20th-century paintings

Creative Space

Learning Gallery

21 22 20 18 23 **4** 19 24 25 17a 26 27 28 31 17 15 29 30 32 33 16 West Wing 14 Sunley Room East Wing 37 9 11 Central 39 38 34 5 Hall 36 40 8 61 60 51 62 59 52 8 6 4 2 45 44 43 41 63 58 54 7 Room 46 42 64 57 55 **1** 1 65 66 56 **2** **3** **5** (i) **6** **7**

Sainsbury Wing

The Ambassadors, Hans Holbein the Younger **5**
The Arnolfini Portrait, Jan Van Eyck **2**
The Baptism of Christ, Piero della Francesca **1**
The Entombment, Michelangelo **3**
The Execution of Maximilian, Edouard Manet **6**
Rembrandt **4**
Sunflowers, Vincent van Gogh **7**
Whistlejacket, George Stubbs **8**

○ Among other works, Rembrandt shows two self-portraits. One at age 34 (room 24, by the painting of a dragon eating a man's face off) is pridefully detailed to declare ego and prosperity; by age 63 (room 23), he's in simple clothes and broadly dolloping paint with a palette knife. The pair makes for a universal story of preening youth giving way to confident old age.

○ Edouard Manet's ***The Execution of Maximilian*** (1867–68, room 41) was sliced into five sections after the artist's death, but Edgar Degas reassembled what he could find; the missing patches lend the firing-squad scene further tension.

○ George Stubbs' stark, life-size portrait of rearing stallion ***Whistlejacket*** (room 34) stops everyone in their tracks; it was painted in 1762 for its proud owner.

○ The Gallery is rich in Peter Paul Rubens, with some 25 works attributed to him. His ***Samson and Delilah*** (1609–10, room 29) is known for Samson's muscular back and Delilah's crimson robe.

There's much more: George Seurat's almost-pointillist *Bathers at Asnieres* (1884, room 41); Van Gogh's *Sunflowers* (1888, room 43); Jan van Eyck's *The Arnolfini Portrait* (Sainsbury Wing, room 56), a mysterious but fabulously skillful depiction of light that dates to 1434, years ahead of its time. **Brueghels. Cézannes. Uccellos.** There's so much art here that you may want to go twice during your visit, and the Gallery is centrally located, so you can.

Trafalgar Square, WC2. www.nationalgallery.org.uk. ⓒ **020/7747-2885.** Free admission. Mon–Thurs and Sat–Sun 10am–6pm; Fri 10am–9pm). Tube: Charing Cross or Leicester Square.

The National Portrait Gallery ★★★ MUSEUM   On paper, the concept of a portrait gallery sounds like Field Trip Hell. But actually, you'll be surprised how the best works capture the sparkle of life behind these charismatic shapers of history. Here, the names from your high school textbook flower into flesh-and-blood people, and the accompanying biographies are so sublimely evocative (Samuel Johnson is described as "massive, ungainly, plagued with nervous tics") that subjects come alive.

Begin by taking the escalator up. The oldest works (Tudors, Jacobeans, Elizabethans) come first, and you'll progress forward in time, coming to photography just about when canvas fatigue sets in. It helps to know a little history so that these pictures ring some bells, so consider visiting near the end of your trip, when some of these names will be fresh in your mind from your tours. The ancient kings and queens have the most heft, partly because it's hard to wrap your brain around the fact that in many cases, the actual people posed alongside these very canvases. One of the most instantly recognizable paintings is the **Ditchley portrait of Elizabeth I** (room 2), in which the queen's jeweled gown spreads like wings and Her Majesty firmly glares at the viewer under stormy skies. Right away, it becomes clear that many artists are slyly commenting on the disposition of their sitters. The troublesome **Henry VIII** is shown in several likenesses. One is a delicate 1537 paper cartoon by Hans Holbein the Younger (for a mural at Whitehall—a rare survivor from that palace), in which the king suspiciously peers with flinty grey eyes—hinting at

Know Before You Go

Your visit to London's major museums will be a lot better if you do these things *before* leaving home.

o **Check what temporary exhibitions are on.** You'll need a ticket, and they sell out.

o **Print maps from the website.** It costs £2 to £3 to pick one up, and they're not detailed.

o **Pick a few items you want to see.** Not just so you can find them (they move around sometimes). Also, signage may be weak and curators unavailable. The more you know, the more you'll love what you see.

o **Check the times for talks and kids' events.** London's museums are always abuzz with activities. Make sure you don't miss the good ones.

a shiftiness that His Majesty probably couldn't recognize in his own likeness, but that all who knew him feared (room 1). You'll also find **George Washington** (he was born an Englishman, after all), and one of the only authoritative images of **Captain James Cook** (room 14), who was so pivotal in colonial expansion. In room 12, look for the **Chevalier D'Eon** (sometimes on loan), a male diplomat and fencing champion who lived as a woman in the late 1700s; in room 10, for the adorable little nose of **William Hogarth** in his terra-cotta bust; and in room 18, for the sketch of **Jane Austen** by her sister Cassandra—friends said it stank, but here it is. The **Brontë Sisters** appear together in an 1834 portrait found folded atop a cupboard in 1914; their alcoholic brother Patrick Branwell Brontë painted himself out but his ghostly image is eerily re-appearing (room 24). The genius of artist John Singer Sargent is immediately apparent in the 1894 likeness of poet **Coventry Patmore** (room 22); with just a few spare brush strokes, you feel like you know him.

Fortunately, the portraits don't stop when cameras were invented. **Margaret Thatcher,** imperiously glaring over the grey gunwale of a dais at the Conservative Party Conference in Brighton, is Paul Brason's fearsome and not-very-fond representation of the Iron Lady (1982, room 32); **Princes William** and **Harry** make appearances in a 2009 sitting (room 32), wearing the uniform of the Household Cavalry, and **Beatrix Potter** (1938, room 31), pictured in front of some sheep, looks as soft and kind as the gran you wish you had. Modern portraits (an impressionistic **Ed Sheeran**, anyone?) change often because there's not enough room to show everything. Just about everything can be photographed (never with flash) or purchased as a poster in the gift shop.

The £3 audio/video guide starts out dull, but by the end, it uses archival recordings, which is cool, and there's a $2 smartphone app (there's free Wi-Fi) of the highlights. Bring kids; the desk lends free discovery trails for them.

Late Shift evenings (Thurs–Fri 6–9pm), with DJs, talks, live music, and sketching sessions, are great fun and a smart way to free up daytime hours to see more attractions. Also consider the pre-theater menu (£20 for two courses, £24 for three) served from 5:30 to 6:30pm in the rooftop Portrait Restaurant (✆ **020/7312-2490**), which has a breathtaking view of Nelson's Column and Big Ben's tower—it's better than the National Gallery's.

St Martin's Place, WC2. www.npg.org.uk. ✆ **020/7312-2463.** Free admission. Sat–Wed 10am–6pm; Thurs–Fri 10am–9pm); last admission 45 min. before closing. Tube: Leicester Square.

Sir John Soane's Museum ★★ MUSEUM A doorman will politely request that you deposit your bags. With good reason: These two town houses on the north side of Lincoln's Inn Fields (fresh off a £7-million expansion that opened up closed rooms) are so overloaded with furniture, paintings, architectural decoration, and sculpture that navigation is a challenge. The Georgian architect, noted for his egotistic neoclassicism (the Bank of England) as much as for his aesthetic materialism, bequeathed his home and its contents as a

All of the following attractions charge no admission fees for their permanent collections. Not a shabby lineup!

museum for "amateurs and students," and so it has been, looking much like this since 1837. It's as if the well-connected eccentric had just popped out to purloin another Greek pilaster, leaving you to roam his groaning wood floors, sussing out the *objets d'art* from the certifiable treasures. His oddball abode, which his will decreed must be left precisely as it was on the day he died, is a melee of art history in which precious paintings and sculpture jostle for space like baubles in a junk shop. Ask to join a tour of the **Picture Room,** built in an 1823 expansion, so you can watch its hidden recesses be opened, revealing layer upon buried layer of works (such as William Hogarth's eight-painting *The Rake's Progress,* a documentary of dissolution), filed inside false walls. Look sharp for Canalettos (which often fetch £9 million at auction) and a J. M. W. Turner (ditto). Curation appears convoluted and haphazard: The guides swear that although sunshine appears to pour onto the masterpieces through skylights, there are UV filters—yet architectural fragments from Whitehall Palace are plainly betrayed to the elements in the courtyard ("It was never covered because that's the way he wanted it," a guide says). You have to wonder how Soane could legally acquire antiquities such as the sarcophagus of Seti I, carved from translucent limestone but stockpiled for £2,000, and you won't know because nearly nothing is marked. (Just how the Hogarth hoarder wanted it, too.) Surf the simulated museum at http://explore.soane.org to get pre-acquainted, or take a guided 1-hr. tour (£12.50; Thurs–Sun noon, also Sat–Sun 11am; book ahead). Mostly, a visit reminds you of the unseemly way in which privileged Englishmen used to stuff their homes with classical art as a way of stocking up on a sense of righteousness—but that doesn't mean it's not wondrous.

13 Lincoln's Inn Fields, WC2. www.soane.org. ✆ **020/7405-2107.** Free admission. Wed–Sun 10am–5pm, last entry 4:30pm; candlelit nights at least once a month (book ahead online). Tube: Holborn.

Other West End Attractions

The Benjamin Franklin House ★ HISTORIC HOME   The only surviving residence of the portly politico is a sort of architectural preserve. Shocker: Franklin lived in this boarding house by the Thames for nearly 16 years, without his wife—he was here for the Boston Tea Party, the enactment of the Stamp Act, and his invention of the armonica—and it was only the Revolution (and scandal) that forced him from his adopted home back to the Colonies. For much of his life Franklin was a fervent Loyalist who, even as late as 1775, felt the differences between Britain and the Colonies could be settled in "half an hour." Tours are conducted by a young actress playing the landlady's daughter, Polly Hewson, who became such a dear friend that she moved to Philadelphia and was with him when he died. In empty rooms, Polly tells wistful tales as recordings chime in with voices from her memory. (Mondays are for architectural tours without the actress.) Rewards are mixed. Exhibits are sparse (one exception is the ghoulish deposit of human bones in the back-yard, likely left over from dissections by Franklin's doctor neighbor). It's humbling to see how this giant man made do with such small quarters. The worn wooden staircase, on which he got his exercise when French trollops weren't available, is so well preserved it feels ghostly.

36 Craven St., WC2. www.benjaminfranklinhouse.org. ℂ **020/7925-1405.** Admission and tour (required) £8 adults, £6 seniors and students, free for children 15 and under. 5 timed tours daily, Mon (architectural tour) and Wed–Sun (historical tour) noon–4:15pm. Tube: Embankment or Charing Cross.

The Temple Church ★★ CHURCH/HISTORIC SITE   For 900 years, this remarkable little sanctum has been a cradle for legal and religious liberties around the world. The oldest part, the Round, was built in 1185 by Knights from the Crusades. Back then, they were considered the good guys, so when befuddled King John ran afoul of his barons, he sought sanctuary here and, under protection of the Knights, hammered out the details of the Magna Carta, which gave common law rights to the people as they never had before. America owes the basis of its Constitution to this building. You can see the stone effigies of nine of the Knights scattered in the Round. Horribly, on May 11, 1941, a Nazi incendiary bomb wrecked this precious place; many of the beautifully carved effigies are now as lumpen and faceless as corpses from Pompeii. The reconstruction of the Temple, which is still a working church serving the legal community in the surrounding Inner and Middle Temple Inns of Court (to which all English barristers must belong), was exacting—notice how the Purbeck Marble columns, sourced from the same Dorset mine as the originals 700 years before, lean slightly according to the architect's plans from the 1200s. It also has world-famous acoustics, a sublime organ, and a top-notch choir, so if you come, time your visit to coincide with the music schedule.

Inner Temple, EC4 (in the quad south of the intersection of Fleet St. and Chancery Lane). www.templechurch.com. ℂ **020/7353-3470.** Admission £5 adults, £3 seniors and students, free for children 16 and under. Generally open Mon–Fri 10am–4pm, but check ahead because hours shift weekly. Tube: Temple or Blackfriars.

CLEOPATRA & "eros"

Two monuments in the West End have been enchanting visitors for years. When he finished his legendary fountain in the middle of Piccadilly Circus in 1893, sculptor Alfred Gilbert thought the playful maritime-themed sculptures on its base would be celebrated. Audiences, however, have minds of their own: They responded instead to the archer god on top. But they got even that bit of admiration wrong—they thought he represented **Eros,** god of erotic love, when Gilbert had actually intended Anteros, god of requited love. Today, Piccadilly Circus isn't a roundabout anymore—it's an interchange—but the ceaseless tourist crowd photographing Gilbert's misunderstood masterpiece at least puts the circus back into Piccadilly. Gilbert's fabulous fountain is now dry and full of McDonald's wrappers, but his misidentified god blesses the city as an icon. (Tube: Piccadilly Circus)

The original Cleopatra's Needles obelisks—which Cleopatra had nothing to do with—were erected in Heliopolis, Egypt, around 1450 B.C., and inscriptions were added 200 years later. The Romans moved the granite spires to Alexandria, where they toppled and were buried in the sand, which preserved them until the early 1800s. After a perilous delivery, London's 224-ton **Cleopatra's Needle** was erected here on the river in 1878 (New York City got one in 1881, and a third went to Paris). Two sphinxes were installed to guard it (some say backward, since they face the sculpture, not away from it). Just 140 years here wrecked what 20 Saharan centuries didn't: Pollution has rendered the hieroglyphs illegible. In 1917, German bombs scarred the western sphinx. The cast iron benches in the area were installed in preparation for its arrival in the 1870s. Look closely; you'll find sphinxes and camels hidden in the armrests. (Tube: Embankment or Temple)

WESTMINSTER & ST JAMES'S

For information on the **Changing the Guard** ceremony, please see p. 190.

Buckingham Palace ★★ PALACE   If you were to fall asleep tonight and wake up inside one of the **State Rooms,** you'd never guess where you were. Is it opulent? No question. But if gilding, teardrop chandeliers, 18th-century portraits, and ceremonial halls could ever be considered standard-issue, Buckingham Palace is your basic palace. Queen Elizabeth's mild taste—call it "respectable decadence" of yellows and creams and pleasant floral arrangements, thank you very much—is partly the reason. Remember, too, that much of this palace was built or remodeled in the 1800s—not so long ago in the scheme of things—and that the queen considers Windsor to be her real home. That's right: Buckingham Palace is a mere *pied-à-terre.*

All tickets are timed and include an audio tour that rushes you around too quickly. (If you want to see highlights of the formal gardens, that's another £9.) The route threads through the public and ceremonial rooms at the back of the Palace—nowhere the Royal Family spends personal time (and besides, tours are held only when they're in Scotland, 2 months a year). Highlights include the 50m-long (164-ft.) **Picture Gallery** filled mostly with works

Changing the Guard at Buckingham Palace is touristy but well-attended.

amassed by George IV, an obsessive collector; the 14m-high (46-ft.) **Ballroom,** where the queen confers knighthoods; the parquet-floored **Music Room,** unaltered since John Nash decorated it in 1831, where the queen's three eldest children were baptized in water brought from the River Jordan; and a stroll through the thick **Garden** in the back yard. It's definitely worth seeing—how often can you toddle around the spare rooms in a queen's house, inspecting artwork given as gifts by some of history's most prominent names? But it's no Versailles. If you're in London any time other than August or September and spot her standard of red, gold, and blue flying above, you'll at least know the queen is home. If it's the Union Jack, she's gone.

Buckingham Palace Rd., SW1. www.royalcollection.org.uk. ✆ **020/7766-7300.** Admission £24 adults, £22 seniors and students, £13.50 children 5–16. Generally open late July to late Aug daily 9:30am–7pm; Sept daily 9:30am–6pm; last admission 1 hr. 45 min. before closing. Tube: Victoria or Green Park.

Churchill War Rooms ★★★ MUSEUM/HISTORIC SITE

One of London's most fascinating museums is the secret command center used by Winston Churchill and his staff during the most harrowing moments of World War II, when it looked like England might become German. We regard the period with nostalgia, but a staggering 30,000 civilians were killed by some 18,000 tons of bombs in London alone and more than 65,000 innocent people were killed in Britain as a whole. Here, in the cellar of the Treasury building, practically next door to 10 Downing St., the core of the British government hunkered down where one errant bomb could have incinerated the lot of them.

When the war ended, the bunker was abandoned, but everything was left just as it was in August 1945. When it came time to make it a museum, everything was intact—from pushpins tracing convoy movements on yellowed world maps to rationed sugar cubes hidden in the back of a clerk's desk drawer. Although the hideout functioned like a small town for 526 people, with sleeping quarters, kitchens, radio rooms, and other facilities that would enable leaders to live undetected for months on end, it feels a lot more like your old elementary school, with its painted brick, linoleum walls, and round clocks.

Midway through, you disappear into the **Churchill Museum,** surely the most cutting-edge biographical museum open at this moment. Exhaustively displaying every conceivable facet of his life (his bowtie, his bowler hat, and even the original front door to 10 Downing St.), it covers the exalted statesman's life from entitled birth through his antics as a journalist in South Africa (where he escaped a kidnapping and became a national hero) to his stints as prime minister. You even learn his favorite cigar (Romeo y Julieta) and brandy (Hine). The entire museum is atwitter with multimedia displays, movies, and archival sounds, but the centerpiece will blow you away: a 15m-long (50-ft.) Lifeline Interactive table, like a long file cabinet illuminated by projections, that covers every month of Churchill's life. Touch a date, and the file "opens" with 4,600 pages of rare documents, photos, or, for critical dates in history, animated Easter eggs that temporarily consume the entire table (select the original Armistice Day or the *Titanic* sinking to see what I mean). You could play for hours, dipping into his life day by day.

Clive Steps, King Charles St., SW1. www.iwm.org.uk. © **020/7930-6961.** Admission £21 adults, £16.80 seniors and students, £10.50 children 5–15; roughly 10% discount for booking ahead online; higher posted prices include a "voluntary donation." Daily 9:30am–6pm; last admission 5pm. Tube: Westminster or St James's Park.

Houses of Parliament ★★ LANDMARK   In olden days, England's rich overlords got together at the king's house, Westminster Palace, to figure out how to manage their peasants. Over time, the king was forced out of the proceedings and most of the Palace burned down. What remains is constructed to express the might of Empire riches and the lofty aesthetics of Gothic-revival architecture. Luckily, the nation allows you to tour a dozen stately halls and even to wander through its vaunted House of Lords and House of Commons when they're not in session. There are now two ways to see it: Choose a 100-min. guided group tour, which presents the usual issues of audibility and pace, or take it easy with the new 2-hr. audio guide (and eavesdrop on groups whenever you want).

The historical highlight is massive **Westminster Hall,** one of the world's most precious spaces and a UNESCO World Heritage Site, built in 1097 by William Rufus, son of William the Conqueror. Richard II commissioned its cherished oak hammer-beam ceiling before he was deposed in the 1390s. Charles I, William Wallace, Sir Thomas More, and Guy Fawkes were all condemned in it, monarchs lie in state in it—and your role in it is to pick up your audio tour. The rest of the Palace is roughly divided into three areas: those for the **House of Lords** (whose members inherit seats upholstered in rose with an unbelievable gilt sitting area where Queen Victoria would preside on designated occasions); the **House of Commons** (by far the more powerful, elected by the people, but plainer, with seats of blue-green under a hanging forest of microphones); and some flabbergasting lobbies, sitting rooms, and the **Robing Room** (golds, browns, burgundies), which the Sovereign flits through when she shows up once a year to kick off sessions. You walk right onto the floor of both Houses. Many delicious details are elucidated, from the knockmarks on the Commons door made by the Crown's emissary, the Black Rod, to the line in the carpet members may not cross when in the throes of vigorous

You can tour portions of the Houses of Parliament.

debates. Booking ahead is advisable; otherwise, try your luck for openings at the ticket office next to the Jewel Tower, across the street.

Overseas visitors are permitted to observe some debates, but the wait can be as long as 2 hr. (line up outside the Cromwell Green visitor entrance). Check ahead, since security concerns may cause the government to review public access. The website also posts times of lower-level "Westminster Hall debates" in a committee room, where anyone can come on a first-come, first-served basis. Question Time is only allowed for U.K. residents by previous arrangement with their MP or a Member of the House of Lords.

The Palace runs an afternoon tea service (p. 89) overlooking the river (not the most posh, but a cool place). Sorry, but Elizabeth Tower (1859) beside the Houses—it contains the 13½-ton bell known as Big Ben plus four smaller bells—is usually only open to U.K. residents, and not at all until about 2021, when its current restoration will be completed. If the green Ayrton Light atop it burns, Parliament is sitting after dark. But see it soon: This aged building will close for several years after 2025 for a much-needed restoration.

Bridge St. and Parliament Sq., SW1. www.parliament.uk/visit. ℗ **020/7219-4114.** Admission £26 adults, £21 seniors and students, £11 children 5–15, free for children 4 and under, add £2 if booked the same day. Tours: Sat and most weekdays during Parliamentary recesses; times vary; always check ahead. Reservations recommended. Tube: Westminster.

Spencer House ★★ HISTORIC HOME   Currently owned by Rothschilds banking company, which hosts diplomatic and corporate events here, this lush home is the only surviving London mansion with an intact 18th-century interior; tours let you see the ground floor and a portion of the first floor. The house was begun in 1756 as a love nest by Diana Spencer's ancestors (and, by extension, the future king's); its lavish gilt and carved decor repeatedly invoke the symbols of fidelity and virility. Great War damage spooked the Spencer clan, who moved out in the 1920s, and since then, they've gradually transferred the most precious elements to their estate at Althorp, 193km (120 miles) north of the city, and replaced them with equally fantastic facsimiles— the library fireplace, for instance, took 4,000 hours to carve. The original Painted Room suite was once at the V&A. Groups are limited to 20, so arrive early to secure a spot.

27 St James's Place, SW1. www.spencerhouse.co.uk. ✆ **020/7514-1958.** Tours £15.50 adults; £12.50 students, seniors, and children 15 and under. Sun 10:30am–4:30pm; closed Jan and Aug. Tube: Green Park.

Tate Britain ★ MUSEUM   Tourists often wonder about the difference between the Tate Modern and this, its sister upstream on the Thames. Well, the Modern is for contemporary art of any origin, and the Britain, besides its calmer and more civilized affect, is mostly for British-made art made after 1500. Its art is far more approachable than the esoteric stuff at Bankside, and you'll see plenty of grade-A work, though not many recognizable masterpieces. Britain has a historic knack for collecting masterpieces, not so much for creating them, so a lot of the work is rich with relevance but highly imitative of classical or Renaissance styles—it's hard to shake the feeling that, artistically speaking, Britain was playing catch-up with the rest of Europe. The oldest portion of the collection, full of documentary or moralist works by William Hogarth, William Blake, and Joshua Reynolds, dips into British life from centuries ago, but it's not until the galleries progress chronologically into the modern era that you find works by visionaries such as Francis Bacon, John Singer Sargent, and James Abbott McNeill Whistler (those last two, granted, were not English but Americans in England) that reveal ebullient colors latent in the national mind.

Descriptions are pedantic ("this picture bridges the historical and the sublime") and paintings are hung salon-style, many at such altitude that lighting glare makes them inscrutable. But the 1-hr. tours (at 11am, noon, 2pm, and 3pm) help get around such shortcomings. The last tour of the day focuses on paintings by J. M. W. Turner, a highlight of the collection (see below).

Beyond temporary charged exhibitions (around £18; in 2019, one is an examination of Vincent van Gogh's relationship with Britain), there's a large, free permanent collection. Beloved paintings are constantly being rotated into storage, a frustrating habit with Tate, but some masterpieces can be relied upon. Turner's trenchant *The Field of Waterloo* (room 1810) was painted in 1818, 3 years after the battle; its shadowy piles of corpses, and of bereaved

The Tate Britain museum is for British-made art made after 1500.

family members searching them, is still considered a daring exposure of the true price of war. The oil-on-canvas ***Carnation, Lily, Lily, Rose*** (1840) by John Singer Sargent depicts children holding paper lanterns so luminous that when it was first exhibited in 1887, its worth was instantly recognized and it was purchased for the nation. John Everett Millais' depiction of a drowning ***Ophelia*** (1840) is also considered a treasure for its phenomenally tricky depiction of water; the artist painted the plants in the summer so he'd get them right and waited until winter to paint his model, a hat-shop girl, in a tub of water. Naturally, she caught a severe cold (he paid for her doctor's bill after her father threatened to sue). Kids love the double vision of ***The Cholmonde-ley Ladies*** (room 1540), two new mothers "born the same day, Married the same day, And brought to Bed the same day"; look closely and you'll realize they're not identical. Check out the sculptures, too, including forms by **Henry Moore,** who gets two rooms, and Barbara Hepworth. But the crowning attraction here is the **Turner Galleries,** with their expansive collection of J. M. W. Turners. Turner (1775–1851), the son of a Covent Garden barber, was a master of landscapes lit by gauzy, perpetual sunrise, and the dozens of paintings testify to both his undying popularity and his doggedly British tendency to convey information mostly by implication. Turner's work is lovely, if sleepy (the precise landscape painter John Constable called them "airy visions

The most fun way to get between the Tates is not the Tube (a circuitous route) but the **Tate Boat** (www.tate.org.uk/visit/tate-boat; ℰ **020/7887-8888**; £8.40 adults, half-off kids 15 and under, Oyster rate 10 percent off, Oyster with Travelcard one-third off), a 220-seat catamaran that zips along the Thames every 40 minutes between the Tate Britain and the Tate Modern during gallery opening times. Along the way, it supplies camera-ready views of the London Eye and the Houses of Parliament. Tate's entertainment! Buy at the piers or at a Tate.

painted with tinted steam"), but it's best appreciated if you understand its influence on subsequent artists. The free Tate App supplies some additional descriptions of major works. Maps are £1. There are two places to eat: a casual underground café and the **Rex Whistler** (p. 92), which in 1927 kicked off the trend of high museum dining.

Millbank, SW1. www.tate.org.uk/britain. ℰ **020/7887-8888.** Free admission. Daily 10am–6pm; closes 9:30pm one Fri every 2 months. Tube: Pimlico.

Westminster Abbey ★★★ HISTORIC SITE/CHURCH   If you have to pick just one church to see in London—nay, one church in the entire *world*—this is the one. The echoes of history are mind-blowing: The current building

Westminster Abbey is the one church you must see.

dates from the 1200s, but it was part of a monastery dating to at least 960. Every English monarch since 1066 has been crowned here (with three minor exceptions: Edward V, Edward VIII, and possibly Mary I). There are 17 monarchs interred here (deaths dating from 1066 to 1760—the crypts here are overstuffed, so now they go to Windsor), as are dozens of great writers and artists. Even if England's tumultuous history and the thought of bodies lying underfoot don't stir your imagination, the interior—in places, as intricate as lace—will earn your appreciation. A visit should take about 3 hours and should begin early, since entry lines (1.3 million tour a year) can be excruciating.

Unlike St Paul's Cathedral (p. 163), which has an airy, stately beauty, the much smaller Westminster is more like time's attic, packed with artifacts, memorials, tombs, and virtuosic shrines—a confluence of God, art, and dense history. It's easy to feel overloaded after just a few minutes. Take your time and don't get swept along in the current of visitors. Let them pass. There are stories to be told in every square meter of this place—name another building where there is such a staggering continuity of a nation's heritage.

A visit is likely to start with a welcome from a volunteer; the Abbey follows the Benedictine tradition, which dictates a warm reception for everyone. It's also still a functioning spiritual center, so there may be calls for prayer or moments of silence as you tour. You'll be in the Nave, passing Darwin's resting place (just after the first blue gate), and it only accelerates from there. Bombastic tombs abound; take your time absorbing their colonialist self-importance. Google one and you'll unravel a tale, such as the one Thomas Banks sculpted (1789) for Sir Eyre Coote, commander of the British Forces in India—"death interrupted his career of glory." Although his battles of conquest slaughtered thousands of Indians, he is attended by a weeping naked savage. All that ponderous stone, yet he (like many others memorialized in the Abbey) is not even buried here—he's in Hampshire.

The royal tombs are clustered in the region of the High Altar, where coronations and funerals are conducted. The most famous rulers of all time are truly *here*—not in story, but in body, a few inches behind marble slabs. Some are stashed in cozy side chapels (which once held medieval shrines before Cromwellians bashed them to pieces during the Reformation; some vandalism is still visible), but the oldest are on the sanctuary side of the ambulatory (aisle). The executed **Mary, Queen of Scots** was belatedly given a crypt of equal stature to her rival, **Elizabeth I,** by Mary's son **James I,** who gave himself only a marker for his own tomb beneath **Henry VII**'s elaborate resting place. Some **Stuart and Hanoverian monarchs** are also here (Charles II, Queen Anne, William and Mary) but don't have elaborate tombs. James I's infant daughter Sophia, who died aged 3 days, was given a creepy bassinet sarcophagus in the Lady Chapel (peer into it using a mirror).

The audio tour only picks up highlights, and that pushes you along too quickly if you're truly interested. The *Treasures of Westminster Abbey* book in the gift shop is useful for identifying oddities and learning about people

Westminster Abbey

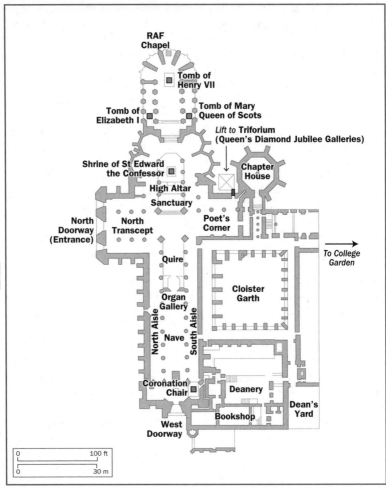

RAF Chapel

Tomb of Henry VII

Tomb of Elizabeth I

Tomb of Mary Queen of Scots

Lift to **Triforium (Queen's Diamond Jubilee Galleries)**

Shrine of St Edward the Confessor

Chapter House

High Altar

Sanctuary

North Doorway (Entrance)

North Transept

Poet's Corner

To College Garden

Quire

Cloister Garth

Organ Gallery

North Aisle

South Aisle

Nave

Coronation Chair

Deanery

Dean's Yard

Bookshop

West Doorway

0   100 ft

0   30 m

buried under them, but it's £15. If you have questions, approach anyone in a red robe; they're "vergers," or officers who attend to the church. They lead 90-min. tours (usually at 10am, but up to five times daily, for £5) and if you stump them, you may win an invitation to the atmospheric Library, a creaking loft that smells of medieval vellum and dust, where an archivist can answer you.

The South Transept is **Poet's Corner,** where Britain's great writers are honored. You'll see many plaques, but 60 percent (Shakespeare, Austen, Carroll, Wilde, the Brontës) are merely memorials. The biggest names who truly lie underfoot are Robert Browning, Geoffrey Chaucer (he was placed here

5

Westminster & St James's

EXPLORING LONDON

first, starting the trend), Charles Dickens, Thomas Hardy (without his heart, which was buried in Dorset), John Gay, Rudyard Kipling, George Frideric Handel (who popularized the use of the Abbey as a concert venue), Dr. Samuel Johnson, Laurence Olivier, Edmund Spenser, and Alfred Lord Tennyson. Ben Jonson is commemorated here, but is actually buried in the Nave near Isaac Newton, Charles Darwin, and new genius on the block, Stephen Hawking. Also in the Nave, in the northwest corner, look out for a batch of prime ministers underfoot.

TOP DON'T-MISS EXHIBITS AT WESTMINSTER ABBEY

o That oak seat in the last niche before your exit is the **Coronation Chair.** Unbelievably, nearly every English monarch since 1308 has been crowned on this excruciating-looking throne. The slot under the seat is for the 152kg (336-lb.) Stone of Scone, said to be used as a pillow by the Bible's Jacob, and a central part of Irish, Scottish, and English coronations since at least 700 B.C. After spending 7 centuries in the Abbey (except for when Scottish nationalists stole it for 4 months in late 1950), the Stone was returned to Scotland in 1996, where it's on view at Edinburgh Castle. It will return for every future coronation.

o **Oliver Cromwell,** who overthrew the monarchy and ran England as a republic, was buried with honors behind the High Altar in 1658. Three years later, after the monarchy was restored, his corpse was dug up, dragged to Tyburn (by the Marble Arch), hanged, decapitated, the body tossed into a common grave, and its head put on display outside the Abbey. (Didn't they realize he was already dead?) Today his much-abused cranium is at Sidney Sussex College in Cambridge. Cromwell's daughter, who died young, was mercifully allowed to remain buried in the Abbey. In the window above the grave, look for a hole that was left after a 1940 Blitz bombing.

o The **High Altar,** with a mosaic floor laid in the year 1268, is where coronations take place. The actual event sounds glamorous, but it's actually excruciating for everyone involved: Some 8,500 spectators are packed into this small space and the monarch's crown weighs a brutal 5.5 pounds.

o The **Quire** is where the choir sings; it comprises about 12 men and 30 or so boys who are educated at the adjoining Westminster Choir School, the last of its type in the U.K. The wooden stalls, in the Gothic style, are Victorian, and are so delicate they're dusted using vacuum cleaners.

A 2018 addition, made out of a very old space never before open to the public, is the 13th-century **Triforium,** a sort of horseshoe-shaped attic 70 feet up, with an astounding view down the length of the sanctuary—a lift tower was grafted to the venerable building just for it. This once-dusty aerie is now a mind-blowing museum about royal connections with the Abbey called the **Queen's Diamond Jubilee Galleries** (book a timed ticket in advance). You'll find such fascinating stuff as Prince William and Kate's marriage license, the lavishly illuminated book the **Litlyngton Missal** (1384), and the startlingly lifelike effigies used in centuries of monarchs' funerals—many, like Mary II, wearing their *original* garments. Back on the ground, look also for the panel concealing the **Chapter House,** which was made between 924 and 1030 and is Britain's oldest door. Time seems suspended in the **Cloister,** or courtyard. Writer Aphra Behn was buried in the East Cloister near the steps of the church when she "dyed" in 1689 (her wry inscription: "Here lies a Proof that Wit can never be Defence enough against Mortality."). Even better gardens are hidden away: Look for the fragrant and fountained **Little Cloister Garden,** blackened by 19th-century coal dust, and beyond that to the right, the wide **College Garden** (open Tues–Thurs), a tempting courtyard with daffodil beds, green lawns, and five plane trees dating to 1850. The garden is thought to be Britain's longest-established one, having been cultivated for nearly a millennium. **Westminster School,** started by the abbey's monks in the 1300s, stands nearby; past students include Christopher Wren, Edward Gibbon, John Gielgud, and pop musicians Thomas Dolby and Gavin Rossdale. (Incidentally, there haven't been monks in this complex for 550 years, yet Londoners persist in calling it an "Abbey.")

Get a real sense of the majesty of the space at a service. Evening prayer services with choirs from around the world are at 5pm weekdays; sung Eucharist is on Sundays at 11am, plus a Sunday organ recital at 5:45pm and evening service with simple hymns at 6:30pm (but check ahead, since services are sometimes shuffled to smaller, but equally historic, chapels). Holy Communion is daily at 8am, Matins are at 10am, and Evensong is Saturdays at 3pm. There's also a daily Eucharist at 12:30pm in the Nave. Next door, pop into **St Margaret's Chapel** (free), which the monks built in 1523 so they'd be left alone in peace. The Germans didn't comply: Some southern windows were destroyed by a bomb and were replaced by plain glass, and in addition to damage to the north wall, Pew 3 remains charred.

Broad Sanctuary, SW1. www.westminster-abbey.org. ✆ **020/7222-5152.** Admission £20 adults, £17 seniors and students, £9 children 6–16, free for children 5 and under; £2 more if you wait to purchase at the Abbey; half-price Wed after 4:30pm. Queen's Diamond Jubilee Galleries £5 more and require a timed ticket. Generally Mon–Tues and Thurs–Fri 9:30am–3:30pm; Wed 9:30am–6pm; Sat 9:30am–1:30pm, but check the online calendar; last admission 1 hr. before closing. Closed Sun for worship. Check ahead for closures. Tube: Westminster.

Other Westminster & St James' Attractions

The Banqueting House ★ HISTORIC SITE   The storied palace of Whitehall was home to some of England's flashiest characters, including Henry VIII. In a wrenching loss for art and architecture—to say nothing of bowling heritage, since Henry had an alley installed—it burned down in 1698. But if you had to pick just one room to survive, it would have been the one that did, designed with Italianate Renaissance assurance by Inigo Jones and completed in 1622. Henry never set foot in it, but another fateful king set his *last* foot in it: In 1649, Charles I walked onto the scaffold from a window that stood in the present-day staircase, and met his doom under an axe wielded by

Cromwell's republicans, many of whom (shades of modern fundamentalism here) thought that by executing the king of Divine Right, they were heralding the return of Christ himself. The reason to come here is to gape at the nine grandiose ceiling murals by Peter Paul Rubens in which the king is portrayed as a god. They give you a bold clue as to why the rabble would want to see His Highness brought low. Thoughtfully, mirrored tables help you inspect the ceiling without craning your head to behold why Charles lost his.

Whitehall at Horseguards Ave., SW1. www.hrp.org.uk. © **084/4482-7777.** Admission £6.50 adults, £5.50 seniors and students (including audio tour), free for children 15 and under; posted rates are higher and include a "voluntary donation"; £1 cheaper if bought online. Daily 10am–5pm; last admission 30 min. before closing. Tube: Charing Cross or Westminster.

Clarence House ★ HISTORIC HOME   The queen dictates who lives at which palace, and she herself lived at this four-story mansion, a part of St James's Palace, before she took the throne. Her mother dwelled here for nearly half a century until her 2002 death at age 101, and now it's chez Charles and Camilla. Charles, having a keener sense of public relations than any royal before him, decided to open the house, where royals have lived since 1827, during the summer when the family is away. You won't get to poke around the Prince's medicine cabinet, though; you can only see the ground floor. Clarence is more like a grand town house than a king's mansion, and that reflects the Windsors' homey, cluttered style, heavy on horse paintings and light on gilding and glitter.

Stableyard Rd., SW1. www.royalcollection.org.uk. © **020/7766-7303.** Admission £10.30 adults, seniors, and students; £6.20 children 5–16. Aug Mon–Fri 10am–4:30pm; Sat–Sun 10am–5:30pm; last admission 1 hr. before closing. Tube: Green Park.

Jewel Tower ★ HISTORIC SITE   Built around 1365, it's one of only two remnants left from the 1834 fire that ravaged the Royal Palace of Westminster. Quiet and easily overlooked, this three-level stone tower, once a moatside storehouse for Edward III's treasures, has walls so thick it was later considered an ideal setting for taking accurate measurements. So you'll see some explanation of weights-and-measures standards and some relics dug up from the moat (including a 1,200-year-old sword, and a bulbous bottle from the Sun, a 17th-c. tavern where Samuel Pepys drank).

Abingdon St., SW1. www.english-heritage.org.uk. © **020/7222-2219.** Admission £5.40 adults, £4.90 seniors and students, £3.20 children 5–15; posted prices are higher and include "gift aid." Apr–Sept daily 10am–6pm; Oct–Nov 2 daily 10am–5pm; Nov 3–Mar Sat–Sun 10am–4pm. Tube: Westminster.

The Queen's Gallery ★ MUSEUM   The queen inherited the mother of all art collections—1 million items including 7,000 paintings, 30,000 watercolors, and half a million prints, to say nothing of sculpture, furniture, and jewelry—but she shows only a tiny fraction here; the booty is also in her palaces such as Kensington and Hampton Court, and on loan. The few works (budget 1 hr.) are undoubtedly exceptional (one of the world's few Vermeers, a Rubens' self-portrait given to Charles I, glittering ephemera by Fabergé), but depending on what temporary exhibition supplements them, they may not be the cream of what she owns, and it may bore kids. The Gallery and the Royal Mews can be seen on a joint ticket (£19 adults, £17 seniors and students, £10 children 5–16).

149 Buckingham Palace Rd., SW1. www.royalcollection.org.uk. © 020/7766-7301. Admission £11 adults, £10 seniors and students, £5.50 children 5–16. Sept–July daily 10am–5:30pm; late July–Sept daily 9:30am–5:30pm; last admission 4:30pm. Tube: Victoria.

The Royal Mews ★ MUSEUM   Most visitors pop in to what amounts to the queen's garage in about 15 minutes. You'll see stables fit for a you-know-who (they barely smell at all) and Her Majesty's Rolls-Royces (many of which, at Prince Charles's behest, run on green fuels). You'll also overdose on learning about regulations for when this set of harnesses may be used and when that leather must be polished. The Queen's Gallery and the Mews can be seen on a joint ticket (£19 adults, £17 seniors and students, £10 children 5–16).

Buckingham Palace Rd., SW1. www.royalcollection.org.uk. © 020/7766-7302. Admission £11 adults, £10 seniors and students, £6.40 children 5–17. Apr–Oct 10am–5pm; Nov–March 10am–4pm; last admission 45 min. before closing. Tube: Victoria.

MARYLEBONE & MAYFAIR

Apsley House ★★ HISTORIC HOME   This is how you'd be rewarded if you became a colonial war hero: You'd get Hyde Park as a backyard. In 1815, Arthur Wellesley defeated Napoleon and became the Duke of Wellington, and later prime minister. The mansion, still in the family (they maintain private rooms), was filled with splendid thank-you gifts showered upon him by grateful nations, including a thousand-piece silver set from the Portuguese court. Still, he never seemed to get his nemesis off his mind: Under the grand staircase stands a colossal nude statue of Napoleon that the little emperor despised; the Duke cherished it as a token of victory. Apsley's supreme art stash, which was largely looted by the French from the Spanish royal family and never went home, includes a few Jan Bruegel the Elders, Diego Velasquez's virtuosic *The Waterseller of Seville* (you can understand why it was the artist's favorite work—just looking at it makes you thirsty); and Correggio's *The Agony in the Garden,* in a case fitted with a keyhole so the Duke could open it and polish it with a silk hankie. The Duke and his best friend lived here together after their wives died, and the whiff of faded masculine glory pervades the place like cigar smoke. In other circumstances, the Duke and Napoleon, who both liked fancy finery and fancier egos, would have been buddies. If you're also visiting Wellington Arch (p. 146), a joint ticket will save a couple of pounds.

149 Piccadilly. www.english-heritage.org.uk. © 0870/333-1181. Admission £10 adults, £9 seniors and students, £6 children 5–17 (including audio tour); posted prices are higher and include "gift aid." Apr–Oct Wed–Sun 11am–5pm; Nov–Mar Sat–Sun 11am–5pm. Check ahead for closures. Tube: Hyde Park Corner.

Handel & Hendrix Museum ★ HISTORIC HOME   Here's a pleasant *Messiah* complex. This Mayfair building, the German-born composer's home from 1723 (he was its first tenant) to his death in 1759, has lived many lives—before the museum's 2001 opening, conservators chipped 28 layers of paint off the interior walls to uncover the original grey color. In its day, it was a factory for his celebrity: Handel would compose in one room, debut his work in another (there are still frequent performances; check the website), sleep in a third, and sell scores and tickets to the public from a ground-floor shop. None of the furniture was his, but Handel fans should investigate the composer's collection at the Foundling Museum (p. 118), where he was a crucial patron. In 2016, the museum expanded to encompass the top floors of a neighboring building, where legendary guitarist Jimi Hendrix lived in 1968 and 1969. Here, in a cozy flat, his girlfriend Kathy Etchingham tried to give him his first stable home; here he made music and love, entertained, filmed interviews (which gave curators images to reconstruct it down to the last detail)—and played Handel records to absorb the genius of his neighbor across the centuries. But Etchingham's nurturing efforts were to no avail; soon after they broke up, he died at age 27 in Notting Hill.

25 Brook St., W1. www.handelhendrix.org. ⓒ **020/7495-1685.** Admission £10 adults, £5 children 5–16 (Handel House only: £7.50 adult, £3 child). Mon–Sat 11am–6pm, last admission 5pm. Tube: Bond Street.

Royal Academy of Arts ★ MUSEUM   Britain's first art school, founded in 1768, relocated here to Burlington House, a Palladian-style mansion away from Piccadilly's fumes (plus a few bars and an exclusive restaurant, The Keeper's House). In 2018, it completed a renovation that connected an adjacent building, linked it with modern elements such as polished concrete and picture windows, and found new space to put some previously stored works on display (the Royal Academy Collection Gallery contains those, plus Michelangelo's only marble sculpture in Britain, an unfinished circular relief of Mary with the babies Jesus and John). But in truth, the main reason to come is whatever crowd-pleasing paid exhibition is on. The biggest event, and always worth it, is the annual **Summer Exhibition,** which without fail since 1769 has displayed the best works from anonymous submissions; careers are made by it. Don't miss the wooden red "Phone Box No. 1" tucked behind the stone front gate—it was the 1924 prototype for what we now recognize as an international icon.

Burlington House, Piccadilly or 6 Burlington Gardens, W1. www.royalacademy.org.uk. ⓒ **020/7300-8000.** Free admission. Sat–Thurs 10am–6pm; Fri 10am–10pm; last admission 30 min. before closing. Tube: Piccadilly Circus or Green Park.

Speakers' Corner ★ LANDMARK   Near the northeast corner of Hyde Park, where Edgware Road meets Bayswater Road, Londoners of yore congregated for public executions. By the early 1800s, the gathered crowds were jeering at hangings instead of cheering them, and the locale's reputation for public outcry became entrenched. An Act of Parliament in 1872 finally legitimized it as a place of free speech, and its tradition of well-intentioned protest

Speaker's Corner in Hyde Park is an authorized place of free speech.

has evolved into a quirky weekend attraction. Laborers and suffragettes fomented social change here, but these days, you're more likely to encounter a rogues' gallery of idealists and religious nutters. Anyone can show up, always on Sunday mornings after 7am, with a soapbox (or, these days, a step-ladder), plus an axe to grind, and orate about anything from Muslim relations to the superiority of 1970s disco—but if they don't have the wit to appease the crowd, they stand a good chance of being jibed, or at the very least vigorously challenged. In true British style, most speakers refrain from profanity. Even the heckling is usually polite. ("Communists, violent racists, vegetarians," reported Arthur Frommer in 1957. "They undergo the finest heckling in the world, a vicious repartee. . . .")

Tube: Marble Arch, exits 4, 5, 8, or 9.

The Wallace Collection ★★★ MUSEUM   A little bit V&A (decorative arts and furniture), a little bit National Gallery (paintings and portraits), but with a boutique French flair, the Wallace celebrates fine living in an extrava-gant 19th-century city mansion, the former Hertford House. Rooms drip with chandeliers, clocks, suits of armor, and furniture, usually of royal provenance, and there's not a clunker among the paintings. While other museums were stocking up on Renaissance works, the Wallaces, visionaries of sorts, were buying 17th- and 18th-century artists for cheap, and now its collection shines.

DEATH TAKES A holiday

If you're a major musical star, stay away from London! It seems a disproportionate number of singers have met untimely ends here (especially in the summer). These houses aren't open to the public, but their grim pasts make them music landmarks:

o **June 22, 1969, 4 Cadogan Lane, Belgravia** (Tube: Sloane Square): **Judy Garland** overdosed on barbiturates (Seconal) and expired in the bathroom of the two-room flat owned by her fifth husband of three months, Mickey Deans. The public outpouring of grief, and its suppression by police in New York City, is credited with starting, or at least fueling, the gay rights movement as we know it today.

o **September 18, 1970, 22 Lansdowne Crescent, Notting Hill** (Tube: Notting Hill Gate): In a basement flat of the Samarkand Hotel, **Jimi Hendrix** washed down nine Vesperax sleeping pills with alcohol. An ambulance was summoned, but arrived too late. The plot thickened 26 years later, when the last person to see him alive, girlfriend Monika Dannemann, was found asphyxiated in a car in Seaford, East Sussex, not long after being accused in court of keeping secrets about Hendrix's final moments.

o **July 29, 1974 and September 7, 1978, Flat 12, 9 Curzon Place, Mayfair** (Tube: Hyde Park Corner): **"Mama" Cass Elliot** of The Mamas and the Papas was found dead in between solo performances at the London Palladium in a flat owned by songwriter Harry Nilsson, who wasn't home. Contrary to lore, she didn't die by choking on a ham sandwich but from a heart attack in her sleep brought on by morbid obesity (she was 165cm/5'5" and weighed 108kg/238 lb.). Four years after Elliot's death, **Keith Moon,** drummer of The Who, died in the same flat. His undoing: chlormethiazole edisylate, a prescribed anti-alcohol drug. Horrified that two of his friends should die while borrowing his apartment, Nilsson quickly sold it to Moon's bandmate Pete Townshend.

o **July 23, 2011, 30 Camden Square, Camden** (Tube: Camden Town): After a period of abstinence, **Amy Winehouse** binged on vodka and succumbed to alcohol poisoning in her bedroom in this 2,500-square-foot townhouse, where she'd lived only a few months. Security guards were there but thought she was only sleeping. For years afterward, fans would leave bottles and cans of booze outside as a macabre tribute.

You might recognize Jean-Honoré Fragonard's *The Swing* (Oval Drawing Room), showing a maiden kicking her slipper to her suitor below. Peter Paul Rubens' *The Rainbow Landscape* is also here (East Drawing Room), as is the world's most complete room of furniture belonging to Marie-Antoinette (Study; look for her initials hidden around a keyhole on one cabinet). Thomas Gainsborough's *Mrs. Mary Robinson "Perdita"* (West Room) depicts the sloe-eyed actress in mid-affair with the Prince of Wales; she holds a token of his love, a miniature portrait, in her right hand. If she exudes suspicion, it's for good reason—the Prince dumped her before the paint was dry. Don't miss the recently restored Great Gallery, a stupendous tour de force of world-class old master paintings. Red folders contain descriptions of pictures, and gold ones are for furniture—the information even tells who owned them before they got here. Be in the Ground Floor State Rooms at the top of the hour, when a chorus of golden musical clocks announce midday direct from the 1700s. Kids should grab a free trail map, which leads them to the most attention-holding works, but adults should get the audio guide which highlights 80 of the best items for £4. The Wallace Restaurant, in the covered courtyard, has an exemplary atmosphere but stupidly high prices, although its French-styled afternoon tea is under £19 or just £7 if you only want tea and scones.

Hertford House, Manchester Sq., W1. www.wallacecollection.org. ☏ **020/7563-9500.** Free admission. Daily 10am–5pm. Tube: Bond Street.

Wellington Arch ★ LANDMARK   When it was finished in 1830, it was intended as a triumphal entry to central London (Marble Arch, at Hyde Park's northern corner, was originally Queen Victoria's triumphal entry to Buckingham Palace). Now it's the equivalent of a shrug. Minor anecdotes of its relocation and the switch from Wellington's original statue on top to a smaller statue (*Peace Descending upon War*, the largest bronze sculpture in Europe) are all this handsome landmark can muster in its little museum, which also discusses the period when the Arch served as a police station. If you buy a joint ticket with the Apsley House, across Piccadilly (p. 142), you'll save a couple of pounds; you can take an elevator up with the admission price.

Hyde Park Corner, Apsley Way, W1. www.english-heritage.org.uk. ☏ **020/7930-2726.** Admission £5.40 adults, £4.90 seniors and students, £3.20 children 5–17; posted prices are higher and include "gift aid." Apr–Sept daily 10am–6pm; Oct daily 10am–5pm; Nov–Mar daily 10am–4pm. Tube: Hyde Park Corner.

KENSINGTON & KNIGHTSBRIDGE

Diana Memorial Fountain ★ LANDMARK   In July 2004, the queen came to Hyde Park, probably grudgingly, to open an unusual gated fountain designed to conjure the memory of the mother of her grandchildren and a longtime thorn in her side, Princess Diana. As designed by American architect Kathryn Gustafson, this graceful, O-shaped fountain undulates down a gentle slope, sending two flumes of water gurgling into a collecting pool. At three points, bridges carry you to the center. Rather than putting you in a state of remembrance, it may put you into a state of wanting to ride it on an inner tube. Reach it from the Alexandra Gate at Kensington Gore, Knightsbridge, up Exhibition Road, and don't confuse it for the Diana, Princess of Wales Playground in Kensington Gardens or the 17th-century Diana Fountain.

Between West Carriage Dr., Rotten Row, and The Serpentine, Hyde Park. www.royal parks.org.uk. ☏ **030/0061-2350.** Free admission. Apr–Aug daily 10am–8pm; Sept daily 10am–7pm; Mar and Oct daily 10am–6pm; Nov–Feb daily 10am–4pm. Check website for maintenance closures. Tube: South Kensington.

Kensington & Knightsbridge

EXPLORING LONDON

Enjoying a summer day at the Princess Diana Memorial Fountain.

Kensington Palace ★ PALACE   Most people know it as the place where Lady Diana raised Princes William and Harry with Prince Charles from 1984 to 1996, but now it's where Prince William, Kate, George, Charlotte, and Louis live when they're in town. (No, you won't find their toothbrushes in the bathroom.) It has been a royal domicile since 1689, when William and Mary took control of an existing home (then in the country, far from town, to ease William's asthma) and made it theirs. Handsome and haughty, with none of the symmetry that defined later English tastes, the redbrick palace is not as ostentatious as you might expect. At least from the outside. Historic Royal Palaces, grasping for currency, installed junky art installations (voices whispering from gramophones, graffiti-like quotations scrawled across carpets and walls) based on scandals that happened here. The venerable palace was stripped of most of its context and now it's a spook house for art snobs. The newly reopened King's State Apartments, pegged to King George III and Queen Caroline, is explained to visitors not with a thoughtful historical dossier but with a scratch-and-sniff guide to odors that might have filled the palace once. Kids may appreciate the costumed characters wandering about, but anyone who can reach the pedals knows it's all style over substance. Queen Victoria has her own section, but she's given the trashy treatment, too—rather than teaching visitors what enabled a girl of 18 to rise to master the most powerful empire in the world, it shows her failing the Bechdel test and living in terms of men: as a good girl, a loving wife, and a grieving widow. It's also misleading: One room draped in black leads you to believe Prince Albert died here, but no, he died at Windsor.

Thankfully, the walk-through still includes the magnificent King's Staircase, lined with delicate canvas panels whose perimeters are rigged with tissue paper slivers that will tear as a warning of shifting or swelling. The staircase is considered so precious that it wasn't opened to the public until 2004, 105 years after the rest of the palace first accepted sightseers. In the Gallery there's a working Anemoscope, which has told the outside wind direction since 1694, and a map of the world as known in that year; you'll also see gowns worn by HM the Queen, Diana, and Princess Margaret, who lived here as well. Overall, though, if you're short on time, this pandering Palace is no longer a must-see.

Kensington Gardens, W8. www.hrp.org.uk. ⓒ **084/4482-7777.** Admission £23 adults, £18.30 seniors and students, £11.50 kids 5–15, including audio tour; higher posted prices include a "voluntary donation"; up to £3.50 cheaper when booked online. Mar–Oct daily 10am–6pm; Nov–Feb daily 10am–5pm; last admission 1 hr. before closing. Tube: High St. Kensington or Queensway.

Natural History Museum ★★ MUSEUM   The commodious NHM, which attracts 4.4 million visitors a year (mostly families, and by far the most of the three big South Ken museums), is good for several hours' wander, but

The dodo bird, now extinct, lives on at the Natural History Museum.

you'll have plenty of company. In all ways, it's a zoo. You get a hall of dinosaur bones, a taxidermist's menagerie, racks of rocks, and case after case of stuffed goners. Mostly, you'll encounter the wildest creatures of all: lurching, wailing, scampering children in all their varieties, because everything here, down to the simplified signage and touchable replicas, is pitched to kids. On weekends and school holidays, the outdoor queue can be an hour long, so go at opening and enter through Exhibition Road for lighter crowds. The trove is rich: At the top of the stairs, the **Treasures** gallery holds such historically meaningful stuff as a dodo skeleton and Britain's only moon rock. The pretend kitchen full of hiding places for insects and **Creepy Crawlies** (the

Green Zone) are longtime visitor favorites, as is the **Red Zone** (the Earth Galleries), anchored by a toned-down, ride-along mock-up of a Japanese supermarket jolted by the 1995 Kobe earthquake. Even the dinosaurs (in the **Blue Zone**) are supplemented by scary robotic estimations of how they sounded and moved. The **Darwin Centre**'s Cocoon looks like a seven-story egg laid in the back atrium; hidden inside are some 20 million bottled specimens (including those that came back on the *Beagle*) on 27km/17 miles of shelves, which you will not see. Most of the discussion here, and throughout the museum, is aimed at a child's mind, with signs answering such unasked questions such as why we study nature, but now and then you'll see an expert through a window into the stacks of the Centre who can use a microphone to respond to more intelligent concerns.

Even if you don't give a hooey about remedial ecology, the cathedral-like 1880 Victorian building is unforgettable. Columns crawl with carved monkeys whimsically clinging to the terra cotta and plants creeping across ceiling panels. Daily Nature Live talks are given at 2:30pm on a huge range of topics; they're put online, too. The Museum's brainiacs even cultivate a garden and pond (the **Orange Zone;** open Apr–Oct) that attract a range of English creatures and flowers. Kids 6 and under can borrow free Explorer backpacks with pith helmets, binoculars, and activities (they tend to run out early on weekends); and those 7 to 14 should look for the hands-on **Investigate** lab in the basement (afternoons are less crowded). All that and the requisite ceiling whale, which washed up on an Irish beach in 1891 and is now stuck to the top of the main Hintze Hall.

Cromwell Rd., SW7. www.nhm.ac.uk. ℘ **020/7942-5000.** Free admission. Daily 10am–5:50pm. Tube: South Kensington.

Royal Albert Hall ★★ CONCERT HALL

In addition to being a great concert venue, the Royal Albert is also one of London's great landmarks, and you don't need a seat to enjoy it. Conceived by Queen Victoria's husband Albert, it opened in 1871, a decade after his death from typhoid (Vicky was so distraught that she didn't speak at the opening ceremonies). If you don't mind stairs, you can take a 1-hr. tour. The hall contains such oddities as Britain's longest single-weave carpet (in the corridors), the Queen's Box (still leased to the monarchy), and a spectacular glass

Royal Albert Hall is one of London's great landmarks.

dome (41m/135 ft. high and supported only at its rim). Only groups can go backstage, however: Some 320 performances a year are presented, many with less than 24 hours' set-up time, and a flow of sightseers would be in the way.

Kensington Gore, SW7. www.royalalberthall.com. ✆ **020/7589-8212.** Free admission to lobby, tours £13.25 adults, £11.25 seniors and students, £6.25 children 18 and under. Tours available most days; times vary, generally 10am–4pm. Tube: South Kensington.

Science Museum ★★ MUSEUM It's really two museums, one old-fashioned and one progressive, that have been grafted together and embellished with a few tacky gimmicks and blatant corporate propaganda, but it's a firm family favorite, attracting 3.4 million visits in 2015. So many interesting exhibitions are on display here that you'll probably run out of time. The old-school section, which began collecting in 1857 and is split over six levels, is an embarrassment of riches from the artifact archives of science and technology: 1969's *Apollo 10* command module; "Puffing Billy," the world's oldest surviving steam engine; and the first Daguerreotype camera from 1839. In 2015, the rare clocks and watches of London's prestigious Clockmakers' Museum, most dating from 1600 to 1850, were added. Upper floors are full of model ships and 1950s computers (second floor, the Information Age), veterinary medicine (fifth floor), and in the hangarlike third floor, aviation. Highlights there: a complete De Havilland Comet, which was the first jetliner (1952), a slice of a jumbo jet, and a modified Vickers Vimy bomber, the first plane to cross the Atlantic without stopping. It was flown by Arthur Whitten Brown, who promptly became the first person to report jet lag. He called it something much less catchy: the "difficulty of adjustment to the sudden change in time." New is the Mathematics gallery (second floor), one of the last projects overseen by the late architect Zaha Hadid, full of lovely swooping forms inspired by the aerodynamic flow around its central object: an experimental Handley Page aircraft from 1929 that was only made possible by math (or as the English call it, "maths").

The high-concept wing buried in the back of the ground floor is easy to miss, but seek it out. A cobalt-blue cavern for interactive games and displays, it bears little relation to the mothballed museum you just crossed through. The Antenna exhibition (ground floor) is exceptionally cutting-edge, and updated regularly with the latest breakthroughs; past topics have included biodegradable cell phones implanted with seeds and building bricks grown from bacteria. The interactive exhibits of Launchpad (third floor; heat-seeking cameras, dry ice, and the like) enchant kids. But not everything in the museum is enchanting. The gift shop (mostly mall-style toys) and guidebook disappoint. And when you've got the actual Model T, why charge an extra £11 for a gimmicky IMAX 3D cinema or £12 on motion simulator rides? Fortunately, the merits override the patronization.

Exhibition Rd., SW7. www.sciencemuseum.org.uk. ✆ **087/0870-4868.** Free admission. Daily 10am–6pm, last admission 5:15pm. Tube: South Kensington.

The interior of the V&A museum is all about the eye candy of objects.

V&A ★★★ MUSEUM If it was pretty, well-made, or valuable, the British Empire wanted to possess it. As a decorative arts repository, the Victoria & Albert, occupying a haughty High Victorian edifice (it was endowed by the proceeds from the first world's fair, the Great Exhibition of 1851), is about the eye candy of objects—not so much for paintings, but some—and if you're paying attention, it tells the story of mankind through the development of style and technique.

As for how to tour it, the ground floor, a jumbled grid of rooms, has lots of good stuff, but lots more bric-a-brac (Korean pots, 1,000-year-old rock crystal jugs from Egypt) that you'll probably walk past with polite but hasty appreciation. Rooms are arranged by country of origin or by medium (ironwork, tapestries, and the like) but you'll want to see the **20th Century** (rooms 74, 76; level 3), which surprises by including objects you may have once kept in your home (a Dyson vacuum cleaner, mobile phones); the U.K.'s only permanent **architecture** gallery (rooms 127–128a; level 4); the ever-popular **fashion** gallery (room 40) for looks both historic and haute; and endless slices of **medieval stained glass** (rooms 83–84; level 3). Wherever you go, if you see a drawer beneath a display case, open it, because many treasures are stored out of the light.

TOP DON'T-MISS EXHIBITS AT THE V&A

o The **Europe 1600–1815 galleries,** to the left as you enter, were recently renovated to be bright, rich, and instructive. They're crammed with 1,100 precious objects including 300-year-old furniture, 18th-century court clothing that looks like it was made yesterday, and even an entire bedchamber from the 1600s. Stream the audio guide from www.vam.ac.uk/europeaudio (there's free Wi-Fi).

o The seven **Raphael Cartoons** (room 48a), 500 years old in 2015, are probably the most priceless items. These giant paper paintings—yes, paper—were created by the hand of Raphael as templates for the weavers of his 10 tapestries for the Sistine Chapel. Before Queen Victoria moved them here, they hung for around 175 years in the purpose-built Cartoon Gallery at Hampton Court Palace (p. 182). The colors are fugitive, meaning they're fading: Christ's red robe, painted with plant-based madder lake, has turned white—his reflection in the water, painted with a different pigment, is still red. Yet the queen recently decided people could take flash photos of it.

o None of the sculptures in the sky-lit **Cast Court** (rooms 46 and 46a) are original. They're casts of the greatest hits in Renaissance art, and they crowd the room like a yard sale. They were put here in 1873 for the poor, who could never hope to see the real articles for themselves. Find Ghiberti's doors to the baptistery at Florence's San Giovanni, whose design kicked off the artistic frenzy of the Renaissance, and Michelangelo's *David,* floppy puppy feet and all; he was fitted with a fig leaf for royal visits. Depressingly, many of these replicas are now in better shape than the originals.

o Tipu Sultan of India hated imperialists. So, in the 1790s he commissioned an automaton of a tiger sinking its fangs into one. A crank on **Tippoo's Tiger** (room 41) activates a clockwork that makes an Englishman's hand flail while a hidden keyboard plays a death knell. To no avail; in the end, Tipu was killed by Europeans and the English brought this home. It has been a favorite since 1808, when it was part of the East India Company's trophy museum.

o The **Great Bed of Ware** (room 57), a 10-by-11-foot four-poster of carved oak that dates to about 1590, was once a tourist attraction at a country inn, renowned enough for Shakespeare to mention it in *Twelfth Night:* "big enough for the bed of Ware." As you admire it, consider that in those days, bed canopies were installed to protect sleepers from insects that might tumble out of their thatched roofs and into their mouths. Canopied beds, a mark of luxury today, were a sign of a humbler home. Nearby is James II's silver-embroidered wedding suit (1673, room 56).

o The **Ardabil carpet** (room 42), the world's oldest dated carpet (copies lay on the floors of 10 Downing St. and Hitler's Berlin office alike), is from 1539. To preserve its dyes, it's lit 10 minutes at a time on every half-hour.

o The **Hereford Screen** (1862, Ironworks balcony) is a liturgical riot by Gilbert Scott, the architect of the "Eros" (p. 130) and the St Pancras Renaissance Hotel (p. 36). It took 38 conservators 13 months to restore the 8-ton choir screen to its full golden, brassy, painted Gothic Revival glory.

o The **Gilbert Collection** (rooms 70–73) of impossibly fine jewel boxes, cameos, silver, and mosaics was amassed by a rich enthusiast who originally gave them to LACMA in California, where he made his fortune. But in a museum-world scandal, he stripped them from it for not showing the whole collection at once. Despite that slap in the face, the V&A still displays only highlights and the galleries may be closed.

o One volume of Da Vinci's legendary **notebooks** is on display in room 64 (Medieval and Renaissance).

o It's hard to forget the riotous figures and tilework of the **Ceramic Staircase** (1860s); originally, every staircase here was to look like this, but when the cost became apparent, even those excessive Victorians satisfied themselves with just one. To find it, turn left after coming through the Exhibition Road entrance.

o The second, third, and fourth levels have less space and therefore are more intuitive. Look for the **Theatre & Performance** collection (103–106b), which lends the spark of modern familiarity to the proceedings; you can see, for example, Vivien Leigh's Oscar, Fred Astaire's tux, Kylie Minogue's dressing room, and costumes from *The Lion King* and *Wicked*.

Questions about what you're seeing will be referred to the Info Desk, which in turn may be referred to a search on the public website. Such is the sad reality of today's heavily touristed museum. That's why planning pays off: Download a map and you'll save £2, and download its free app to see what hot-ticket exhibitions are coming, many of them on topics that pander to a wide paying audience (David Bowie, Pink Floyd) or are blatantly influenced by sponsors (historic underwear). £20 is a typical upcharge for an exhibition here. Free 1-hr. introductory tours are given at 10:30am, and 12:30, 1:30, and 3:30pm, with one for the Medieval and Renaissance galleries at 11:30am and another for the British galleries at 2:30pm. Kids can borrow delightful "Back-Packs" at the Sackler Centre Reception, which contain activity sets that engage them in some of the museum's most eye-catching holdings. More goodies for kids are listed at www.vam.ac.uk/families and exhibited at the Museum of Childhood (p. 174). Even the cafe (the world's first museum restaurant) is gorgeous; have a coffee in the extraordinary Gamble Room (1865–1878), a visual feast in ceramic tile and enameled iron. Also visit the V&A's western exterior; scarred during the Blitz, the stonework was left unrepaired as a memorial.

Cromwell Rd., SW7. www.vam.ac.uk. ℭ **020/7942-2000.** Free admission. Sat–Thurs 10am–5:45pm; Fri 10am–10pm, with reduced gallery openings. Tube: South Kensington.

Other Kensington & Knightsbridge Attractions

Albert Memorial ★ LANDMARK   Albert, Queen Victoria's German-born husband (and, um, first cousin), was a passionate supporter of the arts who piloted Britain from one dazzling creative triumph to another. But when he died suddenly of typhoid (some say Crohn's disease) in 1861 at age 42, the devastated queen abruptly withdrew from the gaiety and remained in mourning until her death in 1901, shaping the Victorian mentality. She arranged for this astounding spire—part bombast, part elegy—to be erected in 1872 opposite the concert hall Albert spearheaded. Some of its nearly 200 figures represent the continents and the sciences, and some, higher up, represent angels and virtues. It's Victorian high-mindedness in stone. At the center, as if on an altar, is Albert himself, gleaming in gold. Guided explanations happen at 2 and 3pm on the first Sunday of each month, March to December (ℭ **020/8969-0104;** no reservations required; 45 min.; £9).

Kensington Gardens. www.royalparks.org.uk. Tube: South Kensington.

The Design Museum ★ MUSEUM Newly relocated to a cavernous landmark modernist building in Kensington, the Design Museum is where you'll find the cool kids of current style and architecture waxing esoteric about their thought processes in themed exhibitions. The top floor balcony celebrates everyday objects (typeface, laptops) that have been designed well. In point of fact, it's more of a gallery than a museum, appealing more to designers than to scholars. Everything is imbued with an awareness of how design can improve the lives of the less fortunate, a notion that's at best Victorian and at worst condescending, and the curators occasionally appear to sell out to sponsors (a recent show rhapsodized about Cartier wristwatches), but the rewards may be richer if there's a good temporary exhibition on. The shop has some interesting finds, as you might suspect.

224–238 Kensington High St., W8. www.designmuseum.org. © **020/3862-5900.** Permanent collection free, exhibitions charge £10–£16. Daily 10am–6pm; last admission 5pm. Tube: High St. Kensington.

THE SOUTH BANK, SOUTHWARK & BOROUGH

Florence Nightingale Museum ★ MUSEUM You probably don't know much about her now, but spend 45 minutes in this small and well-designed biographical museum (on the grounds of the hospital with which she worked) and you'll brim with newfound respect for this consequential person—as a founder of sensible nursing practices, as a leader who took no guff, and ultimately, as an all-around hard-core badass. It's broken into three sections, attractively presented and with kid-friendly elements: her headstrong youth, her fame-making work whipping the troop hospitals of the Crimean War into shape, and her subsequent years of cranky reclusiveness and ceaseless writing.

2 Lambeth Palace Rd., SE1. www.florence-nightingale.co.uk. © **020/7620-0374.** Admission £7.50 adults, £4.80 seniors and students, £3.80 children 15 and under. Daily 10am–5pm; last entry 4:30pm. Tube: Westminster, Waterloo, or Lambeth North.

Garden Museum ★ MUSEUM Here, in a deconsecrated church (the tower, which you can climb, dates to 1377), you'll find artifacts and academic respect paid to the greatest gardeners of Britaindom, including John Tradescant the Elder, a green thumb and seed pioneer who himself was planted in the churchyard in 1638. You'll find an assortment of antique gardening implements, a collection of gardening-related art, plus a few curios such as an original 18th-century bronze season pass token for the Vauxhall Gardens—yes, only horticulture nerds need apply. The museum was set up in 1977 as a way to preserve the abandoned church of St Mary's, but—garden museum irony alert—no one thought to dig down. In 2016, workers discovered a vault containing a collapsing pile of 30 lead coffins topped with a rusted Archbishop's miter cap—like your nightmare's nightmare. One of the corpses is Richard

City & South Bank Attractions

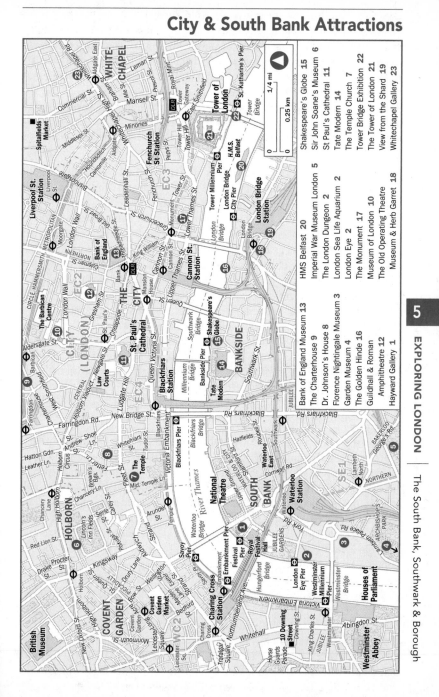

Bank of England Museum 13
The Charterhouse 9
Dr. Johnson's House 8
Florence Nightingale Museum 3
Garden Museum 4
The Golden Hinde 16
Guildhall & Roman
Amphitheatre 12
Hayward Gallery 1

HMS Belfast 20
Imperial War Museum London 5
The London Dungeon 2
London Sea Life Aquarium 2
London Eye 2
The Monument 17
Museum of London 10
The Old Operating Theatre
Museum & Herb Garret 18

Shakespeare's Globe 15
Sir John Soane's Museum 6
St Paul's Cathedral 11
Tate Modern 14
The Temple Church 7
Tower Bridge Exhibition 22
The Tower of London 21
View from the Shard 19
Whitechapel Gallery 23

Bancroft, who oversaw creation of the King James Bible, and as many as five others are Archbishops of Canterbury, like England's popes. You can find the clear, sealed panel leading to their chamber in The Ark. There are other graves to see: Captain Bligh of *Bounty* fame is in the yard. A more cheerful fact: The roundabout outside, at Lambeth Bridge, is where Clark Griswold told his kids, "Big Ben! Parliament!" (You either know it or you don't).

5 Lambeth Palace Rd., SE1. www.gardenmuseum.co.uk. ℮ **020/7401-8865.** Admission £10 adults, £8.50 seniors, £5 students, free for children 5 and under. Church tower another £3. Sun-Fri 10:30am–5pm; Sat 10:30am–6pm (but check ahead). Closed first Mon of month. Tube: Westminster, Waterloo, or Lambeth North.

Imperial War Museum London ★★ MUSEUM   One of London's unexpectedly gripping museums has a deceptive name. It's not just for military buffs, and it's no gun-fondling armory, even if there is a Spitfire hanging from the rafters. Instead of merely showcasing heavy implements of death, which it does, this museum—the latest tenant of the commodious former mental hospital known as Bedlam—takes care to convey the sensations, feelings, and motivations of soldiers and civilians caught in past conflicts. It is ultimately not about weapons but a museum about *people* at war. In addition to easy-to-grasp background on major conflicts, the museum intelligently balances tanks and planes with storytelling that unravels propaganda. In 2014, the IWM was expensively renovated from a brick storehouse into a gleaming facility—while some exhibits were perhaps oversimplified, the First World War Galleries (reserve ahead in peak season) are the most advanced, best-stocked, most comprehensible, and most moving you'll ever see on the topic, followed by the segment on the Holocaust.

Lambeth Rd., SE1. www.iwm.org.uk. ℮ **020/7416-5000.** Free admission. Daily 10am–6pm; last admission 5:30pm. Tube: Lambeth North or Elephant & Castle.

London Eye ★★★ OBSERVATIONAL WHEEL   The Eye was erected in 1999 as the Millennium Wheel, and like many temporary vantage points, it became such a sensation—and a money-spinner—that it was made permanent. It rises above everything in this part of the city—at 135m/443 ft. high, it's 1½ times taller than the Statue of Liberty. The 30-min. ride above the Thames affords an unmatched and unobstructed perspective on the prime tourist territory; there's no narration, but six tablets elucidate what's before you. On a clear day, you can see to Windsor, but even on an average day, the entire West End bows down before you. That's why you should either go as soon as you arrive in the city, to orient yourself, or on your last day in town (my choice), when you can appreciate what you've seen. The whirl is adulterated by a lame "4D Experience" movie (a camera flies over London while a fan and bubbles blow in your face—it's Orlando-fied twaddle) but it's included in the price and you can skip that if you want. Each of the 32 enclosed capsules, which accommodate up to 28 people, is climate-controlled and rotates so gradually that it's easy to forget you're moving—which means this ride will upset only the desperately height-averse. By the time you summit, you'll have true 360-degree views unobstructed by the support frame. The ticket queue often looks positively wicked (book ahead if possible), but it moves quickly, chewing through 15,000 riders a day, 800 per revolution. The Shard (p. 160) is much taller (but costs much more). *Tip:* Booking online saves waiting in the first queue, but you will be bewildered by the ticket options. Basically, a Standard timed ticket will do, although you can pay up to £37 to go anytime you want ("Flexi") rather than stick to a reservation or to wait in a shorter line ("Fast Track").

Riverside Building, County Hall, SE1. www.londoneye.com. No public phone. Advance purchase prices for standard ticket: £23 adults, £19 children 4–15, free for children 3 and under; prices go up as capacity decreases, so book ahead. Walk-up prices 10% higher. Apr–June 10am–9pm; July–August 10am–9:30pm; Jan–Mar and Sept–Dec 10am–8:30pm. Tube: Waterloo or Westminster.

The Old Operating Theatre Museum & Herb Garret ★★

MUSEUM   In the mid-1800s, before general anesthesia, St Thomas' Hospital used the attic of a neighboring church as a space where surgeries, mostly amputations and other quick-hit procedures, could be conducted where students could watch but other patients couldn't hear the agonized screams. When the hospital moved in 1862, it was abandoned, sealed away, and forgotten. It was considered lost until 1956, when an enterprising historian thought to look in the attic, and found the secret surgical stadium behind a wall. Creep up a tight wooden spiral staircase once used by the bell ringer and you'll find the theater, now the centerpiece of a ghoulish, but carefully educational, museum delving into medical methods of the early 1800s, from herbal remedies to leeches. On a recent visit, a 7-year-old boy in a visiting school group nearly passed out during a mock bloodletting show-and-tell; the staff, accustomed to fainters, casually produced a pillow and a glass of water without halting the demonstration, proving that in the old days, medicine was less about science and more about soldiering on. Which you must also do; there are no toilets here.

9a St Thomas St., SE1. www.oldoperatingtheatre.com. ✆ **020/7188-2679.** Admission £6.50 adults, £5 seniors and students, £3.50 children 17 and under. Tues–Sun 10:30am–5pm. Closed late Dec–early Jan. Tube: London Bridge.

Shakespeare's Globe ★ LANDMARK   A painstaking re-creation of an

outdoor Elizabethan theater, it tends to bewitch fans of history and theater, but it can put all others to sleep. Arrive early since the timed 40-min. tours fill up. Get a bad time, and you'll be stuck waiting for far too long in the UnderGlobe, a well-crafted but exhaustible exhibition about Elizabethan theater. Also avoid matinee days, since tours don't run during performances. Opened in 1997, the open-air theater was made using only Elizabethan technology such as saws, pillars made from solid oak trees, 17,000 bundles of Norfolk water reed, and plaster panels mixed with goat's hair (the original recipe called for cow's hair, but the breed they needed is now extinct). The first Globe burned down, aged just 14, when a cannon fired during a performance caused its thatched roof to catch fire; it took a special act of Parliament, plus plenty of hidden sprinkler systems, to permit the construction of this, the first thatched roof in London since the Great Fire. The original theater was the same size (and stood 180m/591 ft. to the southeast), but it crammed in 3,000 luckless souls. Today, just 1,600 are admitted for performances. If you'd like to see the location of the **Rose Theatre,** a true Shakespeare original, go around the corner to 56 Park St., where its foundations, discovered in 1989 and now squatted over by a modern office building, are open for visitors on Saturdays from 10am to 5pm. There's a video on how it was discovered and it also hosts regular performances (www.rosetheatre.org.uk; ✆ **020/7261-9565;** free admission).

21 New Globe Walk, SE1. www.shakespearesglobe.com. ✆ **020/7401-9919.** Exhibition admission £17 adults, £15.50 seniors, £13.50 students, £10 children 5–15. Exhibition: daily 9am–5pm. Theater tours: daily 9:30am–5pm; check ahead for schedule changes. Tube: London Bridge.

Tate Modern ★★★ MUSEUM   In 2000, Bankside's most reviled eyesore, a bleak power station—steely and cavernous, a cathedral to the soulless machinery of industry—was ingeniously converted into the national contemporary art collection of pieces made since 1900. Now it's a temple to the machinery of the art world. It's as integral to the tourist's London as the Quire of Westminster Abbey or the Dome of St Paul's, attracting 4.7 million annual visitors. The mammoth Turbine Hall, cleared of machinery to form a meadowlike expanse of concrete, often hosts works created by major-league artists for its periodic Hyundai Commission. People of every background frolic there as if it were a park.

In 2016, the Tate took on declining attendance by expanding its exhibition spaces by 60 percent with a newly built expansion in back. Now the Turbine Hall connects the original post-industrial, three-level galleries (the riverfront Boiler House) with a twisting 10-story custom-built tower behind them (Blavatnik Building) that's topped with a terrace for views of St Paul's dome. Beneath the new tower, in the power station's former oil tanks, new performance spaces try to engage visitors (check online ahead of time for what's on).

The addition is impressive but it doesn't solve some of the core problems with the Tate: Great works are too often rotated into storage, so there's no guarantee of what you'll find, and the pieces that are on display annoy many visitors as joyless or overly esoteric. The commissions in the Turbine Hall are so massive they take weeks to assemble, so there's a good chance you won't be able to enjoy that part of the experience when you visit. And descriptions dwell on pretentious doubletalk and the incestuous art world culture—"works gathered in this wing capture making as gesture, the trace of an action," whatever that means. On the second floor, rent a multimedia guide of the highlights (£4.50, one version for adults, another for kids, and you can swap between them) on a video device that embellishes on the works' meaning and context. Maps cost £2, so consider going online ahead of time to print floor plans for free. Also see what temporary exhibitions are on—there's usually one blockbuster going.

MUSEUMS: after hours

Many attractions offer extended opening times for evening viewing. Often, extra inducements are tossed in, such as wine and sketch classes at the National Portrait Gallery or DJs at the V&A. These are the major "Lates" events that can really free up your daytime touring to include more sights:

ATTRACTION	LATE OPENING
British Library (p. 110)	Tuesday–Thursday to 8pm
British Museum (p. 114)	Friday to 8:30pm
Design Museum (p. 154)	Friday to 8pm (first of month)
Handel House Museum (p. 143)	Frequent evening concerts
London Canal Museum (p. 194)	Thursday to 7:30pm (first of month)
London Zoo (p. 190)	Friday to 10pm (selected nights)
National Gallery (p. 123)	Friday to 9pm
National Portrait Gallery (p. 126)	Thursday–Friday to 9pm
Natural History Museum (p. 148)	Friday to 10:30pm (last of month)
Royal Academy of Arts (p. 143)	Friday to 10pm
Science Museum (p. 150)	Wednesday to 10pm (last of month)
Sir John Soane's Museum (p. 127)	Tuesday to 9pm (first of month)
Tate Britain (p. 134)	Friday to 10pm (once bi-monthly)
Tate Modern (p. 158)	Friday–Saturday to 10pm
V & A Museum (p. 151)	Friday to 10pm
Wellcome Collection (p. 120)	Friday to 10pm (first of month except Jan & Aug)
Whitechapel Gallery (p. 169)	Thursday to 9pm

The formidable permanent collection, one of the world's best for breadth, is always shifting, not just because the museum owns more than it can display (even with the new tower), but also because works vanish on short-term loans. Some heavy hitters never leave, though. My favorite: Seven of the nine monotonal series created by Mark Rothko for New York City's Four Seasons restaurant, which never fail to put visitors in a meditative mood (one of them, *Black on Maroon,* was restored after a 2012 vandalism incident). There are four free daily guided tours, usually at 11am, noon, 2pm, and 3pm; ask at the ground-floor desk to find out where to join them. At the family desk, open on weekends and busy days, kids pick up free drawing kits or tours based on sounds. One thing not to miss is the shop on the bottom floor. Also carve out refreshment time: The restaurant on Level 6 is a city highlight. I beeline for the 30 first-come bar stools facing floor-to-ceiling glass over St Paul's and the Thames. The fish and chips platter with minty mushy peas has my approval for flavor if not price (£15, but that view!).

Bankside, SE1. www.tate.org.uk/modern. ✆ **020/7887-8888.** Free admission. Sun–Thurs 10am–6pm; Fri–Sat 10am–10pm. Tube: Southwark.

View from the Shard ★ OBSERVATION DECK   In 2013 the Shard, the tallest building in Europe (but not even in the top 50 worldwide), added an extremely expensive observation deck with timed tickets—sunset sells out ahead of time, but if you come during the day, you can come back after dark on the same ticket. The jagged 306m/1,016 ft.-tall tower doesn't exactly fit in with its neighbors. Commerce is the theme, with staff members hustling you to purchase pricey green-screen souvenir photos and champagne hawked for £10 to £12 a glass. After airport-style security and two ear-poppingly fast elevator rides, you emerge 244m/800 feet up to some weird angel-like choir music and vertiginous floor-to-ceiling windows far, far over the city—so far that, after the initial impression, casual visitors aren't likely to figure out most of what they see. A few levels up (you must use stairs for those last three floors), there's a patio shielded at body-level from the elements. You can stay as long as you want—an advantage over the Eye—but there's no seating and no washrooms up there, so take care of business on Earth. There is one novel addition: Point a digital "TellScope" in the distance, and its screen reveals the same view at different times of day. If you have to choose, the London Eye is a more memorable experience than a £31 elevator ride.

Joiner St., SE1. www.theviewfromtheshard.com. ✆ **0844/499-7111.** Admission £31 adults, £25 children 4–15, £5 discount if booked 24 hr. ahead. Apr–Oct daily 10am–10pm; Nov–Mar Sun–Wed 10am–7pm, Thurs–Sat 10am–10pm. Tube: London Bridge.

Other Bankside/Southwark Attractions

Brunel Museum ★ MUSEUM/HISTORIC SITE   Although the engineering contributions of Marc Brunel and his son Isambard Kingdom Brunel are commonly taken for granted, here they're given their due. With the help of a shield system they invented, these pioneers executed the first tunnel to be built under a navigable river. London's soft earth didn't make it easy, though—it took from 1825 to 1843. This red brick building marked by a chimney was where steam engines pumped the seeping water out as diggers toiled. The tunnel, lined with arches and Doric capitals, was a commercial flop that deteriorated into a subterranean red-light district. It later found new purpose, however, as a part of the Overground Line, and it has gained new respect through this museum, which often creates special events to bring guests into the tunnel. Maximize immersion by combining it with a London Walks tour from Bermondsey Station to the museum door (current times are listed on the website; no reservations needed).

Railway Ave., SE16. www.brunel-museum.org.uk. ✆ **020/7231-3840.** Admission £6 adults, £4 seniors, students, and children. Daily 10am–5pm. Tube: Rotherhithe.

The Golden Hinde ★ HISTORIC SHIP   Tucked into one of the few remaining slips that enabled ships to unload in Southwark (another is Hay's Galleria, downstream by the HMS *Belfast* [see below], now a boutique shopping area), is a 1:1 replica of Sir Francis Drake's square-rigged Tudor galleon, which circumnavigated the world from 1577 to 1580. This 1973 version, which is so tiny you will forever feel pity for those old explorers, made its own circumnavigation in 1980. It was recently wrested from the trust that once owned it, and the new owners are trying to put its maintenance back on even keel, as it were. For now, tours are self-guided, but on weekends there may be guided ones if you check the schedule ahead of time.

St Mary Overie Dock, Cathedral Street, SE1. www.goldenhinde.co.uk. ℂ **020/7403-0123.** Admission £5 adults, £3 children 3–16. Daily 10am–5pm. Tube: London Bridge.

HMS *Belfast* ★ HISTORIC SHIP   It's as if the powerful 1938 warship, upon being retired from service in 1965, was motored straight to this dock and opened to visitors the next day. Nearly everything, down to the checked flooring and decaying cables, is exactly as it was, making the boat a fascinating snapshot of mid-20th-century maritime technology, and smart exhibits do a lot to make it come alive again. Authenticity also makes it a devil to navigate, especially if you have any bags with you—sorry, no cloakrooms, sailor. Getting around its labyrinth of decks, engine rooms, ladders, and hatches requires dexterity and a well-calibrated inner compass—it seems the Health and Safety rules that bedevil every aspect of British life do not apply here. You can roam as you wish, visiting every cubby of the ship from kitchen to bridge, touching nearly anything you want, while being thankful that it wasn't you who was chasing German cruisers (the *Belfast* sank the *Scharnhorst*) and backing up the D-Day invasion in this tough tin can. Admission includes an excellent audio guide, but privately, crew members tell me that they wish visitors would pause and ask them questions in person—there's so much more to point out to you. The price is too high for those with a lukewarm interest, but the

HMS *Belfast* and Tower Bridge.

Tom's Kitchen bar, atop the visitor center (a wine bar overlooking a warship—appropriate?), has stellar views of the Tower of London and Tower Bridge—and an afternoon champagne tea that's just £15. Thanks, World War II!

Morgan's Lane, Tooley St., SE1. www.iwm.org.uk. ✆ **020/7940-6300.** Admission £15.45 adults, £12.35 seniors and students, £7.70 children 5–15; higher posted prices include a "voluntary donation"; discounts for booking online. Daily 10am–6pm; last admission 1 hr. before closing. Tube: London Bridge.

THE CITY

Museum of London ★★★ MUSEUM   This repository's miraculous cache of rarities from everyday life would do credit to the greatest national museums of any land, and it's sure to satisfy history buffs. Displays contain so many forehead-smackingly rare or fascinating items that by the time you're two-thirds through it, you'll start to lose track. Exhibits start with local archaeological finds (including elephant vertebrae and a lion skull) before continuing to 3,500-year-old spearheads and swords found in the muck of the Thames. Voices from the past come alive again in chronological order: There's a 1st-century oak ladder that was discovered preserved in a well, Norman chain mail, loaded gambling dice made of bone in the 1400s, a leather bucket used in vain to fight the Great Fire of 1666, a walk-in wooden prison cell from 1750, Selfridge's original bronze Art Deco elevators, and far, far more. The biggest drawback is that you need to budget a few hours, otherwise you'll end up in a mad rush through the entire lower floor covering the Great Fire to now—and it'd be such a shame to miss diver Tom Daley's teeny Stella McCartney swim trunks. You also don't want to miss the Victorian Walk, a kid-friendly re-creation of city streets, shops and all from the 1800s (grab a card at its entrance to know what you're seeing). Also seek out the Lord Mayor's state coach, carved in 1757, which garages here all year awaiting its annual airing at the Lord Mayor's Show in November, and Great Britain's petal from the Olympic flame cauldron, on display alongside a re-creation

A Poignant Pocket Park

Little-known **Postman's Park** is beloved by those lucky enough to have stumbled across it. Hemmed in between buildings, its central feature is the moving **Watts Memorial,** a collection of plaques dedicated to ordinary people who died in acts of "heroic self sacrifice." Have a seat on a bench and ponder John Clinton, 10, "who was drowned near London Bridge in trying to save a companion younger than himself" in July 1894. In 1893, William Freer Lucas tantalizingly "risked poison for himself rather than lessen any chance of saving a child's life and died." Alice Ayres saved three children from a burning house in 1885 "at the cost of her own young life." The commemorations mostly ceased in Edwardian times (poor Leigh Pitt squeaked in after saving a drowning child in 2009), making these forgotten faces obscure once again. (West side of St Martin's-Le-Grand between St Paul's Cathedral and the Barbican Centre; 8am–dusk; Tube: St Paul's or Barbican.)

of a portion of it (the original petals were given to each country they represented).

The museum, built into the Barbican complex beside a Roman wall fragment (it will move to Clerkenwell in 2022), is easy to combine with St Paul's, and it sells one of the best selections of books on city history. It also runs an excellent second museum in East London about Docklands (p. 174). So rich is this city in history that behind the scenes, the Museum also owns the world's largest archaeological archive, which is open for tours a few times a year.

150 London Wall, EC2. www.museumoflondon.org.uk. © **020/7001-9844.** Free admission. Daily 10am–6pm, galleries close 5:40pm. Tube: Barbican or St Paul's.

St Paul's Cathedral ★★★ HISTORIC SITE/CHURCH   The old St Paul's, with its magnificent spire, stood on this site for 600 years before it was claimed by 1666's Great Fire. It was so beloved that when Sir Christopher Wren was commissioned to rebuild London's greatest house of worship, he tried to outdo the original, devoting 40 years to the project and going one further by crowning it with a mighty dome—highly unusual for the time. It was also stark and plain, like the Catholics did their churches, not Gothic and complicated like the Protestants. My, how people talked.

St Paul's cost £750,000 to build, an astronomical sum in 1697 when the first section opened for worship, and now, it costs £3 million a year to run. Wren overspent so badly that decoration was curtailed; the Byzantine-style mosaics over the Quire weren't added until Queen Victoria thought the place needed spiffing up (and some purists are still complaining). Stained glass is still missing, but that just allows the sweep and arch of Wren's design to shine cleanly through. Many foreigners were introduced to the sanctuary during the wedding of Prince Charles and Lady Diana Spencer in 1981, but the pulpit also saw a sermon by Martin Luther King in 1964 and Churchill's funeral the next year. Frustratingly, you're not allowed to take photos on your tour.

The **Great West Doors,** largely unused unless you're important, are 27m high (90 ft.) and on their original hinges; they're so well-hung that even an infirm vicar can swing them open. In 2005, the Cathedral completed a £10.8-million cleaning program; a stone panel beside the doors was left filthy to show just how gloomy centuries of candles had made it in here. The **High Altar** has a canopy supported by single tree trunks that were hollowed out and carved, and its 15th-century crucifix and candlesticks require two men to lift. (They're nailed down, anyway. As one docent, a half-century veteran of Cathedral tours, lamented, "You'd be surprised what people try to steal.") Behind it is the **American Memorial Chapel** to the 28,000 American soldiers who died while based in England in World War II; in a glass case, one leaf of a 500-page book containing their names is turned each day. The **organ,** with 7,000 pipes, was regularly played by Mendelssohn and Handel, and the **lectern** is original. Give special admiration to the impossibly fine limewood carvings in the Quire by Grinling Gibbons—dark wood is original and lighter wood has been replaced or restored. Nearby, there's a monument to prettyboy

St Paul's Cathedral

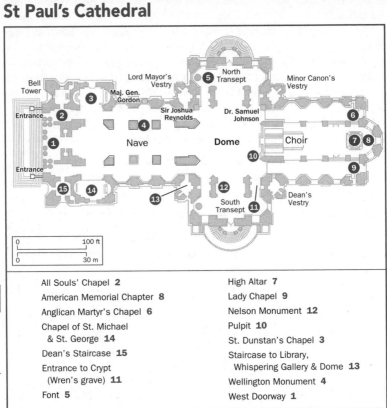

All Souls' Chapel **2**	High Altar **7**
American Memorial Chapter **8**	Lady Chapel **9**
Anglican Martyr's Chapel **6**	Nelson Monument **12**
Chapel of St. Michael & St. George **14**	Pulpit **10**
Dean's Staircase **15**	St. Dunstan's Chapel **3**
Entrance to Crypt (Wren's grave) **11**	Staircase to Library, Whispering Gallery & Dome **13**
Font **5**	Wellington Monument **4**
	West Doorway **1**

poet and cleric **John Donne** that still bears on its urn the scorch marks it suffered in Old St Paul's during the Great Fire (it was the only thing that survived the conflagration).

Eight central pillars support the entire weight of the wood-framed Dome; Wren filled them with loose rubble. In 1925, engineers broke them open to find the debris had settled to the bottom, and they filled them again with liquid concrete. If you're fit, you can mount the 259 steps (each just an awkward 13cm/5 in. tall, but double-wide with some spots to catch your breath) to the circular **Whispering Gallery,** 30m/98 feet above the floor. Famously, its acoustics are so fine you can turn your head and mutter something that can be understood on the opposite side, 33m/108 feet away. That's in theory; so many tourists are usually blabbing to each other that you won't hear a thing, although it is a transcendent place to listen to choir rehearsal on a mid-afternoon. Climb higher (you've gone 378 steps now, and now the stairs get tight) to the **Stone Gallery,** an outdoor terrace just beneath the Dome. Catch your breath, if you choose, for the final 152-step push to the **Golden Gallery**— you'll be scaling the inner skin of the Dome, past ancient oriel windows and along tight metal stairs. There are three domes, in fact—the inner skin with the monochrome paintings by Sir James Thornhill, the leaden outside, and in between, a brick one that holds it all together. That's what you traverse—look sharp for ancient carved graffiti by tourists who preceded you in the 1700s. It's safe, but it's not for those with vertigo or claustrophobia. The spectacular 360-degree city view from the top (85m/279 ft. up), at the base of the Ball and Lantern (you can't go up farther), is so beautiful it defies full appreciation. For more than 250 years, this was the tallest structure in a city that itself was atop the world.

If you miss the **Crypt,** you'll have missed a lot. In addition to memorials to the famous dead (such as Florence Nightingale and plenty of obscure war heroes), you'll find tombs, such as composer Sir Arthur Sullivan's ebullient bronze plate and the tombs of two of Britain's greatest military demigods: **Admiral Horatio Nelson** (whose body was preserved for the trip from the battlefield by soaking in brandy and wine), and **Arthur, Duke of Wellington** (flanked by flags captured on the field of battle; they will hang there until they disintegrate). To the right of the OBE Chapel, in **Artists Corner,** you'll find the graves of the artists **J. M. W. Turner** and **Henry Moore,** plus, under a black slab by a window, **Christopher Wren** himself, who rests inside his masterpiece. "I build for eternity," he once said, and so far, so good: In 2010, the cathedral celebrated 300 years since its completion.

Volunteers, called "supers," lead free 90-min. tours at 10 and 11am, and 1 and 2pm, and half-hour highlights tours six times a day between 10:30am and 3pm. Listen closely, because they are the elder statesmen; many have been here for decades. Lest you forgot it's actually a cathedral, you can also worship here outside of sightseeing hours—for free. If you're hungry, scope out the cafe, one of the cheaper options in this neighborhood. When you're done

The Forgotten Colosseum

Guildhall, a magnificent stone structure originally completed in 1440 but heavily rebuilt time and again, was once where Londoners went to pay taxes but today is used as the City's most regal events space. Partly due to World War II's wrath, the collection at its **Guildhall Art Gallery** is perhaps second-rate (for this city), although its works depicting London can be interesting. But the real reason to come is in the cellar: the foundations of the eastern entrance of **London's Roman Amphitheatre,** 2,000 years old, which were discovered when the gallery was being built in 1987. Once the largest in Britannia, the amphitheater could hold some 7,000 specta- tors at a time when the entire population of London was only about 25,000. Slots carved into one of the rooms suggest there was once a trap door that could release wild animals to fight in the arena. Sometimes it's hard to believe the Romans trod the same streets as you, but here in the darkness deep underground, the bones of their abandoned plaything provide an eerie reminder. (Gresham St., EC2; www. guildhall.cityoflondon.gov.uk; ✆ **020/ 7332-1313;** admission free except for exhibitions; monthly tours £8, booked online; daily 10am–4pm; Tube: Moor- gate or St Paul's.)

inside, head just east to the **One New Change** shopping complex, where the free rooftop terrace has some spectacular close-up views of the Dome—perfect for vacation snaps.

St Paul's Churchyard, EC4. www.stpauls.co.uk. ℗ **020/7246-8357**. Admission £18 adults, £16 seniors and students, £8 children 6–17, free for children 5 and under; up to £2 cheaper online. Mon–Sat 8:30am–4:30pm; Sun open for worship only. Whispering Gallery and Dome 9:30am–4pm. Tube: St Paul's.

Tower Bridge Exhibition ★★
LANDMARK   In the late 1800s, there was no bolder display of a country's technological prowess than a spectacular bridge; consider the Brooklyn Bridge or the Firth of Forth Bridge. This exhibit celebrates one such triumph, Tower Bridge. You may wonder: How did such a monument survive the Blitz when everything around it got flattened? Simple: The Luftwaffe needed its proud towers as a visual landmark. It's always free to walk across the bridge on your own, but visiting this museum is like getting two attractions in one. The first satisfies sightseers who dream of going up in the famous neo-Gothic towers and crossing the high-level observation walkways—it's a close encounter with a world icon. The

Knight's armor is on display at the Tower of London.

second aspect delves into the steam-driven machinery that so impressed the world in 1894; those displays will hook the mechanically inclined. The original bascule-raising equipment, representing the largest use of hydraulic power at the time, remains in fine condition despite being retired in favor of electricity in 1976. The raising of the spans is now controlled by joystick from a cabin across the road from the entrance (check "Bridge Lift Times" on the website to find out when). Recently, a glass floor was installed in a portion of the upper walkway so visitors can get giddy to the sight of the river 42m (138 ft.) below their feet. *Note:* Tickets are discounted if you also buy entry to the Monument (p. 172).

Tower Bridge (on the Tower of London side), SE1. www.towerbridge.org.uk. ℗ **020/7403-3761**. Admission £9.80 adults, £6.80 seniors and students, £4.20 children 5–15; about £1 cheaper online. Apr–Sept daily 10am–6pm; Oct–Mar daily 9:30am–5:30pm; last admission 30 min. before closing. Tube: Tower Hill or Tower Gateway DLR.

The Tower of London ★★★ MUSEUM/HISTORIC SITE   Every morning at 9am, a military guard escorts the keys to the Tower and its huge wooden doors yawn open again for outsiders. It's the most famous castle in the world,

Tower of London

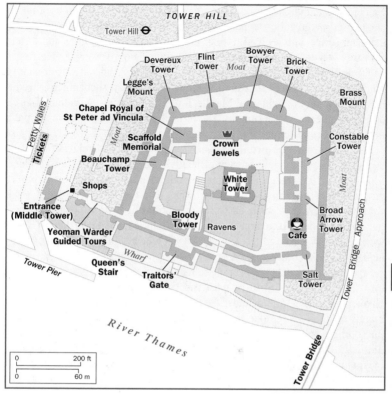

TOWER HILL

Tower Hill

Devereux Tower
Flint Tower
Moat
Bowyer Tower
Brick Tower

Legge's Mount

Brass Mount

Chapel Royal of St Peter ad Vincula

Petty Wales

Tickets

Moat

Scaffold Memorial

Crown Jewels

Constable Tower

Beauchamp Tower

Shops

White Tower

Entrance (Middle Tower)

Bloody Tower

Moat

Broad Arrow Tower

Yeoman Warder Guided Tours

Ravens

Café

Wharf

Tower Pier

Queen's Stair

Traitors' Gate

Salt Tower

Tower Bridge Approach

River Thames

Tower Bridge

0   200 ft
0   60 m

a UNESCO World Heritage Site, and a symbol of not just London, but also of a millennium of English history. Less a tower than a fortified mini-town of stone and timber, its history could fill this book. Suffice it to say that its oldest building, the four-cornered White Tower, went up in 1078, and the compound that grew around it has served as palace, prison, treasury, mint, armory, zoo, and now, a lovingly maintained tourist attraction that no visitor should neglect. Exploring its sprawl should take between 3 and 5 hours.

The key to touring the Tower is to arrive close to opening, since intimidating queues can form by lunchtime for the Crown Jewels, located in the Waterloo Block at the north wall (farthest from the Thames), and the White Tower, in the center. Tickets are sold outside the battlements. Hit the Welcome Centre, just past the Ticket Office, and grab a copy of the free "Daily Programme," which runs down the times and locations of all the free talks, temporary exhibitions, and mini-performances. Plenty are offered—the Tower at times feels like a theme park with 1,000 years of history behind it. As soon as you're in, between the Middle and Byward towers, note the next time of the prime excursion: the 1-hr. **Yeoman Warder Tour,** led with theatrical aplomb by one

167

of the Beefeaters who live in the Tower and preserve it. (There are about 100 Tower residents, including families, but only one of the 35 Beefeaters, Moira Cameron, is female.) The tour (don't come later than 2pm if you want one) is engaging, but juvenile—expect bellowing and histrionics, each reciting an identical script with a gleeful fetish for yarns about beheadings and torture. (In truth, you can count the people executed inside the Tower on your fingers and toes; it was considered an honor to be killed here, since it was private.) If you'd like your history delivered without vaudevillian shenanigans, head to the gift shop on the right after Middle Tower and grab an audio tour (£4), but do it early; headsets can run out. The official guidebooks (£5) here are pretty good, and they certainly help with orientation.

As you enter the **Crown Jewels** exhibition, you'll see archival film of the last time most of the jewels were officially used, at the coronation of Queen Elizabeth in 1952. After passing into a vault, visitors glide via people-movers past cases of glittering, downlit crowns, scepters, and orbs worn (awkwardly—they're 2.3kg/5 lb. each) by generations of British monarchs. Check out the legendary 105-carat Koh-I-Noor diamond, once the largest in the world, which is fixed to the temple of the **Queen Mother's Crown** (1937), along with 2,000 other diamonds; the Indian government has been begging to get the stone back. The 530-carat Cullinan I, the world's largest cut diamond, tops the Sovereign's **Sceptre with the Cross** (1661). The **Imperial State Crown**—ringed with emeralds, the 170-carat Black Prince's ruby, and diamonds aplenty—is the one used in the annual State Opening of Parliament; the solid gold **St Edward's Crown** is for coronations. After those come candlesticks that could support the roof of your house, trumpets, swords, and the inevitable traffic jam around the 1m-wide **Grand Punch Bowl** (1829), an elaborate riot of lions, cherubs, and unicorns that holds 144 bottles' worth and shows what it would look like if punch bowls could go insane. Because Oliver Cromwell liquidated every royal artifact he could get his hands on, everything dates to after the Restoration (the 1660s or later). Clearly, the monarchy has more than made up for the loss.

The four-sided **White Tower** (completed in 1098) is the heart of the fortress, and for more than 200 years, it was the tallest structure in London. Touring its four cavernous levels requires much circuitous stair-climbing, but takes in a wide span of history, including a fine stone chapel, Norman-era fireplaces and toilets, the gleaming

The Ravens, Forevermore

Ravens probably visited the Tower in the 1200s to feast on the dripping corpses of the executed, who were taken from Tower Hill (the public execution ground, near the present-day Tube stop) and hung outside the battlements as a warning. You've probably heard the legend that if the ravens leave the Tower, England will fall, but it's a modern superstition. Nevertheless, seven of the carnivorous birds are kept in cages north of Wakefield Tower; in 2018, one raven died of old age, but it has been replaced by a baby, Poppy. They are fed raw meat, blood-soaked cookies, and the occasional finger from a tourist dumb enough to get too close.

GREAT galleries

Hayward Gallery ★ Hidden on a back rampart of the vital nonprofit Southbank Centre, it hosts terrific blockbuster shows, which have included Ansel Adams, Roy Lichtenstein, 1920s Surrealism, and a 60-artist panorama of modern African art. Always modern, never staid, and a recent multi-year renovation put it back on London's art A List—make an advance booking. It also takes itself quite seriously, which can be good for a laugh. Southbank Centre, Belvedere Rd., SE1. www.southbankcentre.co.uk. ✆ **020/ 3879-9555.** Charge for exhibitions £11–£20. Wed–Mon 11am–7pm; Thurs 11am–9pm. Tube: Waterloo.

House of Illustration ★ This gallery-cum-museum is dedicated to the art of illustration—sometimes the children's book kind (world-famous Roald Dahl illustrator Quentin Blake is on the board), sometimes the magazine kind, always well-selected. You'll find two changing exhibitions at a time plus a fantastic little gift shop. 2 Granary Sq., N1. www.house ofillustration.org.uk. ✆ **020/3696-2020.** Free admission to 1 gallery; charge around £8 for exhibitions. Tues–Sun 10am–6pm, last admission 5:30pm. Tube: King's Cross St Pancras.

Saatchi Gallery ★ This landmark, the only resident in the three-story, 6,500-sq.-m (70,000-sq.-ft.) former Royal Military Asylum building (1801) in Chelsea, used to be unmissable for avant garde contemporary art; now exhibitions are too often shills for luxury brands (Hermés, Rolls-Royce). Only commit if the current fare is a true artists' showcase. Duke of York Square, SW3. www.saatchigallery. com. ✆ **020/7811-3070.** Free admission. Daily 10am–6pm. Tube: Sloane Square.

Stephen Wiltshire Gallery ★★ Stephen Wiltshire, an autistic artistic savant, can draw huge, twisting, intricately detailed ink-and-paper landscapes after seeing the real view for just a few seconds. This collection is located in the **Royal Opera Arcade** off Pall Mall, which dates to 1818—it's the world's oldest shopping arcade, essentially the first indoor shopping mall. 5 Royal Opera Arcade, Pall Mall, SW1. www.stephen wiltshire.co.uk. ✆ **020/7321-2622.** Free admission. Mon–Fri 10am–5:30pm; Sat appointment only. Tube: Charing Cross or Piccadilly Circus.

Whitechapel Gallery ★★ Since 1901, the Whitechapel has reliably led the development of new artistic movements. In 1939, it brought to Britain Picasso's newly painted *Guernica* as part of an exhibition protesting the then-current Spanish Civil War. Later it introduced Jackson Pollock's abstracts. There's always a challenging exhibition, talk, or screening going on. 77–82 Whitechapel Rd., E1. www.whitechapelgallery.org. ✆ **020/7 522-7888.** Free admission. Tues–Wed and Fri–Sun 11am–6pm; Thurs 11am–9pm. Tube: Aldgate East.

Line of Kings collection of the **Royal Armoury** (even small children can't help but notice the exaggerated codpiece of King Henry VIII's intricately etched suit from 1540), and some models depicting the Tower's evolution (it's been much altered, but the six smallest arched windows on the White Tower's south side are original to the 11th c.). Try to time your arrival on the top floor to take one of three daily tours (10:45am, 12:45pm, or 2:15pm) of the nearly 1,000-year-old **Chapel of St John.** After you're finished in here, you'll have an excellent overview of how the whole complex worked.

Once you've got those two areas under your belt, take your time exploring the rest. I suggest a stop in the brick **Beauchamp Tower** (pronounced *beech-um*, built in 1280), where important political prisoners were held and where you can still glimpse graffiti testifying to their suffering. In front of it on Tower Green is the circular glass memorial designating the **Scaffold Site,** where the unlucky few (including sitting Queens Anne Boleyn and Lady Jane Grey) are said to have lost their heads. In reality, we don't know exactly where they were killed, but Queen Victoria wanted a commemorative site set, and because of the evident dangers of displeasing the monarch, this spot was chosen.

The **St Thomas's Tower,** from the 13th century, is closest to the Thames and re-creates King Edward's bedchamber with authentic materials. Beneath it, **Traitor's Gate,** once called Water Gate, originally was used to ferry prisoners in secret from the Thames. Torture was never a part of English law, but it happened here anyway, and the **Bloody Tower** was where some of the worst stuff went down. In truth, there were only 48 recorded cases of torture in the Tower, but that doesn't stop curators from devoting an entire room to a display of (mostly replica) torture devices. Don't forget to climb the ramparts for that classic photo of the Tower Bridge. Skip the Royal Fusiliers Regimental Museum, a dreary hodgepodge of military memorabilia.

Daily at 2:50pm, the guards parade outside the Waterloo Block to the Byward Tower. On Sundays, your admission ticket allows you to attend services at the **Chapel Royal of St. Peter ad Vincula,** the Tower's church with a Tudor-era Spanish chestnut ceiling, at 9:15 or 11am; otherwise, the only way to get in, and to see the marble slab beneath which Boleyn and Grey's decapitated bodies were entombed, is with a Yeoman Warder Tour—salacious tales of gory fates are spun virtually on top of the graves of the people who suffered them, which by any measure is tacky. It's a shame the cheap histrionics of the interpretation strip this ancient Tower of so much depth and dignity.

Tower Hill, EC3. www.hrp.org.uk. ⓒ **084/4482-7777.** Admission £26.80 adults, £20.90 students and seniors, £12.70 children 5–15; higher posted prices include a "voluntary donation"; up to £4 cheaper if purchased online. Mar–Oct Tues–Sat 9am–5:30pm, Sun–Mon 10am–5:30pm; Nov–Feb Tues–Sat 9am–4:30pm, Sun–Mon 10am–4:30pm; last admission 30 min. before closing. Tube: Tower Hill or Tower Gateway DLR.

Other Attractions in The City

Bank of England Museum ★ MUSEUM   The intermittently compelling tale of the B of E is recounted in appealingly patronizing but generous detail, accompanied by plenty of antiques from the vaults. That's fine if you understand finance, but most people lose the plot pretty quickly. Along the way are some fun oddities, including a million-pound note, printed in the early 19th century for internal accounting, and reimbursement claims from families of *Titanic* victims. There's lots of expensive swag, such as a primitive safe from 1700, heaps of silver treasures, and a gold bar so pure (1 part in 10,000 impure) that it was given to Queen Elizabeth as a coronation gift. Guess she didn't need it. It's also fun to watch Her Majesty age on the money over the years. The most popular exhibit is a 28-lb. standard gold bar encased in a clear plastic box, that you're challenged to lift. The rest of the Bank isn't open.

Threadneedle St., EC2. www.bankofengland.co.uk/museum. ℂ **020/7601-5545.** Free admission. Mon–Fri 10am–5pm; last admission 4:30pm. Tube: Bank.

The Charterhouse ★★★ HISTORIC SITE   Once you enter this once-powerful vestige of Medieval England, opened in 2017 after being off limits since 1348, it's hard to believe you're still in Modern London. These ancient collected quads and halls have been a monastery, mansion, school, hospital, home for the poor, and burial ground—it's still the last four, and in fact, you'll meet the skeleton of one longtime resident, a victim of the Black Plague in the 1300s, discovered in the digging for the new Elizabeth Line. A journey so winding makes for a hodgepodge of ancient things to amaze you: gardens and cobbled courtyards, slanted slots used by pre-Henry VIII monks to receive food so they wouldn't have the disturbance of human contact, and a paneled Jacobean chapel (full of carvings of dogs and weapons, its patron's symbols) that miraculously survived the Blitz thanks to the protection of a mere wooden door than now hangs blackened on its hinges. The museum is free to see, but to truly get inside, you must be escorted. One of the 40 "Brothers" (even the women are called "Brothers") who has been lucky enough to be selected to retire here give affectionate tours of what the last 700-odd years have left behind; on the afternoon tours, the smell of lunch still lingers in the great dining hall, for this time-stunned, one-of-a-kind hideaway is still in active use. On one tour I took, the Brother cocked his ear at the sound of church bells in the distance. "St Bartholomew's," he said. "The only set of bells to date from before the Dissolution. 1510, I think." At the Charterhouse, another miracle of survival, we can hear and see exactly what people did half a millennium ago.

Charterhouse Square, EC1. www.thecharterhouse.org. ℂ **020/3818-8873.** Free admission. Tues–Sat 11am–4:45pm. Standard tours £10 (11:30am, noon, 2pm Tues–Sat, 2 and 3:15pm Sun), Brothers' Tours £15 (2:15pm Tues–Thurs, Sat–Sun). Tube: Barbican or Farringdon.

Dr Johnson's House ★ HISTORIC HOME   A rare surviving middle-class home from the 18th century (built in 1700), this slouching and brick-faced abode happens to be that of famous lexicographer Samuel Johnson, who lived here from 1748 to 1759. If you're hoping to learn a lot about him, you'll have to spring for a book in the gift shop. Little substance is provided in the house itself, which fortunately merits some mild interest on its own terms (the corkscrew latch on the front door, which prevented lock-picking from above, is an example). The rooftop garret in which Johnson and six helpers toiled to publish the first comprehensive English dictionary was burned out in the Blitz, ironically, by a barrel of burning ink which flew out of a bombed warehouse; you can still see some scorch marks on the ceiling timbers. Ink defined the house and nearly destroyed it, but it also saved it, because the printers who used it in the intervening years boarded up the walls, preserving them. While you're here, pop round the corner to the wonderful Ye Olde Cheshire Cheese pub (p. 108). Dr. Johnson sure liked to.

17 Gough Sq., EC4. www.drjohnsonshouse.org. © **020/7353-3745.** Admission £7 adults, £6 seniors and students, £3.50 children 5–17. Cash only. May–Sept Mon–Sat 11am–5:30pm; Oct–Apr Mon–Sat 11am–5pm. Tube: Blackfriars.

The Monument ★ LANDMARK   Back in 1677, it was the tallest thing (61m/200 ft.) in town and it made people gasp. Today, it's hemmed in by personality-free glass buildings. The Monument was erected to commemorate the destruction of the city by the Great Fire in 1666. Its height also represents the distance east from its base to the site of Thomas Farynor's bakery in Pudding Lane, where the conflagration began. There's only one thing to do in this fluted column of Portland stone: Climb it. The spiral staircase of 15cm (6-in.) steps, which has no landings, gradually narrows as it ascends to the outdoor observation platform—a popular suicide spot until 1842, when a cage was installed. They'll tell you it's 311 steps to the top, but they're lying—it's 313, if you count the two steps before the box office. Check out the metal band snaking down the north side; it's a lightning rod, and it crosses along a Latin inscription blaming Catholics for starting the fire (the insult was chiseled off in 1831). Tickets are discounted in combo deals with the Tower Bridge Exhibition (p. 166). Go on a pleasant day (unless you'd like a good wind whipping), be prepared to leave large bags downstairs, and ask for your free certificate of accomplishment before you go.

Monument St. at Fish St. Hill, WC4. www.themonument.info. © **020/3627-2552.** Admission £4.50 adults, £3 seniors and students, £2.30 children 15 and under. Cash only. April–Sept daily 9:30am–6pm; Oct–Mar daily 9:30am–5:30pm; last admission 30 min. before closing. Tube: Monument or Bank.

EAST LONDON & DOCKLANDS

The part of London east of the City encompasses many square miles and dozens of separate neighborhoods, but most visitors will only hear it referred to broadly as "East London." It starts around Shoreditch and Whitechapel and, as you go east, begins to incorporate rehabbed former industrial wastelands. **Docklands,** the area bordering the river, is rich in upscale condos and corporate offices. **Greenwich** is a gorgeous villagelike neighborhood on the southern bank of the Thames. And in Stratford, the biggest population center of East London, everything seems newly made, including the Queen Elizabeth Olympic Park.

Dennis Severs' House ★★★ MUSEUM   This 1724 town house was dragged down by a declining neighborhood until the 1970s, when eccentric Californian Dennis Severs purchased it for a pittance, dressed it with antiques, and delighted the intelligentsia with this amusingly pretentious imagination odyssey—he called it "Still Life Drama." Other museums are unrealistically neat and cordoned off, but his house looks lived-in, so the past feels as real as it truly was. As Severs, who died in 1999, put it, "In this house it is not what you *see,* but what you have only just *missed* and are being asked to imagine."

You could go during the day, but it's best on Monday, Wednesday, and Friday after dark for "Silent Night." As you approach, the shutters are drawn and a gas lamp burns. You're admitted by a manservant who speaks little. He motions you to explore the premises, silently and at your own pace. Suddenly, you're in the parlor of a prosperous merchant in the 1700s; the owners seem to be home but in the next room. Candles burn, a fire pops in the hearth, the smell of food wafts in the air, and a black cat dozes in the corner. Out on the street, you hear footsteps and hooves. Room by dusky room, you silently explore corners overflowing with the implements of everyday life. It's as if the residents were just there, leaving toys on the stairs, beds rumpled, mulled wine freshly spilled, tea growing cold. By the time you explore the attic, you'll have accompanied the house and its occupants through its decay into a collapsing slum. "Silent Night" is one of London's most invigorating diversions.

18 Folgate St., E1. www.dennissevershouse.co.uk. ⓒ **020/7247-4013.** Admission £10 Mon daytime or Sun visits, £15 Silent Night visits (£17.50 for Christmas period). Day visits: Sun noon–4pm; selected Mon noon–2pm; last admission 45 min. before closing. Silent Night: Mon, Wed, Fri 5–9pm (reservations required). Tube: Liverpool Street.

Geffrye Museum ★★ MUSEUM This U-shaped line of dignified brick houses, built in 1714 for ironworkers, is closed for renovations until 2020, but you can still visit its restored almshouse for the poor, which is certainly worth an hour to see how charity cases lived back in the day. They were so mean to poor people! Good thing we're not at all mean to them these days. (Check the website for the schedule; £5 adults, free for children 15 and under.)

136 Kingsland Rd., Shoreditch, E2. www.geffrye-museum.org.uk. ✆ **020/7739-9893.** Main museum and gardens closed until 2020. Tube: Hoxton.

Museum of Childhood ★★ MUSEUM The awesome V&A Museum (p. 151) chronicles kid-dom through the ages in this location, pulling from a considerable archive of toys, clothing, dollhouses, books, teddy bears, and games. Objects are placed at kids' eye-level with simplified descriptions. Some young ones don't grasp the concept—toddlers burst into tears when they see a crib behind glass that they can't climb into—but if they're too young for exhibits, bring them to one of the daily kids' activities, such as stories or drawing. Child-rearing history is also addressed; look for the "Princess Bottle" of 1871, which had a reservoir shape that allowed for quick milk dispensing but also incubated bacteria, a fact that wasn't realized until countless babies died. The MoC's double-galleried glass-and-steel hall, which has a cafe, is itself an artifact; it began its life in South Kensington as the home of the nascent V&A collection but was re-erected here in the 1860s—the fish-scale mosaic floor was assembled by female prisoners, many of whom (in an ugly irony) weren't allowed to see their own kids.

Cambridge Heath Rd., E2. www.museumofchildhood.org.uk. ✆ **020/8983-5200.** Free admission. Daily 10am–5:45pm. Tube: Bethnal Green.

Museum of London Docklands ★★★ MUSEUM Most of the city's museums would have you believe that London was always a genteel bastion of refined gentlemen. The real story lies in working men who shortened their own lives to put teacups into more privileged, manicured hands, and in the labor that circulated profits from slavery into banks and onto City gallery walls. Housed in a brick rum-and-coffee warehouse from 1804, the three-floor museum, strong on plain-speaking explanations, traces the history of working on the Thames, starting with Anglo-Saxon times and ending now. You can inspect an intricate model of the medieval London Bridge, which like the Florentine Ponte Vecchio was stacked with homes and businesses but clogged the river's flow so drastically that it was a threat to life. You'll also roam Sailortown, a creepy warren of quayside alleys, all shanties and low doorways, meant to evoke the area's early-19th-century underworld. Finally, the spotlight shifts to the harrowing Blitz, when the East End, taking the brunt of the Reich, was obliterated by fire from the sky and forced to reinvent itself as a corporate citadel. The whole circuit takes 2 to 3 hours. There's also an interactive, river-themed play area for kids, Mudlarks.

No. 1 Warehouse, West India Quay, E14. www.museumoflondon.org.uk/docklands. ✆ **020/7001-9844.** Free admission. Daily 10am–6pm; galleries close 5:40pm. Tube: West India Quay DLR or Canary Wharf.

The Ragged School Museum is a time capsule of a Victorian charity school.

Ragged School Museum ★ MUSEUM   The Victorians weren't very nice people. Although in 1883, as many as 60,000 families lived in a single room, church-run schools still charged a penny a week and had a dress code, and the many kids who couldn't manage ended up on the street. Thomas Bernardo was headed for missionary work abroad when he realized East London kids needed him more than foreigners did; he took in the "ragged" children who couldn't even muster shoes, gave them an education, and made them his "home kids," feeding and nurturing them. From 1877 (when one in four children who lived around here died) to 1908, he used this canalside warehouse as a school—playground in the basement, classrooms (now re-created) up top—and he worked to help the most desperate kids emigrate for better lives. One in 11 Canadians can trace their ancestry to "home" children who went to ragged schools like this one. This little museum is like Bernardo's school: homegrown, rough around the edges, run as a labor of love, and welcoming.

46–50 Copperfield Rd., E3. www.raggedschoolmuseum.org.uk. ✆ **020/8980-6405.** Free admission (suggested donation). Wed–Thurs 10am–5pm; first Sun of the month 2–5pm. Tube: Mile End or Limehouse DLR.

The Royal London Hospital Museum ★ MUSEUM   The Royal London Hospital has been central to London life since 1740, when it was established—supported by donations—to help the desperate condition of the poor. That history has put a lot of cool material in its hodgepodge archive, including letters by unfairly forgotten hero nurse Edith Cavell, forensic files from the Jack the Ripper case, a portion of George Washington's false teeth, and personal belongings of Joseph "The Elephant Man" Merrick, the sweet but luckless soul who lived in rooms on the premises until his death at age 27. You'll see it all, plus lot of skin-crawling archaic medical instruments that will fascinate anyone who works in modern healthcare. This place can keep funky hours; it's always smart to call ahead.

St Augustine with St Philip's Church, Newark St., E1. www.bartshealth.nhs.uk. ℭ **020/ 7377-7608.** Free admission (suggested donation). Tues–Fri 10am–4pm. Tube: White-chapel or Aldgate East.

Up at the O₂ ★★ TOUR   Built on a toxic peninsula wasteland on the Thames in the 1990s, the Millennium Dome was conceived as a showplace for what turned out to be a poorly attended turn-of-the-century exposition. It's supported by a dozen 100m-tall yellow towers, one for each hour on the clock, in honor of the nearby Greenwich Prime Meridian—a preening and meaning-less symbolism that cost £789 million, and then stood empty for half a decade. In 2007, however, it was finally reborn as the city's finest performance arena, with 20,000 seats (p. 246). Now, Londoners can stomp on it like they always wanted. Climbers, about 10 at a time, hook into a safety rigging system and follow a guide over a tensile fabric catwalk laid a few feet over the Dome's roof, to an observation platform at the zenith of the structure. There they pause for 15 minutes of photos of East London (the City is mostly hidden behind Canary Wharf's towers). Beneath them, humming like a ship at sea, is a Dome conquered. The excursion isn't for the height-averse—at your highest, you're 52m (171 ft.) above the ground—and it's not for big eaters or children, either (the weight cutoff is 130kg/286 lb., and you have to be at least 10 years old). But it's also not scary, since you're tethered and the shoes they lend you grip well. If the weather's bad, you get matching jumpsuits like Ooompa-Loompas. The climb, which is more like a stroll up a steep hill, takes 45 minutes; the rest of the 90-min. experience consists of getting harnessed and psyched up.

Peninsula Sq., SE10. www.theO2.co.uk. ℭ**020/8463-2680.** Climbs £30–36, depending on weekday/weekend/holiday/sunset/twilight. Daily 10am to 6–10pm, depending on season. Tube: North Greenwich or North Greenwich ferry.

Greenwich Attractions

Situated on a picturesque slope of the south bank of the Thames, Greenwich once was home to Greenwich Palace, where both Henry VIII and Elizabeth I were born. The last part of the palace to be constructed, the **Queen's House** (1616, Inigo Jones, p. 179), still stands, but most of the grounds were rebuilt in the late Georgian period as the equally palatial Royal Hospital, a convales-cence haven for disabled and veteran sailors now known as the **Old Royal Naval College** (p. 179). High on the hill, in Greenwich Park, is the **Royal Observatory** (p. 180), and between them stands the **National Maritime**

East London & Docklands

EXPLORING LONDON

Museum (p. 178). Many of these treasures are owned by the state, so most entrance fees are waived; you can play the whole day without paying more than a few pounds. Most tourists come to get a photo straddling the **Prime Meridian,** the line that slices through the Observatory and marks zero degrees longitude. Stop by the **Discover Greenwich visitor center,** alongside the *Cutty Sark,* for background information and to pick up a walking tour from the Greenwich Tour Guides Association (www.greenwichtours.co.uk; ✆ **0757/577-2298**). Greenwich offers a Meridian Line tour at noon, or town highlights at 2:15pm. Tours costs £8 adult, £7 seniors/students/kids, and last about 90 minutes.

Cutty Sark ★★ HISTORIC SHIP   The only clipper ship left in the world was launched in 1869; by the end of its 52-year career, it had traveled the equivalent of to the moon and back, carrying cargos including tea, wool, and furniture. By the sunset of its sailing life, it was a decrepit old thing, renamed *Ferreira,* having survived hurricanes in America and the loss of its mast in Cape Town. It was eventually drydocked in Greenwich to show off for tour-

ists, but worse indignities were yet to come: A 2007 fire twisted its iron frame and devastated its hull planking (fortunately, sails, masts, prow, fig-urehead, and deckhouses had been safely stored for a restoration). As you tour its hold, climbing stairs and weaving across decks (and acciden-tally banging your head on low thresholds), note that the white-painted framework you see is origi-nal, while the grey is new. Restoration provided an opportunity for the pres-ent lavish presentation: Today, it's as gorgeous as when Britain dominated the seas, and instead of floating in the Thames, it floats 3.6m (11 ft.) over a dry dock skirted by a glass canopy. At the end of a full ship tour, visitors can peep beneath the streamlined brassed keel. It's a slight cheat, because the hull originally was coated with Muntz metal, bitumen, and felt, but hey, it looks incredible. It'll never be speedy again, but it's never looked hotter. If you're also entering the Royal Observatory (p. 180), buy a combo ticket and save a few pounds.

The brass keel of the *Cutty Sark.*

King William Walk, SE10. www.rmg.co.uk/cuttysark. ✆ **020/8312-6608.** Admission £13.50 adults, £12 seniors and students, £7 children 5–15; higher posted prices include a "voluntary donation"; cheaper if purchased online. Daily 10am–5pm; last admission 4:15pm. Tube: Cutty Sark DLR, Greenwich river ferry, or Greenwich National Rail.

The Fan Museum ★ MUSEUM   This is as niche as museums get, but it's classy and it truly has the best of what it claims to honor—some 4,000 artful specimens, many of them precious, going back a millennium. Fans were necessities in the centuries before air-conditioning, when flames generated constant heat and corsets severely restricted breathing; these tools were the only things that helped ladies remain conscious. There are regular exhibition of the little lifesavers, such as collections of Christmas-themed imagery, Biblical themes, and so on. The museum also offers a reasonably priced afternoon tea at 2:15 and 3:45pm (reservations required)—don't faint, but it's just £9.

12 Crooms Hill, SE10. www.thefanmuseum.org.uk. ⓟ **020/8305-1441.** Admission £5 adults, £3 seniors and students 7–16. Tues–Sat 11am–5pm; Sun noon–5pm. Tube: Cutty Sark DLR, Greenwich river ferry, or Greenwich National Rail.

The National Maritime Museum ★★ MUSEUM   Don't be put off by the topic. The world's largest maritime museum is extraordinarily kid-friendly, brimming with buzzy set-piece toys such as steering simulators and a giant play area that looks like a world map. So it's not as, ahem, dry as most would expect. Because so much of Britain's history from the 17th to 20th centuries was transacted via the high seas, this place isn't just about boats and knots. The facility has an endless supply of Smithsonian-worthy artifacts that would do any museum proud. Highlights include a musical stuffed pig

Gold details on a boat on display at the National Maritime Museum.

clutched in a lifeboat by a *Titanic* passenger; and, most ghoulishly, the blood-stained breeches and bullet-punctured topcoat that Admiral Lord Nelson wore on the day he took his fatal shot (in a new gallery devoted to the man). Get the creeps from relics from Sir John Franklin's ill-fated 1848 Arctic expedition, including lead-lined food tins that likely caused the explorers to go mad and probably eat each other. Also excellent is the Atlantic Worlds display, which plumbs the British role in the slave trade, something few London museums touch upon. The museum also presents the oft-ignored viewpoint that through the East India Company, England looted India—in fact, the English word *looted* has Hindi origins. It's not all so gloomy, though; there are big set pieces such as figureheads, models, antique instruments, and entire wooden vessels. Weekends are full of free kids' events (storytelling, treasure hunts) that bring suburban London families pouring into the gates, and the fun Greenwich Market is running nearby then, too. Maps cost £1.

Romney Rd., Greenwich, SE10. www.nmm.ac.uk. ✆ **020/8858-4422.** Free admission. Daily 10am–5pm. Tube: Cutty Sark DLR, Greenwich river ferry, or Greenwich National Rail.

Old Royal Naval College ★ HISTORIC SITE/LANDMARK This

1696 neoclassical complex, primarily the work of Christopher Wren, is mostly used by a university but offers two main sights: the Painted Hall and the Chapel. The **Painted Hall,** fresh off a major conservation, is adorned with 40,000 square feet of incredible paintings by Sir James Thornhill that took nearly 2 decades to complete. It was the setting for the funeral of Admiral Nelson, but it may never have looked more glorious than today, because recent restoration removed years of candle grime and even crusty food splatters from rowdy pensioners' banquets. The **Chapel,** in the Greek Revival style, is the work of James Stuart. The 90-min. tours by accredited guides run daily at 11:30am and 2pm. If the ORNC's stately symmetry rings a bell, that's because it was used as a stand-in for Paris in the movie musical *Les Misérables.* It's also where you'll find the **Old Brewery** (p. 106), with plenty of garden space where you can kick back with very stiff pints.

Greenwich, SE10. www.ornc.org. ✆ **020/8269-4747.** Free admission. 90-min. tours (reservation line ✆ **020/8269-4799**) £5 adults, free for children 15 and under. Grounds daily 8am–11pm; buildings daily 10am–5pm; Royal Chapel Sun 11am for worship. Tube: Cutty Sark DLR, Greenwich river ferry, or Greenwich National Rail.

The Queen's House ★ HISTORIC HOME Viewed from the river and

framed by the newer Old Royal Naval College, the Queen's House enjoys as elegant a setting as a building could wish for. Inigo Jones took 22 years to come up with a then-revolutionary Palladian-style summer retreat for Charles I's wife, Henrietta Maria. It was completed only in 1638—just before the Civil Wars cut both Charles and his building schemes off at the head, and Henrietta scurried off to France. The house has a few pleasant galleries and displays, including Orazio Gentileschi's *Joseph and Potiphar's Wife,* which, after the house's 2016 restoration, was returned to these walls for the first time since around 1650. The nautilus-shaped Tulip staircase, plus other rooms, are considered to be haunted by an unknown specter, so have a camera ready.

Romney Rd., SE10. www.rmg.co.uk. ℐ **020/8312-6565.** Free admission; guided tours £10 adult, £9 senior; £1 cheaper online. Daily 10am–5pm. Tube: Cutty Sark DLR, Greenwich river ferry, or Greenwich National Rail.

The Royal Observatory ★ HISTORIC SITE/MUSEUM   Commanding a terrific view from the hill in Greenwich Park, with the towers of Canary Wharf spread out in its lap, the Observatory is yet another creation of Christopher Wren (from 1675), and the place from which time zones emanate. Historically the Empire's most important site for celestial observation, it houses significant relics of star-peeping, but the paid areas aren't worth the money. Most of the good stuff—marked on the map in red—is free, including a small Astronomy Centre and an exhibition on time. The only things admission buys you are an unremarkable ceiling-projection planetarium and the sparsely furnished, borderline-interesting Flamsteed House by Wren, which has a collection of 18th-century clocks once used to crack the mystery of measuring longitude (an advance that ushered the English Empire to worldwide dominance). Most people plunk down admission not because they care about those but to gain access to the Meridian Courtyard. The Prime Meridian, located at precisely 0° longitude (the equator is 0° latitude), crosses through the grounds, and hordes of coach tourists pay to wait an hour for an Instagram moment of straddling the line with a foot in two hemispheres at once—but the secret is they don't have to. The line continues down the wall on the walkway north of the courtyard, where the Meridian is free and there's never a wait. In the old days, the red Time Ball fell precisely at 1pm daily so that the city could synchronize its clocks; it still rises at 12:55pm and drops 5 minutes later. You could set your watch by it, but technically, you already do. If you're also visiting the *Cutty Sark* (p. 177), a combo ticket will save you a few pounds, but overall, the ticket structure is needlessly complicated.

Greenwich Park, Greenwich, SE10. www.rmg.co.uk. ℐ **020/8312-6565.** Free admission for most of grounds. Flamsteed House and Meridian Courtyard: £9 adults, £8.10 seniors and students, £5.85 children 4–15. Planetarium: £8 adults, £7 seniors and students, £5.50 children 3–15. Combination ticket: £13 adults, £9.50 seniors and students, £6.50 children 15 and under. Daily 10am–5pm; last admission 4:30pm. Tube: Cutty Sark DLR, Greenwich river ferry, or Greenwich National Rail.

OUTER LONDON

Dulwich Picture Gallery ★★ MUSEUM   A 15-min. train ride from Victoria and an 8-min. walk lands you in a pretty villagelike enclave of South London, where a leafy stroll acclimates one to contemplation and appreciation. Here you'll find one of the world's most vital collections of Old Master paintings of the 1600s and 1700s, kept in just a few rooms. Magnanimous donors made it England's first public gallery (opened 1817), designed with a surplus of light by Sir John Soane (who also left us his own cramped museum;

p. 127). A visit is almost indescribably serene, the better to stare into the Cheshire Cat face of one of its star masterpieces, Rembrandt's *A Girl at a Window*—how did he capture her bemusedly frank expression? A handheld video tour unspools fascinating backstories of 10 works you might otherwise pass by, such as the portrait of young Venetia Stanley, which exists because she was discovered dead in bed and her distraught husband summoned Van Dyck to capture her beautiful corpse. Twist ending: Her beloved might have poisoned her. At the airy cafe, grab tea with Devon clotted cream for £6.

Gallery Rd., Dulwich Village, SE21. www.dulwichpicturegallery.org.uk. *©* **020/8693-5254.** Admission £5 adults, £5 seniors and students, free for children 17 and under; special exhibitions cost more. Tues–Sun 10am–5pm; last entry 4:30pm. National Rail: West Dulwich Station.

Eltham Palace and Gardens ★ HISTORIC HOME

Eltham (*ell*-tum) was once a palace on the level of importance with Hampton Court or Greenwich—Henry VIII was a boy here. Time was not kind to the grounds, though, and by the 1920s, Stephen and Virginia Courtauld, a wealthy childless couple, bought the Tudor ruin to rebuild into an ocean liner-inspired mansion for entertaining their movie-industry friends. The guided tour provides a delightful peek into the eccentricity and insularity of the wealthy—while it worships their entertaining skills, the evidence uncomfortably suggests they were awful people. Stephen was prone to sulking, and their obnoxious pet lemur, Mah-Jongg, liked to bite guests—it bit one Arctic explorer so badly an artery was severed, which postponed his exploration by three months. (Note Jongy's likeness carved into various architectural details.) Most country houses drive home stiff Georgian elegance, but Eltham (strangely, closed Sat) is about the excesses of Art Deco living and a capsule of Britain between the wars. After tearing down sections that might have had Tudor origin, the Courtaulds lived here only 11 years. The surrounding moat and 19 acres of greenery and gardens, however, still feel like they must have 400 years ago.

Court Yard, Eltham, Greenwich, SE9. www.english-heritage.org.uk. *©* **020/8294-2548.** Admission £15 adults, £13.50 seniors and students, £9 kids 5–17; posted prices are higher and include "gift aid." Apr–Sept Sun–Fri 10am–6pm; other periods daily noon–5pm (hours shift seasonally, see website for more information). National Rail: Eltham from Charing Cross.

The Freud Museum ★ HISTORIC HOME

In a hilly Hampstead neighborhood of spacious brick-faced homes, Sigmund Freud, having just fled the Nazis, spent the last year of his life here. His daughter Anna, herself a noted figure in psychoanalysis, lived on in the same house until her own death in 1982. Sigmund's study and library, which came from the doctor's famed offices at Berggasse 19, Vienna, were left precisely as they were on the day he died—which he did on a couch, of course.

20 Maresfield Gardens, NW3. www.freud.org.uk. *©* **020/7435-2002.** Admission £9 adults, £7 seniors, £5 students age 12–16, free for children 11 and under. Wed–Sun noon–5pm. Tube: Hampstead.

Hampton Court Palace ★★ PALACE   A 35-min. commuter train ride from the center of town, Hampton Court *looks* like the ideal palace because it *defined* the ideal. The rambling redbrick mansion was a center for royal life from 1525 to 1737, its forest of chimneys standing regally in 24 hectares (59 acres) of achingly pretty riverside gardens, now painstakingly restored to their 1702 appearance. Visitors come seeking vibrations left by Henry VIII during the 811 days he spent here (yes, that's all; he had more than 60 houses, partly because his court devoured so much food it kept exhausting local resources). The Crown still stocks precious art in many of the 70 public rooms, which start out Tudor and end up Georgian. It can take a whole day to see properly.

The inflexibly programmed audio guide, which follows a handful of themed trails (Young Henry VIII's Story, Henry VIII's Apartments, and so on), is free, but it harps endlessly on the same old stories about King Henry's wives; if you're looking for deeper explanations, research beforehand. What you're told panders to Tudor scandals because curators apparently think it makes history more interesting. On a surface level it does, but ultimately, it reduces this famous location to little more than a stereotypical set of a tawdry bygone play. The staff can't even adequately describe the paintings on the

The entrance at Hampton Court Palace was definitely built to impress.

TAKE THE thames TO HAMPTON OR KEW

From April to September daily, you can take **London River Services** (www.wpsa.co.uk; ✆ **020/7930-2062;** £19 adults, £9.50 children 5–15, cash only) all the way from Westminster in central London to Hampton Court, the way Henry VIII did on his barges. It can be a commitment of 3 hr., however, and tides sometimes play such havoc with schedules that you may arrive too late to see much. You will have to take the train the other way. Trains go twice an hour from Waterloo, take 35 min., and let you off across the river from the Palace: much easier. Kew is simpler: The ferry's round-trip fare is £27 adults and £13.50 children. It goes four times a day and takes 90 min.

walls because the Royal Collection, which loans them, keeps switching their locations at a whim. Days are full of live events, which may include re-enactments of gossipy events by costumed actors; traditional cooking using bygone methods in the **Tudor Kitchens** (a popular stop); bizarre spoken-word performances in the hammer-beamed **Great Hall;** or ghost tours. Whatever you do, don't neglect the 26.7-hectare (66-acre) **gardens**—regally planted with historical accuracy (topiaries, sculpted yews, 300-year-old trees), they're half the reason to visit. Make time to lose yourself in the Northern Gardens' 500-year-old shrubbery **Maze,** installed by William III; kids giggle their way through to the middle of this leafy labyrinth. The well-mannered **South Garden** has the Great Vine, the oldest and largest vine in the world, planted in 1768; its black grapes are sold in the gift shop in early September. Wear strong shoes because the grounds are cobbled. Seeing this consumes half a day; if I had to choose between it and Windsor (p. 290), I'd choose Windsor.

East Molesey, Surrey. www.hrp.org.uk. ✆ **084/4482-7777.** Admission £22.70 adults, £18.10 seniors and students, £11.35 children 5–15; higher posted prices include a "voluntary donation"; up to £2 cheaper if bought online. Mar–late Oct daily 10am–6pm; late Oct–Mar daily 10am–4:30pm; last admission 1 hr. before closing. National Rail: Hampton Court from Waterloo Station.

Royal Botanic Gardens, Kew ★★ PARK/GARDEN   The 121-hectare (300-acre) gardens, with many expansive lawns, earned a spot on the UNESCO list of World Heritage Sites in 2003. As you'd expect, the glasshouses are world-class—there are 2,000 varieties of plants, many descended from specimens collected in the earliest days of international sea trade. Of the seven conservatories, the domed **Palm House,** built from 1844 to 1848 and jungle-warm, is probably the world's most recognizable greenhouse, while the **Temperate House** is the world's largest glasshouse containing the world's largest indoor plant (the 17.7m/58-ft.-tall Chilean wine-palm, planted in 1843—and that's not a typo). It just completed a £41-million restoration, and it's full of some 1,500 species of incredible plants, some once thought lost,

5

EXPLORING LONDON

Outer London

like the *Dombeya mauritiana*, and some, like the *Encephalartos woodii* cycad, extinct in the wild. Other attractions include a bamboo garden, a water lily pond, **Treehouse Towers** (a tree-themed play area for children 3–11), and, it must be said, a heartwarmingly charming village outside the gates. The gardeners are champs; in 1986, they coaxed a bloom from a portea that hadn't flowered in 160 years. Kew's contributions to botanical science are ongoing since 1759, but not mired in the past; it also provides a free app that lets you scan labels to learn more and find blooms. Unless you're a fevered horticulturalist, however, it will ultimately feel like a park you have to pay for—and pay a lot, at that. Also be aware that many of the goodies clamp down in winter (including Kew Palace, included in the price, p. 186), so this is best in the summer.

Kew, Richmond, Surrey. www.kew.org. © **020/8332-5655.** Admission £16 adults, £14 seniors and students, £4 children 16 and under; posted prices are higher and include "voluntary donation"; discounts sometimes available online. Daily 10am–7pm (closes at 6pm in fall and 5:15pm in winter); last entry 1 hr. before closing. Tube: Kew Gardens.

Warner Bros. Studio Tour London—The Making of Harry Potter ★★★ MUSEUM   London's most popular new family outing is like a DVD extra feature that comes to life; it's a full day out, and as gripping as the fine museums can be. On the very lot where the eight movies of history's most successful film franchise were shot, it seems that every set, prop, prosthetic, wig, and wand—and I mean every last thing—was lovingly saved for this polished, informative, and exhaustive walk-though feast. You could spend hours grazing the bounty, from the students' Great Hall to Dumbledore's roost to Dolores Umbridge's den to the actual Diagon Alley. There's not much filler, so book your entry time for early in the day so you'll have time to wander. Even if you care nothing about the movies, you will be blown away by the craftsmanship of items that got barely 2 seconds of screen time. The finale, an astounding 1:24 scale model of Hogwarts Castle embedded with 2,500 fiber optic lights, is 50 feet across and takes up an arena-size room, lit to simulate day and night. Midway through the tour, in an outdoor area containing 4 Privet Dr. and the actual Knight Bus, you'll find one of only four places on Earth where you can taste Butterbeer and Butterbeer ice cream. And you won't *believe* the gift shop. Easy 15-min. trains (don't get on one that takes 40 min.) go three times an hour from Euston Station—but not, fans sigh, from Platform 9¾ at King's Cross. (Although there, an enterprising Potter souvenir stall affixed a sign and sells people pictures.) You will wait just outside the Watford Junction station for the shuttle bus.

Warner Bros. Studios Leavesden, Aerodrome Way, Leavesden, Hertfordshire. www.wbstudiotour.co.uk. © **0345/084-0900.** Admission £41 adults, £33 children 5–15, free for children 4 and under, £132 family of 4; slightly cheaper "Saver" tickets sold online for lower-traffic days. Return train ticket £10–20. Reservations required. Daily. First tours 9–10am, last tours 4–7pm depending on day, closes 2½ hr. after last tour time. National Rail: Watford Junction, then a £2.50 return shuttle bus that meets trains.

Other Outer London Attractions

Fuller's Brewery Tours ★ FACTORY TOUR   Beer has been made on this Thameside property in West London since the 1600s, and Fuller's has been in charge of the brewing since 1845. Now this steampunk-feeling brick complex supplies some 380 pubs with its products, particularly its popular London Pride. They refuse to move to cheaper digs because a new water supply would change the flavor. Its tour is professional and engaging, more educational than bacchanalian—these people are passionate about their heritage. Free samples once you're done!

Chiswick Lane South. www.fullers.co.uk/brewery/book-a-tour. ✆ **020/8996-2000.** Tours £20. Mon–Sat hourly 11am–3pm. No children 15 and under, no tasting under age 18. Reservations required. Tube: Turnham Green, then a 20-min. walk.

Home of Charles Darwin—Down House ★★ HISTORIC HOME Charles Darwin made one of history's most important voyages, but once back in England, he barely left his home here in the idyllic parish village of Downe. Upstairs you'll find out about the man and his life (did you know the scientist who theorized about mutation married his own first cousin?) and downstairs, guided by an audio tour narrated by Sir David Attenborough, you'll explore his study, his greenhouse, and his enchanting garden of lawns and breezy fields. No wonder he never left again. There are two charming country pubs to enjoy while you wait for the bus back; your Oyster card will get you here.

Luxted Rd., Downe, Kent. www.english-heritage.org.uk. ✆ **0370/333-1181.** Admission £12 adults, £10.80 seniors and students, £7.20 children 5–17; posted prices are higher and include "gift aid." Apr–Sept daily 10am–6pm; Oct–Nov daily 10am–5pm; Nov–mid-Feb Sat–Sun 10am–4pm; mid-Feb–Mar Wed–Sun 10am–4pm. National Rail: Bromley South, then bus no. 122 and 7-min. walk.

Horniman Museum ★ MUSEUM   A rich Victorian dilettante collected crazy stuff from all over the world, and rather than let it gather dust, he built a museum in South London. This repository of some 350,000 items has since blossomed into a wild educational ride, with something for everyone, particularly children. To wit: a cherished collection of 7,000 musical instruments (Boosey & Hawkes, once the U.K.'s largest instrument maker, donated its archive) and a huge range of items regarding anthropology (masks, puppets, folk art) and natural history (stuffed creatures galore). There's even a modest aquarium, a cafe, and some gorgeous gardened grounds on a hill with a panorama of London 6 miles north.

100 London Rd., Forest Hill. www.horniman.ac.uk. ✆ **020/8699-1872.** Free admission. Daily 10am–5:30pm. Tube: Forest Hill Overground.

Kenwood House ★★ HISTORIC HOME   Bask in a country-house high without leaving the city. Kenwood is a sublime 18th-century job by Robert Adam with a sigh-inducing southern view across Hampstead Heath, from within the green embrace of 112 acres. Inside, the walls are hung with paintings that would be the envy of the National Gallery, including Vermeer's *The*

Guitar Player, a John Singer Sargent, and a Rembrandt self-portrait. The title character of the 2014 film *Belle* was raised by Lord Mansfield in this house, and the film was shot here. There's no better place to enjoy an English summer than on its acres of lawns or alongside its ornamental pond.

Hampstead Lane, NW3. www.english-heritage.org.uk. ℂ **020/8348-1286.** Free admission, guided tours £16.30 adult, £14.70 seniors and students, £9.80 kids. House: daily 10am–5pm (summer until 6pm); grounds: 8am–dusk. Tube: Archway or Golders Green, then bus no. 210.

Kew Palace and Queen Charlotte's Cottage ★ PALACE   Remember George III? He's the dilettante ruler who, during his reign from 1760 to 1820, lost the American colonies and went crazy from suspected porphyria: See the movie *The Madness of King George* for the tragic tale. Kew Palace is where he spent his childhood and later went insane, and you can tour a piece of his vanished palace, recently restored with scientific exactitude. It's only the size of a standard manor house and lacks interpretation except for some ill-advised histrionic audio enactments that no one pauses to endure. Across Kew Gardens, the little Queen Charlotte's Cottage is an imitation of a humble village home. Its Picnic Room is painted with vines across its vaulted ceiling—work attributed to King George's daughter, Princess Elizabeth. In late April, the Cottage, which is at Kew's southwest end, is surrounded by bluebells in bloom.

Royal Botanic Gardens, Kew, Richmond. www.hrp.org.uk. ℂ **020/8332-5655.** Included in Kew Gardens admission: £15 adults, £14 seniors and students, £3.50 children 16 and under; discounts sometimes available online. Kew Palace: Apr–Oct 10am–5:30pm; closed Nov–Mar. Cottage: Sat–Sun and bank holidays 10am–4pm. Tube: Kew Gardens.

Mandir ★ TEMPLE   The breathtakingly pretty, many-pinnacled Mandir in northwest London is the largest Hindu temple outside of India. This fabulous concoction was completed in 1995, after some 5,500 tons of Italian Carrara marble and Bulgarian limestone were carved in India and assembled by volunteers. Its dome was built without using steel or lead. The interior is as white and lavishly detailed as a doily—it's apt to amaze even people generally unimpressed by such virtuosity. Tourists are welcome—try to be there to witness the musical wick-lighting Arti ceremony at 11:45am. If you're entering, shorts or skirts must fall at least to the knee (although ankle-length is preferable and sarongs are available to borrow); visitors must also remove their shoes.

105–119 Brentfield Rd., NW10. http://londonmandir.baps.org. ℂ **020/8965-2651.** Free admission. Daily 9am–6pm. Tube: Wembley Park, then bus no. 206, or Stonebridge Park, then bus no. 112.

Thames Barrier Visitor Centre ★ LANDMARK/MUSEUM   People forget that London floods. Parliament has been under water, and in 1953, surges killed 307 people in the U.K. At least, London *used* to flood. The Thames Barrier is the city's primary defense against it, comprised of ten 20m (66-ft.) steel-and-concrete gates that can be raised to block the 520m

(1706-ft.) span of the river in just 10 minutes. Most of the time you can't see the gates, which rest on the riverbed, but the piers that raise and lower them are always visible, strung across the river like a row of mini-Sydney Opera Houses. At the visitor center on shore, you plumb the Barrier's construction and, if you're lucky, see a test raise.

1 Unity Way, Woolwich, SE18. www.gov.uk/guidance/the-thames-barrier. ℰ **020/8305-4188.** Admission £4.15 adults, £3.65 seniors and students, £2.65 children 5–15, free for children 4 and under. Thurs–Sun and bank holiday Mon 10:30am–5pm. National Rail: Woolwich Dockyard or Charlton.

Wimbledon Lawn Tennis Museum ★★ MUSEUM   Most of us can't get into the tournament (see "Netting Wimbledon Tickets," below), and there's an 11-year waiting list to become a member to the All England Lawn Tennis & Croquet Club, the official name of Wimbledon. But for us, there's still something worth seeing the rest of the year. The museum is like a Hall of Fame, with an emphasis of course on Wimbledon, with artifacts going back to 1555. The climax, most times of year, is the hallowed room shimmering with the silver men's "Challenge-Cup" and women's "Challenge-Plate," which are the actual Championships trophies inscribed with every winner's name. (The

---

Netting Wimbledon Tickets

It's easy watching the Wimbledon Championships on TV for 2 weeks in late June and early July, but seeing it in person is a trickier matter. High hotel prices are just the beginning. Because tickets for the final matches go to VIPs, you're more likely to catch famous players during the early rounds, when the club's 19 grass courts are all in use. For the price of a "ground pass" (£15–£25, cash only) you can get roaming access to all but three courts (surcharges of £29–£175 are levied for Centre, No. 1, and No. 2 courts, and those tickets are distributed by lottery the previous summer). Around 6,000 ground passes are distributed each morning starting at 7:30am, so arrive many hours before (by 5:30am at the latest) that to camp in Wimbledon Park, Church Road side (no large luggage allowed). If you snag one, you'll probably be inside by noon, before matches begin. You can wander around to your heart's content, drinking Pimm's Cup and eating strawberries and cream, and watching matches on giant screens, but you'll still need to get into the three most important courts. You can try by ballot, but that closes in December. Meanwhile, Ticketmaster (and no one else; www.ticketmaster.co.uk) may release several hundred tickets for Centre Court and Court 3 the day before play. Another clever way to get in is to bum tickets off people as they get tired and leave for the day; just don't offer money—the organizers hate that because they sell unused tickets, too, for charity. Those are resold after 3pm to those already on the grounds (£5–£10). On weekdays and rainy days, your chances of getting unfilled seats for the best courts are better, since people are working or huddling indoors. And after 5pm, ground-pass rates dip to, at most, £18, which isn't such a bad deal since matches continue until 9pm. It's all ridiculously complicated—the English love complicated admission schemes—so check ahead on Wimbledon.com to ensure rules remain the same.

British have never been prouder than they are now that Scotsman Andy Murray brought home the trophy after 77 years.) There is no other museum in the world where a ghostly video apparition of John McEnroe appears in a locker room to vent about opponents. (He comes in peace. No need to duck.) Tennis fans should absolutely spring for the tour of the grounds, too, which is truly all-access, including entry into the Competitors' Complex reserved for players, a photo op in the press conference room where they meet the media, and the all-important Centre Court, where Finals are always played, and always on grass. The guides are fantastic and challenge you to stump them.

Church Rd., SW19. www.wimbledon.com/museum. ℂ **020/8946-6131.** Museum admission £13 adults, £11 seniors and students, £8 children 5–16. Museum with tour: £25 adults, £21 seniors and students, £15 children 5–16 (one free child for each paying adult). Apr–Sept, daily 10am–5:30pm; Oct–Mar daily 10am–5pm. Tube: Southfields, then 15-min. walk or bus no. 493; or National Rail from Waterloo to Wimbledon Station, then bus no. 493.

OVERRATED ATTRACTIONS

In every city, you invariably find attractions that are heavily publicized but, once seen, are revealed to be time poorly spent. London provides a variety of overpriced pursuits catering to people who are ignorant of its treasures—there's even an attraction by the London Eye about the movie *Shrek*, which needless to say you can safely skip. Take our advice: These are overhyped.

ArcelorMittal Orbit OBSERVATION TOWER   This 114.5m-tall (376-ft.) vertical scribble, a publicity exercise by a steel concern that is now failing, has observation decks at 76m (249 ft.) and 80m (262 ft.), but it barely matters when there's not much to look at. It originally overlooked the Olympics, but with the torch and the games gone, it now peers into a stadium many miles from town. So tragic have attendance numbers been than in 2016 it desperately added a 40-second tube slide, the world's longest and tallest—narrow enough to bonk your head and fast enough to smash your phone—that drops from one of the observation levels, wrapping around the structure 12 times. They put a helmet and elbow pads on you, tuck your feet into a cubby at the end of a mat, and send you screaming. It also offers an abseil thrill from 80m/262 feet high (www.wireandsky.co.uk; ℂ **020/3198-0407;** £85; minimum age 14, maximum weight 120kg/264 lb.). Wear a jacket because it gets windy in the exposed areas. And no, it doesn't orbit.

Queen Elizabeth Olympic Park, E20. www.arcelormittalorbit.com. ℂ **0333/800-8099.** Admission £17.50 adults, £13.50 seniors and students, £12.50 children 3–16; tower without slide £12.50 adult, £10.50 senior/student, £7.50 kids 3–16; slight discount when booked online. Slide restricted to people taller than 4'2"/1.3m. Mon–Fri 11am–5pm; Sat–Sun 10am–6pm; last admission 30 min. before closing. Tube: Stratford.

Emirates Air Line OBSERVATION GONDOLA   Opened for the Olympics as a Thames crossing between the ExCeL convention center and the O_2

dome, it's an enclosed, 10-person gondola (you'll share with strangers) with (barely audible) recorded commentary that shuttles between two places most tourists never go. It's too far from the City to be a panoramic substitute for the Eye or the Shard. Don't waste money on the "Experience" package that includes a touristy flight simulator/Emirates PR puffery on the O_2 side. The ride takes 5–10 minutes. It costs what a Tube ride does, and you can use Oyster.

Emirates Cable Car Terminal, Edmund Halley Way, E10, or Royal Docks side 27 Western Gateway, E16. www.emiratesairline.co.uk. ℗ **0843/222-1234.** Admission £4.50 adult, £2.30 children (without Oyster card); or £3.40 adults, £1.70 children 5–15 (with Oyster card). Mon–Fri 7am–11pm; Sat 8am–11pm; Sun 9am–11pm; in winter, closed at 9pm Sun-Thurs. Tube: North Greenwich or Royal Victoria DLR.

The Household Cavalry Museum MUSEUM   Along Whitehall, where guards try mightily to ignore buffoonish tourists who try to get them to crack a smile, this tiny museum pays soporific tribute to the martial ceremonies of the Queen's Life Guard. You might see troopers groom horses through a glass partition or regard cases of uniforms and regalia with glazed eyes, but—nothing against these dedicated men—you won't get much back on your investment. On the hour, mounted dutymen change, and at 11am, the Life Guard changes, but you can see those outside for free.

Horse Guards, Whitehall, SW1. www.householdcavalrymuseum.co.uk. ℗ **020/7930-3070.** Admission £8 adults, £6 seniors and children 5–16. Apr–Oct 10am–6pm; Nov–March 10am–5pm. Tube: Embankment.

The London Dungeon ATTRACTION   Avoid it like the plague. This sophomoric gross-out, with locations in 10 cities, sops up overflow from the London Eye. Costumed actors bray at you as you're led through darkness from set to set, each representing a period of English history as a 13-year-old boy might define them. The climax is a pair of indoor carnival rides. If you dread being picked on by bad stand-up comics, you're going to hate this place. Booking ahead may not save you having to queue. If you can't resist, at least bundle it with a ticket on the London Eye for a discount.

County Hall, Westminster Bridge Rd., SE1. www.thedungeons.com. ℗ **020/7654-0809.** Admission from £31 adults, £26 children 5–15; £7–£8 cheaper booked online. Times change but roughly daily 10am–5pm. Tube: Westminster or Waterloo.

London Sea Life Aquarium AQUARIUM   Sure, it's fun to see sharks under your feet and penguins on a faux floe. But sorry Charlie, the truth is there is nothing here you can't see at other fish zoos. There are more than three dozen other locations worldwide by Sea Life, the McDonald's of fish tanks, and this one feels as cramped as a 16th-century galleon.

County Hall, Westminster Bridge Rd., SE1. www.sealifelondon.co.uk. ℗ **0871/663-1678.** Admission £26 adults, £21 children 3–15, free for children 2 and under; 10% discount online. Mon–Fri 10am–6pm; Sat–Sun 9:30am–7pm; last admission 1 hr. before closing. Tube: Waterloo or Westminster.

ritual ABUSE

I'm only telling you this because I love you: **Changing the Guard,** sometimes called Guard Mounting, is an underwhelming use of your time, even if admission is free. Arrive at Buckingham Palace at least 45 minutes before the 11:30am ceremony if you don't want to face the backs of other tourists. A marching band advances from Birdcage Walk (often, playing themes from *Star Wars, West Side Story,* or ABBA—so much for traditional English customs), then members of the Queen's Life Guard—two if the queen's away, three or four if she's in—do a change around their sentry boxes behind a heavy fence. And that's it, give or take additional prancing. Buckingham Palace (www.royal.gov.uk/changing-guard) sells a $1 smartphone app that will help decode the ritual. It takes place daily May–July, every other day the rest of year, and it gets cancelled in heavy rain (Tube: St James's Park, Victoria, or Green Park).

Guards patrol all day, without crowds, at both Buckingham Palace and at Horse Guards Arch on Whitehall (which does its own, uncrowded change daily at 11am, or 10am Sun). Or park yourself at **Wellington Barracks,** just east of the Palace along Birdcage Walk, by 11am, and catch the Inspection of the Guard that happens before the same guards march over to the Palace for the main event. Then use the day's golden hours for something less touristy.

Ceremony of the Keys at the Tower of London (www.hrp.org.uk; ☎ **020/3166-6278;** Tube: Tower Hill, or Tower Gateway DLR), is held every night at 9:53pm as the Yeomen lock up the Tower of London. It's been a routine for more than 700 years—not even German bombs cancelled it. But it's an awful lot of work for not much payoff: You must enter the Tower at 9:30pm (several hours after closing time, so you can't combine it with a day's visit) and leave around 10:05pm, even though the whole show takes less than 7 minutes—plus, photos aren't allowed. As for the event, the Chief Yeoman Warder approaches the heavy wooden gate with keys and a lantern, is asked "Halt, who comes there?," passes muster, and locks up the gates to a bugle call. The end. If you want to see that, apply for tickets online (admission is free), with a nightly maximum of six places April to October. It sells out 11 months in advance.

The London Zoo ZOO   Yes, it has an esteemed history going back to 1828 as a menagerie for members of the Zoological Society of London. It's just that it's ultimately only a zoo, and a smallish one at that, with few large animals. Sumatran tigers, baby penguins, and a newly renovated monkey aviary are not enough to justify the high ticket price, especially for first-time London visitors who could be exploring the city instead.

Outer Circle Rd., Regent's Park, NW1. www.zsl.org. ☎ **020/7722-333.** Admission £24.30 adults, £22 seniors and students, £18 children 3–15; gate prices slightly higher. Daily 10am to 4pm–6pm, depending on the month. Tube: Camden Town, then bus no. 274.

Madame Tussauds ATTRACTION   Have you ever heard of Katrina Kaif? Zoe and Alfie? Jessica Ennis-Hill? If your answer is no, you won't get much joy out of this ferociously priced, miserably crowded wax trap. The execution of its doppelgangers, which you can usually touch (Harry is behind ropes, girls), is generally superb. But the focus of this world-famous waxworks is on British celebrities. A 5-min., Disney-esque ride, "The Spirit of London," invokes every conceivable London stereotype, from the Artful Dodger to plague victims. As you glide through, you'll suddenly wonder if you're the real dummy here.

Marylebone Rd., W1. www.madame-tussauds.com/london. ℂ **0871/894-3000.** Admission based on time of year and time of day, peaks at £35 adults, £30 children 4–15; £6 less when booked online. Daily 9am to 4–6pm, depending on the week, slightly longer Sat–Sun and holidays. Tours continue at least 45 min. past posted closing time. Tube: Baker St.

The Sherlock Holmes Museum ATTRACTION   Set up a house as if it were really the home of a fictional character, prop up some shabby mannequins, and then charge tourists to see it. That's the scheme and it has worked for years, so well there's often a line and it recently hiked prices 50 percent.

221b Baker St., NW1. www.sherlock-holmes.co.uk. ℂ **020/7224-3688.** Admission £15 adults, £10 children 15 and under. Daily 9:30am–6pm. Tube: Baker St.

OUTDOOR LONDON

Buildings come and go, but London's open spaces have remained unchanged for centuries—they're the city's oldest places. There are often walks and tours scheduled, so check websites to see what's coming.

Epping Forest ★★★ PARK/GARDEN   Mostly because its soil is unsuitable for farming, for a millennium this remained a semi-virgin woodland—it's the best place to get a feel for what Britain was like before humans denuded its land. It's the largest open space in London, 6,000 acres, 12 miles long by 2½ miles wide, and it contains a universe of diversity—650 plant species, 80 ponds where waterfowl splash, and even some 1,500 species of fungi. Getting lost in the woods is feasible, but not likely, since it stretches in a single direction. Henry VII built a timber-framed hunting lodge in 1542 that was inherited by his daughter Elizabeth and, astoundingly, still stands: **Queen Elizabeth's Hunting Lodge** (reach that via the Chingford rail station).

Rangers Rd., Chingford, E4. www.cityoflondon.gov.uk/eppingforest. ℂ **020/8529-6681.** Free admission. Daily 6am–dusk. Lodge: daily 10am–5pm. Tube: Snaresbrook or Wood St. National Rail: Chingford.

The Green Park ★★ PARK/GARDEN   The area south of Mayfair between Hyde Park and St James's Park was once a burial ground for lepers, but now is a simple expanse of meadows and light copses of trees. It doesn't have much to offer except pastoral views, and most visitors find themselves crossing it instead of dawdling in it, although its springtime flower beds (which bloom brightest Mar–Apr) are marvelous. Don't sit in one of those picturesque striped deck chairs unless you've got a few quid to pay as rent.

Piccadilly, SW1. ℂ **030/0061-2350.** Free admission. Daily 24 hr. Tube: Green Park.

FAMOUS graves

London's top tombs don't just belong to royalty. Visit these historic area cemeteries for a tranquil day out and to say hello to some major figures.

Bunhill Fields (Tube: Old St.): *The Pilgrim's Progress*'s John Bunyan, poet William Blake, author Daniel Defoe

Golders Green Crematorium (Tube: Golders Green): Ashes of writers Bram Stoker, Doris Lessing, and Seán O'Casey; musician Keith Moon; dancer Anna Pavlova; actor Peter Sellers; Sigmund Freud

Highgate Cemetery (www.highgate cemetery.org; Tube: Archway): **Karl Marx;** authors **Douglas Adams** and **George Eliot** (East Cemetery, £4 entry); actor **Ralph Richardson;** artist **Lucian Freud** (West Cemetery); and in a private area, **George Michael.**

Kensal Green Cemetery (www.kensal greencemetery.com; Tube: Kensal Green, and National Rail): Writers **Terence Rattigan, Anthony Trollope, Harold Pinter, Wilkie Collins, J. G. Ballard, William Makepeace Thackeray;** engineers **Marc Isambard Brunel** and **Isambard Kingdom Brunel**

Royal Hospital Chelsea (Tube: Sloane Square): **Margaret Thatcher**

St Mary's Church, Battersea (Clapham Junction National Rail): Lapsed rebel **Benedict Arnold** (his crypt is now used as a kindergarten)

St Mary Magdalen Roman Catholic Church Mortlake (Mortlake National Rail): adventurer **Sir Richard Burton** (under a tent made of Carrera marble)

St Nicholas Church, Chiswick (Tube: Stamford Brook): Artists **William Hogarth** and **James McNeill Whistler**

St. Nicholas Church, Deptford Green (Deptford National Rail): Writer **Christopher Marlowe**

Greenwich Park ★★ PARK/GARDEN   Decently sized (74 hectares/183 acres), it was once a deer preserve maintained for royal amusement; a herd of them still have 5 hectares (13 acres) at their disposal. It's been a Royal Park since the 15th century, although the boundary wasn't formally defined until the early 1600s when James I erected a brick wall around it, much of which still survives. On top of its clean-swept main hill are marvelous views of the Canary Wharf district, and the world-famous **Royal Observatory** (p. 180), commissioned in 1675 by Charles II, serves as the intersection point for the Prime Meridian, making it the center of Greenwich Mean Time. Most people combine a visit here with the many other museums of Greenwich (p. 176).

Greenwich Park, SE10. www.royalparks.org.uk. ✆ **030/0061-2000.** Free admission. Daily 6am–9pm. National Rail: Greenwich or Maze Hill, or Cutty Sark DLR or Greenwich ferry.

Hampstead Heath ★★★ PARK/GARDEN   Some 7 million visitors a year come to the 320-hectare (791-acre) Heath, in northwest London, to walk on the grass, get enveloped by thick woods, and take in the view from the magnificent Pergola, a beguiling overgrown Edwardian garden and a true London secret. The Heath is a perennial locale for aimless strolls and (it must

Overlooking Hampstead Heath, Kenwood House is a popular filming location and free to explore.

be confessed, George Michael) furtive trysts. The Heath has several sublime places to rest, including the just-restored **Kenwood House** (p. 185), a sumptuous neoclassical home from 1640; and the inviting and woody **Spaniards Inn** (Spaniards Rd. at Spaniards End, NW3; www.thespaniardshampstead.co.uk; ℭ **020/8731-8406**). The Heath's hilltop is another favored lookout point. The Heath isn't considered a park by locals, but a green space. The difference is irrelevant. It's transporting.

www.cityoflondon.gov.uk/hampstead. ℭ **020/7332-3505.** Daily 7:30am–dusk. Tube: Hampstead or Hampstead Heath Overground.

Hyde Park & Kensington Gardens ★★★ PARK/GARDEN Bordered by Mayfair, Bayswater, and Kensington, these two conjoined areas are the largest park in the middle of the city. Hyde Park is home to a meandering lake called the Serpentine, the famous **Speakers' Corner** (p. 143), and the **Diana Memorial Fountain** (p. 146). The most famous promenade is Rotten Row, probably a corruption of "Route de Roi," or King's Way, which was laid out by William III as his private road to town; it runs along the southern edge of the park from Hyde Park Corner. Kensington Gardens, which flows seamlessly from Hyde Park, only opened to plebes like us in 1851, and it hasn't yet

THE watery park

Sure, everybody knows about London's famous green spaces, but there's one recreation area, stretching from London's northwest to its east through gentrified lanes and industrial wasteland alike, that few tourists are told about. It's the **Regent's Canal,** which threads from Paddington through Camden, Islington, and East London before joining with the Thames (26m/86 ft. lower) just before Canary Wharf. It was completed in 1820 to link with canals all the way to Birmingham and feed the city's massive seagoing trade. In those days, barges were animal-drawn and the districts along the waterway were rat-infested and perilous, but today, it's one of the frontiers for development; many of the horse tracks are leafy promenades, shadowy warehouses have become affluent loft condos, and the use of houseboats has soared 60 percent over the last half-decade. A new development north of King's Cross station is revealing even more glories. Along the shore, you'll pass docks where houseboat barges tie up; their owners can be found topside, making conversation with passersby. The most popular segment is probably the crescent just north of Regent's Park. Set in a former icehouse, the **London Canal Museum** (12–13 New Wharf Rd., N1; www.canalmuseum.org.uk; *℃* **020/7713-0836;** admission £5; Tues–Sun 10am–4:30pm; Tube: Kings Cross St Pancras) is devoted to the waterway and operates tours of its towpath and boat tours of the Islington Tunnel, which stretches for 1.2km (¾ mile) under the streets. **London Waterbus** (www.londonwaterbus.com; *℃* **020/7482-2550**) and **Jason's Trip** (www.jasons.co.uk; no phone) ferry riders in longboats through the 270-foot Maida Hill Tunnel and the glorious villas that line the canal between Little Venice (Tube: Warwick Ave.) and Camden's markets (Tube: Camden Town). Ferries run in either direction, year-round; a ride costs £9 for adults, £7.50 seniors and children 3–16. There are no tourist boats that currently ferry riders east of the locks at Camden.

shed its country-manor quality. You'll also find the **Serpentine Gallery** (west of W. Carriage Dr. and north of Alexandra Gate; www.serpentinegallery.org; *℃* **020/7402-6075;** free admission; Tues–Sun 10am–6pm; Tube: South Kensington), a popular venue for its modern art exhibitions and an art bookshop. Each summer (mid-June–Oct), a leading architect creates a fanciful pavilion there. Volunteers sometimes run guided tours of the park's quirks; check the bulletin boards at each park entrance to see if one is upcoming. Borrow a Boris Bike and cruise around this giant green playground, and don't forget to look for Sir George Frampton's marvelous bronze statue of Peter Pan (1912) near the west shore of the Long Water.

Hyde Park, W2. www.royalparks.org.uk. *℃* **0300/061-2000.** Free admission. Daily 5am–midnight. Tube: Hyde Park Corner, Marble Arch, or Lancaster Gate.

Queen Elizabeth Olympic Park ★ PARK/GARDEN   A dearth of trees and a usual bracing wind make this feel a lot like a theme park in which all of the attractions were torn down. Locals mostly love it because they remember when it was an industrial wasteland. The Pringle-shaped Aquatics Centre and Velopark make for striking architecture, but this park is mostly of interest if you want to see the place you saw on TV—yet the torch is gone, the stadium has been downgraded for a soccer team, and the ArcelorMittal Orbit tower (p. 188) is ultimately pointless. If you do go, Stratford station dumps into a mall (one of the nicest in the city); go up one level and exit near the John Lewis.

Stratford, E20. www.queenelizabetholympicpark.co.uk. ℗ **020/3288-1800.** Free admission. Daily 24 hr. Tube: Stratford.

The Regent's Park ★★★ PARK/GARDEN

It's the people's park (195 hectares/487 acres), best for sunning, strolling grassy expanses—it can take a half-hour to cross it—and darting into the bohemian neighborhoods that fringe it. Once a hunting ground, it was very nearly turned into a development for the buddies of Prince Regent (later King George IV), but only a few of the private terrace homes were built. You will notice Winfield House, on 5 hectares (12 acres) near the western border of the park, which has the largest garden in London after the queen's; the American ambassador lives there—surprised? The most breathtaking entrance is from the south through John Nash's elegant Park Crescent development, by the Regent's Park and Great Portland Street Tube stations. North of the park, just over the Regent's Canal

Summertime in Regent's Park.

and Prince Albert Road, **Primrose Hill Park** (Tube: Chalk Farm or Camden Town) affords a panorama of the city from 62m (203 ft.) high.

Regent's Park, NW1. www.royalparks.gov.uk. © **030/0061-2300.** Free admission. Daily 5am–9pm. Tube: Baker St., Great Portland St., or Regent's Park.

Richmond Park ★★★ PARK/GARDEN   The biggest and wildest park, if you have the time, is 30 minutes from Waterloo station, in Richmond, which was once a distinct village but has been absorbed and yuppified by the greater city. It's more than a park—it's a habitat: 2,500 deliriously green acres brimming with herds of deer (since the 1600s!), 144 species of birds, and 11 of Britain's 17 bat species. Beeline to the Isabella Plantation, a 40-acre woodland garden, in May for a nearly pyrotechnic display of pink rhododendrons and azaleas. The visitor center is by the square in front of Pembroke Lodge, a Georgian mansion. Even if you don't have time to explore the whole park (no one does), you can follow the footpath on the south bank of the Thames for miles, starting by Richmond's waterside pubs and carrying on past ancient oaks (some nearly 800 years old) until you're ready to double back for a second pint.

Richmond-upon-Thames.   www.royalparks.org.uk   and   www.visitrichmond.co.uk. © **0300/061-2200.** Free admission. Daily 7am–7:30pm. Tube or National Rail: Richmond.

St James's Park ★ PARK/GARDEN   The easternmost segment of the contiguous quartet of parks that runs east from Kensington Gardens, it was laid out by James I in 1603 and Buckingham Palace redeveloped it a century later. Its little pond, St James's Park Lake, hosts ducks and other waterfowl. The Russian ambassador made a gift of pelicans to the park in 1667; six (three of them a 2013 gift from the city of Prague) still call it home, and are fed their 13kg (28 lb.) of whiting daily at 2:30pm at the Duck Island Cottage. The park has a fine view of Buckingham Palace's front facade, where royal couples smooch on balconies (but live in a section of the building you can't see). The real draw is people-watching, since a cross-section of all London passes through here. It's not a place for picnics or ball throwing, and there's little in the way of amenities or activities—unless you count voyeurism, and why wouldn't you?

The Mall, SW1. www.royalparks.org.uk. © **0300/061-2350.** Free admission. Daily 5am–midnight. Tube: St James's Park.

Victoria Park ★★ PARK/GARDEN   This was the largest and finest open space in East London when it opened in 1845, the capital's first public park. Bordered by canals and divided in two by Grove Road, it covers an area of just under 87 hectares (220 acres) and contains two lakes, formal gardens, sports facilities, and a bandstand. Other notable features include a Grade II-listed 1862 drinking fountain and two arches from the pre-1831 London Bridge—now turned into benches. In summer, big music events such as

Lovebox come here. The park also forms the central section of the **Jubilee Greenway Walk,** a route marked out in 2009 with glass paving slabs in honor of the queen's Diamond Jubilee, and stretching for exactly 60km (37 miles)—1 kilometer for each year of her reign—from Buckingham Palace to the Olympic Park. She doesn't use it.

Grove Rd., E3. www.towerhamlets.gov.uk/victoriapark. *©* **020/7364-7971.** Free admission. Daily 7am–dusk. Tube: Mile End/Overground, Hackney Wick, or Homerton.

Walking Tours

The best ones are led by government-accredited "Blue Badge" professionals who go through a rigorous historical training program, so always look for a Blue Badge (or, sometimes, Green Badge) guide—there are more than 500 in town, and their trade group has a website, **www.guidelondon.co.uk**, that can match-make them to your interests and schedule. Plenty of other qualified operators cater to custom business (many only cater to groups), but these will let you join individually. Also check that online compendium of day tours, Viator (www.viator.com).

Brit Movie Tours ★★   Most of the tour companies try their hand at Harry Potter and/or James Bond circuits now, but this outfit specializes in movies, filming locations, and cinema history—its excursion exclusively about romantic comedies like *Love Actually* and *Notting Hill* is a particular hoot. A majority of its tours go on weekends only, though, which can cause some scheduling headaches. During the week, a coach tour heads to Highclere Castle (Downton Abbey; £120 adults, £90 kids 3–15).

www.britmovietours.com. *©* **020/7118-1007.** Walking tours around £12–£27 adults and £10–£20 children 15 and under.

City of London Guided Walks ★★   The government that oversees the Square Mile of the oldest part of London gives written and performance-based exams to the experts who lead its excellent weekly tours. The experience is less theatrical and denser with facts than what London Walks (see below) generally provides, and group sizes tend to be smaller, too. There are 18 from which to choose (from thrice weekly to monthly), including ones on Dickens, the City's top 10 sights, and Roman London. Tours are 1½ to 2 hours. Pre-booking is advised, but not essential.

City Information Centre, St Paul's Churchyard, EC4. www.cityoflondonguides.com. Tours £5–8 adults, £6 seniors and students, free for children 11 and under. Tube: St Paul's.

City of Westminster Guides ★★   Westminster, the area of London west of the City that includes the theater district, also contracts officially tested guides to lead tours there. Advance booking isn't required, but tours sometimes only go in summer. Tours are 1½ to 2 hours; locations vary.

www.westminsterguides.org.uk. Tours £12 adults, £9 seniors and students, free for children 11 and under.

The Classic Tour ★   If you don't have all day, this 75-min. whirlwind of the major sites gives you as much style as possible in a limited window of time: You ride on a modified double-decker 1960s Routemaster bus—for decades the standard for commuting Londoners—as a somewhat hammy guide gives you the quick lowdown on everything you pass, from Buckingham Palace to the famous Tower Bridge (which you'll cross).

www.theclassictour.com. Ⓒ **0844/318-7655.** Tours £15 adults, seniors, and students, £12 children 5–15.

Dotmaker Tours ★★   Dotmaker's clever weekend walks delve into offbeat topics such as chimneys, tunnels, the story of sounds like St Paul's bells, where the city dumps its rubbish, and where London's past geniuses have found their inspiration. One tour is designed around taking moments to people-watch and observe the rhythms of the town.

www.dotmakertours.co.uk. Tours generally £12–18 adults, £15 seniors and students. Reservations required.

Eating London Tours ★★   I recommend this 3½-hour, stuff-yourself-silly walking romp though some of the greatest victuals in the East End. You'll get to try eight tastings of flavors that are truly East End and not faked for tourists, from fish and chips to Brick Lane curry to Beigel Bake salt beef to a pint in an old-fashioned pub—all while getting a solid lay of the land from an entertaining guide. It also does a more expensive evening tour of Soho (£94; no kids on that one), of the pubs in Docklands, and of the Indian grub on Brick Lane. Locations vary.

www.eatinglondontours.co.uk. Ⓒ **020/3289-6327,** or 215/688-5571 in U.S. Tours £69 adults, £54 children 13–18, £42 children 12 and under.

Footprints of London ★★★   For walks with sharper focus than standard ones. Truly passionate, accredited guides with a depth of knowledge both own and operate this company, and they come up with topics that are much more diverse and surprising than rivals': hidden maritime artifacts, neighborhood explorations by the famous "poverty maps" of the 1890s, great paintings of London, Charlie Chaplin's Kennington, and even a sing-along combining suffragettes with Winston Churchill and wartime music. Great stuff! Have a look to see what they've concocted for when you visit.

www.footprintsoflondon.com. Tours £12 adults, £9 seniors and students. Reservations recommended but not required.

Free Tours by Foot ★★   Okay, so it's not supposed to be totally free. At the end, you're supposed to pay what you feel it was worth. Fortunately, that means guides work hard for your approval so these tours are highly rated, and there are 4 to 6 choices (from neighborhoods like the City, Piccadilly, or Brixton to single attractions such as the British Museum) every day, so giving up £10 or £15 in thanks should not be too difficult. It also does a few set-price tours such as a £25 afternoon pub crawl.

www.freetoursbyfoot.com/london-tours. Tours mostly by donation. Reserve online.

Greenwich Guided Walks ★   Like London, Greenwich operates its own official tours with carefully vetted guides. There are usually two basic 90-min. tours daily (around noon and 2:15pm, but check ahead) from the Greenwich Tourist Information Centre (Discover Greenwich) taking in the main sights plus the Royal Observatory and the Meridian Line. No booking required.

www.greenwichtours.co.uk. ✆ **07575/772-298.** Tours £8 adults, £7 seniors and students, free for two children 13 and under with paying adult. Tube: Cutty Sark DLR

London Walks ★★★   Undoubtedly one of the city's best tourist services, London Walks' tour list is inspiring. On weekdays, there are often more than a dozen choices, and on weekends, nearly 25, which means that if you ever find yourself with a few hours to kill, you can always find instant occupation. Every tour (most are £10) departs from a Tube stop, and none require reservations, which makes arrangements easy. The marquee tour is probably "Jack the Ripper Haunts," which heads out to the streets of Whitechapel around sunset and, in the pursuit of ghoulish entertainment, employs considerably more grotesquerie than uncontested facts. Many of the group's other walks are more informative, including "The Blitz," "Old Mayfair," Harry Potter filming sites, and even guided tours of the British Museum. Other topics can supply authoritative tours on lesser-visited areas such as Hampstead village or the "Little Venice" near Regent's Canal, places few other touring companies touch. The group also provides guidance (and discounts) for Westminster Abbey, as well as "Great Escapes!" of Bath, Stonehenge, Cambridge, Canterbury, and other day-trip favorites (entry fees and train transit are included in the price, £22–£53); they may go weekly or seasonally. If there's any fault with London Walks, it's that some groups swell to untenable sizes, and many of the guides, although proven knowledgeable when pressed, rely too commonly on canned performance shtick (in fact, many are actors, but then again, histrionics are preferable to a narcotic delivery). The best way to remedy both problems is to pick a tour with narrower appeal; you'll have a better chance to ask questions. Tours are 2 hr.; prices and locations vary.

www.walks.com. ✆ **020/7624-3978.** Tours £10 adults, £8 seniors and students.

Marx Walks ★★   It's often forgotten that Karl Marx fled Prussia and lived in the U.K. for nearly 40 years, where dire conditions shaped everything he wrote, taught, and thought about revolution and the rights of man, which other leaders seized upon for their own uses. This excursion, fine for beginning economists, runs you past the landmarks of his life, many of which are still standing, and culminates at the British Museum, where he studied but you can run off and explore. The guide knows his subject, which makes this one headier than a lot of walking tours.

www.marxwalks.com. ✆ **077/2252-3629**. Tours £10 adults; £8 seniors, students, kids 15 and under. Sun 11am–1pm. Reservations required.

Muggle Tours ★★   Although it's based on a mass-appeal trend, it's worthy. This well-assembled tour dispenses reams of Harry Potter trivia, from the books to the movies and locations from the movies. Groups of 20 start at London Bridge, near Borough Market (p. 94), and wind up in Leicester Square. Because so much London history is folded in, there's enough for non-Potterheads. Book online. Tours are 2½ hr.

www.muggletours.co.uk. ℂ **07917/411-374.** Tours £13 adults, £11 children 11 and under. Tube: London Bridge.

Take Walks ★★★   This company operates in several cities worldwide, but in London, it shines via special access and innovative offerings that make for an intelligent replacement for tour buses. These include the exploration of Parliament, which go into spaces most groups can't, and the walk of famous Highgate Cemetery, which gets you into the locked Western portion. It also sells passes that let you jump in on any of its scheduled tours and "London in a Day," a guided tour that takes care of admission to Westminster Abbey and the Tower of London, a Thames boat ride linking them, and the Changing the Guard.

www.takewalks.com/london-tours. ℂ **888/683-8670** in U.S., or 0845/591-6256 in U.K. Tours £65–£190.

Unseen Tours ★★★   London is more than kings, art, and canned tall tales. See it from a raw angle, and plumb its modern issues, on a walk guided by homeless and former homeless residents. Walks go on five different routes—around Shoreditch, Brick Lane, Covent Garden, London Bridge, and Camden/Primrose Hill. Tours last 2 hr.; locations vary.

www.sockmobevents.org.uk. ℂ **0751/426-6775.** Tours £12 adults, £8 seniors and students.

Escorted Tours

There are many reasons to avoid hop-on, hop-off bus tours. First, they're expensive. Also, after 10 min. of rolling down the streets in these hit-or-miss tourist-processing machines, everything you've seen will blend into a miasma of antiquity. Third, these tours are like playing Russian roulette, because your experience depends on the skill and brains of your guide and/or the quality of the amplification system, over which you have no control. Fourth, gridlock.

Narrated bus tours often make you wait 15 to 30 min. to catch your next leg, which can add up to hours wasted, and although your ticket will be good for 24 hr., don't expect to catch anything from 6pm or so until after 9am the next morning. Day tickets may come with a free walking tour (Changing the Guard, Jack the Ripper) and a hop-on, hop-off pass for the river shuttle boat (although some report that paying customers may crowd out passholders like you). Unfortunately, both of those perks must often be used during the same 24 hr. as the bus ticket's validity, demolishing their usefulness.

HOP-ON, HOP-OFF

It's also possible to buy all-day tickets for hop-on, hop-off access to regular ferry boats on the Thames. See p. 322 in the last chapter for those.

Big Bus Tours Like its competition, it offers three circuitous routes, although two of them (Red and Blue) cover much of the same ground and narration is frequently prerecorded (it's live on Red, recorded on Blue) with out-of-date information. It doesn't matter at which of the 50-odd stops you get on, but since drivers often change at Green Park on Piccadilly, you can avoid that wait by starting there. Most people get on at Marble Arch, Regent Street south of Piccadilly Circus, Charing Cross Road north of Trafalgar Square, or under the South Bank Lion at Westminster Bridge. Prices can be a few pounds higher if you don't book ahead.

48 Buckingham Palace Rd., SW1. www.bigbustours.com. ℂ **020/7808-6753.** 24-hr. tours £33.30 adults, £17.10 children 5–15 (including City Cruise tour and 3 walking tours); walk-up prices slightly higher; 48-hr. tickets additional £7 adults, £5 children. Daily 8:30am–8pm.

Golden Tours Open Top Bus Tours The discount option. Golden Tours is one of the big machines in town, offering every permutation of bus tour and day-trip excursion you can imagine. None are particularly special, but they get the job done at low-ish prices, which means crowds. Its main product is a system of routes granting 24-hr. access to a network of nearly four dozen stops (which can be a waste of money since stops are generally only open from 8am–4:30 or 5pm), plus one free walking tour and one free river boat ride. Its Classic Tour covers most of the core city including South Kensington, and the Essential Tour forgoes South Ken but is the only line with a live narrator. Tickets are good for any line. Commensurate with the lower prices, buses can be shabby.

11a Charing Cross Rd., WC2; 156 Cromwell Rd., SW7; and 4 Fountain Sq., 123–151 Buckingham Palace Rd., SW1. www.hoponhopoffplus.com. ℂ **020/7630-2040** in U.K., and 800/509-2507 in North America. One-day tickets £25 adults, £14 children 5–15, £68 for family of 2 adults and 2 children; 24-hr. tickets £2–£4 more and include 1 river cruise and 1 walking tour. Add £6 adults, £3 children for 2nd 24-hr. period. Daily 9am–4:30pm.

MegaSightseeing.com Spawned by cheap coach line Megabus, it's cheap and cheerful: as little as £1 when booked ahead. For that, you get a one-way, 2-hr. loop around town on an open-topped blue double-decker with three stops (Park Lane, the London Eye, and the Tower of London). Narration is recorded—one of the two voices is a Blue Badge guide—and triggered to play in the right spots by GPS. It even goes across Tower Bridge.

48 Buckingham Palace Rd., SW1. www.megasightseeing.com. No public phone. 2-hr. tours £1 to £7, depending on capacity. Daily 10am–7pm. Must book online.

The Original Tour London Sightseeing Tours, conducted on open-top coaches, are covered for 24 hr. with a ticket, so you can go around five times if your feet hurt. You can catch the bus (three interconnecting circuits that supply solid coverage of the main sights) at any of the 80-odd stops on the routes, but most people begin at Piccadilly Circus, Trafalgar Square, Embankment Station, near Victoria Station, or outside Madame Tussauds. Live narrators appear, without much vigor or inspiration, on the Yellow Line, which covers the broadest swath of town, while other lines are likely to have digital spiels, sometimes too quiet to hear. Two of its routes come with audio/booklet packs for kids, but you have to pick them up at its office.

17–19 Cockspur St., SW1. www.theoriginaltour.com. ✆ **020/8877-1722.** Tours £32 adults, £15 children 5–15; £3 adults, £1.50 children discount online (including river cruise). Mar–Oct daily 8:30am–5:20pm; Nov–Feb Fri–Sun 8:30am–5:20pm, Mon–Thurs 8:30am–4:50pm.

OTHER TOURS

City Cruises   When you take a standard trip on these generously glass-sided and -topped boats, live narrators point out details of interest. The "Red Rover" ticket allows you to hop on and off all day. Boats, which have cafe-bars, depart every 40 min., generally between 9am and 9pm, from four piers: Westminster, London Eye, the Tower, and Greenwich, which covers a lot of the area tourists like seeing. Using it to get to Greenwich can save money off buying several one-way tickets on standard ferries, but simple return tickets are cheaper on the commuters' Thames Clippers (p. 322). The 40-min. **London Eye River Cruise** (www.londoneye.com; ✆ **0870/500-0600;** £13 adults, £6.50 children 5–16; daily 11:45am–4:45pm) from London Eye pier is less of a value because you can't get off to explore.

www.citycruises.com. ✆ **020/774-0400.** Tours £13 single, £17 return. 24-hr. passes: £19 adults, £13 seniors and students, £9.25 children 5–16, £37 for 2 adults and 3 children; 72-hr. passes about £3 more; 10% online discount.

The London Helicopter   Six-seated choppers take off from Battersea and supply an epic bird's-eye view of the city, following the Thames to Greenwich, back to Hammersmith, and returning to Battersea in 12 to 18 min. (the "Buzz" route covers less ground). Your pilot is pressed uncomfortably into double duty as a guide, dispensing dubious information such as dating the *Cutty Sark* 300 years before its actual construction. Never mind; the view is the thing, and it's an unbeatable view. You'll see the Shard from above, the ligature of countless rail lines binding the city together, and flights at 11:30am will spy Changing the Guard in the distance at Buckingham Palace. There are two seats in the front at the dashboard and four in a row along the back, so on shared flights, those two middle passengers get a bad view for the same money.

London Battersea Heliport, The Pod Building, Bridges Court, Battersea, SW11. www.thelondonhelicopter.com. ✆ **020/7887-2626.** Tours £200–£300. Daylight hours only. Tube: Clapham Junction.

Thames RIB Experience   Touristy to the core and annoying to everyone except passengers, this outfit loads groups of about a dozen in semi-inflatable RIB speedboats with twin 245-horsepower engines and flits downriver to Canary Wharf, around the O$_2$, or Greenwich from three far-flung piers. Try in vain to make a lasting memory of St Paul's flying past, your eyes blurry from estuary spray. Tours are 50 to 75 min. Its competition, offering similar thrills: **Thames Rockets** (www.thamesrockets.com; ✆ **020/7928-8933;** £30–£44), which goes from close to the London Eye and from St Katharine's Pier near the Tower of London to Canary Wharf; and **Thames Jet** (www.thamesjet. com; ✆ **020/7740-0400;** £29–£39).

Victoria Embankment, WC2. www.thamesribexperience.com. ✆ **020/3613-2325.** Tours £27–£55 adults, £24–£39 children 15 and under; prices depend on tour length. Tube: Embankment or Charing Cross, Tower Hill, or North Greenwich.

LONDON SHOPPING

B lame Elizabeth I. Sure, the old girl loved her baubles and gold-embroidered bodices, but her biggest contribution to English consumerism was defeating the Spanish Armada. That established England as the dominant player on the high seas, which opened channels of international trade, and soon the Thames was more jammed with bounty than the parking lot at the mall on Christmas Eve. Ever since then, London has had a hankering for the finer things. Grease up your credit card!

Stores across the city generally open at 9 or 10am daily and close at 7 or 8pm, although boutiques may close at 6pm and the department stores and Oxford Street shops are often open as late as 9pm. On Sunday, relatively new terrain for British shopping, 11am or noon to 6pm is common (although arcane laws mean some stores won't make a sale until noon); very few places stay open past then. Expect crowds on weekends, when people pour into town from the countryside.

THE GREAT SHOPPING STREETS

Appropriately for a city obsessed with class, London's prime shopping streets aren't usually defined so much by what they sell as by how much you'll spend to bring home their booty. Most run a website listing which stores they host.

The Arcades of Piccadilly & Old Bond Street

Tube: Green Park: There are several iron-framed, skylighted "arcades" (closed Sun), built by 19th-century blue bloods for shopping along these streets in any weather. The best include the longest one, **Burlington Arcade,** a block-long parallel to Old Bond Street at Piccadilly (silverware, cashmere, handbags, Ladurée *macarons*); the **Royal Arcade,** south of Burlington Gardens (antiques, shoes, watches, and Budd Shirtmakers, in residence since the arcade's 1910 opening); and **Piccadilly Arcade,** across from Burlington

The Burlington Arcade is the longest arcade, running parallel to Old Bond Street.

Arcade (men's tailoring; it leads to Jermyn St. [see below], a heart of haberdashery).

Carnaby Street

Tube: Oxford Circus or Piccadilly Circus: Soho's famous street used to be for the mod crowd, but today its legendary hyper-alternative looks are mostly found on Memory Lane. Instead, expect mainstream sporty choices such as North Face and Vans. Better for browsing is **Kingly Court,** a former timber warehouse converted into a mini-mall for 21-odd restaurants, cafes, and bars. www.carnaby.co.uk. Soho: www.thisissoho.co.uk.

Cecil Court

Tube: Leicester Square: Distinguished by original glazed-tile Victorian storefronts, Cecil Court (it and St Martin's Court just north are said to have inspired Harry Potter's Diagon Alley) was once the cradle of British cinema, but today it's a holdout of the antiquarian book trade that used to dominate Charing Cross Road. Favorites are Marchpane, at 16, a trove of vintage children's literature; Storey's for antique maps at 1 & 3; and Travis & Emery, at 17, specializing in music and books about music. www.cecilcourt.co.uk.

Seven Dials

Tube: Covent Garden: Such a charming wander. Every lane around Covent Garden is an obvious shopping drag, full of the usual brands but increasingly some one-off names. Check out **Neal Street** for shoes, **Long Acre** for big clothing stores, and **Floral Street** for designers. www.sevendials.co.uk and www.coventgardenlondonuk.com.

Jermyn Street

Tube: Piccadilly Circus or Green Park: The quintessential street for the natty man for more than a century. Try Harvie & Hudson, Hilditch & Key (since 1899), Hawes & Curtis, and mahogany-lined Turnbull & Asser (1895)—dresser of Chaplin, Churchill, Prince Charles, Ronald Reagan, William, Harry, and James Bond. There's also a growing number of shoemakers, such as Tricker's, which tend to be better as you move toward St. James's Street. It connects to Piccadilly via Princes Arcade, which is also strong on shoes. www.jermynstreet.net.

King's Road

Tube: Sloane Square or South Kensington: The Chelsea avenue where affluent "Sloaneys" spend is where you go to dream—increasingly, about what King's Road used to be. Most of the unique stores have recently been elbowed aside by the same new names, but you'll find a few independent boutiques, high-end mommy wear, and some designer furnishings. The cafes on Sloane Square remain prime for watching rich kids. www.kingsroadchelsea.london.

Lamb's Conduit Street

Tube: Russell Square: This Bloomsbury lane is the ideal respite after a trip to the British Museum, with dapper men's shoes (Grenson, since 1866), hip young clothing names (Folk, Oliver Spencer), haughty housewares (Darkroom), two Victorian pubs, a wine bar (Noble Rot; p. 74)—and no corporate chains.

New Bond Street

Tube: Bond Street or Green Park: The ultimate high-end purchasing pantheon runs from Oxford Street to Piccadilly, partly as Old Bond Street. Every account-draining trinket maker has a presence, including Sotheby's, Van Cleef & Arpels, Harry Winston, Chopard, and Boucheron. A short walk west, **South Molton Street** continues the luxury, but at a half-step down in expense. Check out Browns (p. 85), which gave Alexander McQueen and John Galliano early validation. www.bondstreet.co.uk.

Oxford Street

Tube: Marble Arch, Bond Street, or Oxford Circus: The king of London shopping streets is on the upswing with the addition of the Elizabeth Line,

New Bond Street offers high-end shopping with stores such as Cartier.

which runs underneath it. The major is also pushing for pedestrianization of nearly half a mile of it, from Oxford Circus west to Selfridges, the grand department store. You'll find other retail giants here, too, including Topshop, H&M, Uniqlo, the ever-mobbed Primark, and a few more lollapalooza stores like John Lewis and Marks & Spencer. www.oxfordstreet.co.uk.

Redchurch Street

Tube: Shoreditch High Street: This 6-block Shoreditch stretch, once rammed with cabinetmakers, today is at the forefront for stylists. The 150-year-old menswear brand Sunspel opened its first retail shop here; Labour & Wait (p. 223) vends desirable kitchen toys; and Terence Conran's super-chic hotel/restaurant/cafe complex Boundary, including the cafe Albion, seals the deal for scenesters. Around the corner, **Boxpark,** a hipster mall comprising five dozen rehabbed shipping containers, hosts both emerging names and not-really slumming corporate brands, while **Cheshire Street** is ideal for vintage discoveries.

Sloane Street

Tube: Knightsbridge: Offshore millionaires come here to feast at the top of the consumerist food chain: Bulgari, Valentino, Miu Miu, Prada, Chanel, and everything else haute and showy. And no farther than you can throw a chocolate truffle, Harvey Nichols and Harrods. www.sloanestreet.co.uk.

Tottenham Court Road

Tube: Tottenham Court Road or Goodge Street: Locals sniff, but Tottenham Court Road's lower half, from Oxford Street north to Store Street, is their drag for cut-rate electronics (including voltage converters). North to Torrington Place, pickings shift to brilliantly designed housewares and furnishings at Habitat (p. 223) and London's doyenne of smart styling, Heal's (p. 223).

Upper Street

Tube: Angel: Islington's chief avenue is a low-key location for boutiques, vintage outfits, and kitchen-sink junk shops, all pleasantly spelled by unpretentious pubs and cafes. While you're south of the Green, explore the sidewalks of **Camden Passage** (p. 213), known for antiques and bric-a-brac.

THE SHOPPING PALACES

Fortnum & Mason ★★★ So venerable is this vendor, which began life in 1707 as the candle maker to Queen Anne, that in 1922 archaeologist Howard Carter used empty F&M boxes to tote home the treasures of King Tut's

Entrance to Fortnum & Mason, a department store known for elegant picnic hampers and gourmet foods.

tomb. The quintessentially British, modestly sized department store, which has a focus on gourmet foods, is renowned for its glamorous food hampers, which were first distributed in the days before World War I, when soldiers' families were responsible for feeding their men on the field. Picnic sets now come with bone china and can cost £300, but you can also pack your own. For the full experience, which will leave your family with no inheritance, head to the first floor to peruse its famous wicker hampers, which you can then fill with goodies from the ground-floor Food Hall and have shipped. Select from a cornucopia of such tongue-teasing triumphs as jarred black truffles and fresh Blue Stilton cheese in ceramic pots. In addition to a huge selection of tea packaged in distinctive canisters (*so* much tea), F&M makes its own "parlour ice" (ice creams), "royal game pie" (loafs of seasonal game meats layered with cheese), and something called Rubies in the Rubble (chutney made from fruits obtained in London's markets). Content yourself, as most do, with a wander through the carpeted upper-floor departments, which are lit by chandelier, serenaded by classical music, and illuminated by a lotuslike atrium skylight. The fragrance department smells like a rose garden. High tea can be taken in the Tea Salon, since 1926 among the city's most sumptuous (reservations ✆ **020/7734-8040**), while lunching ladies can be found in the excellent corner brasserie called 45 Jermyn St., which just replaced the Fountain Restaurant after its 6-decade run. When the clock strikes the hour over the store's Piccadilly entrance, two modern mechanical representations of Mr. Fortnum and Mr. Mason emerge, bow to each other approvingly, and return to business inside.

181 Piccadilly, W1. www.fortnumandmason.com. ✆ **020/7734-8040.** Tube: Green Park or Piccadilly Circus.

Harrods ★   Now owned by the Qatari royal family's financiers, a miraculous holdover from the golden age of shopping has been retooled into a bombastic mall appealing largely to free-spending out-of-towners. Few London-born people bother with it, yet it thrives, proof of just how awash with foreign fortunes the city truly is. Its thronged but terrific Food Hall rooms are a glut of exorbitantly priced meats and cheeses, its ornate seven-floor facade emblazoned like a Christmas tree after dark, its jewelry hall attended by robotic staff plying the husbands of spoiled wives with champagne until they give in. But much floor space, where too-loud rock music blares nonstop, is devoted either to brands you'd find for a third of the price at your local mall or to One-Percenter nonsense such as £150,000 sculptures. The artificial environment, from the overpriced razzmatazz to the clerks wearing straw hats, would be more authentic at Disneyland than in London of old. In the souvenir "emporium" on the second floor (£17 for sandwich-size gusset bags; £15 mugs; teddy bears aplenty), I sense the air has been pumped with the same scent you smell at Disney wherever the company wants to coax customers into purchasing (a trick called "olfactory coding"). Of the many escalator banks, the most interesting is the uproarious Egyptian-themed one at the store's center. At its base is a tacky brass fountain memorial to Dodi Al-Fayed and Princess Diana, who died together in Paris in 1997—his father owned Harrods at the time and campaigned to prove Prince Philip ordered the murder of Diana lest she marry a Muslim. A lipstick-smudged wine glass from the couple's final tryst is preserved along with a ring with which al-Fayed claims his son intended to propose to Diana. Tacky! If you crave a real British department store, visit Fortnum & Mason or Selfridges; if you want to be flabbergasted by the pompous excesses of the jet set, Harrods is the overly shellacked circus for you, but don't be fooled into thinking it's something traditional.

87–135 Brompton Rd., SW1. www.harrods.com. (C) **020/7730-1234.** Tube: Knightsbridge.

Harvey Nichols ★ The shallow anti-heroines Patsy and Edina of *Absolutely Fabulous* spoke of it with the same breathless reverence most people reserve for deities. You'll need the income of a god to afford a single thread of Harvey Nick's women's and men's fashions, and although the British-owned store isn't as popular as it used to be—it's been here since the 1880s—a stroll through this eight-floor spendthrift's heaven is entertaining. Note the lunching ladies on display in the fifth-floor restaurant—think of it as a zoo for old money.

109–125 Knightsbridge, SW1. www.harveynichols.com. (C) **020/7235-5000.** Tube: Knightsbridge.

John Lewis ★★ Every Englishman knows that if you want a sound deal, you go here, where there's a price guarantee; it employs an army of people to scout for the lowest prices in the area, which it matches. That may sound like the gimmick of a low-rent wannabe, but John Lewis, established in 1864, is in fact a respected cooperative owned by its employees, and their interest in its success shows in their attentive service and seemingly limitless product line. It also has some exceptional buyers; you'll find things here no other store carries (the bedding department is renowned). Art fans shouldn't miss the building's eastern face, upon which is mounted an abstract cast-aluminum sculpture, *The Winged Figure* (1960), by one of the most important artists of the 20th century, Dame Barbara Hepworth, whose work is in the Tate Britain (p. 134).

Oxford St. at Holles St. www.johnlewis.com/oxfordstreet. (C) **020/7629-7711.** Tube: Oxford Circus.

Liberty ★★ Founded in 1875, Liberty made its name (and earned some mockery) as an importer of Asian art and as a major proponent of Art Nouveau style. Now its focus is distinctly British. The timber-and-plaster wing looks Tudor, but is actually a 1924 revival constructed from the salvaged timbers of two ships, HMS *Impregnable* and HMS *Hindustan;* the length of the latter ship equals the building's length along Great Marlborough Street. The store's stationery and scarf selections are deservedly celebrated, as are its fabrics (many of which are designed in house or only available briefly), and the beauty hall is one of the best. The soft wooden spaces are creaky and seductive, while the staff service is so obsequious it evokes a bygone era.

210–220 Regent St., W1. www.liberty.co.uk. ℗ **020/7734-1234.** Tube: Oxford Circus.

Marks & Spencer ★★★   The beloved M&S is the country's favorite mid-level department store for good-looking clothing staples. Its own-brand looks, once shoddy and ill-fitting, have been re-envisioned as affordable riffs on well-tailored fashions, and it sells the go-to suit for many a young man starting out in life. M&S is particularly beloved for its underwear, and its bathrobes are preternaturally soft. But its crowning achievement is its giant **food halls** ★★★ (usually tucked underneath the store but sometimes a stand-alone shop called **Simply Food**), which sell an astonishing array of prepared meals, soups and sandwiches, and well-selected yet inexpensive wines. M&S is a national treasure, with nothing like it in other countries, and it's about time the English remembered that.

Flagship: 458 Oxford St., W1. www.marksandspencer.co.uk. ℗ **020/7935-7954.** Tube: Marble Arch.

Selfridges ★★★   Selfridges fills the real-life role in London life that many tourists think Harrods does; aside from Harrods' olive drab sacks, no shopping bag speaks louder about your shopping preferences than a canary yellow screamer from Selfridges. It's unquestionably the better of the two

Selfridges has about a million products for sale and popular ground-floor food counters.

stores, since it's not merely a sprawling sensory treat, but also sells items you'd actually buy. Since its 1909 opening by Harry Gordon Selfridge, an immoderate American marketing genius from Marshall Field's in Chicago (the building was designed by Daniel Burnham, of Manhattan's Flatiron Building fame), Selfridges has pioneered many department store practices. Placing the perfumes near the front door, filling its 27 ground-floor windows with consumerist fantasias, coining the phrase "the customer is always right"—all Selfridges inventions. Some one million products are for sale, and the beauty department is Europe's largest. The thicket of food counters on the ground floor gets busy at lunchtime, and the rest of the store is just as popular at other times; some 17 million visits are recorded each year. Selfridges has traded in history, too; the first public demonstration of television was held on the first floor in 1925, and 3 years later, the store sold the world's first TV set. During much of the Blitz, Churchill's transatlantic conversations with FDR were encoded via a scrambler stashed in the cellar. The store's popularity is enjoying a goose thanks to the series *Mr. Selfridge,* with Jeremy Piven barking his way through the title role, which gives the store the soapy treatment.

400 Oxford St., W1. www.selfridges.com. ℭ **0800/123-400** (U.K.), or 113/369-8040 (overseas). Tube: Bond St. or Marble Arch.

RECOMMENDED STORES

For a city world-famous for shopping, where people from around the world arrive with one fat wallet and leave with 10 stuffed suitcases, there's no way to give proper celebratory due to everything that is wonderful and for sale. Some stores, though, are so original and site-specific that they can sweeten the experience of being in London, even if you don't buy a thing.

Art & Antiques

After Noah ★ More like an upscale junk shop with restoration chops, it makes its name on vintage toys, crockery, bathroom fittings, cheerful celluloid jewelry, and wooden desks and bedsteads (sadly, those are too large to get home). 121 Upper St., N1. www.afternoah.com. ℭ **020/7359-4281.** Tube: Angel.

Blue Mantle ★ For dream renovations back home, the largest antique fireplace showroom in the world salvages the good stuff with warm English touches when developers knock down classic buildings—which is

Window display at After Noah, which resembles an upscale junk shop.

Many London museums are free, which means they must get creative about making money in other ways. Some of their gift shops would be worth a visit even if there weren't priceless exhibits attached. All can be accessed for free.

The British Library (p. 110): Literary totes, toys, and tomes.

Churchill War Rooms (p. 131): WW2 posters, postcards, and novelties.

The Design Museum (p. 154): The selection of clever gadgets and conversation pieces is actually better than the museum itself.

London Transport Museum (p. 121): Tube-themed bags, clothes, reproduction posters. Plus a big selection of train toys and material.

Museum of London (p. 162): Novel city-themed history books and gifts.

Tate Modern (p. 158): Gifts, books about art and London, prints, and the Tate Edit line of slick homewares.

The V&A (p. 151): Gorgeous fabric, handbags, jewelry, stationery, and design glass. A mega-emporium of good taste.

---

happening more than we like. 306–312 Old Kent Rd., SE1. www.bluemantle.co.uk. 020/7703-7437. Tube: Borough.

Camden Passage ★★ Plenty of tourists swing through the booths, so bargains aren't always easy to come by. Still, shimmering examples of china, silverware, cocktail shakers, military medals, coins, and countless other hand-me-downs overflow the cases. Despite the name, it's in Islington. Off Upper St., N1. www.camdenpassageislington.co.uk. Market on Wed, Sat, smaller one Sun. Tube: Angel.

Grays ★★ Not the place to go if you're looking for the lowest deal (it's in Mayfair), but it's definitely a source for variety. There are some 200 vendors, many experts registered in the official antiques societies, split among two buildings, selling everything from Victorian jewelry to toys to strange bric-a-brac and collectible silverware. Weekdays are best. Head into the basement of the Mews building to see the River Tyburn, which was buried by 18th-century redevelopment but now feeds into Grays' goldfish trough. 58 Davies St., W1. www.graysantiques.com. 020/7629-7034. Closed Sun. Tube: Bond St.

LASSCo ★★ From stained glass to paneling and faucets to wood flooring, you'll get an incredible selection of fittings and furniture rescued from museums, churches, pubs, and homes at LASSCo (the London Architectural Salvage and Supply Company). 41 Maltby St., SE1. www.lassco.co.uk. 020/7394-8061. Tube: Bermondsey. Also at Brunswick House: 30 Wandsworth Rd., SW8. 020/7394-2100. Tube: Vauxhall.

We Built This City ★★★ For a souvenir you could only find in London, this colorful boutique stocks art, gifts, and collectibles designed by some 250 local artists, with an emphasis on British themes and this street's rock history. 56b Carnaby St. www.webuilt-thiscity.com. 020/3642-9650. Tube: Oxford Circus.

Books

The territorial nature of publishing means that many books that are for sale in London won't be in print back home. Take time to trawl the used-book stores along **Charing Cross Road** and, off that, the collectibles of **Cecil Court** (p. 205), which runs to St Martin's Lane. The major art museums are strong on titles in their respective disciplines, especially **Tate Modern** (p. 158), **Museum of London** (p. 162), and the **National Portrait Gallery** (p. 126). Performing artists turn to the scripts and theatrical ephemera at the **National Theatre** (Southbank, SE1; https://shop.nationaltheatre.org.uk; ✆ **020/7452-3456;** Tube: Waterloo) and **Samuel French** (at the Royal Court Theatre, Sloane Square; www.royalcourttheatre.com; ✆ **020/7565-5024;** Tube: Sloane Square).

Daunt Books ★★ Lined with oak galleries and lit by a long, central skylight, Daunt prides itself on its travel collection, which is located down a groaning wooden staircase. Everything is arranged by the country it's about—Third Reich histories under Germany, Tolstoy under Russia. It's no slouch in the general interest categories, either. Clerks seem to know what will interest the vaguest browser, and the cashier's desk is always piled with choice curiosities. 83 Marylebone High St., W1. www.daunt books.co.uk. ✆ **020/7224-2295.** Tube: Baker St.

Daunt Books on Marylebone High Street has an extensive travel collection.

Foyles ★★ In business since 1903, this institution has thus far navigated the onslaught of high rents and low readership. After the 1999 death of its off-putting and tyrannical owner, the store was once again passed to the next generation of the Foyle family, and it finally caught up with modernity just in time to avoid closure. Its huge inventory of 200,000 titles straddles both popular and specialty topics. There are small outlets at Waterloo Station and the Royal Festival Hall on Southbank, but this beloved HQ is more like a theme park for readers, full of talks, special events, and signings. If you sign into its free Wi-Fi, you can get walking directions to the shelf containing the title you want. 107 Charing Cross Rd., WC2. www.foyles.co.uk. ✆ **020/7437-5660.** Tube: Tottenham Court Rd.

Hatchards ★★ Although the Duke of Wellington and the queen herself are counted among its customers, Hatchards, the oldest bookseller in the city

(1797), is noted for its signed first editions, as well as for its famous shoplifters: An 18-year-old Noël Coward was apprehended as he stuffed a suitcase full of books. (Characteristically, he talked his way out of trouble.) It has been trading since 1801 at its current location, which means it was selling books before Hardy, Dickens, or the Brontës were writing them. Virginia Woolf wrote about it, too, in *Mrs Dalloway.* You'll find it not far west of Waterstones (below). 187 Piccadilly, W1. www.hatchards.co.uk. ✆ **020/7439-9921.** Tube: Piccadilly Circus.

Housmans Booksellers ★ London supports a vibrant protest community—don't forget this is where Karl Marx fashioned his views that changed the world—and since 1945, the city's preeminent store for radical books has been Housmans. You're not going to find most of the stuff here published back home. Wednesdays at 7pm, an author speaks. 5 Caledonian Rd., N1. www.housmans.com. ✆ **020/7837-4473.** Tube: King's Cross St Pancras.

Ian Allan★ This rather masculine boutique is big on trains (a British obsession), wars (a British specialty), and history (a British necessity). 45–46 Lower Marsh, SE1. www.ianallanpublishing.com. ✆ **020/7401-2100.** Closed Sun. Tube: Waterloo.

Persephone Books ★ Persephone rediscovers and reprints works by forgotten mid-20th-century writers, most of them female—it was responsible for reintroducing *Miss Pettigrew Lives for a Day,* which then became a movie. The shop, on a street brimming with other boutiques, is charming. 59 Lamb's Conduit St., WC1. www.persephonebooks.co.uk. ✆ **020/7242-9292.** Tube: Russell Square.

Stanfords ★★★ Marvelous since 1901, Stanfords trades in globe-trotting goodness, from guides to narratives to fiction with a worldview. Should you accidentally leave your map in your hotel room, beeline to the basement; the floor there is covered with an oversized reproduction of the London A–Z map as well as reams of maps for purchase, especially for walking trails across Britain. 12–14 Long Acre. www.stanfords.co.uk. ✆ **020/7836-1321.** Tube: Covent Garden.

Waterstones ★★★ In a location opened in 1936 as Simpson's clothiers—the Art Deco model for Grace Brothers in the saucy Britcom *Are You Being Served?* (the show's creator was a clerk)—this branch of the giant chain is now Europe's largest bookshop. Even if Waterstones is a Big Gorilla of bookselling, it handles the stewardship of that dubious title with dignity; there are six sweeping floors, an enormous London section, plenty of easy chairs for freeloaders, scads of discount offers, and a dedicated events space for visiting authors. The top floor's panoramic cafe, 5th View, hops after work and into the evening. 203 Piccadilly. www.waterstones.com. ✆ **020/7851-2400.** Tube: Piccadilly Circus.

When you're snooping around the stuffy shops of St James's or Mayfair, keep an eye out for a royal crest near the store's sign. That insignia is a seal of approval—its presence means that the business counts a member of the royal family as a customer and has done so for at least 5 years. To earn Prince Charles's plumed crest, stores have to do even more and prove they abide by a sustainable environmental policy. The Queen is represented by a lion and a unicorn, but William doesn't have any warrants registered yet. Once a business wins a warrant—about 800 have done it, from chandeliers to elevator repair—it's extraordinarily rare to see it withdrawn (to its eternal humiliation, Harrods lost its seal in 2000, and Rigby & Peller which made the Queen's bras since 1960, was ejected in 2018 after its owner wrote a memoir that said too much). Which hotel does the Queen prefer? The Goring (p. 46), which earned its warrant in 2013. More great retailers: Anderson & Sheppard (Prince Charles's clothing), Corney & Barrow (wine), Jeroboams (cheese), and Dewar's (the queen's quaff). But don't ask what specific items businesses are delivering to the Palace; shopkeepers aren't permitted to tattle. To learn which companies supply the Windsors—say, where the queen buys her corgis' dog food—search the current warrant holders at www.royalwarrant.org.

Clothing & Accessories

The clothes you find in the U.K. will not be the same as in major stores elsewhere. Different markets, different tastes, different inventories.

Albam ★★   Unusually, this men's boutique seeks out well-constructed, honest clothing (most made in the U.K.), but doesn't mark it up by insane factors. Although its prices are similar to those of high-casual chain stores, the store has a following among guys because its clothing lasts so long. 23 Beak St., W1. www.albamclothing.com. ✆ **020/3157-7000.** Tube: Piccadilly Circus or Oxford Circus.

Arket ★★   Scandinavian-simple, ethically sourced, it aims a little higher in style and substance than its corporate cousin, H&M. This clean-and-casual newcomer does homewares, too. 224 Regent St., W1. www.arket.com. ✆ **020/3402-9150.** Tube: Oxford Circus. Also at 27–29 Long Acre. Tube: Covent Garden.

Atika ★★   Atika, once called Blitz, has crowned itself Europe's largest vintage shop, a boast I cannot authenticate, but it's true that within its 6,000 square feet, you'll be spoilt for choice. 55–59 Hanbury St., E1. www.atikalondon.co.uk. ✆ **020/7377-0730.** Tube: Shoreditch High Street.

Beyond Retro ★★   A one-stop for classic items (jeans, jackets, boots, and other casuals), it's a haunt of the poor and stylish, who can put together an off-margin look without overdrawing. There's a branch in Soho (58–59 Great Marlborough St., W1; same phone; Tube: Oxford Circus), but this is the location with the cat Tiny, who lives in the store and has become a local mascot. 110–112 Cheshire St., E2. www.beyondretro.com. ✆ **020/7729-9001.** Tube: Shoreditch High Street or Whitechapel.

Browns ★★   Some 100 designers, all of them for higher-end purchasers, fill these five connected shops at the top of Mayfair. For 4 decades, it's been a marketplace for upscale women, but increasingly, it's pitching to a younger and more casual set. 23–27 S. Molton St., W1. www.brownsfashion.com. ✆ **020/7514-0016.** Tube: Bond St.

Burberry Factory Outlet ★   Although its East London location is charmless, light on men's, and somewhat laborious to reach, it's worth it for overstock prices that dip 30 to 70 percent lower than what's on sale in the brand's high-end stores—still expensive, but a lot less than the usual damage. 29–31 Chatham Place, E9. ✆ **020/8328-4287.** Tube/National Rail: Hackney Central.

Cordings ★★   Britain's top manufacturer of Wellington boots, which were invented for the first Duke of Wellington, can be found at this well-heeled and very English emporium of field clothing, suits, waistcoats, tweeds, and knitwear that cost a pretty pound. It has traded here since 1877. 19 Piccadilly, W1. www.cordings.co.uk. ✆ **020/7734-0830.** Closed Sun. Tube: Piccadilly Circus.

Diverse ★   Diverse spotlights white-hot labels, many of which go on to greatness. Clothes tend toward arty, which is to say interesting but not irresistible. 148 Fortress Rd., NW5. www.diverseclothing.com. ✆ **020/7813-7425.** Tube: Tufnell Park.

Dover Street Market ★   A high-minded multidesigner concept, heavy on pretentious industrial architecture, is supported by couture (all of Comme des Garçons' lines) fused with multimedia art installations. 18–1228 Haymarket, SW1. www.doverstreetmarket.com. ✆ **020/7518-0680.** Tube: Piccadilly Circus.

Dover Street Market offers couture fused with multimedia art installations.

The Goodhood Store ★★ Consummately East End, the clothing and "life store" products sold in this popular, half-serious two-story emporium are all about what it means to feel cool. Don a faux-vintage T-shirt printed with inscrutable gibberish, carry home a "The Masses are Asses" mug for your latte, and stock up on the latest on-trend grooming products. Independent, self-knowing—but it only *looks* secondhand. 151 Curtain Rd., EC2. www.goodhoodstore.com. ✆ **020/7729-3600.** Tube: Old Street.

Herbert Johnson ★★ This hatter, in business since 1889, made Indiana Jones' famous fedora, called The Poet Hat, for Steven Spielberg in 1980. That's so awesome, not much more needs to be said, except that it can make a cool hat for you, too. In the Brigg store, 7 Piccadilly Arcade, SW1. www.herbert-johnson.co.uk. ✆ **020/7409-7277.** Closed Sun. Tube: Green Park or Piccadilly Circus.

Jack Wills ★★ "Fabulously British," it brags, but this line still comes off a bit like American Eagle Goes to Eton. It goes for a sporty prep school look with rugby shirts, tweeds, cute striped trunks, and brightly hued jumpers. It has expanded internationally, but here's the three-story flagship. 136 Long Acre, WC2. www.jackwills.com. ✆ **020/7240-8946.** Tube: Leicester Square.

James Smith & Sons ★★★ This shop out of time, hung from the outside with old-style high Victorian lettering, is rattling the rafters inside with handmade umbrellas and walking sticks. That's all it makes, as it has done since 1830, so you can imagine the wonders: handles of hazelnut wood, ebony, buffalo horn, and antler, from £25 to more than £300. Clerks can also fashion a box so you can check your purchase onto the plane. Hazlewood House, 53 New Oxford St., WC1. www.james-smith.co.uk. ✆ **020/7836-4731.** Tube: Holborn or Tottenham Court Rd.

Jimmy Choo ★ The legendary Malaysian cobbler started his luxe line in 1996 with a fashion editor from the British edition of *Vogue*. In London, his home base, he owns a three-level flagship store. 27 New Bond St., W1. www.jimmychoo.com. ✆ **020/7493-5858.** Tube: Bond St.

Joules ★★ Tongue-in-cheek, summery British clothing in whites and brights for a jaunty day out (especially for women). Unit 15, Waterloo Station, N1. www.joules.com. ✆ **020/7928-1323.** Tube: Waterloo.

Levisons ★★ In an old storefront with the vintage smell of bygone closets, find early-era men's jackets and suits you could only locate in England—Harris tweeds, school uniforms, tailored peacoats. The stock changes weekly. In fact, all of Cheshire Street is lined with boutiques for unusual vintage finds. 1 Cheshire St., E2. www.levisons.co.uk. ✆ **020/3609-2224.** Tube: Shoreditch High Street.

Lock & Co. ★ Exquisitely crafted classic British hats (Panamas and bowlers, for men, women, and kids, too) are made by this hatter dating to 1765. Their hats have been favored by Wilde, Churchill, Prince Charles, Oddjob from *Goldfinger,* and even the queen—it tailors the inside of her crowns. 6 St James's St., SW1. www.lockhatters.co.uk. ✆ **020/7930-8874.** Tube: Green Park.

Mango ★   Take the cream of high fashion and make it accessible for the typical English young woman—that's the formula at this slightly upmarket label, which does well when you want your look to be colorful, casual, and maybe even beachy. 225–235 Oxford St., W1. www.mango.com. ℂ **020/7534-3505.** Tube: Oxford Circus.

Misan ★★   Uncover a wealth of unique fabrics at this well-regarded Soho showcase and stock up on beautiful stuff you won't find imported at home. 4 Berwick St., W1. www.misan.co.uk. ℂ **020/3556-9806.** Closed Sun. Tube: Piccadilly Circus.

Monsoon ★   One of the favored High Street brands for women, Monsoon's outfits are for independent dressers who favor bright hues and aren't afraid of a few embellishments. It also does good eveningwear. 498–500 Oxford St., W1. www.monsoon.co.uk. ℂ **020/7491-3004.** Tube: Marble Arch.

New Look ★★   Another reliable and very successful High Street chain, New Look does a huge amount of cute casual wear fashionably and cheaply. Its specialty is women's clothes, but it does a few men's, and it captures trends without going overboard. 500–502 Oxford St., W1. www.newlook.co.uk. ℂ **020/7290-7860.** Tube: Marble Arch.

Nick Tentis ★   This London-born men's designer (favored by Eddie Redmayne and Martin Freeman) revitalizes the Savile Row neighborhood's fusty looks with ready-to-wear suits in youthful, Mod-culture cuts and modern, sometimes daring, fabrics. 37 Savile Row, W1. www.nicktentis.com. ℂ **020/7287-1966.** Tube: Piccadilly Circus or Oxford Circus.

Office ★★★   The H&M of footwear rips off designer styles cheaply but effectively. You'll find it everywhere in town, but one of the most convenient locations is here, in the Seven Dials area of Covent Garden. Office's major competition **Schuh,** found around town, mostly stocks other brands (although it has its own sub-line). 57 Neal St., WC2. www.office.co.uk. ℂ **020/7379-1896.** Tube: Covent Garden.

Philip Treacy ★★   If you're invited to Ascot, it would be churlish not to be seen in one of Philip Treacy's world-famous designs in *haute couture* hats, bonnets, or fascinators. If you're not, you're welcome to go home with a £1,200 white elephant. 69 Elizabeth St., SW1. www.philiptreacy.co.uk. ℂ **020/7730-3992.** Closed Sun. Tube: Victoria or Sloane Square.

Hats at Philip Treacy.

WHAT CAN I bring home?

Although you should always claim edibles when you pass through Customs, very few things will be confiscated. Most stuff, including baked goods, honeys, vinegars, condiments, roasted coffee, teas, candy bars, crisps, pickles, and homemade dishes are good to go. And Cadbury chocolate! Stores can't import it to the U.S. now, so grab all you can! Always check your country's requirements, but these things are certain to make the inspector dog's nose twitch:

- Meat and anything containing meat, be it dried, canned, or bouillon.
- Fresh fruit and vegetables.
- Runny cheeses, but not firm ones (rule of thumb: If you have to keep it chilled, leave it behind).
- Rice. As if you would import rice.
- Plants, soil, wood, and seeds (nonedible). Ask the nursery whether you need paperwork, because many varieties are permitted. And be warned that officers in Australia respond to wood like it's kryptonite.

Primark ★★★   The most intense, most crowded, most oppressive store on Oxford Street roils with young families stuffing baskets with cheap-as-chips fashionable outfits, shoes, luggage, and outrageously lowballed accessories. Unfortunately, we're also talking about a clientele that discards garments wherever they want, staff that deals with the rubble using big push brooms, no washrooms, and products that won't last a year. But the bargains! Oh, the bargains—most stuff is less than £10, and £1 deals are common. You just can't help leaving with sacksful. "The devil wears Primark," mutter the snobs. 213 Oxford St., W1. www.primark.co.uk. © **020/7495-0420.** Tube: Marble Arch. Also at 14–18 Oxford St., W1. © **020/7580-5510.** Tube: Tottenham Court Rd.

River Island ★★   Another of the popular, affordable women's High Street fashion brands, River Island is headquartered in West London and designs most of its wares in-house. Dresses are affordable, shoes are cool, leather jackets well-cut, and there's a kid's line. In 2013, Rihanna tried her hand at formulating a collection for the brand. Police had to restrain the crowd. The course of fashion did not change. 473 Oxford St. (© **0844/826-9835**), 207–213 Oxford St. (© **0844/847-2666**), and 309 Oxford St. (© **0844/395-1011**), W1. www.riverisland.com. Tube: Oxford Circus.

Rokit ★★   Because it's been cool for longer than many of its competitors have been in business, Rokit has a following. Probably the largest collection in the city, it sells retro and vintage threads, shoes, and accessories that are funky and hipster-prone, from 1950s industrial uniforms to tracksuits. 42 Shelton St., WC2. www.rokit.co.uk. © **020/7836-6547.** Tube: Covent Garden. Also in Whitechapel (101 and 107 Brick Lane, E1; © **020/7375-3864;** Tube: Shoreditch High Street) and Camden (225 Camden High St., NW1; © **020/7267-3046;** Tube: Camden Town).

Topshop ★★★   At this 8,361-sq.-m (90,000-sq.-ft.) store, the range of accessories is dizzying—you can even get tattooed or pierced if you're so inclined. It's not just women, either, because the incorporated **Topman** is crammed with deal seekers, too, and its colorful socks are legion and fun. Designs are at the vanguard of youth fashion, yet the prices are defiantly low, which makes this forward-thinking store a primary stop. 214 Oxford St., W1. www.topshop.com. ✆ 020/7636-7700. Tube: Oxford St.

World's End ★ For a few years in the 1970s, Vivienne Westwood's shop was the coolest place on the planet. The clock at this guerilla boutique still runs backwards, but London's punk heyday is long over, and Westwood went from rebel to royalty. Never mind the bargains—her Anglomania label is a living museum, but it's not cheap. Still, the fanciful couture inventions, flowing with fabric, are outlandish enough to enchant. 430 Kings Rd., SW10. www.worldsendshop.co.uk. ✆ 020/7352-6551. Closed Sun. Tube: Fulham Broadway.

Food

Don't neglect the many fine foodie markets (p. 225) or the food halls of the shopping palaces (earlier in this chapter). *One warning:* Don't buy tea from a touristy shop. It'll be old and awful. You have a rare chance to patronize world-famous purveyors like **Twinings** (below) or **Fortnum & Mason** (p. 208).

A. Gold ★★ English food has been a punchline for so long that even the British were starting to believe the reputation. A. Gold looks longstanding because of its vintage fittings, but it's actually a newcomer. It peddles country comfort food that you can't even find at the English supermarkets anymore, such as Cornish salted sardine filets, Romney's Kendal mint cakes, Geo.

Twinings, the queen's tea and coffee merchant.

Watkins Anchovy Sauce, and Yorkshire brack—okay, those names aren't helping, are they? 42 Brushfield St., E1. www.agoldshop.com. ✆ **020/7247-2487.** Closes 4pm. Tube: Liverpool Street.

Dark Sugars Cocoa House ★★ Sublime handmade chocolates and truffles (gin and lime, stem ginger and honey, and more) sourced from a family farm in Ghana are the addictive wares at this Brick Lane success story. The golden "pearl" orbs containing smooth hazelnut nougat are delicate and divine, and the shop makes incredible hot chocolates—try it with chili—and even vegan versions. They don't deliver to North America, so indulge here. There's a small shop at 141 Brick Lane, but this flagship is larger. 124–126 Brick Lane, E1. www.darksugars.co.uk. ✆ **074/294-7260.** Tube: Liverpool Street or Shoreditch High Street.

Twinings ★★ Does this tea boutique rely on tourist traffic? Definitely. But it's still steeped in tradition, having taken over from a coffee shop in this narrow, portrait-lined location in 1706. Here you can sample, taste, mix-and-match, and savor the leaf in all its varieties—or just peruse its little tea museum. 216 Strand, WC2. www.twinings.co.uk. ✆ **020/7353-3511.** Tube: Temple.

Health & Beauty

Boots ★ Do I dare suggest you patronize the ubiquitous High Street brand that has devoured all other drugstores? Yes, I certainly do. Something like 80 percent of fragrance sales in the U.K. are conducted over Boots' counters, and the chain's endless 3-for-2 promotions almost always include something worth taking home, be it Berocca vitamins or other hard-to-get items. Makeup costs a few pounds less than at most other stores. It's authentically British, too—its founder, John Campbell Boot, the second Baron Trent, has his picture in the National Portrait Gallery. Multiple locations. www.boots.co.uk.

Neal's Yard Remedies ★★★ At the forefront of Britain's powerful green movement, this shop supplies beauty aids, holistic treatments, massage oils, and even make-your-own-cosmetics ingredients, all cruelty-free, clear of toxins, and naturally formulated. Its products—London's answer to the New

---

Humidorable

Cigars are big business in London, and not just because the city was once the capital of the world tobacco trade. Many wealthy visitors from Arab countries are not permitted to drink alcohol by dint of their religion but they may enjoy a fine stogie, so most finer hotels offer humidors as well as cocktail bars. Dating to 1787, **James J. Fox** claims to be the oldest cigar merchant in the world, and its pedigree is peerless: Oscar Wilde indulged himself here, and Winston Churchill slouched in its weary brown leather armchair while he perused the Coronas. Come to inhale the rich, musky aroma, to select one of its fine bowl pipes, or even to smoke—the city's public smoking ban does not apply here. (19 St James's St., SW1. www.jjfox.co.uk. ✆ 020/7930-3787. Tube: Green Park.)

York beauty boutique Kiehl's—are respected for their quality. 15 Neal's Yard, W1. www.nealsyardremedies.com. ℭ **020/7379-7222.** Tube: Covent Garden.

Penhaligon's ★★★ I don't enjoy the mental image of Prince Charles lighting a Lily of the Valley candle and anointing his body with English Fern eau de toilette, but the fact is that Penhaligon's, established in 1870, is listed as an official supplier of "toilet requisites" to the Prince of Wales, so it may be happening right now. The company hand-squeezes and custom designs its own fragrances for both men and women—generally floral-based and gentle—and sidelines in luxury shaving and grooming products. Another picturesque location is at 16–17 Burlington Arcade (Tube: Green Park). 41 Wellington St., WC2. www.penhaligons.co.uk. ℭ **020/7629-1416.** Tube: Covent Garden.

Housewares

Conran Shop ★★ Gorgeous, contemporary, smartly selected pieces made Conran's name in housewares; its flagship store is a master class in elegant urban furnishings and desirable home accessories. Its building is just as worthy: the 1911 Art Nouveau headquarters of the Michelin Tire Company, coated with decorative tiles of era racing cars and the Michelin Man (aka Bibendum). The newer location in Marylebone, however, is more convenient (55 Marylebone High St., W1; ℭ **020/7723-2223;** Tube: Baker Street). 81 Fulham Rd., SW3. www.conranshop.co.uk. ℭ **020/7589-7401.** Tube: South Kensington.

Habitat ★★★ Consider it not for furniture but for its cheerful linens, kitchen tools, and bath fabrics. In pursuit of this department store's mandate (set by founder Sir Terence Conran) to bring high design to the masses at affordable prices, A-list artists (Tracey Emin, Manolo Blahnik) have been recruited to contribute temporary items, and products are always peppy and practical. Although this store is Habitat's showpiece, a nice-size outpost is at 208 King's Rd. in Chelsea (Tube: Sloane Square or South Kensington). 196–199 Tottenham Court Rd., W1. www.habitat.co.uk. ℭ **084/4499-1122.** Tube: Goodge Street.

Heal's ★★ A stalwart since 1810, but not stuffy like one, Heal's (like Liberty, p. 210), was instrumental in forwarding the Arts and Crafts movement in England. Its furniture and housewares, which are usually defined by chic shapes, have proven so influential that in 1978 it donated its archive to the Victoria & Albert museum. The kitchen department is popular. 196 Tottenham Court Rd., W1. www.heals.co.uk. ℭ **020/7636-1666.** Tube: Goodge Street.

Labour and Wait ★★ The most expensive dustpan you'll ever own will be the envy of dirt everywhere. This store's gorgeously designed kitchenware, bathroom items, gardening tools, and stationery—from vintage enamel to new sculptural metalwork—will put some chic into your chores. Even its location, an emerald-tiled former pub, is functionally fabulous, and its neighbors along Redchurch Street, selling clothes and interior items, are just as stylish. 85 Redchurch St., E2. www.labourandwait.co.uk. ℭ **020/7729-6253.** Closed Mon. Tube: Shoreditch High Street.

Pitfield London ★★   Funky and smart homewares and kitchenwares that are, as the kids say, "carefully edited." This means they're often one-offs or artist-made (bamboo cups and plates, for example) or hard-to-find (vintage Bakelite radios). Find it here and no one will have anything like it back home. 31–35 Pitfield St., N1. www.pitfieldlondon.com. ☎ **020/7490-6852.** Tube: Old Street.

Stationery

Paperchase ★★★   Paperchase does for stationery what Habitat does for chairs and tables: imbues them with infectious style, bold colors, and wit. Its journal selection is incomparable. Starting in summer, stock up on holiday cards, not only because they're much cheaper in the U.K. than abroad, but also because some proceeds go to charity (but be aware that the non-standard envelope sizes may require extra postage back home). There are many so-so branches, but this three-floor flagship is a big paper cut above. There's even a cafe. 213–215 Tottenham Court Rd., W1. www.paperchase.co.uk. ☎ **020/7467-6200.** Tube: Goodge Street.

Ryman Stationery ★   If you're into office supplies (admit it—it's time to come out of the supply closet), the ubiquitous chain, which makes an appearance on almost every busy U.K. shopping street, is a good place to stock up on hard-to-find English-size A4 paper, clamp binders (not common in the U.S.), and convenient "box files" (also absent from other countries' stationers), available in a spectrum of sprightly colors. Multiple locations. www. ryman.co.uk.

Smythson of Bond Street ★★★   In addition to a line of leather journals, organizers, and handbags, this firm, now in its 14th decade, does stationery impeccably. The queen, a one-woman thank-you note industry, buys her paper here. The cotton-fiber content is probably higher than in your bedsheets. 131-132 New Bond St., W1. www.smythson.com. ☎ **020/3535-8009.** Closed Sun. Tube: Bond Street or Oxford Circus.

Toys

Hamleys ★★★   Remote-control helicopters in your hair, magicians at your elbow, rugrats at your knees. This high-octane toy store is run by a gaggle of cheerful young floor staff, themselves kids at heart, who giddily demonstrate the latest toys. The experience will send you into sensory overload. Seven floors are stuffed with amusements—the fifth floor is nothing but sweets. Depending on when you go, there may be free pirate face painting, a caricaturist, or even a beach party. It's one of the world's few department stores devoted just to children, and the only must-see toy store in London—even if you don't have kids. 188–196 Regent St., W1. www.hamleys.com. ☎ **0871/ 704-1977.** Tube: Oxford Circus.

LONDON'S GREATEST MARKETS

Unfortunately, with the inexorable spread of megastores, outdoor markets that have been feeding Central Londoners since the Dark Ages are finding themselves extinguished. The following markets soldier on. Not every market sells something you can take home, unless you count memories: For example, the **Columbia Road Flower Market** (Sun at 8am; Tube: Old Street), is an Eden for English blooms, which get cheaper around 2pm, near closing time. **Borough Market,** which is fully described on p. 94, is all about prepared foods or things you can't get past Customs. Even if you aren't keen to buy anything, however, stroll down one of these market lanes. Whether for gourmets, tourists, or locals, it's like a front-row seat to the ongoing opera of everyday life, and a taste of London as it once was.

> ### Market Hours
>
> Unless otherwise noted, markets are mostly outdoors and generally kick off around 8 or 9am in the morning and start packing up around 3pm.

Berwick Street Market ★

Berwick St. around Broadwick St. Daily 9am–6pm except Sun. Tube: Piccadilly Circus.

Good for: The last daily street market in the West End, dating to the crowded days of the 1840s, is now being produced by developers. Gone are the Cockney calls, in are the overpriced baked goods and Apple Pay—convenient, but false.

Also check out: The gourmand-pleasing specialty shops lining the route.

Brick Lane Markets ★★★

Brick Lane at Buxton St. www.bricklanemarket.com. ✆ **020/7770-6028.** Tube: Shoreditch High Street.

Good for: The Vintage Market (Thurs–Sun, clothes), Backyard Market (Sat–Sun, crafts), Boiler House (Sat–Sun, food), and Tea Rooms (Sat–Sun, antiques). As you can see, Sundays are a banner day: UpMarket for trendy fashions, antiques, food stalls, and Spitalfields Market (below) are also in full swing.

Also check out: The Beigel Bake (p. 100) for London's version of a bagel.

Brixton Market ★

Electric Ave. at Pope's Rd. www.brixtonmarket.net. Mon–Sat. Tube: Brixton.

Good for: Exotic produce, spices, halal meats, music from soul to reggae and hip-hop.

Also check out: Brixton Village, stalls selling African and Caribbean clothes, foods, and housewares. Check its calendar for the theme of the day.

Camden Markets ★★

Camden High St. at Buck St. www.camdenlock.net. Daily (Sat–Sun best). Tube: Camden Town.

Good for: A rambling warren of 700 stalls for vintage wear, sunglasses, leather, goth gear, and fast foods, partly in a canal-side setting, and favored by tourists. Between the Lock Market, the Market Hall, the Horse Stables, and Camden Lock Village across the street, the crowds are utterly exhausting.

Also check out: Stables Market, on the other side of the railway off Chalk Farm Road, sells vintage clothes, antiques, and pop culture knick-knacks; Electric Market (on Camden High St.) is an indoor fair of vinyl, programs, and film posters (Sat) and retro and punk clothes (Sun).

Chapel Market ★

Penton St., Islington. Tues–Sun. Tube: Angel.

Good for: Cheese, dumplings, meat pies, toiletries—a real catch-all working-class market that actually feeds workaday Londoners.

Also check out: The antithesis of a market, the gleaming Angel Central mall, dominates the eastern end of the street; it's New London versus Old London.

Greenwich Markets ★★

11A Greenwich Market. www.greenwichmarketlondon.com. Daily 10am–5:30pm (Sat–Sun best). Tube: Cutty Sark DLR or Greenwich National Rail.

Good for: 40 stalls of antiques (Tues, Thurs, Fri), plus crafts, honeys, breads, and cakes under a historic market roof.

Also check out: The cafes lining the covered Craft Market.

Leadenhall Market ★★

Gracechurch St., EC3. Space pen 24 hrs., businesses keep own hours. Tube: Monument.

Good for: The shops are high-end and the cafes always packed with suited City workers, but what a locale! The glorious wrought iron-and-glass canopy (1882), once shelter for a meat market, is an architectural treasure. In the first Harry Potter film, this is where The Leaky Cauldron is found.

Also check out: The Monument (p. 172), two streets away.

Portobello Road Market ★

www.portobelloroad.co.uk. ℂ **020/7727-7684.** Mon–Wed 9am–6pm; Thurs 9am–1pm; Fri–Sat 9am–7pm. Best on Sat. Tube: Notting Hill Gate or Westbourne Park.

Good for: Antiques, hot foods, jewelry, vintage clothes, tourist tat by the ton. Overcrowded and overrated, but thanks to the movies, it's not going anywhere.

Also check out: The packed pubs along the route; the galleries and antiques shops in the storefronts, where prices can be better than at the stalls.

Queen's Market ★

Green St. at Queen's Rd. www.newham.gov.uk. ☏ **020/8475-8971.** Tues and Thurs–Sat 9am–6pm. Tube: Upton Park.

Good for: 80 stalls and 60 local stores for ingredients from Asia, Africa, Russia, the Caribbean, and elsewhere; international clothes and rugs. Although it's not very posh, it is very Everyday London. Sunday is a quieter day.

Also check out: Its defenders' website, www.friendsofqueensmarket.org.uk, which has argued their market is half as expensive as Wal-Mart.

Riverside Walk Market ★★

Southbank under the Waterloo Bridge. Daily noon–7pm in good weather. Tube: Waterloo.

Good for: Tables of used books, maps, lithographs, and wood engravings. Small, but the setting is its own destination.

Also check out: Lower Marsh Market (www.lowermarshmarket.co.uk) on Lower Marsh between Westminster Bridge and Baylis roads (south of Waterloo station), a classic produce market.

Spitalfields Market ★★

Commercial St. between Brushfield St. and Lamb St. www.spitalfields.co.uk. Daily. Tube: Liverpool Street.

Good for: Prepared world food, handmade housewares, jewelry, vintage posters. It's the most gentrified market in town, and especially on Saturdays, there

Riverside Walk Market at Southbank Centre has an outdoor used-book market.

HACK THE tax attack

First, good news: When you see a price in England, that's the full price. Tax is always included. Now, the bad news: That tax is usually charged at a rate of 20 percent. It's called VAT (Value-Added Tax), and it goes to enviable programs such as national health care, so that any British citizen who gets sick doesn't have to go bankrupt to get well.

And more good news: Tourists can get a little VAT back. As long as the store you're patronizing participates in the VAT Retail Export Scheme (many don't) and you get the paperwork while you're there (stores have varying minimum-purchase requirements), you can apply for a refund, minus a dismaying chunk for fees. The only tangible purchases it doesn't work for are vehicles, unmounted gemstones, and anything requiring an export license (except antiques). The system mostly benefits those who spend hundreds or thousands of pounds, not tourists packing casual finds.

To get money back:

- Be a non–European Union visitor to the U.K.
- Obtain stamped tax refund documents from each retailer. At big stores, you may have to wait in line with ID and receipts for as long as a half-hour and the store may take a cut of several pounds as a processing fee.
- On the day you leave Britain, present that document to the VAT refund desk at the airport. The line may be extreme. You must also have the goods on hand, so have your travel documents but don't check your bags yet. This process can take up to 2 hours, and even then you may only get £7 back for every £100 spent, so decide if it's really worth the hassle.

Britain maintains information via www.hmrc.gov.uk. or ✆ **0300/200-3700**

are one-of-a-kind clothing items. Sit-down restaurants surround it. The market's success was a linchpin in East London's revitalization.

Also check out: Visit the Style Market for fashions on Saturday afternoons.

Walthamstow Market ★

Walthamstow Market St. Tues–Sat. Tube: Walthamstow.

Good for: 450 non-touristy stalls selling everything from knockoff clothes to junky food to Chinese-made batteries—it's the longest market street in Europe.

Also check out: You may not have the energy to see much else in this multicultural neighborhood—the market itself is a kilometer long.

LONDON NIGHTLIFE

L et no one tell you that London tucks itself into bed early. Perhaps that was true in your grandfather's day—not now. The Tube may shut down after midnight on week-nights, but the main lines now go all night on weekends, so for the intrepid, the entertainment can rollick until morning. With hundreds of theaters, nightclubs, cinemas, and bars, London offers more on a single night than many cities muster in an entire year.

That said, London's nights aren't perfect. The city's prevailing liquor laws force places to often unceremoniously evict their clien-tele in mid-toast. Whereas in Spain, Greece, and New York, the night rarely begins before 1am, that's usually when floors are being mopped at many spots. If you require just one more cocktail to close the deal, a very few clubs will serve until 3am, and they come and go; ask your new friends at the bar which after-hours place is the cool one right now. Where the Night Tube doesn't go, the Night Bus system (p. 320) does, but it's a buzzkill to end a festive night of drinking with your legs crossed on an infrequent and slow-moving bus.

GETTING THE SCOOP Complete listings information for entertainment is published Saturdays in the London papers, but you don't have to wait until you arrive. Excellent online sources for things to do include **Londonist.com, LondonCalling.com, TimeOut.com/ London, Townfish.com,** and the Twitter accounts Handpicked London (**@LDN**) and **@LeCool_London** (nightlife). **@Skint London** helps with finding cheap or free activities. These sources are good, too:

- **Visit London** (www.visitlondon.com): "What's On" in the "Things to Do" section is assiduously updated and covers all hours of the day.
- The *Evening Standard* (www.standard.co.uk/go/london): This free paper appears at Tube stop entrances in midafternoon—Thursday and Friday, there's an accompanying lifestyle maga-zine, *ES*, in a nearby stack. Its *Go London* section also runs down things to do. All are available online for free.

THEATER

If you leave London without seeing at least one stage show, then you'll have missed one of this city's most glittering attractions: This is where Shakespeare defined great writing and Gilbert and Sullivan shaped modern musical theater. The great work continues to this day, and if you doubt it, look at the lists of Oscar, Emmy, and Tony winners from the past decade.

Whenever you hear the phrase "West End" in relation to shows, think of the term as describing the 60-odd top-tier theaters in the middle of town. These are the shows that most tourists flock to see, but that doesn't mean they're always the best—the West End is increasingly clogged with mediocre dramas propped up by Hollywood names and by so-called "jukebox" musicals that are intentionally simplified so tourists who can't speak English can have fun.

Many West End shows begin their lives at companies found elsewhere in town at "Off West End" or "Fringe" stages. For challenging work mounted by producers intent on taking artistic risks, look to them. Many of them have designed and built facilities expressly for pumping out fresh projects. The stars perform here, too—all at prices that are half what you'd shell out for a West End show created by committee.

It's easy to make a night of it. Most theaters have a bar, and Off West End companies might even have their own mid- to high-end restaurants.

Curtain times range from 7:30 to 8pm for evening shows; matinees start anywhere between 2 and 4pm. Every theater is different, so check your ticket. Nearly all shows are closed, or "dark," on Sundays.

Theater Tickets for Less

Even at full price, West End shows cost dramatically less than Broadway's. Considering £30 tickets are typical even for musicals, you can actually afford to see a few. If you are desperate to see a specific show, book tickets directly with the production before you leave home to ensure you won't be left out. Check the **Society of London Theatre,** or SOLT (www.officiallondontheatre. co.uk), the trade association for theater owners and producers (established in 1908), for a season rundown and discounts. Keep in mind that many other websites will deliver you to third parties who charge a premium of as much as 20 percent for your booking. Only use that method if you'd be heartbroken to miss a particular show.

Many theaters post steep **student discounts,** but distribution methods vary—students are advised to check the websites of the major theaters and sign up ahead of time. And bring your student ID, or you will be denied.

Given a lead time of a few days or weeks, anyone can find some discounts on **LastMinute.com, LoveTheatre.com** (click "Special Offers"), and the free app **TodayTix.** Check all three, since deals vary between them. TodayTix is particularly useful since it also handles "**rush tickets**" (a daily allotment of low-cost tickets, usually for popular productions) for many shows. The musical *Hamilton* distributes £10 rush seats by lottery via its own app while

saving ON THE STAGE

Apart from using TKTS, how can you save on a show?

o **Matinees are often cheaper than evening shows.** Unfortunately, they also cut into your daylight touring time.

o **Ask about standing room tickets and "day seats."** Many theaters sell standing room (£10–£20). "Day seats," or "rush seats," are a daily allotment of cheap seats, but you'll either have to queue at the theater in the morning or have a quick

trigger finger on the TodayTix app, which handles some shows.

o **Buy at the box office** to avoid paying booking fees.

o **In one of the older theaters, you can often settle for a restricted-view seat.** You may have to crane your neck to see around the edge of a balcony or a pillar, but you'll be in the room. They cost about a third of top-price seats. **Theatre monkey.com** posts theater-specific ratings.

The Book of Mormon's lottery is only in person. (See box, above, for more tips.)

On the day of the show, **TKTS** (south side of Leicester Square; www.tkts. co.uk; Mon–Sat 10am–7pm, Sun 11am–4:30pm; £3 charge; Tube: Leicester Square), operated by SOLT, has same-day seats for as much as half off—the best stuff is sold in the first hour of opening. While the white-hot tickets won't be found here, about 80 percent of West End shows are—TKTS posts a list of going deals (but no show descriptions) on its website so you can know if it's worth the visit.

The West End is dotted with closet-size stalls hawking tickets to major shows and concerts. Don't deal with them. They are for audiences who simply *must* get tickets to their chosen show regardless of the fees—as high as 25 percent over cost. Before you give your money to any of these outfits, check the directory of the self-policing **Society of Ticket Agents and Retailers** (www.star.org.uk; © **01904/234-737**) to find out who is reputable. Scalpers, called **touts** here, routinely issue counterfeit tickets or abscond with your cash. Some sightseeing discount cards also brag about discounts, but their deals are mostly for the longest-running, touristy shows and they don't save you nearly as much as TKTS would—only around £20 off the top price.

London's Landmark Performance Places

The Barbican Centre ★★   In the 1950s, earnest but misguided city fathers turned their attentions toward redeveloping a bombed-out crater. The end result was a forbidding mixed-use concrete complex that took more than 20 years to finish. They optimistically planned for lively crowds by adding Europe's largest arts and conference center, too, with a concert hall, two theaters, three cinemas, and two galleries, and now they're the best thing about the place—and one of the best things about London arts in general. You can't always find something going on in all of its venues, and even when things are

The Barbican Centre was built in a bombed-out crater.

rocking full-tilt, the bunkered Barbican is so windswept it makes *Blade Runner* look like Candy Land, but what does play here is rarely dull. It's nearly impossible to classify the Barbican's fare, since it hosts a wide range of the world's great orchestras (including the London Symphony Orchestra and the BBC Symphony Orchestra), singers, and composers, plus a handful of banner festivals each year, particularly in the realm of contemporary music and experimental theater. Its cinemas often screen films fresh from major festival triumphs. Silk St., EC2. www.barbican.org.uk. © **020/7638-8891.** Tube: Barbican.

The Bridge Theatre ★   In late 2017, a major new venue opened by City Hall, by the southern foot of Tower Bridge, with an emphasis on well-produced new work. The Bridge was instantly A-list, attracting heavy-hitters Ben Whishaw, Rory Kinnear, and Simon Russell Beale in *Julius Caesar* directed by former National Theatre director Nicholas Hytner, and in early 2019, mounting *A Very Very Very Dark Matter*, a new play by Martin McDonagh. 3 Potters Field Park, SE1. www.bridgetheatre.co.uk. © **0333/320-0051.** Tube: London Bridge.

The Bush Theatre ★★★   The Bush, which for more than 45 years has showcased a formidable output from new writers, started as a pub theater; in 2011, thanks to a lifesaving campaign that rallied support from the likes of Judi Dench and Daniel Radcliffe, it got its own complex in a disused Victorian library. Besides attracting exciting writers, it brings in stars (like Kate Beckinsale and the late Alan Rickman) who want to reconnect with audiences. 7 Uxbridge Rd., W12. www.bushtheatre.co.uk. ℂ **020/8743-5050.** Tube: Shepherds Bush.

Donmar Warehouse ★★★   You can't often snag a last-minute ticket to this 250-seat house without standing in line for returns. Its productions, mostly limited runs of vividly reconceived revivals, are edgy and buzzy. Past coups for this comfortably converted brewery warehouse include the *Cabaret* revival that introduced Alan Cumming to the world, as well as appearances by world-class performers such as Ian McKellen and Nicole Kidman. The front row of full-price tickets are dished out each Monday at 10am sharp for performances 2 weeks later, with a maximum of two tickets per person. 41 Earlham St., WC2. www.donmarwarehouse.com. ℂ **020/3282-3808.** Tube: Covent Garden.

Menier Chocolate Factory ★★   In an intimate setting among exposed beams and cast-iron columns, a converted you-know-what from the 1870s is where some of the city's hottest musical revivals have been mounted. Its *Sunday in the Park with George* and *A Little Night Music* transferred to the West End and later to Broadway. This company, which also does non-musical plays, is one of the few to do Sunday shows; it's dark on Mondays. 51–53 Southwark St., SE1. www.menierchocolatefactory.com. ℂ **020/7378-1713.** Tube: London Bridge.

The Old Vic is home to intellectual dramas.

Old Vic ★   Hitmaking director Matthew Warchus (*Matilda*) is now in charge, drawing celebrities like Vanessa Redgrave, Kim Cattrall, and, last season, *Star Wars*' John Boyega; acting legend Glenda Jackson was even coaxed back on stage here after a quarter century in Parliament. The place is known for mounting intellectual, meat-and-potatoes drama—stuff actors love to sink their teeth into—as well as lively fare such as the musical *Groundhog Day,* which it exported to Broadway. The 200-year-old building is pulling bigger crowds than ever before, and The Pit Bar, downstairs, is a stylish pre- and post-show hangout. The Cut at Waterloo Rd., SE1. www.oldvictheatre.com. ℂ **0844/871-7628.** Tube: Waterloo or Southwark.

Royal Court Theatre ★★   The preeminent writer's theater (it also hosts the Samuel French theater bookshop), the Royal Court has fought censorship and unveiled international brilliance for so long that it's now a preeminent actor's theater as well. On the east side of jaunty Sloane Square, it devotes a hefty portion of its schedule to important premieres by the likes of Bruce Norris and Caryl Churchill and performances from fierce actors. Among the plays it gave the world include *Look Back in Anger, The Rocky Horror Picture Show* (in its upstairs studio theater), George Bernard Shaw's *Major Barbara* and *Heartbreak House,* and Jez Butterworth's *The Ferryman.* Sloane Square, SW1. www.royalcourttheatre.com. ℂ **020/7565-5000.** Tube: Sloane Square.

Royal National Theatre ★★★ The government-subsidized powerhouse people simply call The National is the country's, and possibly the world's, most noted showpiece for top-flight drama and classical acting. Laurence Olivier was its first director, and the tradition of world-class performances has been unerring: Judi Dench, Ralph Fiennes, Anthony Hopkins, Maggie Smith, and Benedict Cumberbatch have been regulars. The National always mounts a diverse repertoire of British works in its three permanent theaters, spanning Shakespeare to classic musicals (the *Oklahoma!* that made Hugh Jackman a star) to emotional spectacles (*War Horse* began here) to world premieres of well-made plays by the world's best playwrights. The 2019 season includes a return engagement of last year's raved-about revival of Stephen Sondheim's *Follies.* The brutalist riverside complex is a pleasure to spend time in, with several places to eat, caffeinate, or tipple, and on sunny days, lounge in orange beach chairs on South Bank. The fascinating (and free) Sherling High-Level Walkway allows anyone off the street to watch the activity backstage; there's even a periscope so kids can peer over railings into the scenery shops. To find that, head down the eastern side road toward the Dorfman, go inside, and take the lift to the second level. As the people's theater, the National's pricing is populist. Some 100,000 tickets a year are discounted to £15 in what's called the Travelex season. Catch one of the 75-minute tours (£11–£15) showing off the inner workings or costume department, or shop in the lobby bookstore, a performing arts nirvana. South Bank, SE1. www.nationaltheatre.org.uk. ℂ **020/7452-3000.** Tube: Waterloo.

Sadler's Wells is an established center for dance.

Sadler's Wells ★ Sadler's Wells has been a part of the fabric of London life for so long (since 1683) that its current two-house home, dating to 1998, is actually the sixth. You can turn to this Islington establishment to catch some of the world's greatest companies in movement- or rhythm-based performances that transcend

Performers at Shakespeare's Globe, an open-air theater on the southern bank of the Thames.

language. Its specialties are ballet (Matthew Bourne is a frequent guest artist), contemporary dance, and daring opera. It also programs the Peacock Theatre on Portugal Street near the Holborn Tube. Rosebery Ave., EC1. www.sadlerswells. com. ✆ **020/7863-8000.** Tube: Angel.

Shakespeare's Globe ★★ This reconstruction of an Elizabethan theater on the Thames (see p. 157 for architectural details) is a serious concern that attracts the finest classically trained performers, thanks partly to its founding artistic director (1995–2005), Oscar-winning actor Mark Rylance. The tone for quality that he set is maintained today—in 2017, the artistic director was fired, in part, for the anachronistic sin of using artificial lighting. Groundling ("Yard") tickets to stand for the show have been £5 for 22 years now. The season at the open-air Globe is spring through fall, but in a 340-seat Jacobean indoor theater, the Sam Wanamaker (named in honor of the American actor who fought to reconstruct the Globe), there's something happening year-round. The smaller candle-lit Wanamaker, premiered Rylance in *Farinelli and the King*, which went to Broadway in 2017. In season (Apr–Oct), its Thames-facing wall is posted with a full performance calendar. 21 New Globe Walk, Bankside, SE1. www.shakespearesglobe.com. ✆ **020/7401-9919.** Tube: Southwark or Mansion House.

THE QUIRKS OF LONDON theatergoing

London theater can be a strange experience for outsiders:

○ Programs are not free; they cost from £4 (for plays) to £6 (for musicals). Big productions may only sell a glossy souvenir brochure, for £7 to £10.

○ Some seats are equipped with plastic opera glasses, which can be rented for the show with a 50p or £1 coin.

○ What North American theaters call "orchestra" seats, London houses call the "stalls." And instead of a "mezzanine," they have a "Dress Circle," and above that, "Upper Circle" or "Royal Circle." If there happens to be a third, topmost level, that is the "balcony," or sometimes, the "gallery." And because many theaters were constructed in a class-obsessed era, there may be a separate street entrance for each area.

○ The break between acts is called an "interval," not "intermission."

○ The big snack? Ice cream, sold by ushers (or "attendants").

○ Older theaters are required to deploy the "fire curtain," which seals the stage from the auditorium in the event of flames, once during every performance. It's usually done discreetly during the interval.

○ Leave big bags at the hotel, not just because of security (they will be searched), but also because these old seats can be knee-knockers. And ladies, cover your knees, because in the Circles, they will likely be at head-level of the person sitting in front of you.

Southbank Centre ★★★ Like the Barbican, this is a bleak canvas-colored slab architects don't know quite how to fix. It was conceived as a postwar pick-me-up, but age was not kind; despite a peerless Thames location, it's a forbidding architectural scowl, looking more like a pile of sidewalk curbs than an artistic capital. It's perkier on the inside, however. Some 1,000 programs a year go down at its three concert venues, as well as in its huge central hall, which has a cafe and is open to everybody. Dance, film, classical and contemporary music, and the London Jazz Festival fill the bill, which is prolific if self-important. Don't miss the Undercroft, the hideous concrete negative space under the building along the Thames. When the Centre went up, this area was thought to be useless, so skateboarders and street artists claimed the architectural mistake. Recently, landlords tried to evict them for shops, but too late—the skaters proved too beloved. Belvedere Rd., SE1. www.southbankcentre.co.uk. ℗ **020/3879-9555.** Tube: Waterloo.

London's Great Smaller Theaters

Almeida Theatre ★★ The inviting Almeida, which has its own contemporary pub, is gaining esteem by bounds—recent performers have included Ralph Fiennes, Juliet Stevenson, Vanessa Redgrave, and Matt Smith. It also sticks to its guns, mounting intelligent plays (some new, some unfairly forgotten, many new) without much regard for pushback. It has added *Ink, King*

Charles III, and *American Psycho–The Musical* to the canon. Almeida St. off Upper St., N1. www.almeida.co.uk. © **020/7359-4404.** Tube: Angel.

Hackney Empire ★ One of London's greatest and most ornate old houses (1901) was where, once upon a time, you could catch Charlie Chaplin as a vaudeville act. The ever-changing slate still presents the best of variety, but with an urban, multicultural twist: kids' shows, opera, Christmas panto-mime, hip-hop drama, and concerts. 291 Mare St., E8. www.hackneyempire.co.uk. © **020/8985-2424.** Tube: Hackney Central Overground.

Lyric Hammersmith ★ Riding high after the 2014 opening of a £16.5-million expansion, this venue's core may look like a fusty Victorian jewel-box theater, but you'll find spectacular stuff—a mix of multimedia-based shows, avant-garde experiments, and an annual Christmas show to write home about. Its kids' shows are its bread and butter. Lyric Square, King St., S6. www.lyric.co.uk. © **020/8741-6850.** Tube: Hammersmith.

The Print Room ★ As the Coronet, this place was built as a small variety house in 1898, but for most of the 20th century it was a cinema—this is where Hugh Grant's character wistfully attended a movie starring his estranged girl-friend (Julia Roberts) in *Notting Hill*. Now it's one of the most respected up-and-coming Fringe theaters, specializing in revitalizing ignored works by great writers. 103 Notting Hill Gate, W11. www.the-print-room.org. © **020/3642-6606.** Tube: Notting Hill Gate.

Roundhouse ★★ Located in a rehabbed 1846 locomotive shed, the Roundhouse picks up on the maverick spirit of neighboring Camden with a frisky, fast-changing lineup of innovative musical dramas and spectaculars, many of them given a crowd-pleasing, dance-inflected, shock-to-the-system twist. In the 1960s, it was one of London's most important stages, particularly for counterculture concerts. In more recent seasons, you're just as likely to see one-off comedy events, poetry slams, or concerts. Chalk Farm Rd., NW1. www.roundhouse.org.uk. © **030/0678-9222.** Tube: Chalk Farm.

Soho Theatre ★ The Soho functions like a one-building arts festival; it casts a wide net in looking for the latest voices in theater, comedy, and caba-ret. On weekend days, come for kids' shows. Its Theatre Bar is a fine hangout even sans tickets. 21 Dean St., W1. www.sohotheatre.com. © **020/7478-0100.** Tube: Tottenham Court Rd.

The Unicorn Theatre ★ A children's theater that caters to kids without suffering from a debilitating case of preciousness, the Unicorn runs at least two productions, one for each of its theater spaces. Some are script-based and some sensory-based for younger kids and kids with autism. Many are designed to expose kids to other cultures, places, and classic stories. If only every city had a kids' facility as lush. 147 Tooley St., SE1. www.unicorntheatre.com. © **020/7645-0560.** Tube: London Bridge.

Young Vic ★ Spry and in top form, this company programs a mixed bag of jarring plays (in early 2019, *The Convert* by Danai Gurira from the film *Black Panther*), conversational touchstones (*Yerma*), edgy musicals (*The Scottsboro Boys*), and affordable opera, then stands back and hopes for frisson. It often achieves it, and if it fails, it doesn't dally long, since it has three theaters (seating 500, 160, and 80) to fill. There's nearly always something high-quality to plumb here. 66 The Cut, SE1. www.youngvic.org. ℂ **020/7922-2922.** Tube: Waterloo or Southwark.

Pub Theaters

For something easy, cheap, and daring, try this option. In the early 1970s, a new form of alternative theater swept London: the pub theater. Often just a tatty back room where you can bring your beer from the scruffy front bar, your typical theater pub is where some of the city's most affordable, idiosyncratic, let's-try-this-and-see-if-it-works stuff is found—which is why they launched so many megastar actors to fame. Four proven ones, all charging £15 or less for most shows, are:

The Etcetera Theatre ★★ Odd, challenging fare (sometimes several different shows a night) are presented in this very small black box. 265 Camden High St., NW1. www.etceteratheatre.com. ℂ **020/7482-4857.** Tube: Camden Town.

Hen & Chickens ★ Frequent comedy bookings as well as strong writing are presented by the resident company, Unrestricted View. 109 St Paul's Rd., N1. www.henandchickens.com. ℂ **020/7354-8246.** Tube: Highbury & Islington.

The King's Head ★★★ Alums include Kenneth Branagh, Clive Owen, Joanna Lumley, Ben Kingsley, Juliet Stevenson, Hugh Grant, and John Hurt in their younger, braver, poorer days. 115 Upper St., N1. www.kingsheadtheatre. com. ℂ **020/7226-8561.** Tube: Angel.

Old Red Lion ★ The very pubby ORL hires its 60-seat space to a variety of aspiring producers and hosts the occasional comedy night. 418 St John St., EC1. www.oldredliontheatre.co.uk. ℂ **0333/012-4963.** Tube: Angel.

OPERA

Opera can be a budget-breaker. Frugal travelers should try the street singers who perform daily at the **Covent Garden Piazza** (Tube: Covent Garden). That's not a joke: Performers are auditioned before being awarded buskers' licenses, so the caliber is high. Also check to see if there's a touring opera putting down stakes at Sadler's Wells (p. 234). Of course, nothing compares to these institutions:

English National Opera ★★ With the Royal Opera entrenched as the country's premium company, the ENO at the gorgeous London Coliseum (built in 1904) is the progressive one that angles for younger audiences. Tightening purse strings have made it slimmer and more crowd-pleasing; its 2016 revival of Glenn Close in *Sunset Boulevard* went to Broadway. The slate consists of both progressive choices and classics: A season usually includes one world premiere, four revivals, and two new collaborations. Its "Secret Seat" program gets you a seat worth £50 or more by paying just £30—I recommend it because the balcony is distant indeed. St Martin's Lane, WC2. www. eno.org. ℃ **020/7845-9300.** Tube: Leicester Square.

Royal Opera House ★★ Opera fans don't need to be reminded of the role the ROH plays on the world scene, but outsiders might be surprised at how inviting and attractive its terrace and cafe are. The main house, which is shared by the Royal Opera (conducted by Antonio Pappano until 2020) and the equally prestigious Royal Ballet (now past its 70th year here), is supplemented with two smaller spaces for chamber opera and studio dance. Happily, 40 percent of the tickets cost £40 or less—if you move quickly—and surtitles appear on little screens or monitors. There are three daytime tours available, too, one for backstage, one for the set and costume workshops, and one for its 2,256-seat, horseshoe-shaped auditorium (℃ **020/7304-4000;** £8–£12; 75 min.; children 7 and under not permitted; sells out 2–3 months ahead, calendar

Covent Garden's Royal Opera House hosts both opera and ballet.

online). Bow St., Covent Garden, WC2. www.roh.org.uk. ℭ **020/7304-4000.** Tube: Covent Garden.

DANCE PERFORMANCE

London's dance scene has yet to achieve the vibrancy of New York's or Germany's, but that's not to say there's nothing to see; it's just that some of the best terpsichorean productions are put on by visiting companies, not by Londoners. The first thing to do is check the schedules at the Barbican (p. 231), Roundhouse (p. 237), Sadler's Wells (p. 234), and Southbank Centre (p. 236), which present a cornucopia of performance genres. The country's largest company, **Royal Ballet ★★**, shares space with the Royal Opera (above). The adventurous **English National Ballet ★** tours Britain much of the time but finds itself in London often (www.ballet.org.uk; ℭ **020/7581-1245**), especially for its December *Nutcracker.*

    The Place ★★★ (17 Duke's Rd., WC1; www.theplace.org.uk; ℭ **020/7121-1100;** Tube: Euston) is known for contemporary dance—specifically, as the home of the Richard Alston Dance Company—and the host venue of some 100 companies a year from around the world. The lucky tenant of a gleaming translucent building by the same team that designed the Tate Modern, **Trinity Laban** (Creekside, Greenwich, SW8; www.trinitylaban.ac.uk; ℭ **020/8691-8600;** Cutty Sark DLR or Greenwich National Rail) puts on a mixed bill of works from around the world and by up-and-comers from its conservatory.

CLASSICAL MUSIC

Cadogan Hall ★   With 900 seats, this onetime Christian Scientist church (built 1907 in the Byzantine Revival style) is now the home of the Royal Philharmonic Orchestra and, in summer, the BBC Proms, which books it during the summer for its chamber music as a supplement to its concerts at Royal Albert Hall. 5 Sloane Terrace, SW1. www.cadoganhall.com. ℭ **020/7730-4500.** Tube: Sloane Square.

King's Place ★★   If you find yourself bored in London, it's not King's Place's fault. The relatively new development behind King's Cross (it shares a building with *The Guardian*) has become the city's most versatile, exciting venue, with spaces for multiple galleries, chamber groups, and orchestras. Comedy, folk music, jazz, interviews with world notables—surprises abound. 90 York Way, N1. www.kingsplace.co.uk. ℭ **020/7520-1490.** Tube: King's Cross St Pancras.

Royal Albert Hall ★★★   Imposing, ornate, and adored by music lovers worldwide, the RAH is one of the few performance arenas on earth where, once they have performed there, artists can truly claim to have made it. During the summer, the storied BBC Promenade Concerts (the Proms) fill this historic, 5,200-seat circular hall with classical music, but the rest of the year, the space books a hodgepodge of movies in concert (the house organ is 21m/69

St Martin-in-the-Fields in Trafalgar Square offers candlelight concerts and lunchtime performances.

ft. tall and has 10,000 pipes), arena-style musicals, Cirque du Soleil, tours—even tennis matches. See p. 149 for tour information. Kensington Gore, SW7. www.royalalberthall.com. © **0845/401-5034.** Tube: South Kensington.

St Martin-in-the-Fields ★★★ Right in the thick of Trafalgar Square, this handsome church's evening candlelight concerts and lunchtime performances are London traditions. It's non-fussy with clean acoustics. Trafalgar Square, WC2. www.smitf.org. © **020/7766-1136.** Tube: Charing Cross or Leicester Square.

Wigmore Hall ★★ Opened in 1901 as a recital hall for the Bechstein piano showroom that was next door, it was seized (along with the company) as enemy property in World War I. A nasty start, but in time performers came to include Ravel, Saint-Saëns, Britten, and Artur Rubinstein. Today the hall, notable for a bombastic Arts and Crafts cupola over the stage, is known for ideal acoustics and a roster of some 450 concerts, mostly classical, each year. Some nights, there's free music in the bar. 36 Wigmore St., W1. www.wigmore-hall.org.uk. © **020/7935-2141.** Tube: Bond St.

PRINCE CHARLES CINEMA: THE WORLD'S silliest MOVIE THEATER?

The family-friendly "Sing-a-Long-a" *The Sound of Music*, a silly participatory screening of the 1965 classic, was born in 1999 at the eccentric **Prince Charles Cinema** (7 Leicester Place; www.prince charlescinema.com; © **020/7494-3654; Tube:** Leicester Square) and swept the world thereafter. Participants—some of whom arrive dressed as Nazis and nuns, without regard to gender—receive a "magic moment" bag with edelweiss, curtain swatches, and a party popper to deploy at the moment of Maria and the Captain's kiss. And it hasn't stopped with "Do-Re-Mi." On Friday nights, other Netflix favorites are given the call-and-response treatment, *Grease, The Greatest Showman, Moulin Rouge,* and *Dirty Dancing* among them. On other nights, it's an all-night Disney musical pajama party. Or a *Labyrinth* Masquerade Ball. Or a *Mean Girls* "bitch-along." Or full 70mm projections of essential cinematic masterpieces such as *Lawrence of Arabia, Die Hard* or, um, *Big Trouble in Little China.*

THE MUSIC SCENE

Just as many of London's live music venues don't draw a heavy line between the genres they present, no rigid division exists between gig venues and dance venues; in fact, many spaces switch from live music to dance in a single evening. That's one of the things that makes the city's nightlife so vibrant, but it's also why it's important to check programming in advance. Students can often get discounts on entry—as if you needed any more proof that education is valued in England. Bring your ID—under 18s aren't usually admitted.

Live Music, Including Jazz, Pop, Folk & Rock

Dozens of theaters and arenas in town book concerts by recognizable names, but it would be fruitless to list them since they're almost all rented by promoters and don't always have something going on. The better advice is to stay on top of who's playing by checking *Time Out* (www.timeout.com/london) or *New Musical Express* (NME; www.nme.com). Since big shows sell out months in advance, the best recourse is to book ahead via **See Tickets** (www. seetickets.com; ✆ **087/1220-0260**); **Stargreen** (www.stargreen.com; ✆ **020/ 7734-8932**), which has a small office at 20/21a Argyll St., outside the Oxford Circus Tube station; **Ticketweb** (www.ticketweb.co.uk; ✆ **0333/321-9990**); or its partner **Ticketmaster** (www.ticketmaster.co.uk; ✆ **0333/321-9999**), all of which levy fees but let you buy from abroad. Also visit **Southbank London.com** to see what's playing in all the South Bank venues.

The 100 Club ★★   Many decades have passed since this was a prime hangout for U.S. servicemen homesick for the jazzy sounds of Glenn Miller (who died serving in the U.K., you'll remember) and his colleagues. In 1976, after passing through an R&B and jazz period that had Louis Armstrong puckering up for audiences, it sponsored the world's first punk festival, and bands like the Sex Pistols—unsigned at the time—took the stage. This battered red-walled basement institution with good sightlines and expensive drinks still can't decide which era to honor, so it careens between punk, swing, R&B, jazz, and up-and-coming bands. 100 Oxford St., W1. www.the100club.co.uk. ✆ **020/ 7636-0933.** Cover £10–£21, 25% discounts often available in advance. Music starts around 8:30pm. Tube: Tottenham Court Road.

The Betsey Trotwood ★★   This adorable, wood-floored Victorian pub has three levels, two with cozy performance spaces, and hosts bluegrass, comedy, and a few singer-songwriters a month—such as Jason Mraz early in his career. 56 Farringdon Rd., EC1. www.facebook.com/TheBetseyTrotwood. ✆ **020/7253-4285.** Tube: Farringdon.

The Borderline ★   A Soho institution since the 1980s, this tiny basement space (which holds 275 people, uncomfortably) was recently renovated to install much-needed air-conditioning and upgrade its sound system. It books country, folk, Britpop, and blues. Cheap beer, young crowd. There are club nights, too: electro, hip-hop, R&B, pop. Orange Yard, Manette St., W1. www.borderline.london. ℗ **0844/847-1678.** Cover: live music around £15. Tube: Tottenham Court Rd.

The Camden Assembly ★   When it was known as Barfly, this dark, intimate bar/performance space in Camden was the launch pad for a thousand indie bands, some of which actually ended up soaring (Coldplay, Blur, and the like). Today it offers a good mix of club nights and concerts for students, musicians, and old-time locals. Gentrification has tamed the overzealous moshers. When the bands wrap up, a house DJ spins for a few more hours while the audience chills. 49 Chalk Farm Rd., NW1. www.camdenassembly.com. ℗ **020/7424-0800.** Cover under £10. Tube: Chalk Farm.

Dingwalls ★   An ever-popular house of rock, folk, and acoustic guitar since 1973, this former industrial space by Camden Lock with a good sound system grants audiences the dignity of sitting at tables to enjoy the music. Performers here have included Mumford and Sons, Jello Biafra, and Foo Fighters, but now and then you'll find something like burlesque or Molly Hatchet. Middle Yard, NW1. www.dingwalls.com. ℗ **01920/823-098.** Cover ranges from "pay what you roll" on a die to £22. Tube: Camden Town.

Dublin Castle ★   Any bar that proclaims itself the birthplace of the 1970s ditty band Madness would not, on the surface, seem to be a place you'd want to enter without prior insobriety. But it has street cred—it was the first bar in London to win a late liquor license from the government, so it became an important nightspot. Really no more than a threadbare, greenish pub with a teeny backroom stage, it hosts bands struggling to make it—and a few (Blur, for one, and Madness, for two) that actually have. On weekends, late-night DJs spin. 94 Parkway, NW1. www.thedublincastle.com. ℗ **020/7485-1773.** Cover £6–£10. Tube: Camden Town.

Electric Ballroom ★★   One of those dicey, utilitarian halls (ca. 1938) that never loses the lingering smell of old beer, the Electric Ballroom has hosted the likes of Sid Vicious, The Clash, Prince, and U2. Steel yourself for a steady roster of punk, goth, industrial, glam, hardcore, metal, and other sensory abusers (like British pro wrestling and Kiefer Sutherland's band). Their aficionados could hardly inflict more architectural damage to the premises than what's already been done by the ravages of time and benign neglect. The divine Ultimate Power club event is all power ballads, all night long. 184 Camden High St., NW1. www.electricballroom.co.uk. ℗ **020/7485-9007.** Cover: live music £15–£20, club nights £7–£14. Tube: Camden Town.

The Garage ★★   This 600-person concert space has so much cred as a modern choice for indie and rock that Harry Styles chose it for a surprise gig in 2017. Overpriced drinks in cans, intimate but loud; you know the drill. 20–22 Highbury Corner, N5. www.thegarage.london. ℗ **020/7619-6720.** Tube and National Rail: Highbury & Islington.

Camden's Jazz Café is a lively venue for music acts such as British soul singer Nate James.

Green Note ★★   This welcoming vegetarian cafe/bar books acoustic live gigs, from folk to jazz, roots to singer-songwriters. Softened by pillows and upholstered seating, it's a laid-back scene with no dancing. You can eat in the front room (tapas at sensible prices, no meat, all organic) and hear the music, or a cover charge will let you swing into the bar in the back room just for the show. 106 Parkway, NW1. www.greennote.co.uk. ℰ **020/7485-9899.** Opens 7pm. Cover £2–£15. Tube: Camden Town.

Jazz After Dark ★   Trios, funk, and soul singers, all packed on a tiny stage (so tiny, it's wise to book a table). Amy Winehouse used to come—it's said she applied for a job but they gave her a gig instead. Who knows how true that is, but the cellar vibe is why visitors manage to overlook the grumpy owner and weak drinks. You know it's no good—but dammit, it has a certain charm. 9 Greek St., W1. www.jazzafterdark.co.uk. ℰ **020/7734-0545.** Cover: live music £15. Until 2am. Tube: Camden Town.

Jazz Café ★★★   The prime Camden venue for "names" keeps the music going until 2am, usually in the form of acts (jazz, soul, bluesy vocalists) seen up close. Converted from a bank and renovated with Deco touches in 2016, it has both cabaret tables and an upstairs gallery with food. In the past, there have been occasional club nights for EDM or Cuban dancing, so check the

schedule. 5 Parkway, NW1. www.thejazzcafelondon.com. ✆ **020/7485-6834.** Cover: live music £10–£14. Until 3am Sat–Sun. Tube: Camden Town.

Koko ★   Favored today by visiting indie bands, in its first life as the Camden Hippodrome this pretty 1,500-person multilevel space saw performances by Charlie Chaplin. In the 1970s and '80s, it became an epicenter for pop—the Eurythmics, Boy George, and Wham! played their earliest gigs here, and it's where Madonna made her U.K. debut. The name Koko brings respect, although the setting isn't intimate and the sound can be muddy. Club nights are fun: Buttoned Down Disco is the first Saturday of the month. 1A Camden Rd., NW1. www.koko.uk.com. ✆ **087/0432-5527.** Cover under £10, student discounts before midnight. Tube: Mornington Crescent.

Pizza Express Live ★★   Unlikely as it may seem, this restaurant chain holds lunchtime and night concerts in a few on-site jazz clubs. The cellar **Jazz Club** in Soho (10 Dean St., W1; ✆ **020/7439-4962;** Tube: Tottenham Court Rd.) has seen respected acts such as Jamie Cullum, Norah Jones, and Roy Haynes. There's also an upscale supper club for live music and talks by notables at the **Pheasantry** in Chelsea (152 Kings Rd., SW3; Tube: Sloane Square). www.pizzaexpresslive.com. Cover: live music £10–£45, free Thurs.

Ronnie Scott's Jazz Club ★   Since the 1960s, when it was first recommended in Frommer's, Ronnie Scott's has been London's standard bearer for stylish, American-style jazz, and it honors a long tradition of pairing visiting U.S. greats with local acts. But the old dive got ritzy—after a £2.1-million renovation, the 255-seater began charging prices in the £45 range. Still, it's true that the club draws names, including Patti Austin, Van Morrison, Tom Waits, Cleo Laine, Chaka Khan, and Kyle Eastwood, and it's also true that, like its landmark neon sign promises, it's open until 3am, which is rare in these parts. 47 Frith St., W1. www.ronniescotts.co.uk. ✆ **020/7439-0747.** Tube: Leicester Square.

Scala ★★   When it was a cinema, Stanley Kubrick shut it down for screening *A Clockwork Orange* without permission. Good thing he did, or this 1920 theater might not have been reborn as a pleasing place to catch an acoustic or lyrical band. Its three levels give nearly everyone a good view of the stage, fostering a sense of intimacy appropriate to its (standing) capacity of around 1,000 people. A warren of rooms confuses the drunk ones and conceals the shy ones. Weekdays, it hosts gigs by indie bands, and weekends, it turns to club nights (the long-running Face Down, every first Fri, is rock). 275 Pentonville Rd., N1. www.scala.co.uk. ✆ **020/7833-2022.** Cover £8–£15. Tube: King's Cross St Pancras.

The Water Rats ★★   If you're not a headbanger, the singer-songwriters here may appeal more than Camden's squalling sets. Once it was a pub known as the Pindar of Wakefield; Bob Dylan made his U.K. debut on its back-room stage in 1962, Oasis braved London audiences for the first time there in 1994, and Katy Perry played it before arenas—and returned for a nostalgia gig in 2017. A recent revamp gave it decent seating, but the food should be rebuffed. 328 Grays Inn Rd., WC1. www.thewaterratsvenue.london. ✆ **020/7209-8747.** Cover from £7 for several bands. Until midnight Mon–Fri, 1am Sat–Sun. Tube: King's Cross St Pancras.

Major Venues

If you want to get into the big-name gigs, you have to book ahead, before you arrive. Grittier, midsize venues, mostly repurposed century-old music halls, include **Bush Hall** (www.bushhallmusic.co.uk); the **O₂ Academy Brixton** (www.O2academybrixton.co.uk), good for metal and alt-rock; the **O₂ Academy Islington** (www.O2academyislington.co.uk); the Art Deco **Eventim Apollo** in Hammersmith (www.eventimapollo.com); the **O₂ Empire Shepherds Bush** (www.O2shepherdsbushempire.co.uk); and the **Electric Ballroom** and **Koko** (see above). The most massive venues—where your favorite artist will look like a tiny, bouncing smudge on the far side of an ocean of sweaty fans—include the **London Stadium** (www.london-stadium.com), originally the main stadium at Queen Elizabeth Olympic Park, re-opened as a concert venue and the home of West Ham United FC; and **SSE Arena Wembley** (www.ssearena.co.uk).

The O₂   The £789-million boondoggle on the Thames in East London is a dome 10 times the volume of St Paul's. It's where gargantuan acts from Dolly to Gaga to Kylie to Monty Python appear, packing in their own religious followings, in a 20,000-place arena (ladies, there are 550 toilets for you, too) fringed by a mall for food and clubs. Michael Jackson was in rehearsal for a concert series for the O₂ when he died; during the 2012 Olympics, it hosted gymnastics and basketball. For those not keen to see their favorite artist reduced to a speck on a distant platform, there's O₂'s "intimate" performance space, **Indigo at the O₂** (✆ **020/8463-2700**), although even that is still plenty big, with 2,800 places. An acoustically superior, contemporary room, it has four bars, and attracts major comics and talent (the late Prince, Black Eyed Peas). If you aren't carrying a ticket for a show, there's not much to do there except eat—there are no retail stores—but if you need something more jolting, you can climb above it, at the **Up at the O₂** roof-walking attraction (p. 176). Thames Clippers (p. 322) docks here, too. Peninsula Square, London, SE10. www.theo2.co.uk. ✆ **020/8463-2000.** Tube and ferry: North Greenwich.

Clubs

The city's dance scene, being embedded in the style scene, is various and shifting, and by the time you read this, the variety will have shifted again. Aside from club nights at the venues listed above (see "Live Music," p. 242), the best source for tips on parties you stand a chance of getting into is *Time Out* (www.timeout.com/london/clubs). The clubs around Shoreditch, Old Street, and King's Cross were until recently the markers of cool, but both gentrification and development have squeezed the scene northeast to Dalston, which makes getting home in the middle of the night expensive—freelance cabbies charge double. Covers nudge toward £20.

The king of clubs remains **Fabric** (77a Charterhouse St., EC1; www.fabric london.com; ℂ **020/7336-8898;** Tube: Farringdon or Barbican), a former butchery that for more than a decade has set a world standard. Its all-weekend parties (from Sat 10pm 'til the cock crows on Mon) are engineered to drill teeth-chattering bass frequencies into the souls of those who dare to submit. Buy early to pay as little as £10. The City is not lost to the nerds yet; the pedigreed managers of **XOYO** (32–37 Cowper St., EC2; www.xoyo.co.uk; ℂ **020/ 7729-5959;** Tube: Old St.) turned a former printworks into a stripped-down sound tank, and succeeded. The **Ministry of Sound** (103 Gaunt St., SE1; www.ministryofsound.com; ℂ **020/7740-8600;** Tube: Elephant & Castle) is known around the planet for its top-notch sound system, upper-crust DJs, and extreme cover charges in the low £30s if you wait until the door.

Ravers currently favor the new superclub **Printworks** (Surrey Quays Road, SE16; www.printworkslondon.co.uk; ℂ **020/8498-4934;** Tube: Canada Water), in a cavernous former printing factory, where the glow-stick electronic crowd—6,000 at a time—have been known to begin proceedings at noon and go all day. It's been called the answer to Berlin's legendary Berghain. World-class DJs head to **Phonox** (418 Brixton Rd., SW9; www. phonox.co.uk; ℂ **020/7095-9411;** Tube: Brixton), which starts as a bar but opens into an all-night event. It's so carefully produced that smartphone use is banned on the dance floor. Otherwise, wander Dalston and its environs for cutting-edge venues and basement clubs. Huge windows overlooking a decommissioned gasworks make partying memorable at the vast, post-industrial **Oval Space** (29–32 The Oval, E2; www.ovalspace.co.uk; ℂ **020/7183-4422;** Cambridge Heath National Rail), with its eclectic programming of alternative and progressive music. Its **Pickle Factory** is more intimate, attracting cult dance names. **93 Feet East** (150 Brick Lane, E1; www.93feeteast. co.uk; ℂ **020/7770-6006;** Tube: Liverpool St. or Shoreditch High St.), was one of the first pioneers to reclaim disused industrial space in Spitalfields for the hipsters; it mounts a mix of experimental electronic music, live bands, club nights, and day parties. The **Dalston Superstore** (117 Kingsland High St., E8; www.dalstonsuperstore.com; ℂ **020/7254-2273;** Dalston Kingsland Overground) is a pansexual party mix of DJs, disco, and ravey go-go boys. **The Nest** (36–44 Stoke Newington Rd., N16; www.ilovethenest.com; ℂ **020/7354-9993;** Dalston Junction National Rail) is intimate, affordable, and at times sweaty, but has the quality lineup and sound system of a mini-Fabric.

COMEDY CLUBS

London's comedy scene is dominated by Edinburgh's. Each August in the Scottish capital, seemingly all of Britain attends the city's famous festival season, where sharp minds vie for awards, audiences, and perversely, that shiniest of brass rings, a major London booking. The rest of the year, it seems that half the stages in town are either helping artists groom material for Edinburgh (June and July schedules are packed with new shows) or cashing in on its past successes. The fevered competition has created a comedy scene that has less in common with the stand-and-discuss neuroses of New York clubs and more to do with the brittle high concepts of, say, Russell Brand or Ricky Gervais. You may miss a few local references, but you're sure to appreciate the wit. All comedy venues serve food and drink, and tickets are almost always under £10 unless it's a big name or a very central location. Main shows are usually at 7:30 or 8pm. The tiny **Angel Comedy Club** (2 Camden Walk, N1; www.angelcomedy.co.uk; no phone; Tube: Angel), even though it's in the back of the Camden Head pub, is (legit) one of the best places in town to catch smart up-and-comers, and it's (legit) free to enter; just get there by 7pm on weekends (shows start daily at 8pm) to avoid being shut out. It's on the upswing and, as a consequence, added a second space nearby, which it named The Bill Murray. A Saturday night stand-up showcase is the main event at **Amused Moose** (Sanctum Soho Hotel, 20 Warwick St., W1; www.amused moose.com; ℂ **020/7287-3727;** Tube: Piccadilly Circus); big-name comics like Eddie Izzard or Stephen Merchant sometimes appear here, without a peep of advance word, to test out new material. The cluttered **Canal Café Theatre** (The Bridge House, Delamere Terrace, W2; www.canalcafetheatre.com; ℂ **020/7289-6054;** Tube: Warwick Ave.) puts on a dozen shows a week; its biggest draw is "NewsRevue" (www.newsrevue.com; runs Thurs–Sat), a weekly send-up of current events running since 1979, which gives it the Guinness world record for longest-running live comedy show. The 400-seat **Comedy Store** (1a Oxendon St., SW1; www.thecomedystore.co.uk; ℂ **0844/871-7699;** Tube: Leicester Square or Piccadilly Circus) was created in 1979 in imitation of clubs popular in New York; it launched both Eddy Izzard and Jennifer Saunders. Today it presents improv on Wednesday and Sunday, and mainstream stand-up sets the other nights of the week. In a former wood warehouse 20 minutes from the center of town, **Pleasance Theatre Islington** (Carpenters Mews, North Rd., N7; www.pleasance.co.uk; ℂ **020/7609-1800;** Tube: Caledonian Rd.) has stronger ties than most to Edinburgh; it operates the Scottish festival's chief comedy venue and it starts previewing entrants in the spring.

CINEMA

Major movie premieres attended by major movie stars are routinely held at a handful of giant cinemas around Leicester Square. Chief among them is the **Odeon** (24–26 Leicester Square, WC2; www.odeon.co.uk; ℂ **087/1224-4007;** Tube: Leicester Square), opened in 1937 and intensely renovated in 2018; it's the largest cinema in the country. But tickets for Leicester Square theaters can cost over £20. For better prices—in even more historic houses—look elsewhere. Because so many handsome old cinemas have survived, movie-going can still feel like an event. In most theaters, you even select your seats when you buy your ticket—London was doing that long before America was.

BFI Southbank ★★★ The programming of the British Film Institute (BFI) is mind-bogglingly broad and savvy, from classics to mainstream to historic—more than 1,000 titles a year. For example, on one day in a recent July, its three screens unspooled a retrospective of Indian director Satyajit Ray, Alfred Hitchcock's *Dial M for Murder* in 3D, a mid-century series from the largely forgotten Boulting Brothers, and outdoor screenings of Gothic monster schlock. As the country's preeminent archive and exhibitor, it also programs plenty of talks, special previews, and the occasional free screening. The on-premises **Mediatheque** is a free video arcade for quiet, on-demand viewing of tons of titles you'd never see abroad because of rights issues. The shop stocks an incomparable list of rare DVDs, including many treasures the BFI has restored and re-released, such as Charlie Chaplin's early Keystone and Mutual films, and war-era British propaganda films, which you can only find here. There are also two popular bars, one in the lobby and one on the water. Belvedere Rd., South Bank, SE1. https://whatson.bfi.org.uk. ✆ **020/7255-1444.** Tube: Waterloo.

The Electric Cinema in Notting Hill offers comfortable leather seats with footstools and wine baskets.

The Electric Cinema ★★★ It's one of the world's great screens: Leather seats are softer and deeper than anything you have at home, and each one is equipped with a footstool, table, and a wine basket—it's a luxurious, romantic way to pass a few hours. The bar in the back of the house sells everything from crudités to booze, and downstairs is a barrel-roofed diner. Meanwhile, films, which change daily, hop between first-run and well-received art house movies—nothing too obscure. Shockingly, this place stood derelict from 1993 to 2001, and only a fierce campaign saved it. Now it's run by the exclusive Soho House, which opened a private club here and replaced some seats with bookable beds and sofas. Its outpost in Shoreditch is a new build and not so richly historic. 191 Portobello Rd., W11. www.electriccinema.co.uk. ✆ **020/7908-9696.** Tube: Ladbroke Grove or Notting Hill Gate.

Phoenix Cinema ★ Thought to be the oldest purpose-built cinema in the U.K., the Phoenix was constructed as the Premier Electric Theatre in 1910; by 1985, despite its handsome Edwardian barrel-vault ceiling, it was nose-to-nose with the wrecker's ball until fans (including director Mike Leigh) rallied. It screens an immense range of films from across eras and borders, plus frequent transmissions of live theater. It also has a liquor license. 52 High Rd., East Finchley, N2. www.phoenixcinema.co.uk. ✆ **020/8444-6789.** Tube: East Finchley.

GAY & LESBIAN SCENE

London's gay and lesbian scene is collapsing in the face of development. The last few years saw the unthinkable closure of Camden's half-century-old drag landmark The Black Cap, and several important Soho bars including Madame Jojo's and Molly Moggs have been forced out or have been sold. Nevertheless, the city still has one of the most varied scenes in the world. The music seems to crank a few notches louder when the jolly and outrageous **Pride London** (www.prideinlondon.org) season rolls along, in late June or early July.

Daily gay-oriented pursuits have traditionally been centered around Soho, where the bars and clubs take on a festive, anyone-is-welcome flair, and after work, guys spill into the streets. But as a mark of a truly integrated city, now nearly every neighborhood has its own pubs and gay nights. Where you spend an evening depends on your proclivities and willingness to commute. At most places, there aren't usually cover charges unless an event or show is on, when they're about £5 at bars and £11 for clubs. Lesbians who want to go out at night must usually plan a little because most girls' events take the form of weekly scheduled nights in bars that might cater to other niches during the rest of the week.

The weekly **Boyz** (www.boyz.co.uk) and **QX Magazine** (www.qxmagazine.com) publish schedules that favor club events. *Time Out* also has a weekly "Gay and Lesbian" section that dwells more on clubbing than on well-rounded pursuits.

There are many smaller venues, but these standout venues in every flavor are welcoming to tourists and will provide a good overview of the culture.

Bethnal Green Working Men's Club ★★   Serving drag, quiz nights, cabaret hosted by an unmoored Mariah Carey spoof performer—the straight-friendly hipster roster is louche and camp (check the theme ahead of time) but reliably messy. 42–44 Pollard Row, E2. www.workersplaytime.net. ✆ **020/7739-7170.** Cover £10. Tube: Bethnal Green.

Comptons ★★   This old two-level pub wears the tatty garb of a bygone saloon but it's one of Soho's most beloved hangouts for men who are out of their bubble-gum years. **Admiral Duncan,** across the street, and the **Duke of Wellington** ("Duke of Welly's"), where Old Compton Street T-bones into Wardour Street a few steps west, cater to the same professional age group. 51–53 Old Compton St., W1. www.comptonsofsoho.co.uk. ✆ **020/7096-5470.** Tube: Piccadilly Circus.

G-A-Y ★★   It's about partying, cruising, and dancing. The main event is the Saturday night club at Heaven, near Charing Cross Station. No other dance club in Europe, gay or straight, comes close to attracting such a pantheon of legendary live performances: Kylie, the Spice Girls, Cyndi Lauper, Bjork, and, of course, Madge, all performed here and have been known to return impromptu. Increasingly, however, there's nothing more exciting than *RuPaul's Drag Race* contestants. Every night, G-A-Y also runs a light pre-show hangout, G-A-Y Bar, where a young, twink crowd steeps in cheery Europop and watches videos on the plasma screens. And you can imagine the vibe at its G-A-Y Late venue, which goes until 3am. **Club:** Heaven, Under the Arches, Villiers St., WC2. Tube: Charing Cross or Embankment. **Bar:** 30 Old Compton St., W1. www.g-a-y.co.uk. ✆ **020/7494-2756.** Tube: Leicester Square. **Late:** 5 Goslett Yard, W1. ✆ **020/7734-9858.** Tube: Tottenham Court Rd.

Ku Bar ★★   A manageably sized, young-skewing, three-level lounge is the place you go when you don't want a scene but you wouldn't mind being served by shirtless boys. It has a later license: until 3am Monday to Saturday. 30 Lisle and 25 Frith sts., WC2. www.ku-bar.co.uk. ✆ **020/7437-4303.** Tube: Leicester Square.

Royal Vauxhall Tavern ★★★   A 2013 biography revealed that Diana, Princess of Wales, once secretly attended this gay drag landmark dressed as a man. Two years later, it became the first U.K. building to gain protection for its status as an LGBTQ landmark. Inside, anything still goes. There are three shows a night, all transgressive, or just dancing, and when the party's thumping, this little brick building literally leaks dance-floor fog. 372 Kennington Lane, SE11. www.vauxhalltavern.com. ✆ **020/7820-1222.** Tube: Vauxhall.

She Soho ★   She's one of London's only 7-days-a-week lesbian bars, and given that there aren't too many part-time girl bars, either, it attracts a wide spectrum of types—even tag-along men. 23a Old Compton St., W1. www.she-soho.com. ✆ **020/7437-4303.** Tube: Piccadilly Circus.

XXL London ★★★ London's biggest dance night for "bears" (for the uninitiated, those are men who would never dream of shaving their chests like the young "twinks" do), it's colossal beyond belief. Its arched-ceilinged dance floors—actually you're in vaults beneath a railway—get super sweaty, which must account for why thousands of assembled men would ever want to strip off their shirts and grind. 1 Invicta Plaza, South Bank, Blackfriars Rd. at Southwark St., SE1. www.xxl-london.com. ℂ **020/7403-4001.** Wed and Sat. Cover £15. Tube: Southwark.

The Yard ★★ On weekends, all the cute jock types are here, cramming the courtyard-like space, or watching the action from the Loft lounge area upstairs. Weekdays, it's more subdued and a place for the after-work crowd, but it's always straight-friendly. Developers are licking their chops over the space. 57 Rupert St., W1. www.yardbar.co.uk. ℂ **020/7437-2652.** Tube: Piccadilly Circus.

WALKING TOURS OF LONDON

Paying for a bus tour seems smart in principle. But you'll glimpse monuments only briefly and hear only one or two eye-glazing facts about them as you whiz past. No coach tour convinces you that the things you're seeing are quite real, or allows you to mull on what's before you, or lets you breathe in the atmosphere. Get close to London. Don't pass it. Touch it—so that it can touch you.

WALKING TOUR 1: WESTMINSTER, WHITEHALL & TRAFALGAR SQUARE

START:	**Westminster Tube station**
FINISH:	**Trafalgar Square**
TIME:	**Allow 60 minutes, not including time spent in attractions**
BEST TIME:	**Be at the starting line just before noon to hear Big Ben deliver its longest chime of the day**
WORST TIME:	**After working hours, when energy drains out of the area**

When most people hear the word "London," this is the area they picture: the Houses of Parliament, the wash of the Thames, the gong of Big Ben, and the Georgian facade of No. 10 Downing St. Kings and queens, prime ministers and executioners, despots and assassins—this is where they converged to shape a millennium of events, at the command center for England and the British Empire. History buffs, lace up.

---

1 Westminster Tube Station

The best train to take here is the Jubilee line, which was added at great expense in 1999. The station's concrete-grey, 36m-deep (118-ft.) cavern, ascended by escalators from the Jubilee's platforms, is one of the city's finest new spaces, providing a modern-day analog to the majestic space of Westminster Abbey nearby. Portcullis House, where many MPs (Members of Parliament) keep offices, is overhead.

Walking Tour 1: Westminster, Whitehall & Trafalgar Square

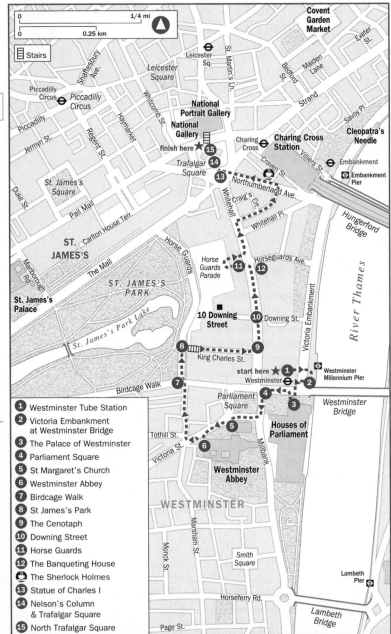

Stairs

0 — 1/4 mi
0 — 0.25 km

Covent Garden Market

Exeter St.

Leicester Sq.

St. Martin's Ln.

Leicester Square

Bedford St.

Maiden Lane

Strand

Savoy Pl.

Piccadilly Circus

Piccadilly Circus

Piccadilly

Jermyn St.

Shaftesbury Ave.

Whitcomb St.

Haymarket

Regent St.

National Portrait Gallery

National Gallery

finish here

Charing Cross

Charing Cross Station

Cleopatra's Needle

Villiers St.

Craven St.

Embankment

Embankment Pier

Trafalgar Square

Northumberland Ave.

Craig's Crt.

Whitehall

Whitehall Pl.

Hungerford Bridge

ST. JAMES'S SQUARE

Duke St.

Pall Mall

Carlton House Terr.

Horse Guards

ST. JAMES'S

The Mall

Marlborough Rd.

St. James's Palace

ST. JAMES'S PARK

St. James's Park Lake

Horse Guards Parade

Horseguards Ave.

River Thames

10 Downing Street

Downing St.

Victoria Embankment

King Charles St.

start here

Westminster

Westminster Millennium Pier

Birdcage Walk

Parliament Square

Westminster Bridge

Tothill St.

Houses of Parliament

Victoria St.

Westminster Abbey

Marsham St.

Millbank

Westminster Bridge

WESTMINSTER

Monck St.

Smith Square

Lambeth Pier

Horseferry Rd.

Page St.

Lambeth Bridge

① Westminster Tube Station
② Victoria Embankment at Westminster Bridge
③ The Palace of Westminster
④ Parliament Square
⑤ St Margaret's Church
⑥ Westminster Abbey
⑦ Birdcage Walk
⑧ St James's Park
⑨ The Cenotaph
⑩ Downing Street
⑪ Horse Guards
⑫ The Banqueting House
🕵 The Sherlock Holmes
⑬ Statue of Charles I
⑭ Nelson's Column & Trafalgar Square
⑮ North Trafalgar Square

The Victoria Embankment features gardens, statues, and glorious Thames views.

Find your way to the Westminster Underground station, Exit 1, and walk outside.

2 Victoria Embankment at Westminster Bridge

Once you're outside, you'll see the River Thames. If you stood here in 1858, in the midst of what came to be known as The Great Stink, you'd have choked on the fumes rising from the fetid effluvia floating in the river below. Until then, the city had no sewers to speak of—only pipes that dumped into the water. The solution was the Victoria Embankment, a daring engineering project, completed in 1870, that saved engineers from having to dig up the whole city. They simply built a new riverbank, laid sewers along it, paired that with new Underground railway tracks, and topped the unattractive additions with a garden and a road. Destructive, but effective—how Victorian.

Today, the embankments' benches are raised to allow a good view of the water, and it's dotted with triumphant statuary like Boudicca in her bladed chariot, which you can also see from here. This tribal queen rose up against the Romans; she failed politically but, as you see, succeeded aesthetically.

The London Eye, spinning on the opposite bank, had a tricky birth in 1999; it was constructed lying flat over the river, resting on pontoons, and then it was laboriously hoisted upright and into place. The mock-baroque building behind it is County Hall—it looks old, but it only dates to the early 20th century—which was once the seat of the London city government.

At the bridge's opposite landing, you can see the South Bank Lion. Weighing 14 tons, 3.6m (12 ft.) tall, and eager-eyed and floppy-pawed as a puppy, he was carved in 1837 by the Coade Stone Factory, which once stood where County Hall stands today. Made of a durable, synthetic ceramic stone formulated by a mother-daughter team, the lion stood proudly for over a century, painted red, atop the Red Lion Brewery that was located past the London Eye. Blitz bomb damage destroyed his roost, but at the request of King George VI, he was saved and placed just feet from his birthplace.

Go back into Westminster station, head down the corridor, and turn left before the set of four stairs. Leave the station via Exit 3, marked Houses of Parliament.

3 The Palace of Westminster

You're now standing under the iconic Elizabeth Tower of the Houses of Parliament, once called St Stephen's Tower but renamed in 2012 in honor of QE2's Diamond Jubilee. This is as close as you can get to it—it's covered in scaffolding until 2021 for its biggest restoration since its installation. Beneath that metal bramble, assorted crowns, kings, and crests are carved into the facade. These buildings may look like they're from the Gothic period, but in fact they date to 1859, when they rose from the ashes of the old Parliament House, destroyed by a nightmarish fire in 1834. Big Ben, the name of the largest of four bells inside (2.7m/9 ft. in diameter, 13 tons), was named for the portly commissioner of works who oversaw its installation. (There's actually a bigger bell in town: Great Paul at St Paul's is 2 tons heavier.) Each side of the Clock Tower's four faces is 6.9m (23 ft.) long. Since 1923, the very earliest days of wireless, the BBC has broadcast the 16-note prelude (called "Westminster Quarters" and replicated in doorbells around the world) of Big Ben before its news summaries. Thanks to a crack that developed in the 1860s, the bell is now slightly off from its original note—E above middle C—but you won't hear it today because of the ongoing works. This Big Ben is actually a ringer; the first Big Ben actually cracked within three months after being struck by bad hammers. A slightly smaller version was recast by the Whitechapel Bell Foundry which, 107 years earlier, also made America's Liberty Bell, which also cracked. Apparently, that happened a lot to big bells and it didn't affect business. But what cracked bells couldn't do, gentrification did: After 450 years of bell-making and 250 years in Whitechapel, the foundry finally shuttered forever in May 2017.

This plot of land has been used by royals since 1050, when Edward the Confessor built a palace here, away from the hubbub of the walled city. Kings ceased living on this block as of Henry VIII, when nearby Whitehall became his main London pad, followed in later reigns by St James's and, currently, Buckingham palaces. But Parliament's land is nationally owned, so technically it meets in Westminster Palace.

Head away from the river to:

4 Parliament Square

The heavy metal bars on the spiked fence that distances you from this building are not there out of mere paranoia; as far back as the thwarted Gunpowder Plot of 1605, the Houses of Parliament have been a target for would-be revolutionaries. Prime Minister Spencer Perceval was fatally shot on the steps of the House of Commons by a former convict on May 11, 1812, and in the Blitz, the buildings were smashed on more than a dozen occasions, including one (May 10, 1941) that caused the near-total destruction of the House of Commons.

The section of the Houses that juts into the yards, behind the statue of Oliver Cromwell, is Westminster Hall, from 1097, one of the only survivors from the 1834 fire. Charles I, Sir Thomas More, and Guy Fawkes were all condemned to death in the Hall.

For more on visiting the **Houses of Parliament,** see p. 132.

Turn left and walk in front of the Houses of Parliament. Use the first crosswalk to your right, heading toward the church. At the far side of the church, enter the gate to see:

5 St Margaret's Church

The little side church by Westminster Abbey (p. 136), the one with the four sundials on its tower, is the Church of Saint Margaret, dating to the early 1500s and much changed over the years. Sir Walter Raleigh, who

8

WALKING TOURS OF LONDON | Walking Tour 1: Westminster, Whitehall & Trafalgar Square

Parliament Square is an important stop on your walking tour.

was executed outside the Palace of Westminster, is buried inside, and both the poet Milton and Winston Churchill married their wives here.

You can see the statues of Parliament Square better from here. Probably the most famous one is that of American president Abraham Lincoln, at the western end; it's a copy of one in Chicago by Augustus Saint-Gaudens. During the anticapitalist protests of 2000, the statue of Winston Churchill that stands here received a temporary Mohawk made of grassy turf. This square has always attracted well-intentioned screw-ups: In 1868, the world's first traffic light was erected here. Gas powered, it blew up.

Follow the footpath to the front of:

6 Westminster Abbey

The lawn beside the abbey—yes, the one you just walked across—is in fact a disused graveyard. In a city this old, you simply can't avoid treading on final resting places. There are an unknown number of plague pits scattered through the city, into which thousands of victims were hastily dumped to avoid the spread of disease, and several city parks likely had the germ of their beginnings, so to speak, as potter's fields—group graves for paupers.

Although most of the Abbey is in the Early English style, the stern western towers above you now were the 18th-century work of Nicholas Hawksmoor, a protégé of Christopher Wren. Hawksmoor's designs are famous for emphasizing the forbidding, angry side of God; some critics accuse him of using architecture to frighten people into piety. Most of the time the people who use this main entrance in an official capacity do so in a crown, a gown, or a coffin. For more on visiting **Westminster Abbey,** see p. 136.

If you peer down Broad Sanctuary, which becomes Victoria Street, you can see the Italianate tower of Westminster Cathedral, the primary cathedral of England. Good news, Catholics: The English don't execute you anymore!

Cross the street to your right (Broad Sanctuary), and cross again. You should be a block west of Parliament Square on Storey's Gate now. Walk straight until you find yourself at the corner of St James's Park. You're at:

7 Birdcage Walk

You've just walked past a variety of European Union offices; the proximity to the Houses of Parliament has appealed to paper-pushers for centuries. The military has a presence here, too. The road that heads to the left, Birdcage Walk, leads to the front of Buckingham Palace. Halfway down, you'll find the Wellington Barracks, the headquarters of the Guards Division, where a battalion of one of the queen's five regiments of foot guards (Grenadier, Coldstream, Scots, Irish, and Welsh) bunks down. There's also a small, curio-packed Guards Museum (www.theguardsmuseum.com;

© **020/7414-3271;** daily 10am–4pm; £6), where you learn that their tall "busby" helmets are made of Canadian brown bearskin. Who knew?

Storey's Gate, the street you just walked, was named for the keeper of Charles II's aviary. Birdcage Walk, the street you're now on, was named after a royal aviary that stood in St James's Park; until 1928, only the Hereditary Royal Falconer was permitted to drive on Birdcage Walk. The park continues its tradition of hosting bird menageries; the pond is a haven for ducks and geese, and a small flock of pelicans has been in residence since the 1600s. They are fed fresh fish daily at 2:30pm.

Cross Birdcage Walk and walk 1 block up Horse Guards Road, passing the Treasury Building on your right, until you reach Clive Steps at King Charles Street on the right. On your left, peek into:

8 St James's Park

See if you can spot the lake in the park. The body of water was originally a formal canal belonging to St James's Palace, the official royal residence from the burning of Whitehall in 1698 to the time Victoria moved into Buckingham Palace in 1837. The old canal was prim and straight in the French style and outfitted with gondolas, a gift of the Doge of Venice. In winter, as Samuel Pepys described in the 1600s, it would freeze over, and people would frolic upon it using skates made of bone. It was later sculpted into something calculated to appear more random and thus more English. St James's Palace, which is not open to the public (except for

Clarence House, in summer; p. 141), is located on the north (far) side of the park. You might be able to make out a rustic-looking shack just inside the park. That's Duck Island Cottage, built in 1840 as a dwelling for the bird keeper. Not shabby for a servant's quarters.

You'd think that if London were under attack from flying bombers that you'd be much safer if you were a little farther from the Houses of Parliament. Yet in the basement of the sturdy 1907 Treasury Building, Britain's leaders orchestrated their country's "finest hour." Unbeknownst to the world, it was the hideout of Winston Churchill and his cabinet. Famously, but hardly wisely, that daredevil

St James's Park offers pleasant strolling around a graceful pond with ducks.

Churchill went onto the roof of the building so he could watch one of Goering's air raids slam the city. The cellar, preserved down to its typing pool and pushpins, is now the **Churchill War Rooms** (p. 131), a superlative museum paying homage to the bulldoggy prime minister.

Who is Robert Clive, the cutlass-wielding subject of this statue on the steps? He was the general who helped the East India Company conquer India and Bengal, partly through a series of underhanded bribes, thus delivering the region into the control of the British Empire for nearly 2 centuries. Don't be too hard on this hardened colonialist; the opium-addicted fellow committed suicide by stabbing himself with a penknife.

Walk down King Charles Street and through the arches at the end. You are now on Parliament Street. Look into the center of it. The somber stone column in the traffic island is:

9 The Cenotaph

The Cenotaph (from the Greek words for "empty" and "tomb") is a simple but elegiac memorial to those killed in the two World Wars. A 1919 plaster parade prop that was made permanent in stone by Edwin Lutyens the next year, it was executed with inconceivable restraint when you consider that nearly a million British subjects died in the Great War alone. Its inscription to the "Glorious Dead," coined by Rudyard Kipling, is repeated on other memorials in Commonwealth nations; the Cenotaphs in Auckland, New Zealand, and in London, Canada, are replicas. Uniformed servicemen and -women will always salute it as they pass, and on the Sunday closest to November 11, Britain's Remembrance Day, the sovereign lays the first wreath while other members of the Royal Family observe from the balcony of the Foreign Office. You may see flowers around it, or possibly silk poppies (red flowers with black centers), the national symbol of remembrance.

Walk left up Parliament Street, which becomes Whitehall. In about 30m (98 ft.) on the left, you reach a black fence with glass lanterns. Look inside the gates. This is:

10 Downing Street

On the right, by the tree and tough to make out, is No. 10, the official home of the prime minister. It's famous for its lion's head knocker—although to be frank, if you have to knock, you aren't welcome. Once, you could walk around in there, but Margaret

Entrance to Downing Street is heavily secured.

Thatcher made many enemies, so you'll have to make do with peering down the lane through metal bars. Such security was a long time coming. In 1842, a lunatic shot and killed the secretary to the prime minister, mistaking him for the big man; and in 1912, suffragette Emmeline Pankhurst and friends pelted the house with stones, breaking four windows, in one of many acts of civil disobedience in the fight for voting rights for women. If sentries prevent you from approaching, then the prime minister might be on the move. Prepare for the black gates to burst open, spew forth an armada of cars, and watch the prime minister's Jaguar blast onto Whitehall as if fleeing a bank heist.

The lane was laid out by George Downing, the second man to graduate from Harvard University in America and by all accounts a shady individual, a turncoat, and a slumlord. He's one of history's great scoundrels; his underhanded dealings resulted in Dutch-held Manhattan being swiped by the British and the slave trade multiplying in the Colonies. Strange that the most important street in British politics should bear his name.

Downing built No. 10 (then, no. 5) as part of a row of terraced houses in the late 1600s, fully intending for it to fall apart after a few years (instead of actually laying bricks, he just painted on lines with mortar). Yet George II had his eye on the house, and he kicked out a man named Mr. Chicken—further information about him, tantalizingly, is lost to the mists of time—to give it as a gift to the first prime minister, Robert Walpole, in 1730. Walpole insisted that the house be used by future First Lords of the Treasury, his official capacity. He also connected it to a grand home behind it on Horse Guards, now nicknamed The House at the Back—this deceptive Georgian facade actually conceals 160 rooms. No. 10 is also connected with nos. 11 and 12, and it's even linked to Buckingham Palace and Q-Whitehall, a sprawling war bunker, by long underground tunnels. Many prime ministers elected to live in their own homes, using No. 10 for meetings, but not William Pitt, who moved in upon becoming prime minister at the virtually pubescent age of 24 in 1783. He lived here for more than 20 years, longer than any other prime minister, until his death at 46. Whitehall became a slum in the mid-1800s, and the house fell out of fashion, but then it served as the nerve center for the two World Wars and became indispensable to the British spirit. You can see the original front door, now replaced by a stronger one, on display at the Churchill Museum at the Cabinet War Rooms (p. 131), two stops back.

A little up Whitehall from Downing Street, look for the bronze monument to "The Women of World War II," which depicts no women, but rather their uniforms and hats, hanging on pegs as if they'd been put away after a job well done. The implication of this 6.6m-tall (22-ft.) tableau is, of course, that the women went back to the kitchen after briefly filling a more robust societal role. This sly bit of statuary-as-commentary was unveiled by the queen in 2005. Some 80 percent of the cost of the memorial was raised by a baroness who won money on ITV's *Who Wants to Be a Millionaire?*

Continue up Whitehall, past the monumental government buildings. In about 60m (200 ft.), you will reach another black gate broken by two stone guardhouses. Head inside the yard to view:

11 Horse Guards

Built in the Palladian style between 1750 and 1758 on a former jousting field of Whitehall Palace, the Horse Guards is the official (but little-used) entrance to the grounds of St James's Palace and Buckingham Palace. Two mounted cavalry troops are posted in the guardhouses every day from 10am to 4pm, and they're changed hourly. At 11am daily and 10am Sunday, the guard on duty is relieved by a dozen men who march in from The Mall behind, accompanied (when the queen is in town) by a trumpeter, a standard bearer, and an officer. Don't try to crack up guards with your shenanigans. You'll look boorish and rude—and they still won't react.

If you think the clock tower arch looks small, you're right. Its designer made it that way so that its proportions would match the rest of the building. Walk through the clock tower arch to reach the graveled Horse Guards Parade, the city's largest non-park gathering space, which you may recognize as the setting for volleyball during the Olympic Games.

Return from the yard to Whitehall. Across the street you'll see:

12 The Banqueting House

Built by Inigo Jones, this is not a home but it is the last remaining portion of the great Whitehall Palace. Inside is a bombastic ceiling by Rubens depicting the king as a god. That vainglorious posture, and the king's grabs for more power, led to the gory event that happened on this spot on January 30, 1649. If you were standing here then, you would have been in the crowd that watched King Charles I mount the scaffold (wearing two shirts so that he wouldn't shiver—he was no true god, after all), place his head on the block, and be decapitated, handing the reins of the country to a military dictatorship led by Oliver Cromwell. When the executioner held the head aloft, one witness said there was a queasy silence, followed by "such a groan by the thousands then present, as I never heard before and I desire I may never hear again." Charles I was buried privately at Windsor, not at Westminster Abbey, to avoid more unpleasant scenes. If you want to see what poor Charles looked like, hang on for the next stop. The regicide was somewhat for naught; by 1660, the country grew weary of its leadership and Charles I's son, the hedonistic spendthrift Charles II, was back on daddy's throne. In revenge, the second Charles chose the Banqueting House as the site for his restoration party, and then had the nerve to show up late. England was royal again—and how. For more on visiting the Banqueting House, see p. 140.

Continue up Whitehall. Take the next right, Great Scotland Yard (the corner of Scotland Place was the "visitor's entrance" of the Ministry of Magic in the Harry Potter movies), and then cross Northumberland Avenue, veer slightly left, and head into Craven Passage.

The Sherlock Holmes 🍺

Time for a pint and maybe some traditional English pub grub, so head to **The Sherlock Holmes** (10–11 Northumberland St.). In 1957, a collection of Arthur Conan Doyle memorabilia was assembled as a tourist attraction for the huge Festival of Britain that gave London the Southbank Centre, and it became the centerpiece of this pub. It's nowhere near 221B Baker St., but it has a roof garden and a terrace.

Return to Northumberland Avenue and turn right. When you reach Trafalgar Square, cross the street so you're in the oval traffic island.

13 Statue of Charles I

That this bronze statue stands here is a miracle. It's of Charles I, pre-headectomy, and is a precious Carolinian original from 1633. When the king was beheaded, the Royal Family was deposed (permanently, so people thought). The owner of this statue was commanded to destroy it, but he was clever enough to bury it instead. After the Restoration, it was dug up and placed here, in about 1675. That was even before Trafalgar Square existed (the zone was, as an equestrian statue suggests, used as stables). Charles wasn't a tall man, and boosting him with a horse went some way toward making the luckless fellow seem imposing. Someone stole his sword in 1867, and he went into hiding again during the Blitz, but otherwise, this is one of the oldest things in this part of London that remains in its original place. Its pedestal, unloved and weathered, could use a restoration, too.

This is a good spot, free of traffic and obstructions, to survey your surroundings and take some photos. Look back down Whitehall, from where you just came, and you'll see Big Ben's tower. To the right, the vista through Admiralty Arch concludes in the distance with the grand Victoria Memorial and Buckingham Palace. Important buildings for two Commonwealth nations stand astride Trafalgar Square: Canada House to the left (west) and South Africa House to the right (east; its country's name is inscribed in Afrikaans as Suid-Afrika).

Cross again so that you're on the south side of:

14 Nelson's Column & Trafalgar Square

Why is Lord Nelson atop that column? Money. The Admiral sacrificed his life in 1805 to defeat Napoleon Bonaparte's naval aspirations at the Battle of Trafalgar, thus securing Britain's dominance over the oceans— and pumping untold wealth into London. In the late 1800s, lightning struck Lord Nelson—or at any rate his statue—damaging his left arm. It took until 2006 for the city to finally eliminate the bronze bands that held him together, repairing him with the same Craigleith sandstone with which he was constructed in 1843. During the work, they realized that the monument is actually 4.8m (16 ft.) shorter than guidebooks had been claiming for generations—it's 51m (167 ft.) from the street to the crown of his hat. The man himself is 5.5m (18 ft.) tall. The column's base is lined with four bronze reliefs that were said to be cast using metal from French cannon captured at the battle that each one depicts. All are guarded by four huge lions by Queen Victoria's favorite painter, Edwin Landseer (1867), the mascots of the square. You might think such animals don't belong here, but in the 1950s, under their noses, archeologists found prehistoric deposits with remains of rhinos, elephants, hippos, and yes, cave lions. Landseer was onto something.

Lutyens, who did the Cenotaph (p. 260), also designed the plaza's two fountains (from 1845 originals), which were ostensibly for beautification but conveniently prevented citizens from gathering in numbers. Trafalgar Square has long been the setting for demonstrations that turned from complaint to unrestful, such as infamous riots over poll taxes and unemployment. The English gather here for happy things, too, as they did for the announcement of V-E Day (May 8, 1945), and as they still do for festivals and free summer performances. In the southeast corner, you'll see a stone booth big enough for a single person, built in 1926. Once a closet for a phone that was used to summon backup, now it's used mostly to store chemicals for the fountains.

You may have heard about Trafalgar's Square's famous pigeons. So where are they? Banished for overactive excretion. Until the early 1990s, the square swarmed with them—the fluttering flock was estimated to peak at 35,000—and vendors made a living from selling bird feed to tourists. Eventually, the GLC, London's government, grew tired of shoveling streaky poo off the statues and decided to return the square to its original function as a great public space to edify its great museum, the National Gallery. They began feeding the pigeons themselves first thing in the morning, and then hired a team of hawks (from the superhero-sounding Hawkforce, tended by a leather-gloved keeper), to patrol the square. The flock learned to chow down and then clear out for the day; anyone who feeds the birds is subject to a £500 fine.

Head to the other side of the fountains to:

15 North Trafalgar Square

At night when landmarks are picked out by lights, the views down Whitehall are sublime. Most of the statues dotting the square are of forgotten military men and nobles: James II (1686; in front of the National Gallery) is finely crafted, but he looks ridiculous, pointing limply in those Roman robes. He was deposed in the Glorious Revolution just two years after the statue was cast. It used to stand outside the Banqueting House; for years, detractors joked he was pointing in the direction he planned to flee. (And yes, that's George Washington, who wrested the Colonies from the Crown, standing nearby. Feelings are no longer hard—he was a gift from

Virginia a century ago. Urban legend has it the pedestal contains a layer of Virginia earth so he can be said to remain on American soil.) The northwestern plinth of Trafalgar Square was designed for an equestrian statue of its own, but money ran out and it stood empty from 1841. More than 150 years later, the naked spot was named The Fourth Plinth and filled by works commissioned by a subversive panel of top artists. Sculptures show for 12 to 18 months, and they get the city talking. Marc Quinn's *Alison Lapper Pregnant* (2005) depicted a snow-white, nude woman born with limb deformities and heavy with child, and *Hahn/Cock* (2013) was Katharina Fritsch's two-story, ultramarine rooster, a sly send-up of the pompous military iconography elsewhere in the square. In early 2018 it's David Shrigley's elongated thumbs-up *Really Good* (2016), followed by Michael Rakowitz's re-creation, out of Iraqi date-syrup cans, of a statue destroyed by ISIS.

Along the north terrace, by the Café on the Square, look for the Imperial Standards of Length, which were set into the wall in 1876 and moved in 2003 when the central stairs were installed. They are the literal yardsticks against which all other British yardsticks are measured, showing inches, feet, and yards, plus mostly obsolete measures such as links, chains, perches, and poles.

And now, reward yourself with a visit to the loo, left of the stairs, and a spot of tea in the cafe. Or, if you crave some more substantial victuals, head over to the street east of the square to St Martin-in-the-Fields church, finished in 1724. Its combination of spire and classical portico was controversial at the time, but today, it pleases people of all persuasions with its excellent Café in the Crypt (p. 82). And, of course, two of the city's greatest museums, the National Gallery (p. 123) and the National Portrait Gallery (p. 126), share the same block and tower above you now.

WALKING TOUR 2: ST PAUL'S & SOUTHWARK

START:	**St Paul's Tube station**
FINISH:	**The George Inn, near London Bridge Tube station**
TIME:	**2 hours, not including restaurant breaks or attractions**
BEST TIMES:	**Weekend days in good weather, when the area is abuzz; Borough Market is most vital from Thursday to Saturday**
WORST TIMES:	**After dark, when cobbled streets are too dark to see well**

It was the best of advertisements, it was the worst of advertisements. Charles Dickens' novels, largely social protests wearing the cloak of entertainment, made readers feel as if they'd traveled to London when they never left their own armchairs. Trouble is, the city that Dickens has primed visitors to expect—the foggy, coal-smudged metropolis teeming with pickpockets and virtuous orphans—is nowhere to be found. Partly thanks to Dickens' work, London reformed itself. On this tour, you'll explore what's left of its darker

Walking Tour 2: St Paul's & Southwark

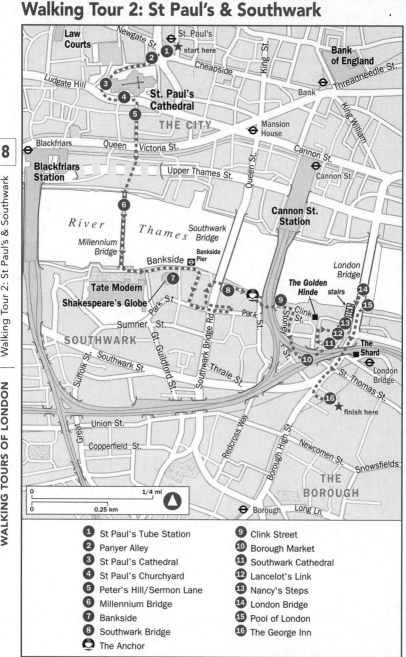

1. St Paul's Tube Station
2. Panyer Alley
3. St Paul's Cathedral
4. St Paul's Churchyard
5. Peter's Hill/Sermon Lane
6. Millennium Bridge
7. Bankside
8. Southwark Bridge
   The Anchor
9. Clink Street
10. Borough Market
11. Southwark Cathedral
12. Lancelot's Link
13. Nancy's Steps
14. London Bridge
15. Pool of London
16. The George Inn

side—from the libertine London of Shakespeare's day to the desperate one Dickens sought to solve with his pen. Along the way, you'll enjoy gourmet food and a beer on the Thames, which conceals a body count of its own.

1 St Paul's Tube Station

If you just took the Central Line here, you rode what was once called the Central Railway. In the first 75 years of the Underground, train lines were independently owned, and separate tickets were required each time a passenger changed trains. Fares were cumbersome, calculated according to the distance traveled and the class of carriage chosen. When the Central Railway held its grand opening in 1900, in the presence of American wit Mark Twain (who lived in London at the time), it soared above its competitors by dint of several innovations, the most important of which was that anyone could ride as far as they wanted on a flat fare. The so-called "Twopenny Tube," which had one class of carriage like today's Tube trains, was a sensation. Gilbert and Sullivan, swept along, amended a line in their operetta *Patience* from a reference to the threepenny bus to "the very delectable, highly respectable Twopenny Tube." The Central Railway helped democratize public transit and accelerated expansion into the suburbs—even if authorities eventually went back to the old format of charging passengers by distance. The St Paul's station opened on July 30, 1900, as Post Office station—the city's main Post Office was then across the street (hence the name of Postman's Park just north; p. 162).

Exit the St Paul's Underground station and turn left, toward:

2 Panyer Alley

Panyer Alley, where you're standing, was named for the basketmakers, or panyers, who once traded here. Look for a plaque on the wall depicting a child sitting on a basket. This plaque, the so-called Panyer Stone, is dated "August the 27, 1688," and reads, "When you have sought / the citty round / yet still this is / the highest ground." The artists behind this stone surely knew that Ludgate is not the highest point in The City; that's Cornhill, which is about 30cm (12 in.) higher. But the sign has been here so long that it would quite literally be a crime to take it down.

Head left, toward St Paul's, and make a right through the pedestrian alley, Paternoster Row, to Paternoster Square. Go through the ornate arch at the far left:

3 St Paul's Cathedral

The area you've just walked through, Paternoster Row, ranks among the most sacred in London. There have been major houses of worship on the plot of St Paul's as far back as 604, and for centuries these narrow surrounding streets have teemed with ecclesiastical scribes and clergy, as well as untold hordes of supplicants desperate for a handout from the merciful church. Paternoster Row was later known as the center of literary London, first for its publishers—who replaced the scribes—and later

St Paul's Cathedral.

for its book market. This is where Shakespeare bought the historical texts that inspired him to write his plays. Yet what you'll see today is modern; even the 23m-tall (75-ft.) column in Paternoster Square was created only a few years ago to appear older than it is. Why would planners permit the wholesale demolition of such a rich heritage? They didn't. This was Ground Zero of the Blitz in 1940. The Germans, recognizing that the destruction of St Paul's would demoralize the nation, focused their power on it, and the spillover devastated everything around it. Every firefighter was called to the cathedral, saving it at the expense of just about everything else.

The ornate stone archway that you pass through, however, is a true antique. It's Temple Gate, one of eight ancient gateways to The City of London, which originally stood where Strand becomes Fleet Street from 1672. Charles Dickens described it in *Bleak House* as "a leaden-headed old obstruction." It was dismantled in 1878 and was destined for a dump somewhere when a visionary stepped in and brought the stones home. After spending more than a century in the hinterland of his family's Hertfordshire estate (and being spared the Blitz), the gate, possibly designed by Christopher Wren, was restored and re-erected here in November 2004. The seven other gates, including Aldgate and Moorgate, were all lost over time.

In front of the cathedral, a statue of Queen Anne, who ruled England when St Paul's was completed, looks down Ludgate Hill. In attendance are ladies symbolizing England, France, Ireland, and North America, which she considered her subjects. The statue is an 1886 copy of the 1712 original, which (like Temple Gate once did) now resides, in scabby condition, in the countryside.

Herbert Mason's iconic photograph of St Paul's dome, snapped during the mighty conflagration that engulfed London after air raids on December 29 and 30, 1940, was taken from Ludgate Hill. Next time you see that picture, note that it's lit by firelight. For more on visiting St Paul's, see p. 163.

Skirt the cathedral along the busy street called:

4 St Paul's Churchyard

At the crossing, go over the street. Now's a good time to duck into The City of London Information Centre (Mon–Sat 9:30am–5:30pm, Sun 10am–4pm), located inside the origami-style, wing-roofed building, and stock up on free tourist brochures and timetables. It also runs daily guided walks in the afternoon.

If you don't need information, turn left. If you do use the office, when you come out again, turn right. After the patch of grass, turn right again. You can see down Peter's Hill to a white pedestrian bridge over the river. Stroll down:

5 Peter's Hill/Sermon Lane

On the right is the Firefighters National Memorial, which depicts a young man gesturing wildly toward St Paul's as two others grapple desperately with a hose. It's impossible to exaggerate the devastation caused by the Blitz, both in property and in lives. The superheated firestorms created damage greater in area than those of the Great Fire of 1666. More than 20,000 people were killed, and 1.4 million left homeless. The names of some 1,000 victims, all volunteer firefighters defeated by the wild blaze and collapsing buildings, are inscribed on the octagonal base. Winston Churchill dubbed this monument "The Heroes with Grimy Faces." For their families, the survival of St Paul's Cathedral amidst utter devastation remains a testament to their sacrifice. Keep going toward the river.

Go onto the:

6 Millennium Bridge

You're now on the steel Millennium Bridge, the central city's first new crossing over the Thames since the Tower Bridge in 1894. Its design, which features side-located suspension cables that sag about six times shallower than a conventional suspension bridge's supports do, was a little too advanced for its own good. When the bridge opened in 2000, it was discovered that the shifting weight of pedestrians caused it to sway, and people had to grasp the rails for support. (At the start of *Harry Potter and the Half-Blood Prince,* Death Eaters attack the bridge and make it wobble—that was an inside joke for Londoners.) Engineers closed the 325m (1,066-ft.) span, poured in another £5.2 million to solve the issue, and reopened it in 2002. Now locals love it because it has transformed accessibility to the river's southern bank, and they're planning more foot crossings. It's still not perfect—it's plagued by joggers with little regard for idle strollers—but crossing the river here, in view of many of the city's landmarks, young and old, makes for some stirring photos.

Straight ahead is the monumental Tate Modern (p. 158), signaled by its factory-like "campanile" smokestack, which from 1952 to 1981 belched exhaust from the Bankside Power Station. Energy has been a fundamental part of the district's character for generations. The power station replaced an earlier one that dusted everything near it with a coating of soot, and that plant, too, supplanted a foul gasworks. Before that, the district was the domain of a legion of coal merchants who shuttled their filthy wares around town in shallow boats. These "lightermen" worked from docks that lined the entire southern shore, where land was cheaper than it was in The City on the northern side. The building you see before you is a direct descendant of the way of life that prevailed on the bank in the 1700s.

How deep is the Thames? The river fluctuates greatly with tides (so it's dangerous for swimming—in fact, that's illegal between Putney and the Thames Barrier), but depending on when you measure around here, it's generally 8.9m (29 ft.) deep at highest tide and 1.8m (6 ft.) at low tide. The Thames' moodiness is the main reason Southwark, the side of the river where the Tate Modern sits, was written off for so many centuries. Until medieval times, the low-lying southern bank was boggy and mostly uninhabitable, so was instead thought of as part of Surrey, the county south of London. Londoners made use of the waterlogged land by turning it into gardens for secret trysts and fish farms (the Pike Garden, or Pye Garden, stood pretty much in front of you around the Tate's eastern flank). It wasn't until the latter part of the 1700s that people figured out how to drain the water and settle the area fully. Southwark was where you went for a rowdy time—that is, until the Puritans quashed the fun in 1642.

Before you completely cross the river, look down at the debris near the river wall. Turn back for a stupendous view of St Paul's dome symmetrically rising from the center of the bridge.

Once you're on the opposite bank, with the river in front of you, turn right. Stand midway between the cluster of houses and the building with the thatched roof. You're on:

7 Bankside

This river promenade also continues west, past the Tate Modern, to the London Eye and the Houses of Parliament. In *Four Weddings and a Funeral,* when Hugh Grant told Andie MacDowell he loved her (in the words of David Cassidy), he did it farther along this walkway by the

National Film Theatre. There's no better place to stroll, people-watch, and appreciate the sweep of the city.

As late as the 1960s, the path you're on, which at this place is called Bankside, was a vehicular street bearing two-way traffic, as it had been since the 1600s. Each building on the street owned rights to the docks or water-stairs on the river opposite it, so tenants were usually people who needed access to the water, such as ferrymen or sailors. The four-story white house at the left of the blind Cardinal Cap Alley, no. 49, was built around 1710 on the foundations of a pub, the Cardinal's Cap, which itself was built in 1547 to entertain the people who came to Southwark to carouse. No. 49 was home to successive generations of coal merchants, but not, as its plaque purports, to Sir Christopher Wren as he built St Paul's. Wren did live nearby, but in a building that was torn down when the power station needed land. This plaque hung on that vanished home, but was appropriated by a D.I.Y. revisionist in the mid–20th century. No. 49 has received its own biography, *The House by the Thames* by Gillian Tindall.

To the left is Shakespeare's Globe Theatre (p. 157), which made a premature exit in its own era, only to be rebuilt in ours. The circular Globe's stage is even at the same compass point as the 1599 original's. Interestingly, the city's theatrical life was centered here from about 1587 to 1642, when it was illegal to operate a theater in The City proper. Once the laws relaxed, the entertainment venues moved back into town, where they've been ever since.

Southwark was the Tudor version of a multiplex, and the biggest blockbuster was bear-baiting—the spectacle of vicious dogs let loose upon tethered bears. Even Henry VIII and Elizabeth I were huge fans; he had a bear pit installed at Whitehall Palace, and she barred Parliament from banning the pursuit on Sundays. One and a half blocks past the Globe, squeeze between modern buildings down an alley called Bear Gardens to find a small courtyard, three-quarters of the way down the street. That's the rough location of the Davies Amphitheatre, one of the most popular bear pits. Samuel Pepys wrote in his diary in 1666 of attending one such slaughter where he "saw some good sport of the bull's tossing the dogs—one into the very boxes. But it is a very rude and nasty pleasure."

Under a modern office building in the next street, Rose Alley, lie the foundations of another theater known to have premiered plays by Shakespeare, the Rose (p. 158). It lasted from 1587 to about 1606. The Swan stood nearby, too, although we may never find the footprint. The Rose's footprint gave us vital clues about what Elizabethan theaters looked like—architects also studied sketches made of it by a Dutch tourist in 1596. (Are you sketching your trip?)

Historians think they know where the original Globe stood. If you'd like to see it, head down Bear Gardens (between two modern buildings) one block to Park Street, turn left and go under the bridge, and just after it, past the buildings on the right, you'll find slightly red cobbles showing locations of fragments archeologists found in 1989. Not very suggestive, is it? In 1949, it was even drearier. It lay behind the gate of the decrepit Anchor Brewery, and when American actor Sam Wanamaker (father of Zoë, who played Madam Hooch in the Harry Potter movies) dropped by to pay pilgrimage, the indignity of the meager plaque (still there) so enraged him that he resolved to rebuild the Globe as a living home for England's great theatrical tradition—which is what came to pass, albeit 4 years after his 1993 death. Oscar-winning actor Mark Rylance was its first artistic director, serving for a decade.

Continue along the river, keeping it to your left. You'll go through a pedestrian tunnel under:

8 Southwark Bridge

On the wall of the tunnel, you'll see illustrations of skaters and revelers at the bygone "Frost Fairs" that, starting in 1564, were regularly held on the icy Thames. No matter how many winters you spend in London, you'll never see the Thames freeze over. But back then, they had the London Bridge, a few hundred yards downstream. Its 19 arches were so narrow, and its supports so thick, that the river's flow became sluggish, allowing water (and the outhouse filth that churned within it) to freeze. By contrast, during outgoing tides the rush was so fierce that boats capsized and passengers (few of whom knew how to swim, given the filth) drowned. When the bridge was dismantled in 1814, the Frost Fairs melted into history.

Take a look underneath Southwark Bridge where it meets the shore. You can still discern the remains of some water-stairs, dating to before the construction of the first bridge here in 1819. Back then, getting across the river usually required boatmen, the taxi drivers of their day. Ferrymen would court business by shouting destinations to theatergoers after their plays: "Eastward ho!" or "Westward ho!"

In 1912, this bridge's central 72m (236-ft.) span was the largest ever attempted in cast iron.

The Anchor 🍺

Few pubs are more idyllic than the **Anchor** (p. 102), situated where Bankside meets the railway viaduct. The riverside patio is open in good weather; otherwise, the interior is charming. This pub was once controlled, as nearly all pubs once were, by a brewery; it was Barclay Perkins, located just behind it from 1790 until about 1980. Even before that, it was a fixture; in 1666, Samuel Pepys watched the Great Fire rage from here before coming to his senses and hurrying across the river to rescue his possessions from his home in Seething Lane, near the Tower of London. In the 1950s, the Anchor was considered a slum and nearly was demolished.

After the Anchor, the path jogs inland. Take the first left onto:

9 Clink Street

Pass under the railway arch. In a few moments, you've gone from Elizabethan Southwark (theaters, bear-baiting) to Georgian Southwark (coal merchants, breweries). Now you're in Victorian Southwark, a claustrophobic underworld teeming with fetid-smelling industry and river rats. You can almost hear distant reverberations on this narrow wharfside street. You might even call the sensation Dickensian, and you wouldn't be wrong, since when the writer was 12 years old, his father was thrown into a debtor's prison near where you're standing, off the Borough High Street.

Clink Street was a service lane in the centuries when the Thames wharves were thriving.

Prisons were something of a cottage industry for the area; the Clink Street Prison stood here from 1127, when the Bishop of Winchester built it as a lockup for his Winchester Palace, until 1780, when the anti-Catholic Gordon riots saw the dismal hole destroyed. Although the Clink gave its name as slang to all prisons that came after it, no one knows for sure how it got the name itself—Flemish or Middle English words for latch are likely the origin. Suffice to say it was awful—and so is the "museum" here that purports to tell its story. Avoid it.

In the 1800s, warehousing goods instead of people became this street's stock-in-trade. You'll still see hints of the street's past maritime uses, from wooden loft doors to cranes used to hoist crates into upper floors, but in recent years even the original cobbles were removed. Today, these spaces house media companies and architects. During the week, you'll see them in their fashionable clothes, strutting in their Italian shoes across pavers that until recently were the original rounded cobbles.

The latter Bishops of Winchester were not nice guys. Henry II (1133–89) gave them control of this neighborhood, and because it was outside the jurisdiction of the city, they could pretty much get away with whatever they wanted to. Principally, they cultivated countless brothels and skimmed the profits for themselves—which is how Southwark got its rep as a den of vice. Anyone who annoyed them (heretics, troublemakers) wound up in the Clink, where no one was likely to find them again. As you continue down Clink Street, past the modern building with the rounded grid of windows, on your right you'll see all that's left of the Bishops' palace: a fragment of old stone wall, dating to the 1300s, with a round panel of stone tracery at the top. That tracery once held a rose window, which lit the palace's great hall. This fragment was forgotten behind a wall until a warehouse fire exposed it again. Double back to Stoney Street.

Turn down Stoney Street and walk under the railway. On your left, you'll see:

10 Borough Market

Stop at the frilly grey portico.

The mood of the neighborhood has changed drastically again. To your left, behind the portico, is Borough Market, a fantasy for the tongue (described in gastronomic detail on p. 94) and the oldest fruit and vegetable market in the city. A market has been held around here since A.D. 43, when Roman soldiers noted passing a market on their way to sack The City. More reliable records date it to 1014, when it served the denizens on the old London Bridge, the city's only river crossing. The cream-grey portico is not original to this place; it's the cast-iron Flower Hall of Covent Garden, rescued when the Royal Opera House was renovated in 2003. If it seems to blend seamlessly, it's because it was made around the same time as the rest of the Borough Market structure (1859–60). You are standing very near the spot, by the Wheatsheaf pub, where police swiftly put an end to a ghastly Saturday night terrorist attack by knife-wielding attackers in June 2017.

The Market is best known for gourmet supplies. Park Street, which runs into Stoney Street, looks as quaint as a movie-set version of old England; in fact, it was used in *Harry Potter and the Prisoner of Azkaban,* and no. 7A was the entrance of The Leaky Cauldron. The Market itself has appeared in films including *Howard's End* and *Bridget Jones's Diary.* The city's first railway, a 6.4km (4-mile) run to Greenwich, plowed its route .8km (½ mile) east of here in 1836. Even after tunneling technology improved, railway tycoons thought nothing of barricading thriving neighborhoods with massive brick viaducts, cutting them off from each other and creating slums. On your tour, you have crossed under a number of railway viaducts built that way, and shortly, you'll see how narrowly one of England's most historic churches averted its own destruction.

Enter the market to the right of the portico and walk straight. Cross the next street and enter the brick arch marked Green Market. Before you is:

11 Southwark Cathedral

(If for some reason the Green Market arch is closed, turn left down Bedale St.—it's not marked—until you see a church appear on your right.)

Before you stands the oldest Gothic church in the city, and the oldest building in Southwark. You'll see its tower appear in every old drawing of the city. In Roman times, it was the site of a villa. Its Christian chapter was begun by the daughter of a ferryman in the 7th century; it was rebuilt in the 850s and again 300 years later. There was once a monastery and a

Southwark Cathedral.

chapel in this yard, where office workers now lunch on gourmet items from Borough Market, but those came and went, too. Southwark teemed with the poor, with factory workers, and with grubby river men. One such blue-collar child was John Harvard, one of nine kids of a man who owned a tavern and butcher shop just northeast of here. John was baptized in this church in the early 1600s, but when he grew up, he fled this slum for the Massachusetts Bay Colony, where Harvard University was later named for him. In time the place was limping along as a humble parish church called St Saviour's and dissolving into dilapidation. The rerouting of London Bridge Road sheared away several small chapels, and in 1863, the rumbling railway forced its way alongside the yard. But by 1905, its fortunes reversed when it was elevated to a cathedral, and now it's so well cared for that it's hard to discern its true age and sordid past.

The cathedral has some beautiful painted monuments, including one of England's oldest wooden effigies (1280). Shakespeare's brother Edmond was buried here in 1607, as was Philip Henslowe, who built the Rose, in an unmarked grave. Other worthwhile sights include Edwardian stained-glass tributes to the Bard's plays, the Harvard Chapel with masonry from the Norman period, and some of the original ceiling bosses, carved in 1469 and saved when things got bad. How bad? During Elizabeth I's reign, the retro-choir (the part behind the altar) was walled off and rented to a baker. Later on, vestrymen discovered the baker was also raising swine in there.

Just north of the cathedral, running parallel to its nave, a separate entrance leads into a glass-roofed corridor, which traces the line of an alley that was called:

12 Lancelot's Link

Nelson Mandela opened this addition in 2001. Have a look at the display inside, which preserves surprising discoveries made in this small area during a 1999 renovation. Look down into the well on the far right, and you'll see the original paving stones from the Roman road that cut through this space in the 1st century. You crossed over this same road several times already today; you were standing above it when you entered Borough Market. Other relics, piled on top of each other, include a stone coffin, probably from the 1200s, with a carved slot for the head, and a kiln from the 1600s, soot marks intact—bits of the Delftware made here have been found as far away as Williamsburg, Virginia.

Back down the corridor, exit. Go through the yard into the lane (it's Montague Close; the Thames is in front of you). Turn right, and just before the overpass, look left for:

13 Nancy's Steps

These are popularly held to be the location, in the Dickens novel *Oliver Twist,* where Noah Claypool eavesdrops on a conversation that leads to Nancy's murder by Bill Sykes. In the book, those steps faced the Thames, but these steps are in fact a rare surviving remnant of the New London Bridge, built here in 1821 as a replacement for the 600-year-old, overcrowded London Bridge. (The steps that Dickens wrote about were sold in 1968 to an American oilman. Locals superciliously quip he was duped, but, in fact, he knew exactly what he was doing and preserved what the English wouldn't. He had most of the New London Bridge shipped, stone by stone, to Lake Havasu, Arizona, to form a tourist attraction, and there it remains today, standing near a marina on a desert lake.) These steps were left behind and attached to the existing London Bridge, a featureless 1973 replacement.

Just so you know, the modern London Bridge was not the source of the nursery rhyme "London Bridge Is Falling Down"—that either referred to the burning of a wooden version in 1013, during a skirmish between Danes and Norwegians; or to Henry III's "fair lady" Queen Eleanor, who skimmed the tolls of the medieval bridge for her own purse, leaving its maintenance in a parlous state.

Climb the stairs to the road above. You're now on:

14 London Bridge

At the top of the stairs, you'll see a pedestal topped by a dragon, the symbol of the city, holding London's crest. You'll see these dragons at several of the city's medieval borders. About 30m (98 ft.) east of here, under modern buildings, is where you would have entered the Stone Gateway, the entry to the disaster-prone medieval London Bridge. For more than 3 centuries, tar-dipped heads of executed criminals were impaled on pikes and stuck atop the Gateway as a vivid warning to would-be ne'er-do-wells.

Turn to the right to use the crosswalk. Go to the opposite side of the street and walk onto London Bridge, over the river. Don't cross the river—just enjoy the view of the:

15 Pool of London

This section of the Thames between London Bridge and the Tower Bridge is known as the Pool of London. It may be quiet now, but for nearly 2,000 years, it was the heart of international trade. So many goods passed through here that warehouses along the southern bank became known as "London's Larder." Ships finally became so large that they had to unload downstream, closer to the sea. The section of river in front of you, parallel to this bridge, is where the medieval London Bridge stood.

Across the river from the Tower, you'll just make out an egg-shaped glass building. That's City Hall (2002), designed by Norman Foster (who also did the Millennium Bridge) to be ergonomic, with a huge spiral staircase curling around its atrium and "smart" windows that open on hot days. Just like a politician, it has no edge and you can't tell if it's coming or going. Former London mayor Ken Livingstone, a man not known for tact or restraint, called it "a glass testicle." Anyone can have a ball in its public spaces from 8:30am to 5:30pm on weekdays (www.london.gov.uk).

Turn around and follow London Bridge inland, keeping on the left side of the road. This street becomes Borough High Street. You will pass under a railway arch. Just after you pass Southwark Street forking off to the right, look for "The George" sign. It marks:

16 The George Inn

Because the London Bridge was the only crossing to the city from the south for so many centuries, this area became the equivalent of a train depot, and it was dotted with inns, stables, coach yards, and pubs. Everyone going to or coming from southern England or Europe stopped here, often spending the night before pushing into the shoulder-to-shoulder crowds of London Bridge. If you've ever read *The Canterbury Tales,* you'll recall that in 1386, the pilgrims began their journey to the shrine of Thomas à Becket from the Tabard Inn. Until 1873, that was located a short walk farther down Borough High Street, on the left. The George, described on p. 103, is the last survivor from this bustling coaching era. Although the wooden building, which once encircled the entire yard, dates to 1677, the inn was here for at least another 130 years before that, if not longer. We know it was typical of the time because John Stow, in *A Survey of London* (1598), termed it "a common hostelry for travelers." A drink here makes a fitting end to your journey through time. Look up and you'll see the jagged glass spire of The Shard (p. 160), Europe's tallest building, peering down as you sit where people have lifted beer for nearly half a millennium.

WALKING TOUR 3: SOHO & ST GILES: POP, SHOP & MARX

START:	**Oxford Circus Tube station**
FINISH:	**Goodge Street Tube station**
TIME:	**2 hours, not including shopping or restaurant breaks**
BEST TIMES:	**Weekdays, when Berwick Street's market is on and Oxford Street is slightly less crowded**
WORST TIMES:	**Evening rush hour, when Oxford Circus Tube stop is positively rammed, and after dark, when stores and markets close**

All churched out? London is more than stories about dead queens and bloody uprisings. It's always been cosmopolitan, too, and the flash point for trends that ripple out to the rest of the world. Songs first sung at the clubs of Soho soon caused toes to tap on the other side of the planet, and fashion trends born

8

Walking Tour 3: Soho & St Giles: Pop, Shop & Marx

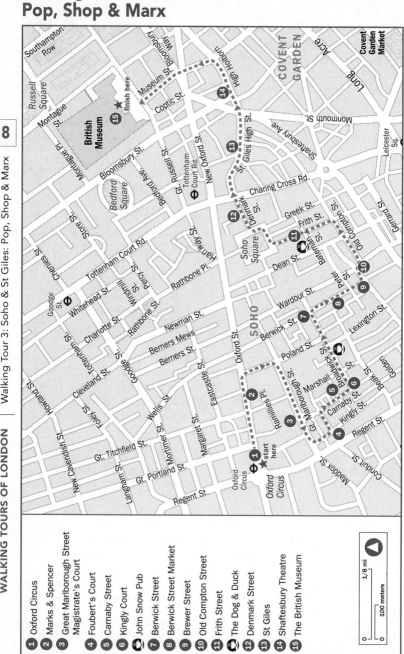

1 Oxford Circus
2 Marks & Spencer
3 Great Marlborough Street Magistrate's Court
4 Foubert's Court
5 Carnaby Street
6 Kingly Court
7 John Snow Pub
8 Berwick Street
9 Berwick Street Market
10 Brewer Street
11 Old Compton Street
12 Frith Street
13 The Dog & Duck
14 Denmark Street
15 St Giles
16 Shaftesbury Theatre
17 The British Museum

0 ___ 1/8 mi
0 ___ 100 meters

on Carnaby Street remain internationally iconic 40 years later. Bring along your credit cards as we roam some of the city's best shopping streets and touch upon a few leftovers from London's recent past, including forgotten air-raid shelters and the settings for some good, old-fashioned sex scandals. This is the London you found out about from the radio and the runways, not from your social studies teacher.

1 Oxford Circus

Leave the Tube station using Exit 2. Position yourself out of the fray.

You are in the thick of mile-long **Regent Street,** which to the right is punctuated by the witches-hat steeple of All Souls Church and to the left curves toward Piccadilly Circus. When the Prince Regent, later George IV, was planning his new pet project, Regent's Park, he decided he also wanted a road to connect his house to it. He chose this particular location because, in his mind, it would provide a suitable demarcation line between the gentry of Mayfair, to the west, and the rabble of the traders who lived in Soho, to the east. George tapped John Nash to do the job, completed in 1825. Originally, the sidewalks were covered by stone colonnades, but when those attracted prostitutes, they were removed, and most of the original buildings were later rebuilt—the only Nash original is now All Souls. Even if most of the facades you see now mask more modern buildings, few streets in London impart such a sweeping, uplifting feeling, though few are also as congested with the hoi polloi George would have spurned.

The bustling intersection known as Oxford Circus.

The other avenue intersecting before you is Oxford Street, following the same line as a Roman road. George's class-centered definition of the landscape has more or less held: The exclusive shops of Oxford Street still lie west of Regent Street, and the downmarket stores tend to be east of it. Having a presence on Oxford Street is considered crucial for brands with mass appeal.

Head right, east on Oxford Street. You will pass Argyll Street on the right. When you pass Ramillies Street, prepare to stop in front of:

2 Marks & Spencer

London has a love-hate relationship with Oxford Street. People come here to shop by the thousands, but they often despair of the crush of the experience. Charles Dickens, Jr., described the street thusly in 1888: "It ought to be the finest thoroughfare in the world. As a matter of fact it is not by any means, and though it is, like all the other thoroughfares, improving, it still contains many houses which even in a third-rate street would be considered mean." We're only going to walk down a sample of Oxford Street. It's usually so crowded, that's as much as you can probably handle if you're keeping one eye on this book.

Marks & Spencer (p. 211), or M&S, dates to 1894 and is the favored British department store for staples. Perhaps proof of its appeal is that the chain can afford to run two giant frontages on Oxford Street; its flagship store is remarkably near here, between Bond Street and Marble Arch Tube stations. Its Food Halls (at this store, in the cellar) are well known as an ideal place to pick up prepared foods, sandwiches, and inexpensive but well-selected wines.

Turn right at Poland Street, walk 1 block, and turn right again onto Great Marlborough Street. Soon on your right, at nos. 19–21, you'll see a stout white building. That's the:

3 Great Marlborough Street Magistrate's Court

Charles Dickens worked here as a reporter just before hitting it big as a novelist, and a variety of other big names appeared before the judges here, including the Marquess of Queensbury (defending himself from Oscar Wilde's libel charge). When this neighborhood turned bohemian in the Swinging '60s, the court began trying a string of drug charges against the likes of Mick Jagger, Johnny Rotten, Keith Richards, Francis Bacon, and, curiously (and coming full circle), the guy who wrote the musical *Oliver!*, Lionel Bart. It's now a hotel, but I suggest you go inside briefly, because much of the old judicial fittings were left intact. You can have a cocktail in one of the old jail cells—now converted into private booths— or even peek into a restaurant slotted into the authoritative Number One court, which still has its witness stand, bench, wood paneling, and vaulted glass ceiling.

Beyond the Courthouse Hotel on the left, you'll see a Tudor-style building of black beams and white plaster. This is Liberty (p. 210), famous for its haute fabrics. It's also famous for its building—it was made in 1924 using wood recycled from junked ships.

Great Marlborough Street runs into Regent Street. Turn left there and walk the short distance to:

4 Foubert's Court

Times have been better on Regent Street. Walmart-style box stores in the suburbs have put the screws on the destination shops of the city, and this avenue has seen long-termers lose their sizzle. Dickins & Jones, a department store at the corner you just turned, closed its doors in early 2006 after nearly 170 years, and the same old shopping mall brands are moving in.

Two doors farther from Foubert's Court, though, at nos. 188–196, is a well-loved holdover from the street's glory days. It's Hamleys (p. 224), one of the largest toy stores in the world. Some 5 million customers pour through its doors every year, but since the sales force is famous for putting on a nonstop show on every floor, it's understandable if many of those customers come to gawp and not to buy. If you go into Hamleys, when and if you come out again, turn right and go back to Foubert's Court.

Walk down the very short Foubert's Court for 1 block; you'll see "Carnaby" on a metal arch. Go under it and head 1 block. Go right, and now you'll see a larger arch on:

5 Carnaby Street

Yes, those obnoxious arches proclaim your location with a self-promotion that proves this street is no longer the super-cool, forward-trending street of the kids in the know. It's more of a mall with an edge. The days of Swinging London, when men could cruise from store to store trying on hip-hugging black trousers and frilly shirts, are behind it. *Time* magazine spilled the secret of Carnaby Street in 1966, and by the 1970s, it was pedestrianized as a shopping street, making hipness a matter of retrospect.

Carnaby Street has little left of its 1960s Swinging London cachet.

Just after you cross Ganton Street, where Broadwick Street hits Carnaby Street, duck into the passageway on the right:

6 Kingly Court

Clever entrepreneurs led Carnaby Street's rebirth with this development, a lively gathering of bars and restaurants in a former timber warehouse.

Slip out the back door of Kingly Court, opposite its front door, and hang a left on Kingly Street. No. 9 is the Bag 'O Nails pub, where future Wings-mates Paul McCartney and Linda Eastman first clapped eyes on each other—and also where in 1961 John Profumo met Christine Keeler, kicking off the notorious Profumo Affair. It's also where Fleetwood Mac's John McVie proposed to Christine. (The free audio touring app Carnaby Echoes dives into the music history of the neighborhood.)

Return to Kingly Court. Retrace your steps out of it, cross Carnaby Street, and head down Broadwick Street. You'll stop around:

John Snow Pub ☕

So grateful were Dr. Snow's neighbors that they renamed their pub for him, albeit a century later. It stands at no. 39, at Lexington Street, on the site of his practice. Raise a pint in his honor here, as we read the words of Dr. Snow himself: "I feel it my duty to endeavor to convince you of the physical evils sustained to your health by using intoxicating liquors even in the greatest moderation." (Oops.)

Kingly Court is a lively gathering of bars and restaurants in a former timber warehouse.

Continue on Broadwick Street to:

7 Berwick Street

About 170 years ago, this block was a foul slum. French, Greek, and Italian immigrants fled hard times and revolutions by cramming into these tight streets, and by the 1850s, cholera was storming through the overstuffed city. An 1854 outbreak killed 500 people in barely 10 days. Common wisdom at the time held that the disease was spread through the air—a reasonable conclusion, given how terrible the sewage-smeared city smelled—but a local anesthetist, John Snow (for whom the pub you just visited was named) had a different theory. Suspecting polluted water was the cause, he got permission to inspect the public pump at Broad Street, now Broadwick Street (in the block before Berwick St.) and found that it was being contaminated with sewage leaking from no. 40, at the corner of Broadwick and Poland streets. The saga was recently retold in the book *The Ghost Map* by Steven Johnson, and in 2015 the site of no. 40 was dug up to build this new building.

When you reach Berwick Street, look left. Think of this location as the modern-day Abbey Road. It's where, in 1995, Oasis photographed the cover of *(What's the Story) Morning Glory?,* one of the seminal CDs of the age. The photographer shot from farther down the street, aiming south, toward where you're standing. (Noel Gallagher, with characteristic tact, said he thought the album cover was "s**t.")

And here's another slice of rock history: One miniblock farther down Broadwick Street at no. 7, the corner shop covered in striking rust-colored tiles (now Sounds of the Universe record store, a local landmark for world music) was the Bricklayers Arms pub. Brian Jones auditioned the Rolling Stones here in 1962, and they held formative rehearsals upstairs. Across the road at no. 6 is Agent Provocateur, a noted lingerie shop, a hint of how unsavory the area once was. The word "Soho" is probably derived from a hunting cry used when this area was parkland—it's nice to see that some folks around here are still on the hunt.

Turn south on Berwick Street. Walk down it to:

8 Berwick Street Market

This is the vestige of the last great weekday market in the center of the city—it's been in operation at least since the 1840s (vestry records indicate some illicit trading was going on as far back as 1778). London's first publicly available grapefruit was sold here in 1890. Now that the Cockney produce sellers have been mostly elbowed aside for gourmet nibbles, the market again caters to those with exotic, expensive tastes.

Pass over Peter Street and under Maurice House, going under the crossover and winding up on:

9 Brewer Street

From the late 1700s to the 1950s, it was impossible for a single gentleman to pass unpropositioned through Soho. A 1959 act chased the open salesmanship indoors, to be replaced by drinking joints where men could buy lap time with a lady, and by the 1970s, even those were forced to seek a lower profile. By law, today's displays are not permitted to titillate, complying with the British reputation (inaccurate in my book) for sexual modesty.

It was in this fleshy carnival that Laura Henderson bought a theater near Great Windmill and Archer streets (across the intersection from No. 20, where Karl Marx's *The Communist Manifesto* was commissioned in 1847, by the way). She got around indecency laws by ensuring that the performers in her naughty entertainment, the Revudeville, never moved a muscle. Famously, the Windmill never closed, not even during the Blitz. You might have seen it in the film *Mrs Henderson Presents* (2005). By the 1950s, Soho was a den of gang warfare and prostitution, full of craftsmen of every sort—costumers, ostrich feather trimmers, gun makers—until the Conservative government re-zoned the neighborhoods to admit offices, and the old ways were priced out.

Go left to Wardour Street, make a right and then a quick left. You'll be at the head of:

10 Old Compton Street

First, note the church of St Anne's, a few yards down Wardour Street, on the left. It was built in 1685, possibly by Wren (which ones weren't?), 2.5m (8 ft.) higher than the street because it went on top of a graveyard for 60,000 bodies (until 1853, when burials stopped, the neighborhood reeked from it). Everything save the church's tower was creamed by the Nazis.

Walk down Old Compton Street, Soho's de facto main street, which is busy round the clock and a center of gay life. No. 54 is the Admiral Duncan, where Dylan Thomas once drank (then again, where didn't he?). It was here, in 1999, that Nazi sympathizer David Copeland planted a bomb stuffed with 500 nails, which killed three people and injured many more. Copeland, an obvious madman, also bombed the South Asian population of Brick Lane and blacks in Brixton, but his only fatalities were here.

On the corner of Dean Street, look right. Down the block on the left, at no. 49, is the French House, more commonly called the French Pub. During World War II, it was the drinking haunt of Charles de Gaulle; here the exiled leader formed the Free French government and army. The street beyond the French House is Shaftesbury Avenue, the famous theatrical thoroughfare; many of the side streets between Old Compton and Shaftesbury contain the stage doors for the major playhouses, where famous actors report to work. Now look left, north up Dean Street. In no. 28, Karl Marx dwelled in abject poverty with his wife and several kids, but no running water or toilet. Three of his kids died while he was in residence in Soho in the early 1850s, and he had to borrow £2 for a coffin for one baby. No wonder he thought Marxism would be better.

Turn left at:

11 Frith Street

Bar Italia, the stylish cafe at no. 22, is a nightlife landmark of its own (p. 82). Upstairs is where, in 1925, John Logie Baird privately tested a homemade invention he called "noctovision," using his grocer's delivery boy as a test subject. The next year, he unveiled an improved model for the science nerds of the Royal Institution upstairs in this building. (Unsatisfied, he made another attempt in 1928 that involved hooking up a fresh human eyeball he'd rushed by taxicab from Charing Cross Ophthalmic Hospital. It created a mess.) Baird's system, which used a spinning disc, was eventually discarded, but it debuted ahead of American Philo T. Farnsworth's more famous electronic version. Within a decade, the BBC was broadcasting "television"—its new name—regularly. In the 1940s, Baird invented the first color picture tube.

Walk up three doors. For 10 months starting in September 1764, the 8-year-old Mozart lived with his father and sister at a house at no. 20 (the building was replaced in 1858). While he was in London, the prodigy amused King George III, wrote his first two symphonies, and befriended fellow composer J.C. Bach, who mentored him. By the 1800s, Soho's Wardour Street was the violin-making center of Europe. Music history of another kind happened at no. 47, which in 1969 hosted the first public performance of The Who's *Tommy,* and then Jimi Hendrix's last performance, in 1970.

The Dog & Duck ☕

You should totally stop at another pub now. I mean, how often are you in London? This one, at 18 Bateman St., is a beauty, rich with Victorian tilework and mahogany paneling. If it puts you in a literary frame of mind, perhaps you're sensing vibrations. It was a favorite of George Orwell—he toasted with absinthe here when he learned he'd sold *Animal Farm* to a publisher.

Turn right into Bateman Street (pub behind you), go one block, then left at Greek Street. Take the first right, the alley of Manette Street, and continue to Charing Cross Road. Cross using the crosswalk on your left and keep going straight along Denmark Street.

12 Denmark Street

Look up, and you'll see the 35-story Centre Point development. Built in 1964 with government concessions, it was kept empty for years by its greedy owner, Harry Hyams, partly to hold out for astronomical rents and partly to get off the tax hook even as the city struggled through a homeless crisis. In 1974, a hundred squatters occupied it to make a point. The charity Centrepoint, which started in the basement of St Anne's Church in Soho and grew into a force, derisively took its name from the waste.

Denmark Street, recently decimated by Elizabeth Line construction and lined with a now-paltry scattering of specialists in musical instruments, is just a hundred yards long, but it's dense with stories. This is

London's version of New York's Tin Pan Alley—a nucleus for the British popular music industry. At no. 4, the Rolling Stones recorded their first album at Regent Sounds Studios (now The Alley Cat Club). On the roof of No. 20, Bernie Taupin wrote the lyric for "Your Song" (1970), his first hit with Elton John, during a break from work, which is why the words reference sitting on a roof. Charlie Chaplin wrote the tune of the iconic "Smile" in 2 hours here. David Bowie, The Kinks, Jimi Hendrix, Bob Marley, the Sex Pistols, and Black Sabbath all had countless formative moments—buying guitars, hiring bands, recording albums—along Denmark Street. It's all in the past now.

Keep following this road. It hangs slightly right, then is renamed St Giles High Street.

13 St Giles

You are standing in the worst slum in London. In the middle 1800s, the census counted more than 50,000 paupers within a few hundred squalid square feet. One eight-roomed house was stuffed with 107 luckless souls. People called poor neighborhoods "rookeries" because inhabitants were packed, shoeless and shivering, into single rooms like birds in nests. This is the London of *Oliver Twist*'s Fagin and his haggard gang of orphan pickpockets, of William Hogarth's "Gin Lane" prints warning of the villainy of drink among the destitute, including kids. This is the lawless labyrinth teeming with penniless immigrants, sex workers, drug addicts, thieves, and rats. This spot is so far gone that in World War II, even Hitler didn't bother to bomb it.

Except it's not. Not anymore. The new toybox-colorful development by Renzo Piano tells you nothing of the depravity that shocked and reformed the heartlessness of English society. Most of the remnants of poverty were bulldozed aside by development, as happens in our age. But the church on the right, St Giles-in-the-Fields, has origins back to Saxon times (1101), but this one was built in the 1730s because the architectural integrity of the previous one had been compromised by the huge number of plague victims buried all around it. The interior is fairly standard as churches go, but note The Angel pub (on Saint Giles High Street) just past it.

Until the late 1700s, St Giles was the last church on the wagon route from Newgate Prison to the gallows at the village of Tyburn a mile away (now near Marble Arch). The convoys of doomed criminals rolled as many as eight times a year, and it was the equivalent of a major sporting event. Thousands of people would line the route to watch the condemned be dispatched to their maker, and as they passed taverns, they would be offered one last draught of ale. The pub that stood here (in the past, called The Bowl) is recorded as being where many prisoners drank their last beer on this mortal plane. The phrase "on the wagon" may stem from this grisly ritual.

The British Museum was established to give all classes access to antiquities and learning.

Continue straight to the Shaftesbury Theatre.

14 Shaftesbury Theatre

The Shaftesbury was built in 1911 as the New Prince's Theatre, and it has been one of the most important independent houses ever since. In 1923, the sibling dance team of Fred and Adele Astaire cemented their international stardom with *Stop Flirting*; Prince Edward, future abdicator and a man fatefully obsessed with Americans, attended almost nightly. Adele was soon swept off her feet by a duke, leaving Fred with the (then) unlikely prospect of finding a career alone. We know how all that turned out. Other past tenants: Peter O'Toole, Anthony Hopkins, the London premieres of *Pal Joey* (1954), *How to Succeed in Business Without Really Trying* (1963), *Hair* (1968), *Follies* (1987), *Rent* (1998), and *Hairspray* (2007).

Two short blocks later, you'll be where Museum Street and Drury Lane both cross High Holborn (the road you're on). Turn left onto Museum Street. In 3 blocks, one of them pedestrianized, you will find yourself standing before the world-famous British Museum (fully explained on p. 114).

15 The British Museum

When it received its charter from George II, in 1753, the idea was revolutionary: A museum not owned by either the king or a church, free for the masses to use, and dedicated to the advancement of a broad range of disciplines. It was called the National Museum, and as you've just learned, at the time, acres of slums roiled just outside its doorstep. But, in a miracle of liberal-leaning benevolence, the country was determined to improve itself. Even the filthy souls who inhabited mid-19th-century Soho and St Giles were welcomed here. And now, so are you.

DAY TRIPS FROM LONDON

Y ou've flown all the way to England. It would be a shame to miss seeing some of the sights that make it special—the rolling countryside, the stately mansions, the ageless villages built on slow-flowing rivers. An excursion enriches you with two experiences for the price of one: You'll taste everyday English life while you immerse yourself in world-famous landmarks.

Britain has comprehensive transport, but it's not quick as mercury. Because of traffic and a dearth of superhighways, you can expect a 48km (30-mile) trip to take an hour, so a spot that's 129 to 161km (80–100 miles) each way, such as Stonehenge or Bath, will require you to rise at dawn if you want to buy yourself much touring time at all. Going by bus is often less expensive than by rail, but the inefficient journey will involve narrow roads.

The tourist offices listed will be able, for a fee (£4–£5, plus 10 percent of the room rate), to hook you up with a bed for the night, should you decide that you'd rather not trek back to London right away. You can find lots more information at **Visit England** (www. visitengland.com) and **Visit Britain** (www.visitbritain.com).

For in-depth coverage of everything outside of London, bring a copy of *Frommer's England & Scotland.* For casual day-trippers, though, here's what you need to know to dash out of the city and see the best of these destinations.

WINDSOR & ETON

Buckingham Palace is a mere *pied-à-terre.* The queen actually prefers this great castle, which dominates the skyline of town like a cloud of stone. Windsor Castle (32km/20 miles west of London) has been the home of the Royal Family for some 900 years, far longer than anything in London. Queen Victoria is buried in the backyard (although they don't phrase it quite that way). Despite the inevitable crowds, this is unmissable.

Essentials

GETTING THERE The price difference between transport options is negligible. Riding the rails is quicker, so it's got the edge.

Trains (www.nationalrail.co.uk; ℭ **03457/48-49-50,** or 020/7278-5240 from overseas; 38–56 min.; £12–£24) go directly from Waterloo station to Windsor & Eton Riverside or from Paddington to Windsor & Eton Central with a change at Slough. Both Windsor stations are a 3-min. walk from the Castle. Trains requiring no changes leave twice an hour, and trains requiring a change leave a little more frequently. Or take coach 702 by **Green Line** (www.green line702.co.uk; ℭ **0118/959-4000;** 1 hr. 45 min.; £15 single before noon, £9 single after noon, or £40 for 4 traveling together). Nos. 700, 701, or 702 leave from Hyde Park Corner or Victoria Coach Station, south of Victoria Station.

VISITOR INFORMATION Stop by **Windsor Royal Shopping** (Old Booking Hall, Windsor Royal Station, Thames St.; www.windsor.gov.uk; ℭ **01753/743-900**). From there (or www.windsorwalks.co.uk), you can be referred to Blue Badge guides for **town walks.**

TOURS The Original Tour (www.theoriginaltour.com; ℭ **020/8877-1722**), a worldwide hop-on, hop-off brand, recently added a route here. But the most appealing way to see the area is by **boat,** departing from Windsor Promenade, Barry Avenue, for a 40-min. round-trip with fine views of the castle. Tours are operated by **French Brothers,** Clewer Boathouse, Clewer Court Rd., Windsor (www.frenchbrothers.co.uk; ℭ **01753/851-900;** 40-min. trip £9 adults, £8.30 seniors, £6 children 3–13, cheaper online; 2-hr. trip £16 adults, £14.75 seniors, £10.70 children 3–13).

Exploring Windsor

Legoland Windsor (www.legoland.co.uk; ℭ **0871/222-2001;** Mar–Oct; £36–£60 seniors and children 3–15, cheaper in advance online), 2 miles from town, has top-notch rides catering to small children and some impressive Lego constructions. The Green Line coach from London goes there, as do shuttles from Windsor's Theatre Royal. The tourist office sells discounted tickets for late-afternoon entry.

Windsor Castle ★ You may have had your fill of palaces in London proper, but you haven't seen the best. A fortress and a royal home for more than 900 years, it was expanded by each successive monarch who dwelled in it—more battlements for the warlike ones, more finery for the aesthetes. The resulting sprawl, which dominates the town from nearly every angle, is the queen's favorite residence—she spends lots of time here—and its history is richer than that of Buckingham Palace.

The castle's **State Apartments** are sumptuous enough to be daunting, and a tour through them—available unless there's a state visit—includes entrance to some mind-bogglingly historic rooms. Around a million people file through every year, so sharpen your elbows. *Warning:* There are no cafes (they're building one for 2018), so eat first.

The palace has a cache of priceless furniture (some of it solid silver), paintings, ephemera (look for the bullet that killed Lord Nelson, sealed in a locket), and weaponry, all of which, frustratingly, the audio guide, signage, and £5

St George's Chapel at Windsor Castle, where Prince Harry and Meghan Markle were wed in 2018.

souvenir book do little to describe, so the only recourse is to pepper staff with questions. In 1992, one-fifth of the castle area was engulfed by an accidental fire; the queen recounted her despair over that, plus the breakup of two of her children's marriages, in her now-famous "annus horribilus" Christmas speech to the nation, and much effort and funding went into returning everything to the way it was before. In fact, the queen originally opened Buckingham Palace to visitors to fund the restoration.

St George's Hall, one of the repaired areas, is the queen's chosen room for banquets. Kids love **Queen Mary's Doll's House,** a preposterously extravagant toy built for the allegedly grown-up Queen Mary in the 1920s with working electricity, elevators, plumbing, specially written library books, and other details so extravagant they're borderline offensive. From October to March, the tour also includes the **Semi-State Rooms,** George IV's private area, considered by many to be among the best-preserved Georgian interiors in England. In August and September, you can climb the **Round Tower** for views, and sometimes in January and midsummer, the castle's ancient **Great Kitchen** is open. There's also a **Changing the Guard** ceremony at 11am (Mon–Sat, but alternate days Aug–Mar; check the website). **St George's Chapel** (closed Sun), a delicately vaulted Gothic spectacle opened by Henry VIII, is his final resting place and that of nine other monarchs, including

Elizabeth II's father (George VI). Elizabeth II's mother (the Queen Mum) and sister (Princess Margaret) are with him in a side chapel; it's safe to assume that this is where she will wind up one day as well. Happy things happen here, too: It's where Prince Harry married Meghan Markle in 2018.

The Castle is the superstar here, but supporting roles are played by the succinctly named **Great Park** adjoining it, and the 4.8km (3-mile) pin-straight **Long Walk** that culminates with an equestrian statue of George III. **Frogmore,** open a pitiful few days in the summer, is the house where Victoria and Albert share their mausoleum. Just south of the castle is the **Guildhall,** where Prince Charles and Camilla Parker-Bowles had a quiet civil marriage in April 2005; it's no St Paul's, where in 1981 Charles wed his first wife, what's-her-name, but it is also the work of Christopher Wren (note its delicate arches). The building was apparently designed without the center columns, which made councilors nervous; Wren threw up some columns but left them an inch shy of the ceiling, just to prove that his architecture was sound.

Castle Hill. www.royalcollection.org.uk. ℭ **020/7766-7304.** Admission £21.20 adults, £19.30 students and seniors, £12.30 children 5–16, free for children 4 and under, £54.70 family of 5 (2 adults and 3 children 16 and under), cheaper if the State Apartments are closed. Mar–Oct daily 9:30am–5:15pm, last admission 4pm; Nov–Feb daily 9:45am–4:15pm, last admission 3pm. Closed for periods in Apr, June, and Dec, when the royal family is in residence. National Rail: Windsor Central or Windsor & Eton Riverside.

Eton College ★

A 15-min. walk over a footbridge on the Thames (narrow at this western remove), you're in a world served by snooty stationers and haberdashers. Eton is probably the most exclusive boys' school on Earth. Princes Harry and William are alums, known as Old Etonians, as are kings and princes from around the world. There's a museum in its wine cellars—and the fact this school has a wine cellar tells you what kind of rich these kids are. Be nice to them. They're tomorrow's dictators.

Keats Lane, Eton, Windsor. www.eton college.com. ℭ **01753/370-600.** Admission £10. 90-min. tours May–early Sept. Fri at 2 and 4pm. Reservations required.

Clocktower and entrance to Eton College.

BATH

Easily roamed on foot, Bath, about 161km (100 miles) west of London, is revered as a splendid example of Georgian architecture—to tourists, Bath is resolutely stuck in that past. The pleasing sandstone hue of its buildings set

Saving on Your Excursion's Rail Ticket

Train fares listed in this section are provided as a guideline; National Rail pricing schemes are complicated and unpredictable. The good news is that for all of the destinations served by trains, if you return to London on the same day that you leave it, you can pay just a little more than the price of the usual one-way (single) ticket. Rail clerks call this a "day return." More tips:

○ Do not wait until the day of travel. Last-minute fares are outrageous.

○ Tickets tend to be most costly on Fridays, when Londoners head out of town.

○ You can find incredible deals (up to 70 percent off) if you happen to be among the first customers to get tickets for a given departure. Book starting 12 weeks out.

○ Prices are highest for "open" tickets with no restrictions, so opt for the restricted fare since you probably won't need to change your plans.

against the slate-grey British sky, the assiduously planned symmetry of its streets, the illusion that Jane Austen (who lived here in 1800–05) is taking tea within one of its 18th-century Palladian town houses—Bath's magic comes from its consistent and regal design. No wonder the upper crust of the 1700s found it so fashionable, and no wonder their descendants have not dared to alter it. And no wonder UNESCO inscribed it as a World Heritage Site—a rarity for an entire city.

Essentials

GETTING THERE   The fastest **trains** (www.nationalrail.co.uk; ✆ **08457/ 48-49-50**; 90 min., twice an hour; £40 return with advance purchase) leave from Paddington and let off in Bath Spa, an ugly section of town about 5 minutes' walk from the good stuff. Because buses take twice as long, I don't recommend National Express (www.nationalexpress.com; ✆ **08705/80-80-80**; 3 hr.; £9 single). Most of the major tour bus companies (see box on p. 303) come here, combining with Stonehenge (p. 304) for about £75.

VISITOR INFORMATION   Visit Bath/Bath Tourist Information Centre (Bridgwater House, 2 Terrace Walk; www.visitbath.co.uk; ✆ **01225/614-420**; open daily; tourism@bathtourism.co.uk).

TOURS   For nearly 90 years, the mayor's office has furnished professionally guided, free 2-hr. **Walking Tours of Bath** (www.bathguides.org.uk; Sun–Fri 10:30am and 2pm, Sat 10:30am; May–Aug also Tues and Thurs 6pm). Meet outside the Roman Baths near Bath Abbey. Download the free **Official Bath App** for orientation. You can also purchase 50-min. walking tours on downloadable MP3s from **Tourist Tracks** (www.tourist-tracks.com; £5 for two).

Exploring Bath

Begin your tour of Georgian Bath at **Queen Square** for some of the famous streets laid out by John Wood the Elder (1704–54). Walk up to the **Circus,** three Palladian crescents arranged in a circle, with 524 different carved emblems above the doors. His son designed the **Royal Crescent,** an elegant half-moon row of town houses. Robert Adam put up **Pulteney Bridge,** a shop-lined crossing of the River Avon, in 1773, just as a similar bridge in the same medieval style, London Bridge, was crumbling.

Roman Baths ★   The Romans (ca. A.D. 60) were the first to recognize the tourism potential of the natural hot springs, which bubble at a rate of 250,000 gallons a day. Springs were re-developed or re-bored every few centuries; the current buildings are mostly from the 1800s, but Roman artifacts are occasionally found, and the restoration and accompanying museum are excellent. The Victorians mounted a proud colonnade around the excavation, and water has long been drawn in the adjoining Pump Room; you can drink a glass of the sulfuric stuff if you like, or settle down for a pricey lunch in neoclassical style. It's been the done thing in Bath since your great-great-great-grandma was in bloomers.

Bath Abbey Church Yard, Stall St. www.romanbaths.co.uk. ✆ **01225/477-785.** Admission £16.50–£17.50 adults, £14.50–£16.50 seniors and students, £10.25–£14.50 children 6–16 (higher prices are July–Aug). July–Aug daily 9am–9pm; Sept–Oct and Mar–June daily 9am–5pm; Nov–Feb daily 9:30am–5pm; last exit 1 hr. after closing.

No. 1 Royal Crescent ★   First-time visitors are blown away by the sweep and elegance of the Royal Crescent, a dazzling 30-house development that took some 8 years to complete, from 1767 to 1775. Its first house, which recently absorbed the old servants' quarters in a massive restoration that religiously presents daily life in those days, is worth a swing-by if you want the full Regency effect.

1 Royal Crescent. www.no1royalcrescent.org.uk. ✆ **01225/428-126.** Admission £10.30 adults, £8.80 students and seniors, £5.10 children 6–16, family ticket £25.40. Daily 10am–5pm; last admission 4pm.

Fashion Museum & Assembly Rooms ★   The grand **Assembly Rooms,** designed by the younger John Wood and completed in 1771, once played host to dances, recitals, and tea parties. Damaged in World War II, the elegant rooms have been restored and look much as they did when Jane Austen and Thomas Gainsborough attended events here. Housed in the same building, the **Fashion Museum** offers audio tours through the history of fashion from the 16th century to the present day through some 165 dressed mannequins. Exhibits change every 6 months. There's also a "Corsets and Crinolines" display where enthusiastic visitors can experience the masochism of period garments.

Bennett St. www.fashionmuseum.co.uk. ✆ **01225/477-789.** Assembly Rooms: free admission. Fashion Museum admission (includes audio tour): £9 adults, £8 students and seniors, £7 children 6–16, £29 family ticket, free for children 5 and under. Mar–Oct daily 10:30am–5pm; Nov–Feb daily 10:30am–4pm; last exit 1 hr. after closing.

Jane Austen Centre ★   This small homage to Britain's favorite 19th-century writer isn't in her house, but Miss Austen did live up the hill (at no. 25)

Taking Tea in Bath

Yes, it's super-touristy—just go with it. The Regency stiffness of Bath is bound to give you a craving for that quintessentially English tradition of afternoon tea served with jam, clotted cream, and scones. Try the **Pump Room** at the Roman Baths (above), which serves "Bath buns" (sweet buns sprinkled with sugar), or **Sally Lunn's** at 4 North Parade Passage (www.sallylunns.co.uk; ✆ **01225/461-634**), which makes such a big deal of its light Sally Lunn buns you'd swear you'd even heard of them before, which you haven't. The latter's building itself is one of the oldest in Bath, dating from 1482, and shows little hint of any changes with its crooked floors and low ceilings. For £8 to £13, you can sample a range of cream teas, which include toasted and buttered buns served with strawberry jam and clotted cream. The **Regency Tea Rooms** at the Jane Austen Centre offer "Tea with Mr. Darcy" sets (yes, I know . . .) for £18 to £56 for two, and basic cream tea from £9.

for a few months in 1805. Exhibits and a video convey a sense of what life was like when Austen lived in Bath between 1801 and 1806. Ladies can also learn the esoteric skill of using a fan to attract an admirer. Wholesome, corny fun. Allow at least 45 min. The tearoom is worth a visit (see "Taking Tea in Bath," above).

40 Gay St. www.janeausten.co.uk. ✆ **01225/443-000.** Admission £12 adults, £10.50 seniors, £9.50 students, £6.20 children 6–16, £28 family ticket. Apr–Oct daily 9:45am–5:30pm; Nov–Mar Sun–Fri 10am–4pm, Sat 9:45am–5:30pm.

OXFORD

Whereas the face of London, 92km (57 miles) east, has been forcibly reshaped by the pressures of war, disaster, and commerce, Oxford was made stronger by them. When plague killed townspeople, the colleges snapped up their houses, and when the Reformation cleaned out the churches, the colleges took their land, too. Academies used the extra space to carve out some of the most beautiful college buildings in the world. Here, the reverence for education borders on the ecclesiastical. Yet Oxford is no cloister; it's a decidedly modern city—thriving, sophisticated, and busy.

Essentials

GETTING THERE The least expensive, easiest method is by coach, since companies compete for students with regular buses rolling round the clock. The so-called **Oxford Tube** bus (www.oxfordtube.com; ✆ **01865/772-250;** 100 min. with no traffic; £16 adult, £12 senior over 60 or student age 16–26; £19/£15 same-day return), with Wi-Fi and power sockets, leaves every 10 to 20 minutes at all hours. It picks passengers up near the Tube stations at Marble Arch, Victoria, Notting Hill Gate, and Shepherd's Bush. Give rush hours wide berth. **Trains** (www.nationalrail.co.uk; ✆ **08457/48-49-50;** 1 hr.; £15–£27 single with advance purchase) go from Paddington or Marylebone stations to Oxford, sometimes via Reading.

VISITOR INFORMATION In addition to selling (yes, selling—not giving) maps and guides, the **Oxford Information Centre** (15–16 Broad St.; www.experienceoxfordshire.org; ℭ **01865/686-441**) offers daily walking tours using accredited guides. You can download free maps of the city from Visit Britain (www.visitbritain.com).

TOURS The Information Centre offers excellent **theme tours** such as "Harry Potter and Alice in Wonderland," "C.S. Lewis and J.R.R. Tolkien," and general university tours; book ahead. **Oxford River Cruises** (www.oxford rivercruises.com; ℭ **01865/987-147**) runs several boat tours along the River Thames; the tranquil 50-min. Oxford Experience (cheaper online: £12 adults, £6 children 15 and under; reservations suggested) is popular. You can also purchase various walking tours on downloadable MP3s from **Tourist Tracks** (www.tourist-tracks.com; £3, or £7.50 for three).

Exploring Oxford

Wandering Oxford's cobbled streets and ducking into its colleges to soak up their hidden loveliness makes for a happy afternoon, particularly for fans of architecture. Many of the most iconic building clusters in this city of 140,000 (30,000 of whom are students) are collected together in the center of town. Oxford, like Cambridge (p. 300), comprises individual colleges that feed off a central university system. Each of the 39 colleges has its own campus, tradition, character, and disciplines—and each has finicky hours, so always check ahead before planning a day. Unfortunately, many close their grassy inner sanctums to visitors. During the school terms (mid-Jan to mid-Mar, late Apr

Oxford students in academic gowns stroll under Hertford Bridge, aka the Bridge of Sighs.

to mid-June, Oct to early Dec), some university buildings required for study (libraries, residence halls) are closed to the public, or only open on Saturdays. At all times of year, watch out for zooming bicyclists; an unwritten law appears to grant them ownership of the city.

To get the most out of Oxford, poke around, looking inside cloisters and above rooftops. The doors between the inner and outer quadrangles of **Balliol College** (Broad St. and St Giles; www.balliol.ox.ac.uk; ℂ **01865/27-77-77**; £3 adults, £1 seniors and students; daily 10am–5pm) still bear scorch marks from where Bloody Mary burned two Protestants alive for refusing to recant. Viewpoints are popular attractions here: The 22m (72-ft.) rectangular **Carfax Tower** (£2.30 adults, £1.20 children 15 and under; Apr–Sept daily 10am–5:30pm, Oct–Mar daily 10am–4:30pm) is the last remaining chunk of the 13th-century St Martin's Church; it has only 99 steps so it's not too taxing, which may be why it's a well-known suicide spot. It's located by the crossroads of the city center. Other popular panoramas are from the octagonal cupola above Sir Christopher Wren's **Sheldonian Theatre** (Broad St.; www. sheldon.ox.ac.uk; ℂ **01865/277-299**; £3.50, £8 with guided tour; Mon–Sat 10am–4:30pm, also Sun in July–Aug, closes at 3pm Dec–Jan; check ahead for closures). Perhaps the top view is from the **University Church of St Mary the Virgin** (www.university-church.ox.ac.uk; ℂ **01865/279-113**; £4 adult, £3 senior, student, and child; daily 9am–5pm, closes 6pm July–Aug, last tower admissions 30 min. before closing).

The Ashmolean Museum ★   Offering more than just a pretty facade, the Ashmolean was founded way back in 1683, literally before anyone knew

what the word "museum" meant. It houses an important hodgepodge of antiquities and art on par with (but on a smaller scale than) the British Museum, including a lantern carried by Guy Fawkes during the foiled Gunpowder Plot; the Anglo-Saxon Alfred Jewel of gold, enamel, and rock crystal; a Stradivarius violin; and assorted Old Masters paintings. Oh, and you know, minor stuff by Raphael and Michelangelo.

Beaumont St. at St Giles. www.ashmolean. org. ℂ **01865/278-000.** Free admission. Tues–Sun 10am–5pm. Closed Dec 24–26.

Christ Church ★   The largest, most beautiful, and most popular college to visit looms large in children's literature; it was copied for Hogwarts School in the Harry Potter films, and it was where Lewis Carroll (aka

The stairway leading to Christ Church College's dining hall may look familiar from the Harry Potter movies.

mathematician Charles Dodgson) befriended the little girl for whom he wrote *Alice in Wonderland*. The college chapel, which dates from the 12th century, also serves as Oxford Cathedral for the local diocese. Bowler-hatted "custodians" still patrol the pristine lawns, and Christ Church Meadow, still grazed by cattle, is a delightful place to watch punters on the rivers Isis and Cherwell. Just being here makes you feel smarter.

St Aldate's. www.chch.ox.ac.uk. ℂ **01865/276-150.** Tours £8–10 adults, £7–9 seniors, students, and children 5–17, free for children 4 and under. Mon–Sat 9am–5pm; Sun 2–5pm. Last admission 4:30pm. Closed for week around Christmas and New Year's.

Magdalen College ★ Pronounced "*Maud*-lin," it is one of the largest and most peaceful colleges here; its tower is the city's highest point, and its chapel is carved with breathtaking detail. Its site has a virtual tour to prep you on your explorations. U.S. Supreme Court justice Stephen Breyer attended.

High St. www.magd.ox.ac.uk. ℂ **01865/276-000.** Admission £6 adults, £5 seniors, students, and children. July–Sept daily noon–7pm; Oct–June daily 1–6pm or dusk (whichever is earlier). Closed for a week around Christmas and New Year's.

Old Bodleian Library ★ The main research library in a town that made its name in research, "the Bod" opened in 1602 and has been burrowing under the streets of Oxford, trying to find new places to store its multiplying collection (11 million tomes and counting), ever since. The round **Radcliffe Camera** ("Rad Cam"; open via guided tours at the Bodleian) was built in the 1740s to house scientific books. It stands on the north side of Radcliffe Square.

Catte St. www.bodleian.ox.ac.uk. ℂ **01865/287-400.** Admission £1, Divinity School only; £14 for 90-min. "Extended tour" including reading rooms, £8 for standard 60-min tour, or £6 for 30-min. "Mini tour"; check current tour times online. Mon–Fri 9am–5pm; Sat 9am–4:30pm; Sun 11am–5pm. Closed for week around Christmas and New Year's.

The Pitt Rivers Museum ★ An imposing 1886 cast-iron cathedral-like building, not unlike a railway station, houses an oft-freakish blend of folk art and anthropology—think shrunken heads and bundles of poisoned arrows brought back by British explorers over hundreds of years. It is, to use an academic term, totally gnarly.

Parks Rd. www.prm.ox.ac.uk. ℂ **01865/270-927.** Free admission. Tues–Sun 10am–4:30pm; Mon noon–4:30pm.

Punting the River Cherwell

Punting on the River Cherwell is an essential if slightly eccentric Oxford pastime. From mid-March to October at the **Cherwell Boathouse,** Bardwell Road (www.cherwellboathouse.co.uk; ℂ **01865/515-978**), you can rent a punt (a flat-bottomed boat for up to five people, maneuvered by a long pole and a small oar) for £17 (Mon–Fri) to £19 (Sat–Sun) per hour. **Magdalen Bridge Boathouse,** the Old Horse Ford, High Street (www.oxfordpunting.co.uk; ℂ **01865/202-643**), charges £22 per hour, daily 10am until dusk. Both outfits will give you some basic training.

BLETCHLEY PARK: ENIGMA no more

For decades, it was top secret. Few people realized what had happened during World War II in these rotting temporary wooden huts, which were nearly bulldozed for a housing development. But in time, we learned what codebreaker Alan Turing and his brilliant team accomplished at **Bletchley Park** (www.bletchleypark. org.uk; ℂ **01908/640-404**), hidden from the world on a former estate 88km (55 miles) northwest of London. Here they cracked the Enigma machine code, breaking the German blockade that threatened to starve an entire country. In 2014, the year their story, *The Imitation Game*, was released, the fully restored Bletchley Park campus was opened as a fascinating day out. It's like a spy novel set in a park, suffused in the urgency, intrigue, and excitement of those terrifying years when computers were born and Nazis were a few chess moves away from storming England. You can tour more than a dozen buildings around its soothing central pond, exploring the methods, experiments, and lucky breaks that enabled round-the-clock workers—including many gifted women—to translate a jumble of meaningless letters into life-saving intercepted secrets. The cramped, rudimentary Huts 3, 6, and 8, dressed to look like they probably did then (no one is sure—photographs were forbidden), were the heart of the operation, but you can also tour the ground floor of the mansion that served as its command post and outbuildings that housed the computers, which were later dismantled down to the rivets to prevent anyone from duplicating them. Head to the basement of Block B, where modern fans have rebuilt one. The number of Enigma-related artifacts and the level of codebreaking detail can be head-spinning, so children may tire quickly, but interested adults could spend 3 or 4 absorbed hours wrapping their heads around it, a pursuit made easier by the three cafes spread around its grassy acres. Admission costs £18.50 adults, £16.25 seniors and students 12–17, £10.75 children age 12–17, £48.25 family ticket. It's open daily, 9:30am–5pm from March to October (the rest of the year it's 9:30am–4pm). Last admission is 1 hour before closing

Next door, you'll find the **National Museum of Computing** (www.tnmoc. org; ℂ **01908/374-708;** admission £7.50 adults, £5 seniors, students, and children), where volunteers are rebuilding historic systems that were lost to time, including Bletchley's own Colossus. That exhibit is open daily, but the rest of the museum, including the world's largest collection of historic computers, is only open Thursday, Saturday, and Sunday from noon to 5pm. The level of computing detail there isn't for everyone.

Trains to Bletchley leave Euston a few times an hour (50 min.; £17 return in advance) and the gates are only 182m (200 yards) from the station; sit on the left of the carriage for good views of the Grand Union Canal as you go. If you fancy a country drive, Avis, Enterprise, and Budget are clustered near the Bletchley train station.

OUTSIDE OXFORD

Blenheim Palace ★   Within 30 minutes, the half-hourly S3 bus (www. stagecoachbus.com; 30 min.; £4.50; buy on board) from the Oxford train station or Gloucester Green whisks visitors to Hensington Road, Woodstock, and the gates of the birthplace of Winston Churchill, now a UNESCO World Heritage Site. The British rarely remind you that their oh-so-English savior was, in fact, half American; his mom Jennie, who was from Brooklyn, married an English lord, and Winston was born here in 1874, several hundred years into the palace's history. A few decades later, the home was saved from financial ruin when the Duke of Marlborough married another American, a Vanderbilt; their descendants still live here for part of the year. Tours of the grounds, landscaped by Capability Brown, and the state rooms, which are in excellent nick, take about 3 hr. Its app contains audio guides.

Hensington Rd., Woodstock, Oxfordshire. www.blenheimpalace.com. ℭ **01993/810-530.** Admission palace and grounds £26 adults, £23 seniors and students, £14.50 children 5–16, £62.50 family ticket, £7–£10 less for grounds only. Daily 10:30am–5:30pm; last admission 4:45pm.

CAMBRIDGE

Oxford is a city in its own right, but Cambridge, in the marshes 79km (49 miles) northeast of London, would barely have a pulse without its university. That makes Cambridge manageable—it's also cheaper to visit. It feels in some ways like a typical English town, with a daily market for crafts and food on its central square, Market Hill. Its best rewards come when you wander through randomly chosen iron gates or along a river path—that's when the inviting little town really opens up.

Essentials

GETTING THERE   Nonstop **coaches** from National Express (www.national express.com; ℭ **08705/80-80-80;** 2½ hr.; £7–£8 single) leave hourly from Victoria Coach station; don't get off at Trumpington, but wait for the city center stop. There are **trains** from Liverpool Street or King's Cross, but be warned that Cambridge's station is several miles from the city center, so you will need to bike or call a taxi; coaches are the smarter way to travel. If you insist, though, note that some trains take about 45 min. and some take twice that, so ask about journey times (www.nationalrail.co.uk; ℭ **08457/48-49-50;** 45–90 min.; £10–£23).

VISITOR INFORMATION   **Cambridge Visitor Information Centre** (The Guildhall, Peas Hill; www.visitcambridge.org; info@visitcambridge.org; ℭ **01223/791-500**; closed Sun) sells maps and guides but won't dispense them for free. You can download free maps of the city from Visit Britain (www.visitbritain.com).

TOURS   The **Cambridge Visitor Information Centre** (see "Visitor Information," above) has several types of walking tours of the city, from £6 to £19 for adults, and up to £7 for children 11 and under. Book tours at www.visit cambridge.org/official-tours (ℭ **01223/791-501**). You can also purchase hour-long walking tours on downloadable MP3s from **Tourist Tracks** (www.tourist-tracks.com; £5 for two).

Exploring Cambridge

Like Oxford, Cambridge's glory is the elaborate and ancient architecture of its colleges. However, unlike in Oxford, it's easy to venture into the cloistered grounds of many of Cambridge's colleges, though doing so usually requires a few quid. (Cambridge took shape in the early 13th c., after a squabble in Oxford drove several scholars to leave there and establish a second educational capital. The oldest Cambridge College, Peterhouse, was founded in 1284.) Mill Lane leads to the River Cam, where you can rent a punting boat for £6 or sit at The Mill pub overlooking the water. (If you want to seem savvy to Cambridge traditions, punt from the back of the boat. In Oxford, they punt from the front.) The meadows along the Cam, known as the **Backs,** make for idyllic walks.

The head of Oliver Cromwell, which was impaled outside Westminster Hall in London as a warning against regicide (albeit 3 years after the man died of natural causes), was finally buried within an antechapel (not open to visitors) at Sidney Sussex College in 1960. It's in an unmarked grave to keep pranksters from pinching the much-abused thing. That's Cambridge in a nutshell: It has many secrets, but since it's still a working university town, marvels won't be handed to you. You have to wander, wonder, and ask questions. Outside of term (terms run mid-Jan to mid-Mar, late Apr to mid-June, and Oct to early Dec), colleges aren't open, and street life is at a minimum.

King's College, Cambridge, is known for its magnificent chapel.

Fitzwilliam Museum ★ Cambridge's most storied attraction is a first-rate neoclassical building full of applied arts and Old Masters that a city 10 times Cambridge's size (population 108,000) would covet. If a colonial Englishman could carry it home on a ship, it's here: precious antiquities from Rome, Greece, Egypt, Asia, and paintings by every famous name under the European sun.

Trumpington St., near Peterhouse. www.fitzmuseum.cam.ac.uk. ℰ **01223/332-900.** Free admission; donations appreciated. Tues–Sat 10am–5pm; Sun noon–5pm. Closed Mon, Good Friday, Dec 24–26 and 31, and Jan 1. Sat guided tours at 2:30pm (£6).

King's College Chapel ★ For some reason, the marauding Puritans neglected to smash the 16th-century stained-glass windows of this chapel—they probably thought they were too divine to destroy, just as you will. The chapel's fanned and vaulted ceiling, a work of craftsmanship that stuns even those who care little for such things, was completed at the behest of Henry VII. Its famous choristers sing at services during term time. Some Saturdays (check ahead), there's a £6 guided tour.

King's Parade. www.kings.cam.ac.uk. © **01223/331-212.** Admission £9 adults, £6 students and seniors, free for children 11 and under. Mon–Fri 9:45am–3:30pm; Sat 9:30am–3:15pm; Sun 1:15–2:30pm; check website ahead for changes.

Pembroke College ★   The third-oldest college in town is one of the best, distinguished by the oldest gatehouse in Cambridge and by a chapel with an ornate plaster ceiling, which was the first completed work by Christopher Wren (after finishing this, the man seemed never to rest again). Unlike many of the colleges, Pembroke never charges visitors to poke around its common areas.

Trumpington St. www.pem.cam.ac.uk. © **01223/33-81-00.** Free admission. Daily 2–5pm, except mid-May to mid-June when closed for exams.

Queen's College ★   Founded in 1448 by the wife of Henry VI and the wife of Edward IV, Queen's is regarded as the most beautiful of Cambridge's colleges. Entry and exit are by the old porter's lodge in Queens' Lane. Tourists are often told that the wooden **Mathematical Bridge** (1749) spanning the Cam behind it (see it from Silver St.) was constructed using no nails, and

Punting under the Mathematical Bridge on the River Cam.

THE TRADE-OFF WITH escorted tours

Arranging your own day trips using public transportation will almost always be the most cost-effective method, but there are cogent reasons for choosing a guided coach tour. It's simply quicker to allow someone else to drive you around, making sure you cram a laundry list of major sites into a short time span, and consuming spoon-fed nuggets of information about each place. What you learn won't have much depth, but at least you'll have been there.

You'll pay a pretty penny to be seated on that bus: Most tours cost at least £70 a day, not including food. You get a richer experience (and one that doesn't have you idling in traffic or waiting for other tour members to catch up), when you do it yourself. But some people desperately want to soak up as many sights as they can, even if it means viewing sights as a blur from the motorway. For them, here are the major players in the coach-tour biz, sold aggressively through concierges at expensive hotels (who love getting the commissions):

- **Evan Evans Tours** (www.evanevans tours.co.uk; ✆ 020/7950-1777 in the U.K., 800/422-9022 in the U.S.)
- **Gray Line's Golden Tours** (www. goldentours.co.uk; ✆ 020/7630-2028 in the U.K., 800/509-2507 in the U.S.)
- **Premium Tours** (www.premiumtours. co.uk; ✆ 020/7713-1311 in the U.K., 800/931-0141 in the U.S.)
- **Rabbies** (www.rabbies.com; ✆ 0131/226-3133 in the U.K.)

Better yet are the more affordable **London Walks** (www.walks.com; ✆ 020/7624-3978), which run frequent day trips (p. 199). These use public transportation and don't include admission fees, but you'll have a guide every step of the way to show you how it's all done.

when curious students disassembled it to figure out how, they couldn't put it back together without using screws. The college is curiously defensive about the tale, saying that anyone who believes this "cannot have a serious grasp on reality."

Silver St. www.quns.cam.ac.uk. ✆ **01223/335-511.** Admission £3.50 adults (including guide booklet), free for children 9 and under. Mid-Jun–Sept and Nov–mid-May daily 10am–4:30pm; Oct Mon–Fri 2–4:30pm, Sat–Sun 10am–4:30pm. Closed late May to late June.

Trinity College ★   Trinity is the largest and most endowed of Cambridge's 31 colleges. Sir Isaac Newton first calculated the speed of sound here, at Neville's Court, and Lord Byron used to bathe naked in the Great Court's fountain with his pet bear. (The University forbade students from having dogs, but there was no rule against bears.) In *Chariots of Fire*, sprinters tried to get around the .8-hectare (2-acre) yard in the time it took for its clock to strike 12. Your attempts will not be appreciated.

Trinity St. www.trin.cam.ac.uk. ✆ **01223/338-400.** Free admission. The Wren Library: Mon–Fri noon–2pm; Sat 10:30am–12:30pm. Various other areas open at different times and may incur a £3 charge; inquire at the porter's lodge.

STONEHENGE & SALISBURY

Stonehenge is a circle of rocks. If it's raining, it's a damned circle of rocks. But people still ask to go, and if that's their dream, then they should do it. Just understand that it may not blow you away.

Most coach tours offer an itinerary that combines Stonehenge with Bath (p. 292); bus and train connections make it difficult to do that if you're traveling independently. However, it's quite doable to combine Stonehenge with a visit to Salisbury, a lovely and relatively well-preserved cathedral town.

Essentials

GETTING THERE This one's a pain. Trains don't go directly to Stonehenge; the nearest station is in Salisbury, nearly 16km (10 miles) south.

Mysterious Stonehenge has drawn visitors since before 1562.

So the easiest way to get here is to drive. The rocks are located 3.2km (2 miles) west of Amesbury in Wiltshire on the junction of A303 and A344/360. If you must do public transportation, take a half-hourly **train** (www.national rail.co.uk; ℭ **08457/48-49-50;** 90 min.; £25 return with advance purchase) from Waterloo station to Salisbury station. There used to be a cheap public bus to the rocks from there, but it says a lot about the values of local tourism authorities that they replaced that route entirely with the expensive but convenient Stonehenge Tour Bus by **Wilts & Dorset Buses** (www.thestonehenge tour.info; ℭ **0845/0727-093;** 30 min.; round-trip £15 adults, £10 children 5–15, buy from driver), which leaves from Salisbury station seven times a day between 10am and 4pm. A few extra buses are tossed in during the summer; check its website for updated schedules. Many tour companies offer round-trip all-day coach tours from London that take 10 or 11 hr. One of them is **Premium Tours** (see above) for £51 adults, £48 seniors, and £41 children 3 to 16. Versions that also include Bath cost about £30 more.

VISITOR INFORMATION Salisbury and Stonehenge (Fish Row, Salisbury; www.visitwiltshire.co.uk; ℭ **01722/342-860**). Visit Wiltshire produces a free app (called Visit Wiltshire) that rounds up the area's offerings.

TOURS You can easily see Salisbury on foot, either on your own or by taking a guided daytime or evening walk run by **Salisbury City Guides** (www. salisburycityguides.co.uk; ℭ **07873/212-941**). Tickets are £6 for adults, £3 for students, and free for kids.

HIGHCLERE CASTLE, the real *DOWNTON ABBEY*

The 8th Earl and Countess of Carnarvon still dwell under the sandstone turrets of **Highclere Castle** (Highclere Park, Newbury; www.highclerecastle.co.uk; ℂ **01635/253-204;** admission £23 adults, £21 students and seniors, £14.50 children 4–16; last admission at 4pm, grounds close at 6pm), known to TV viewers as the idyllic and stately *Downton Abbey*. Time and spendthrift earls took their toll on this historic home, and as recently as 2009, more than 50 rooms were uninhabitable due to mold and leaks. The current Earl faces repair bills running around £12 million, so he welcomes visitors to spend the day exploring the 1,000 acres of private rolling Berkshire countryside. He also rents out to film production: The upstairs scenes of the ITV/PBS show were shot on the ground floor and first floor using the house's actual furniture, though downstairs scenes were shot on a soundstage in Ealing, west London. That's partly because at Highclere, the basement is full not of kitchens but of mummy stuff: The 5th Earl was the guy who bankrolled Howard Carter's 1923 emptying of King Tut's tomb in Luxor, so unseen beneath Lord Grantham's feet lie items taken from the tombs of Egypt. Highclere is only open 60 to 70 days a year, and they're scattered all over the calendar—typically Easter Week, bank holiday weekends, and from July to mid-September. Taking a group tour guarantees a ticket, but those sell out months ahead and herd you along. If you show up independently (download the Highclere Castle guide app for $3 first) at 10am or by 2pm at the latest, you can usually get a walk-up ticket even though advance tickets are

Highclere Castle, better known to TV viewers as *Downton Abbey*.

sold out. Only once you have a ticket can you also sign up for the £30 afternoon tea in its Coach House (no children for that). Getting here on your own involves taking a 52-min. train from Paddington (from £24) or a National Express bus (1¾ hr.; from £10) to the adorable town of Newbury (stop to admire the longboats on the Kennet and Avon canal and peruse the century-old village department store, Camp Hopson) and then a £15 taxi (try www.cabco33333.com, ℂ **01635/33333;** or www.newburytaxi.co.uk, ℂ **01635/44444**).

Exploring Stonehenge & Salisbury

Stonehenge ★ Construction on this bucket-list site began about 5,000 years ago; the first recorded day trips to the megalith were in 1562. Arranged in such a way that it aligns with the rising of the sun during the midsummer solstice, this Neolithic circle of stones is certainly Britain's most important ancient wonder, and it's a UNESCO World Heritage Site (together with Avebury, a far less interesting, but still important, line of rocks 39km/24 miles north). Whether its builders, who remain anonymous, worshiped the sun or merely appreciated astronomy is only the beginning of the mystery. We also can only make educated guesses as to how these prehistoric people, using only rudimentary tools, managed to hoist these slabs from Wales to here, and then into place. Even if you don't salivate over such long-ago feats of ingenuity, the distinctive profile of the stones, surrounded by empty plains, "henge" earthworks, and hundreds of lumpen burial mounds, will surely feel iconic.

You're not allowed to walk amongst the rocks the way visitors once were; you have to stick to a footpath that curves near the circle but keeps the formation at a safe distance, good for pretty photographs but bad for curiosity. Most tourists like you and me are kept at arm's length (exception: Clark Griswold, who managed to topple them like dominoes in *National Lampoon's European Vacation*), but you can apply in advance for a 1-hr. "Circle Access" pass to stroll with about 29 others among the rocks—no touching—timed in the very early morning or after it closes for the day. The application is at the English Heritage website (see below). Otherwise, you'll have a limited experience—a disappointment for many who trudge 129km/80 miles west of London to have it. Alternatively, climb **Amesbury Hill,** clearly visible 2.4km (1½ miles) up the A303. From here, you'll get a free panoramic view. Check opening times before heading out; closings are occasional.

At the junction of A303 and A344. www.english-heritage.org.uk/stonehenge. ⓒ **08703/ 331-181.** Admission £17.50 adults, £15.80 students aged 5–17 and seniors, £10.50 children 5–15, £45.50 family ticket; higher posted prices include a "voluntary donation." June–Aug daily 9am–8pm; Apr–May and Sept–mid-Oct daily 9:30am–7pm; mid-Oct–Mar daily 9:30am–5pm; last admission 2 hr. before closing. Train: Salisbury, then Stonehenge Tour Bus.

Old Sarum ★ Believed to have been an Iron Age fortification, Old Sarum was used again by the Saxons and flourished as a walled town into the Middle Ages. The Normans built a cathedral; parts of that were taken down to build the city of "New Sarum," later known as Salisbury, leaving behind dramatically sited remains with unforgettable views of Salisbury and rolling green hills, not to mention the opportunity to commune with grazing sheep.

2 mi N of Salisbury off A345. Castle Rd. www.english-heritage.org.uk/oldsarum. ⓒ **01722/335-398.** Admission £5.20 adults, £4.70 seniors and students, £3.10 children 5–15; higher posted prices include a "voluntary donation." Apr–Sept daily 10am–6pm; Mar and Oct daily 10am–5pm; Nov–Feb daily 10am–4pm. Bus: X5, 8, or 501, every 30 min. during the day, from Salisbury bus station.

Salisbury Cathedral ★ Built with uncommon efficiency between 1220 and 1258 and barely touched since, this early English Gothic masterpiece is considered by many to be the most breathtaking church in the world. After you've seen it, and lost yourself in gazing at it and sighing, the rest of your time in Salisbury will be contentedly spent walking medieval streets, which were laid in a loose grid and give the city an airy character. The cathedral complex's octagonal Chapter House holds one of four surviving copies of the Magna Carta signed by King John in 1215. (Two more are in London at the British Library; p. 110.)

Salisbury Cathedral is an early English Gothic masterpiece.

The Close. www.salisburycathedral.org. uk. ℂ **01722/555-120.** Admission voluntary donation £8 adults, £7 seniors, £5 students, free for children 7–17, £15 family. Mon–Sat 9am–5pm; Sun noon–4pm. Chapter House closes 5:45pm (4:30pm Nov–Mar) and all morning Sun.

CANTERBURY

The ecclesiastical capital of England, Canterbury (62 miles southeast of London) feels like a seat of English charm itself, with the squared spire of its great Gothic Cathedral rising from the cobbled cluster of its village. You can still find traces of the original city walls and punt on the calm water that meanders through town. It's also easy to explore on foot; starting your explorations at The Goods Shed, a market for luscious English dairy, meat, and alcohol (with its own gourmet restaurant; www.thegoodsshed.co.uk), conveniently beside the Canterbury West railway station.

Essentials

GETTING THERE Two National Rail stations, Canterbury East and Canterbury West, are both conveniently just outside the city walls. High-speed trains from Charing Cross, St Pancras, and Victoria take 60–90 min. (www.nationalrail.co.uk; ℂ **08457/48-49-50;** £38 return in advance). Buses are not recommended for a day trip; trains are quick and deliver you right to the town.

VISITOR INFORMATION Canterbury Visitor Information (the Beaney House of Art and Knowledge, 18 High St.; www.canterbury.co.uk; ℂ **01227/862-162**).

TOURS The popular **Canterbury Punting Company** (Water Lane; www.canterburypunting.co.uk; ℂ **07786/332-666;** £12 adults, £10 seniors and students, £6 kids) lets you ply the river, past medieval buildings in an ancient channel that weaves through town, on a wide, flat boat that crawls oh-so-slowly under the hanging bowers.

Exploring Canterbury

Canterbury Cathedral ★★

The original modern tourist attraction, it's where the pilgrims were headed in Chaucer's *The Canterbury Tales* (1478). They were going to pay their respects to archbishop Thomas Becket, who was murdered in the northwest transept, next to what is now the Chapel of Our Lady Martyrdom. Henry VIII tore down that shrine in a typical fit of pique, but this transporting place is still one of the most visited sites in Britain. The cathedral, along with **St Augustine's Abbey** and **St Martin's Church** (the oldest still-functioning church in the English-speaking world; both were founded around 597), form a World Heritage Site. Look for the medieval tombs of King Henry IV and Edward the Black Prince; Becket lies in the Trinity Chapel, near the high altar.

The square Gothic tower of Canterbury Cathedral rises above the town's cobbled medieval lanes.

The stained glass depicting his reported miracles is regarded as some of England's finest; fortunately, the cathedral's windows survived Hitler's bombs by being removed and hidden away.

The Precincts. www.canterbury-cathedral.org. ☏ **01227/762-862.** Admission £12.50 adults, £11.50 seniors and students, £8.50 children 17 and under. Mon–Sat 9am–5:30pm, until 5pm in winter; Sun 12:30–2:30pm all year.

PLANNING YOUR TRIP TO LONDON

First of all, relax. Getting to London isn't as tricky as it used to be. Some 19.1 million tourists journeyed to London in 2017 (but with Brexit advancing, numbers are showing signs of softening). Still, the London hospitality and tourist industries know a thing or two about helping foreigners. Finding airfare isn't much harder than finding a cross-country flight. Being ready for the rest (money, electricity) is simply a matter of having the facts.

GETTING THERE

By Plane

Transatlantic flights almost always land at **Heathrow,** Europe's busiest international airport (LHR; 17 miles west), or **Gatwick,** perhaps the most disliked (LGW; 31 miles south). With a few minor exceptions, the other four airports, **Stansted** (STN; 37 miles northeast), **Luton** (LTN; 34 miles northwest), **London City** (LCY; in London's Docklands area), and **Southend** (SEN; 42 miles east) serve flights from Europe; they're where cut-rate flyers and executive jets tend to go.

FINDING THE LOWEST AIRFARE

The central question is *when* are they? London is such a popular destination (it's served by more flights from the United States than any other European city) that plenty of airlines vie to carry you across—although the ones that are not American-run are usually of higher quality. If you're not redeeming frequent-flier miles (book very far ahead if you are), there are five rules to finding bargains:

1. **Fly on days when traffic is lightest.** Some airlines post calendars that show you when their best prices are, or test fare trends on a site such as **Hopper.com.**
2. **Depart after dinner.** This saves you from paying another hotel night, since you'll arrive in the morning. You're also likely to find lower fares, because business travelers like day flights.
3. **Go off-season.** London's weather isn't extreme, so there's really not a no-go month. November through March yield the

AIRPORT	COST/AVG. TIME USING NATIONAL RAIL	HOURS OF RAIL SERVICE
Heathrow (LHR), HeathrowAirport.com	Heathrow Express (www.heathrow express.com): £22 single, £37 return, kids 14 and under free*/15 min.	5:10am to 11:33pm
Gatwick (LGW), GatwickAirport.com	Gatwick Express (www.gatwickexpress. com): £20 single/£36 return (in person), £18/£32 (online), kids £10/£17.50 and £9/£15.50/30 min. OR Thameslink (www.thameslinkrailway.com): £11–£20 single/30 to 50 min.	Four times hourly 5am to 12:30am
Luton (LTN), www. London-Luton.co.uk	Thameslink & Great Northern (www. thameslinkrailway.com): £17 single including 5-min. shuttle bus, 45 min.	Six times hourly 5am to midnight; hourly midnight to 5am
Stansted (STN), StanstedAirport.com	From £17 single, £28 return/47 min.	Four times hourly 4:40am to 12:30am (also a 3:40am train on Mon, Fri, and Sat)
London City (LCY), LondonCityAirport.com	N/A	DLR: 5:30am to midnight
London Southend (SEN), www.southend airport.com	Greater Anglia: About £17 single/53 min.	4am to midnight

*Ticket machine or online fare. Tickets £5 more if you wait to pay on board. Advance purchase more than a month ahead is lower.

10

Getting There

PLANNING YOUR TRIP TO LONDON

lowest airfares and hotel rates, although the late-December holidays and the last week of November (Thanksgiving in U.S.) can be busy, too. Summer prices (June–Sept) soar over a grand.

4. **Search for fares for or on a weekend.** Many major airlines post lower prices to fly then. You might also save money by booking your seat at 3am. That's because unpaid-for reservations are flushed out of the system at midnight, and prices often sink when the system becomes aware of an increase in supply.

5. **Try a bargain airline.** Norwegian Air Shuttle (www.norwegian.com) and WOW Air (www.wowair.com) are reliable.

6. **Don't buy last-minute.** Desperation has a price.

Monitor airline newsletters, sale pages, Twitter accounts, and sites for sales. Both **Airfarewatchdog.com** and **Yapta.com** spit out emails when airfare drops.

RAIL SERVICE TO	COST/TIME USING TUBE OR DLR	COST/AVG. TIME FOR NATIONAL EXPRESS SHUTTLE SERVICE TO CENTRAL LONDON	COST/AVG. TIME TO AIRPORT BY TAXI
Paddington	£6 cash or £5.10 Oyster/ Elizabeth Line (30 min.) or Piccadilly Line (75 min.)	£8.50 single, £4.25 kids 3 to 15, free for kids 2 and under (www.national express.com)/50–70 min.	£65–£85/ 70 min.
Gatwick Express: Victoria; T&GN: St Pancras, Farringdon, Blackfriars, or London Bridge	N/A	£5–8 each way, £5 kids 3 to 15, free for kids 2 and under (www.national express.com)/90 min,	£100/ 70 min.
St Pancras, Blackfriars, or London Bridge	N/A	From £11 (www.national express.com)/90 min. (runs 24 hr.)	£100/ 80 min.**
Liverpool Street	N/A	From £12 single (www. nationalexpress.com)/60– 100 min.	£99/ 80 min.**
N/A	£4.90 cash, £3.30 Oyster/ 25 min. on Docklands Light Railway	N/A	£25–£40/ 20–40 min.
Liverpool Street	N/A	N/A	£80–£100/ 60 to 80 min.**

** As if you'd be daft enough to want a taxi after seeing those prices and times, you're more likely to find one by booking ahead. Check www.london-luton.co.uk, www.stansted airport.com, and www.southendairport.com for list of the latest approved companies. Addison Lee (www.addisonlee.com) is an established minicab company, and Heathrow has a partnership with Green Tomato Cars (U.K.: ℭ **0800/599-9099;** www.greentomato cars.com). All services offer discounted prices for children.

Primary websites that collect quotes from a variety of sources (whether they be airlines or other websites) include **Expedia.com, Kayak.com, Mobissimo.com,** and **Momondo.com.** Always canvas multiple sites, because each has odd gaps in coverage because of how they obtain quotes. Always compare your best price with what the airline is offering, because that price might be lowest of all. Some sites have small booking fees of $5 to $10, and many force you to accept nonrefundable tickets for the cheapest prices. If you're hitting a wall, search for transatlantic itineraries that allow for one or two stops, since routes that include stops in Reykjavik or Frankfurt (on Icelandair or Lufthansa, respectively) can produce hidden bargains. No matter which airline you go with, prepare yourself for added taxes and fees, which are usually $500 or higher round-trip from the USA—London's airport fees are truly noxious.

Most times of the year, the least expensive way to reach London is with an **air-hotel package** (p. 58), which combines discounted airfare with discounted nights in a hotel. Most air-hotel deals will allow you to fly back days after your hotel allotment runs out, and at no extra charge. Keep in mind that for those, solo travelers always pay a little more, typically $250.

AIRPORT TRANSPORTATION OPTIONS

Fares and trip duration can be found in the chart, p. 310.

BY TRAIN   Always take the train. Every airport offers some kind of rail connection to the central city, and that's the smartest option to take. Tickets can be bought at kiosks in the arrivals halls, at machines before the platform, or online ahead of time, when you'll get a discount. You'll rarely have to wait more than 20 minutes for the next train, and it's not required to pre-book.

Heathrow Express trains (www.heathrowexpress.com; ☏ 08456/00-15-15) zoom to Paddington every quarter-hour. First Class is a waste of money; Express Saver, the cheapest option (purchase online, on its app, or at vending machines, and buying round-trip is cheapest), is plenty plush. Weekend one-way tickets are just £5.50 if you book at least 90 days ahead. It uses commuter-style carriages and leaves half-hourly. Both trains arrive at Paddington, where you can hop the Tube system or a taxi (above Platform 12). New this year, there are now two lines on the **London Underground** (both cost £6 cash or £5.10 Oyster, which is explained on p. 318) that take you to the city. The classic one is the **Piccadilly Line.** It takes a slow 75 min., but the upside is that line cuts right through town so you don't have to change for the Tube at Paddington the way you do if you take Heathrow Express. This year also sees the gradual introduction of the new **Elizabeth Line** (see "The Underground," p. 315). That's quicker (30 min.) but when it reaches Paddington, you'll have to haul your bags downstairs to join the rest of the Tube system. (Still, take it; it costs much less than Heathrow Express yet only takes 15 min. longer for the same destination.) Come December 2019, the Elizabeth Line will become a one-seat ride from Heathrow all the way to East London, making 6 stops as it crosses the central city, and it'll be a dream. *Bus option:* If you need to go in the middle of the night and the Tube isn't running, Night Bus N9 goes to and from Trafalgar Square and Heathrow, taking about 75 min.

Gatwick Express trains (www.gatwickexpress.com; ☏ 084/5850-530) run from Victoria. On **Thameslink & Great Northern** (www.thameslinkrailway. com; ☏ 0345/026-4700), you can get to Gatwick via Blackfriars, City Thameslink (near St Paul's), Farringdon, or St Pancras stations four times an hour—service usually ends around 11:45pm, but check ahead, since timings change.

Stansted Express (www.stanstedexpress.com; ☏ 0845/600-7245) runs from Liverpool Street station. **Luton** has rail service from St Pancras, Farringdon, City Thameslink, and Blackfriars stations by **Thameslink & Great Northern** (www.thameslinkrailway.com; ☏ 0345/026-4700). The correct stop is Luton Airport Parkway Station, linked by a 10-min. shuttle (5am–midnight) to the terminals.

City Airport is linked so expediently and affordably by the Docklands Light Railway that it doesn't support commuter rail or coach service. **London**

Southend (www.southendairport.com) is so well-connected to a shiny new station by **Greater Anglia** rail from Liverpool Street that buses don't bother to go there, so the train is the sole option.

BY BUS **National Express** (www.nationalexpress.com; ✆ **0871/781-8181**) buses will take you from all airports (except Southend or City) for around £10 each. With extreme advance purchase, **EasyBus** (www.easybus.com) can be a few pounds cheaper (from Gatwick, Stansted, and Luton).

BY TAXI OR CAR SERVICE Because of traffic and price, taking a metered **taxi** (£46–£100) to the city the way you might at home does not have our hearty recommendation. **Uber** drivers can only be hailed once you leave the terminal, and then they pick you up at the Short Stay Car Park. Door-to-door **car service** (£50–£60) can take 45 minutes to 2 hours, so the train-taxi or train-Tube combo is often faster (although on trains you'll have to contend with your luggage). You can book cars ahead, which often saves about 25 percent off the price of a taxi: Check each airport's website for a current list of the latest approved companies. **Addison Lee** (www.addisonlee.com; ✆ **020/7407-9000**) is an established minicab company, the website **Minicabit.com** surveys companies for the best prices, and Heathrow has a partnership with **Green Tomato Cars** (www.greentomatocars.com; ✆ **020/8568-0022**). Also try **Airport Cars UK** (www.airportcars-uk.com; ✆ **0330/088-2222**) and **Carrot Cars** (www.carrotcars.co.uk; ✆ **020/7005-0557**), which serve all airports.

driving IN LONDON?

Don't! Roads are clogged. In bad traffic, a trip from Heathrow to the western fringe of London can take 2 hr. And once you're in the city, just about every technology is deployed against you. There's a hefty fee just to drive to the city center. Roads are confusingly one-way. Cameras catch and ticket your honest driving errors. Parking is a fantasy. Many North Americans think of cars as the default transportation mode, but in London, trains are the thing. The only time to *maybe* drive a car is if you're on a cross-country tour—but in cities, it won't be easy for you.

The cheapest coach and van services for each airport are listed in the chart, and they all drop you off at standardized stops such as major train stations. For Gatwick, Stansted, and Luton, in addition to the usual National Express coach options, there's the no-frills **easyBus** (www.easybus.co.uk). Unless you book far in advance, it may not beat the National Express prices.

If you insist upon wheels (don't!), reserving ahead from home yields the best prices. Try to return your car outside the congestion-charge zone to avoid charges and aggravation. You will find similar rates among **Nova Car Hire** (www.novacarhire.com), **Auto Europe** (www.autoeurope.com), **Europe By Car** (www.ebctravel.com), **Europcar** (www.europcar.com), and **Holiday Autos** (www.holidayautos.com). Also check the major names like Avis, Hertz, and Budget, in case they can do better. Air-conditioning, something you won't need, adds about £5 to the daily bill. Fuel, or *petrol*, is even more expensive than at home, and although most rentals include unlimited mileage, not all do. **Note:** Many rental cars are stick-shift models, which means you'll be driving on the left in a foreign land with a stick shift. Don't!

Also look into the app **Splitcab** (www.splitcab.co.uk), which matchmakes you with other people going in the same direction to cut costs; prices start around £12 from Heathrow to Central London.

By Long-Distance Rail

For trips from northwestern Europe, the train is the dignified way to go. Train stations take you right to the middle of town. We're living in marvelous times: The Channel Tunnel opened 2 decades ago (although they *still* seem to be working out the kinks), so you can reach the heart of London in an incredible 2 hours and 15 minutes from Paris. You can literally ride both the Tube and the Métro before lunch. In fact, you can ride both a black taxi and Space Mountain before lunch, since one Eurostar route alights in the middle of Disneyland Resort. Eurostar links London's St Pancras station with Paris, Brussels (less than 2 hr.), Lille, and Calais, and from there, you can go just about anywhere using other trains. In 2018, after decades of dreams, it finally finished the line to Amsterdam, too (3 hr. 41 min.).

Book via **Eurostar** (www.eurostar.co.uk; ✆ **03432/186-186** in the U.K., or 44-1233/61-75-75 outside of it; phone bookings are $7 more) itself or the U.S.-based **Rail Europe** (www.raileurope.com; ✆ **800/361-7245** in North America), which also sells European rail passes. Check both sites, since prices can differ, but do it early, because rates boom as availability decreases. Advance-purchase deals to Paris regularly go as low as £29 each way.

By Bus

A few coach companies also travel between the U.K. and the Continent, usually crossing the Channel with a ferry. Because of the pressure put on the market by mushrooming no-frills airlines, rates are extremely low. You'll pay as little as £21 one-way to Paris via **Eurolines** (www.eurolines.eu; ✆ **+33 11/41-86-24-21**; 8–10 hr. each way). Brussels or Amsterdam are £15 with a 7-day advance purchase. Also look at **Flixbus** (which absorbed some Megabus routes; www.flixbus.com), which goes from Victoria to multiple destinations around Europe (say, Antwerp from 17€, or five cities for 99€). *The trade-off:* It can take all day, sunrise to sunset, to reach Paris by this method. Discouraged? The website **CheckMyBus.com** searches all the available carriers.

Some other companies arrange full-on organized tours of Europe's greatest hits—but never for less than you could do independently; choose one only because you'd enjoy having company: **Contiki** (www.contiki.com; ✆ **866/266-8454**) is geared toward a party-hearty under-35 crowd, **Tucan Travel Adventure Tours** (www.tucantravel.com; ✆ **855/444-9110** in the U.S.) is for social scrimpers, and **Fanatics** (www.thefanatics.com; ✆ **020/7240-3233**) is for followers of organized sports.

By Boat

Ferry travel is obsolete, mostly used by people who need to transfer cars. No ferry to Europe or Ireland sails directly to London. You'll have to get down to the southern coast (for France), Portsmouth (for Spain), or Liverpool or Wales

(Ireland). Fares are around £56 each way with a car and including taxes (150 min.) on **P&O Ferries** (www.poferries.com; ☎ **01304/44-88-6884**) or **DFDS** (www.dfdsseaways.com; ☎ **0208/574-7235**), both of which do Dover–Calais. Ferries between Wales and Ireland are operated by **Irish Ferries** (www.irish-ferries.ie; ☎ **0818/300-400** in the Republic of Ireland, or ☎ **353/818-300-400** in Northern Ireland/U.K.) and **Stena Line** (www.stenaline.com; ☎ **01/204-7777**). The aggregator **DirectFerries.co.uk** sells European routes from a rapidly diminishing roster of companies.

If you despise flying, one ocean liner still makes the storied 7-day trip between New York City and Southampton, which connects by rail to London in an hour. That's the *Queen Mary 2* (www.cunard.com; ☎ **800/728-6273**), intermittently scheduled. Fares start around $900 per person one-way, including all your meals. Pack your tuxedos and gowns for the formal nights.

GETTING AROUND LONDON

There are three practical methods for taming London's sprawl: by Tube (historic and enchanting, but expensive); by bus (less expensive and less glamorous, but more edifying and often quicker); and by foot (the best method, but not always possible). Taxis are overpriced, Ubers require mobile data usage, and driving a car is lunacy.

A significant savings strategy is to choose a hotel that's within walking distance of lots of the things you want to do. Fortunately, the city's extremely walkable. Tube trains go shockingly slowly (34kmph/21 mph is the *average* and has been for more than 100 years); and in the center of town, stops are remarkably close together and the stairs can wear you out. In fact, if your journey is only two or three stations, you'll often find it less strenuous to simply walk.

The Underground

Londoners call their 402km (249-mile) metro system the Underground, its official name, or just as commonly, "the Tube." Its elegant, distinctive logo—a red "roundel" bisected by a blue bar—debuted in 1913 as one of the world's first corporate symbols, and it remains one of the city's most ubiquitous sights. The Tube is much more dignified than most American systems. In fact, seats are upholstered—that's because the British know how to take care of nice things. And yet there's no older subway system on earth—the first section opened in 1863 while America was fighting its Civil War—and it often acts its age, with frequent delays and shutdowns. Check posters and whiteboards in the ticket hall to see what "engineering works" are scheduled.

The Tube is an attraction unto itself. It's fun to seek out vestiges of the early system (1907 tilework on the Piccadilly Line; the fake house facades built at 23–24 Leinster Gardens to hide exposed tracks; abandoned stations like the one at Strand and Surrey Street). If such "urban archaeology" fascinates you, visit the **London Transport Museum** in Covent Garden (p. 121), one of the city's family-friendly highlights.

There are 13 named lines, plus the Docklands Light Railway (DLR), which serves East London, and a tram line in South London. Lines are color-coded: The Piccadilly is a peacock purple, the Bakerloo could be considered Sherlock Holmes brown, and so on. In 2019, the newly dug, £14.8-billion Elizabeth Line joins them in stages. For the first half of the year, the segment running across the city between Paddington Tube stop and East London (Abbey Wood) will be running, and so will service between Paddington's train station (above ground) and Heathrow. In December 2019, the various services will be stitched together in one continuous route. There's no way to exaggerate how excited natives are to finally have a quick train line that links East London to West London; it has never existed before. What's more, they'll all have step-free access, once unheard of on the Tube. All told, the Underground serves nearly 300 stations.

The Tube shuts down nightly from Sunday to Thursday. Exact times for first and final trains are posted in each station (using the 24-hr. clock), but the Tube generally operates from 5:30am (0530) to just after midnight (0000), and Sundays 7am (0700) to 11:30pm (2330). On Friday and Saturday nights, many lines in Central London run every 10 minutes all night long: **"Night Tube"** trains are the Piccadilly, Victoria, Central, and Jubilee lines, plus the Charing Cross branch of the Northern line and a slice of the Overground between Islington and New Cross Gate. Still, if you plan to take the train after midnight, always check the Night Tube map and schedule beforehand. **Transport for London** (TfL) offers 24-hour information at ✆ **0343/222-1234.**

What happens if you miss the last train? Don't worry—you're not stranded, although your trip may take longer or cost more. Just turn to the city's network of 24-hr. and Night Bus routes (p. 320).

HOW TO FIND YOUR WAY ON THE TUBE

Navigating is mostly foolproof. Look for signs pointing to the color and name of the line you want. Pretty soon, more signs separate you according to the direction you want to go in, based on the Tube map. If you know the name/color of the line you want, as well as the direction of your destination, the signs will march you, anthill-like, to the platform you need. Nearly every station is combed with staircases. You'll shuffle through warrens of cylindrical tunnels, many of them faced in custard-yellow tiles and overly full of commuters, and you'll scale alpine escalators lined with ads. Stand to the right so "climbers" can pass you.

On the DLR (the Overground) and commuter trains, the carriage may not automatically open. Push the illuminated button and it will.

One of the groovier things about the Underground is the electronic displays on platforms that tell you how long it'll be until the next train. A 24-hr. information service is also available at ✆ **0343/222-1234.** The best resource is the TfL Journey Planner, online at **www.tfl.gov.uk/gettingaround**. For specific journey information using a mobile device, you can text your start-point and end-point—as full postcodes (what tourist knows those?), or station or stop names, in the format "A to B"—to ✆ **60835.** TfL will fire off a text with the

frustrations OF THE TUBE

The Tube lists everything about itself in exhaustive detail at **www.tfl.gov.uk**, which contains more maps, planners, and FAQs than a normal person can use. As endearing as the Tube is, it is not perfect. In fact, it can be so dehumanizing that it has had to put up signs begging people not to abuse its staff (sad but true). Be prepared for a few things:

1. **Stairs.** Most stations are as intricate as anthills. Passengers are sadistically corralled up staircases, around platforms, down more staircases, and through still more staircases. Even stations equipped with extremely long escalators (Angel has the longest one in the system—59m/194 ft.) perversely require passengers to climb a final flight to reach the street. So if you bring luggage into the Tube, be able to hoist your stuff for at least 15 stairs at a time. (This is where backpacks make sense—but don't be the person who leaves it on while on a crowded carriage.) For a list of which stations are step-free (there are only 66 so far), contact **Transport for London Access & Mobility** (www.tfl.gov.uk; ✆ **020/7941-4600**).

2. **Delays.** When you enter a station, look for a sign with the names and colors of the Tube lines on it. Beside each line, you'll see a status bar reading "Good service," "Severe delays," or the like. Trust this sign—it's updated every 10 minutes and lines close without warning. If you note "Minor delays," don't worry. Do worry about labor strikes—they're unpleasantly common.

3. **Heat.** The network can be stuffy. In summer, health advisories are issued to passengers. The worst lines: Bakerloo, Central, and Northern. The best: Circle and District. Air-conditioning is being added—slowly.

4. **Hellish rush hours.** Shoulder-to-shoulder, silently shuffling through airless underground cylinders. It's memorable in the wrong way.

5. **Tough weekends.** Unlike modern systems, which generally have two sets of rails in each direction, London's ancient system has one set, so entire lines have to shut down when maintenance is required. Weekends are when this happens. This is a major reason why it's smart to stay in central London, where you don't depend on a single Tube line. Check in the ticket hall to see what "engineering works" are scheduled.

quickest route and scheduled times. The best resource is the free app **Citymapper,** which tells you which Tube, bus, or train to use, how long it takes, and includes mapped walking directions to the nearest stop. The **UK Bus Checker** app shows 3D maps of routes and where the next bus is.

The most confusing lines for tourists are the Northern line (black on the maps) and the District line (green). Owing mostly to the petty backbiting of the Victorians who built these lines as individual businesses, they split and take several paths. You can handle it. Platform displays and signs on the front of the trains tell you its final destination before you board, so you can figure out the direction. You won't get too far off course if you mess up. If you ride the DLR (and you should—it provides a lovely rooftop-level glide through the brickwork of the old East End and the monolithic towers of Canary Wharf), those lines split variously, too, but there are lots of chances to rectify mistakes.

The **Underground's website** provides the excellent "London's Rail and Tube Services Map" at www.tfl.gov.uk/maps/track/national-rail. It's a truer picture than the Tube map alone because it shows all the places your fare card can take you by rail. (Buses are on separate maps.) The site also has terrific simplified bus maps that show you routes from any neighborhood. Plug in your hotel's address, access Citymapper via Wi-Fi, and you'll have your options.

FARES, PASSES & TICKETS

London Underground (**www.tfl.gov.uk/tickets**) provides 1.1 billion rides a year—and seemingly every passenger pays a different fare. Rates go up every January (these rates were current at press time and will give you a sense of proportion). Britain's system is so complicated that it's accused of having been engineered to bewilder travelers into paying more than they have to. But it can be boiled down to this: **Get an Oyster card and load it with money.** I'll explain.

How much you pay: The center of town—basically everything the Circle line envelops, plus a wee bit of padding—is zone 1. Heading outside of town, in a concentric pattern, come zones 2 through 6. Most tourists stick to zones 1 and 2; very few popular sights are outside those (Wimbledon, Hampton Court, and Kew being the main exceptions). Your fare is calculated by how many zones you go through, and the lower the zone number, the less you pay. If a station appears to straddle zones, you'll pay the cheaper zone's rate. One-way tickets are called "singles" and round-trips are "return."

Astonishingly, **kids 10 and under travel for free** when accompanied by an adult. Adults must buy their own ticket and then ask the staff to wave Junior through the entry gate. Ask an agent about the going discounts for kids.

There are essentially three ticket types for visiting adults.

1. **Via Oyster Pay As You Go (PAYG).** This is the best option, and it's what locals use. Rub this credit card–size pass on yellow dots at the turnstiles and you get the lowest fares. You load it with cash and it debits as you go, no tickets required, on all forms of in-city public transit. No matter how many times you ride the Tube (debited at £2.40 in zone 1—that's a lot better than the £4.90 cash fare!) and bus (debited as £1.50—you can't pay cash on a bus), the maximum taken off your card in a single day will **always be less** than what an equivalent Day Travelcard (see below) would cost. Which makes it the cheapest. Nonstop Oyster use will always peak at £6.60 for anytime travel in zones 1 and 2 (£4.50 if you only took buses), versus the flat rate of £12.30 you'd have paid if you'd bought an equivalent Travelcard. It's called "price capping," and it resets daily at 4:30am. Getting an Oyster usually requires a £5 deposit, but you can get that back before you skip town at any Tube ticket office (there's even one at Heathrow; ID may be requested). The card won't get erased if you keep it beside your mobile phone. And if you don't use up all the money you put on it, you can get a refund as long as there's less than £10 value left on your card. (Travelcards offer no refunds for unused monies.) So. **Buy an**

Oyster card. They're sold at vending machines when you enter the Tube and then you can use it on buses, too.

2. **Via Travelcard.** Aimed at tourists, this is an unlimited pass for 1 or 7 days on the Tube, rail, and bus. "Day Anytime" Travelcards for zones 1 through 3 with no timing restrictions are £12.30. If you find you have to pop into a zone that isn't covered by your card, buy an extension from the ticket window before starting your journey; it's usually £1.50 to £2 more. 7-Day Travelcards cost adults £33 for travel in zones 1 and 2. For Travelcard prices that include more zones, visit **www.tfl.gov.uk/tickets**. You can load a Travelcard purchase onto an Oyster. *Downside:* Unlike PAYG, you may end up paying for rides you never use.

3. **In cash, per ride.** You could, but don't. To travel a mile in zone 1 on the Underground, the cash fare is £4.90 (more than $7). I did the math: It costs 3½ times more to pay cash to go a mile on the Tube than to go a mile in transatlantic First Class. What's more, bus drivers don't even take cash anymore. They *do* take Oyster.

The Tube does offer **contactless payment** on turnstiles' yellow dots—charges are exactly the same as with Oyster—but there's no telling if your card issuer or bank supports it. Apple Pay and American Express equipped with contactless payment should work. Visit **www.tfl.gov.uk/fares-and-payments/contactless** and confer with your issuer to make an educated guess whether you can use this method. If you do use Apple Pay, complete fingerprint recognition as you approach the turnstiles or you'll hold everyone else up. Frankly, for visitors, an Oyster card is more surefire.

From *Europe on $5 a Day*, 1969–1970

"For those who have played the sardine in New York's subway, the London "underground" is a revelation. Quiet, clean, comfortable; the normal fare ranges from 6 to 18¢, depending on the length of the ride, but your average trip should cost no more than around 9¢."

How to use tickets: Since pricing depends on how far you've gone, you must touch your Oyster card to the big yellow reader dot both before you board *and* after your trip—even if there are no turnstiles (so don't forget). On the DLR, the dot may be at street level.

The same goes if you have a paper ticket for any train; keep it handy because you'll need it to get back out at the end. If you can't find it, you'll have to fork over the maximum rate. Inspectors regularly check passengers' tickets and they won't hesitate to fine you because they feed on the power.

How to pay at a vending machine: If you are using a swipe credit card to buy tickets from a vending machine, don't pull your card out of the vending machine too quickly, or it will falsely tell you it's declined. (Underground machines never hesitate to claim something is wrong with your card. Don't believe them. Try a few times.) Vending machines usually accept cash and coins. If your credit card issuer offers a version of your card embedded with a SIM chip, order one ahead of your trip—it makes a lot of transactions a lot easier in London, where chip cards are the norm.

Buy ahead?: Although TfL will mail Oysters or Travelcards ahead of time, that's a waste. You can purchase them at any Tube stop without shipping fees.

Buses

The Tube and buses are seen as one piece, so the same payment systems work on both. Buses are what smart Londoners use. The buses in your city may not come often, but London's are frequent (every 5 min. or so on weekdays), plentiful (some 100 routes in central London and 700 in the wider city), and surprisingly fast (many zoom in dedicated lanes). Sitting on the second level of a candy-apple red double-decker, watching the big landmarks roll past, is one of London's priceless pleasures. Best of all, the bus is cheaper than the Tube.

The 1-day Oyster PAYG price cap for bus-only travel is £4.50, no matter the zone. Travelcards and Oysters (per trip £1.50; buy in Tube stations) are the best way to pay. You can make **free transfers** between as many buses as you want within a 1-hour window. Don't ride without paying: Surprise card inspections are common. Note that bus passes and Travelcards expire at 4:30am the day after you buy them. The TfL supplies 24-hr. information at ✆ **0343/222-1234.**

Drivers do not accept money, and very few bus shelters have automated ticket machines (cash only, and don't expect change), so you **must** have an Oyster card or Travelcard (get one in any Tube stop). All stations have easy-to-read maps that tell you where to catch the buses going to your destination. Major intersections have multiple stops named with letters, and each stop services different routes; check the map in the bus shelter to find the letter stop you need. Many shelters even have electronic boards that approximate the arrival time of the next bus.

Board the bus in front, by the driver, and tap your card on the big yellow dot to check in. An automated voice announces stops with plenty of warning.

10

Getting Around London

PLANNING YOUR TRIP TO LONDON

RED-LETTER double-deckers

A few routes are truly world-class, linking legendary sights. With routes like these, you won't need to splurge on those tedious hop-on, hop-off tour buses:

- The **15 bus,** which crosses the city northwest to southeast, takes in Paddington, Oxford Street, Piccadilly Circus, Trafalgar Square, Fleet Street, St Paul's, and the Tower of London. And it has antique Routemaster vehicles.
- The **10** passes Royal Albert Hall, Kensington Gardens, Knightsbridge

(a block north of Harrods), Hyde Park Corner, Marble Arch, Oxford Street, Goodge Street (for the British Museum), and King's Cross Station.

- The **159** links Paddington, Oxford Circus, Trafalgar Square, and Westminster.
- The **RV1** hits Covent Garden, Waterloo, the Tate Modern, and as a bonus, you get to ride over the Tower Bridge to the Tower of London.

Press a button on a handrail to request a halt before the next one. (Unlike on Tubes and trains, which are charged by how far you go, buses are one price so you should *not* tap again at the end.) Get off via the door at the middle. Newer buses have reinstated a rear-door design with its own conductor, so on those, you can leap off that back entrance and break your neck whenever you like.

Routes that start with N are Night Buses, which tote clubbers home after the Tube stops around midnight; many connect tediously in Trafalgar Square, so pee before setting off. London has trams, too, charged like buses, but they're in areas where tourists are unlikely to go.

National Rail

These are the rail lines that aren't operated by the Underground. These comfortable, standard-size trains go to suburbs, distant cities, and to neighborhoods the Victorians didn't tunnel the Tube to, and they operate on a regular, reliable, published timetable—on maps, they are denoted by two red parallel lines with a zig-zag line connecting them. These lines, which for comfort are actually preferable to the Underground, are covered by Travelcards and Oyster PAYG for roughly the same price as the Tube as long as you stay in the zone system. (The major stations have information desks if you're unsure about Oyster's validity on any journey.) You must tap Oyster at the start *and* at the completion of each journey or you'll be charged as if you took the train to the end of the line. If you accidentally tap in for a wrong or missed train, alert staff. They can ensure you aren't penalized.

There are many termini, but you don't have to hunt by trial and error. Check **TheTrainLine.com** website or app, call the 24-hr. operators at **National Rail Enquiries** (www.nationalrail.co.uk; © **08457/48-49-50**), or plug your journey into your favorite map app such as the free **Citymapper.** Alternatively, each station posts timetables. Schedules are listed by destination; find the place you're going, and the departures will be listed in 24-hr. time.

National Rail stations (not Eurostar or the Underground) accept discount cards for certain folks. Each card requires proof of eligibility (passport, ISIC student ID), but since they can be used for trips to distant cities, they pay for themselves quickly if you're doing lots of rail-riding. Get them at rail stations:

○ The **Senior Railcard** (www.senior-railcard.co.uk; £30 a year): Discounts of about 33 percent for those 60 or over.

○ The **16–25 Railcard** (www.16-25railcard.co.uk; £30 a year): Discounts of 33 percent for those 16 to 25, plus full-time students of any age. It requires a passport-size photo, which may be uploaded from a computer. If you're applying in the U.K., bring a passport photo for that purpose.

○ The **Family & Friends Railcard** (www.family-railcard.co.uk; £30 a year) is for at least one adult and one child age 5 to 15, with a maximum of three adults and four kids on one ticket; at least one child must travel at all times. It awards adults 33 percent off and kids 60 percent off. But know that two kids age 4 and under can travel with an adult for free at all times, even without this card.

Ferries

Partly thanks to the dedication of a series of mayors, London's river ferry services are now one of the most pleasurable ways to get around. The boats, nicknamed River Bus, cover a surprising amount of terrain quickly. Some of their most useful stops include right outside the London Eye, the Tate Modern, the Tower of London, Greenwich, and the O_2. Getting from Greenwich to Embankment takes all of 45 idyllic min. (but on weekends, you may have to wait 30 min. for a boat back). You can go right under the famous Tower Bridge—and because it's intended for commuters, it's at a fraction of the price of a tourist boat.

Fares depend on how far you're going, but for a trip from Westminster to Greenwich, expect a one-way fare around £8.40 (£6.50 with Oyster). You will always save money if you buy a return trip instead of two one-ways, and always ask if your Oyster card or Travelcard grants a discount. The fast catamarans of **Thames Clippers** (www.thamesclippers.com; © **020/7930-2062;** generally 6:30am–10:30pm; bookable via its app) go every 20 min. during the day and are much cheaper and plentiful than the narrated tour boats. The RB1 route is particularly useful, hitting most of the major tourist stops plus Greenwich and the O_2. *One snag:* On weekends, the queue to return from Greenwich can be 40 min. to an hour long. River Roamer passes, which allow you to take as many trips as you want on a single day after 9am, cost £18.50 for adults, £37 for a family of two adults and up to three kids. You can buy at the piers or, for a discount of a few quid, buy ahead via the Thames Clippers Tickets app, downloadable via www.thamesclippers.com/route-time-table/book-tickets-with-ticketing-app. **Thames River Services** (www.thamesriver services.co.uk; © **020/7930-4097**) is a sightseeing version of the Clippers and offers a £12.75 single/£16.75 return (£8/£10.50 children) ride from Westminster to Greenwich. It calls these "sightseeing" trips but note that it's not fully guided and the Clippers are just as good. You can pay with Oyster.

Bikes

Scattered throughout town, you'll see racks of identical red bikes in racks. They're yours to borrow, day or night! They are called **Santander Cycles** (www.tfl.gov.uk/modes/cycling/santander-cycles), but Londoners call them **Boris Bikes,** after the blowsy former mayor who brought them here (or **Barclays Bikes** after a previous sponsor), and they provide more than 10.3 million rides a year. Interestingly, it's been reported this is the only part of Transport for London that makes a profit.

It works like this: You choose one and pull it out of the rack by lifting the seat. You ride it to any other docking station in the city with a free space, and you park it by slotting the front wheel in until a green light appears on the dock. When you're ready to ride somewhere else, just get another bike. You buy the right to borrow bikes for 24 hr. for £2, and that gets you 30 min. (payments are on your credit card) every time you pull a bike out of the rack. Go past that, and you pay the same rate: £2 per extra 30 min. The idea is for you to use a bike as you need it, not to keep it with you all day. You are required to follow the same traffic rules that cars do, which won't be easy, although the city's huge parks are safer places to cycle. Locations of nearby docks are listed on every pylon. Use the free apps **Santander Cycles** or **Citymapper** to find nearby stations with space.

Taxis

Even Londoners think taxis are crazy expensive. It's not the fault of the cabbies. They're the best in the world. Before they're given their wheels, every London taxi driver (there are some 24,000 of them) must go through a grueling training period so comprehensive that it's dubbed, simply, "The Knowledge." On Sundays, you'll see trainees zipping around on mopeds with clipboards affixed above their dashboards. Cabbies arrive inculcated with directions to every alley, mews, avenue, shortcut, and square in the city, and if they don't know, they'll find the answer so discreetly you won't catch the gaffe. They're even trained in first aid, childbirth, and assisting after an acid attack—so breathe easy. And then there are those adorable vehicles: bulbous as Depression Era jalopies, roomy as a studio apartment, yet able to do complete U-turns within a single lane of traffic.

But for this admittedly peerless carriage, you'll pay a £2.60 minimum. Trips of up to 1.6km (1 mile) cost £6 to £9.40 during working hours; 3.2km (2-mile) trips are £9 to £14.60; 6.4km (4-mile) trips are £16 to £23; and trips of around 9.6km (6 miles) hit you for a painful £24 to £31. Rates rise when you're most likely to need a taxi: by about 10 percent from 8 to 10pm or all day on weekends, and roughly another 20 percent from 10pm until dawn. Trips that start at Heathrow cost an extra £2.80, and trips around Christmas and New Year's Day tack on £4. Mercifully, there is no charge for extra passengers or for luggage. It has become customary to tip 10 percent, but most people just round up to the nearest pound. Some taxis accept credit cards (don't count on it), but mostly they are a cash-only concern.

CAN I do that?

Some things that are considered sins back home may lead to legal pleasures in London. Which means they're not sinful as long as you're on British soil! To wit:

- The drinking age is 18. But if you're having your first legit night out, take it easy, because beers here have higher alcohol content than in many countries.

- There are no open container laws. That means you can drink beer in public. The one exception is on public transportation, where you need a drink the most.

- You may smoke Cuban cigars. Get them at any tobacconist and puff away. If you're American, though, don't try smuggling them home.

- Absinthe, the brutal quaff nicknamed "The Green Fairy," is available here. Drink up because American Customs frowns on many versions of it.

- The age of consent is 16 no matter the sexual preference.

Taxis are often called "black cabs," although in fact 12 colors are registered, including "thistle blue" and "nightfire red." **Minicabs,** which are hire cars that operate separately from the traditional black cab system, are easy to find using apps. Don't accept a ride from an unsolicited one. Among the top free apps that can hail the nearest ride: **Splitcab** (www.splitcab.co.uk), which finds people going your way to share the cost (and gives women the option of female-driven cars); **Kabbee** (www.kabbee.com; ☎ **0203/515-1111**), which canvasses cab fleets for the best fixed price; **Minicabit** (www.minicabit.com); taxi-calling app **MyTaxi** (once called Hailo; https://uk.mytaxi.com); independent share ride app **Uber** (www.uber.com), which is at odds with city regulators and may not last; and London's reigning power minicab operator, **Addison Lee** (www.addisonlee.com), which makes more than £100 million in bookings a year from its free app alone.

Renting a Car

Are you insane? Rare is the local who drives in central London, where there's a mandatory daily "congestion charge" of £11.50 (don't believe me? see **www.cclondon.com**), and where parking rates look like your rent back home. Streets were cramped enough when people rode horses, and now they're dogged with one-way rules and police cameras that will ticket you for even honest errors, which you'll definitely make since you're just visiting. You'll go crazy and broke, so why do it? If you're driving out of the city for a tour of the country, fine, but *do not* rent a car for a London vacation.

GETTING AROUND THE U.K.

By Train

The original railway builders plowed their stations into every town of size, making it easy to see the highlights of the United Kingdom without getting near a car. The British whine about the declining quality of the service, but Americans, Canadians, and Australians will be blown away by the speed (and the cost, if they don't book ahead) of the system. Find tickets to all destinations through **National Rail** (www.nationalrail.co.uk; ☎ **08457/48-49-50**) or the indispensable **TrainLine.com.** Seats are sold 12 weeks ahead, and early-bird bookings can yield some marvelous deals, such as £26 for a 4-hr. trip to Scotland (£125 last-minute is common). When hunting for tickets, always search for "off-peak" (non-rush hour) trips going or coming from London in general, not a specific London station, because each London terminal serves various cities. **SplitTicketing.com** also searches the rail companies' byzantine fare schedules to tell you journey configurations that can save you many pounds. Unfortunately, not every train company website accepts international credit cards; Trainline does.

Tickets bought reasonably well in advance will still be cheaper than what you'd pay for the same trips on a **BritRail pass** (www.britrail.com; must purchase outside the U.K.), good on long-distance trains but not on local London transport. Few tourists ride rails with the near-daily regularity that would make a timed pass pay for itself. Check prices against the U.S. seller **Rail Europe** (www.raileurope.com; ℭ **800/622-8600**), as quotes vary.

By Bus

National Express (www.nationalexpress.com; ℭ **0871/781-8181**) is the least expensive way to get from city to city in Britain (but not the fastest—that's usually the train). Because the country is not very big, it rarely takes more than a few hours to reach anyplace by bus. Even Scotland is only 5 hr. away. A major carrier with scads of departures, **Megabus** (https://uk.megabus.com; ℭ **090/0160-0900,** or 44-141-352-4444), which serves more than 100 cities across Europe, charges as little as £1.50 for early bookings, although £19 to £45 for Edinburgh is a more typical rate. It accepts bookings 2 months ahead; book online to avoid phone fees. Both coach services depart from the miserable Victoria Coach Station, located behind Victoria railway station (www.tfl. gov.uk/coaches).

What's the best place to hear about inexpensive ground tours? Hostels. Drop into one; most of their lobbies are papered with brochures. Don't neglect their bulletin boards, either, since you may catch wind of a shared-ride situation that'll often cost you no more than your share of the gasoline (in Britain, *petrol*).

By Car

The only reason you might want to rent a car is if you're headed out of town (see "Driving in London?" on p. 313 for car rental tips).

WHEN TO GO

CLIMATE   It's always time to visit London. It doesn't rain as much as they say and it hasn't been foggy since they got rid of coal. Even though it's approximately at the same latitude of Edmonton, Alberta, weather patterns keep the environment from being extreme. It gets cold in the winter, but rarely snowed in. It gets warm in the summer, but rarely blisteringly so (in fact, most buildings don't even have air-conditioning). The winter months are generally more humid than the summer ones, but experience only slightly more rain. Locals use the free, reliable **Met Office Weather Forecast app,** by the U.K.'s national weather service, to pinpoint forecasts by GPS.

London's Average Daytime Temperatures & Rainfall

	JAN	FEB	MAR	APR	MAY	JUNE	JULY	AUG	SEPT	OCT	NOV	DEC
TEMP. (°F)	39	39	43	46	52	58	62	62	57	51	44	42
TEMP. (°C)	3	3	6	7	11	14	16	16	13	10	6	5
RAINFALL (in.)	1.6	1.4	1.6	1.6	1.7	1.8	1.3	2.1	2	2.4	2.2	1.9
RAINFALL (mm)	41	36	40	40	45	47	34	54	51	61	57	48

SEASONAL CONSIDERATIONS The principal art season (for theater, concerts, art shows) falls between September and May, leaving the summer months for festivals and park-going. A few royal attractions, such as the state rooms of Buckingham Palace, are only open in the summer when the Royal Family decamps to Scotland. In summer, when the weather is warmest, the sun sets after 10pm, and half of Europe takes its annual holiday, airfares are higher, as are hotel rates. Summertime queues for most tourist attractions, such as the London Eye and the Tower of London, might make you wish you'd come in March. For decent prices and lighter crowds, go in spring or fall—April and October seem to have the best confluence of mild weather, pretty plantings, and tolerable crowds. Prices are lowest in mid-winter, but a number of minor sights, such as historic houses, sometimes close from November to March, and the biggest annual events take place during the warmer months.

London's Public Holidays

England observes **eight public holidays** (also known as "bank holidays"): New Year's Day (Jan 1); Good Friday and Easter Monday (usually Apr); May Bank Holiday (first Mon in May); Spring Bank Holiday (usually last Mon in May, but occasionally the first in June); August Bank Holiday (last Mon in Aug); Christmas Day (Dec 25) followed by Boxing Day (Dec 26)—you'll find it hard to even get around on those last two dates. If a date falls on a weekend, the holiday rolls over to the following Monday.

London's Calendar of Events

Special events are an integral part of London's calendar, and many regular happenings draw tourists from around the world. Find even more events at London's **city website** (www.london.gov.uk/events), at the **official tourism site** (www.visitlondon.com), the blogs **Londonist** (www.londonist.com) and **IanVisits** (www.ianvisits.co.uk), and *Time Out* **magazine** (www.timeout.com/london).

JANUARY

London New Year's Day Parade. As many as 10,000 dancers, acrobats, musicians, and performers (heavy on the marching bands) promenade from Parliament Square to Piccadilly for 500,000 spectators and TV audiences. www.lnydp.com, ☎ 020/3275-0190. January 1.

Chinese New Year Festival. In conjunction with the Chinese New Year, the streets around Leicester Square come alive with dragon and lion dances, children's parades, performances, screenings, and fireworks displays. www.chinatownlondon.org.

Get into London Theatre. Theatre gets a jolt of new audiences during this promotional period during which producers cooperate to sell some 75,000 tickets at big discounts. www.getintolondontheatre.co.uk. Early January to February.

London International Mime Festival. Not just for silent clowns, but also for funky puppets and ingenious physical tomfoolery, it's held at venues around town. www. mimelondon.com, ☎ **020/7637-5661.** Mid-January.

FEBRUARY

London Fashion Week. Collections are unveiled for press and buyers at a biannual fashion festival also held in September. It's tough to get a runway show ticket, but there's a raft of slick events and parties across the city. www.londonfashionweek. co.uk. Mid-February and mid-September.

MARCH

St Patrick's Festival. When you're this close to Dublin and you consider England's long rivalry with the Emerald Isle, you can expect 3 days of raging Irish pride—parades, music, and food stalls around Trafalgar Square, where the fountains gush green. The city also sponsors concerts and craft fairs promoting Irish culture and heritage. It's not just about drinking—it just looks that way. www.london. gov.uk, ☎ 020/7983-4000. March 17.

BADA Antiques & Fine Art Fair. Sponsored by the British Antique Dealers' Association, it's considered to be the best in Britain for such collectors. Some 100 exhibitors move into a mighty tent in Duke of York's Square, in Chelsea, for the 7-day sales event. Don't expect a bargain. www.badafair.com, ☎ 020/7589-6108. Mid- to late March.

Oxford and Cambridge Boat Race. This popular annual event (since 1829), held on the Thames in Hammersmith, takes less than a half-hour, but the after-party rollicks into the night and the good-natured rivalry is undying. www.theboatrace.org. Late March or early April.

APRIL

London Marathon. Although it draws some 35,000 runners, the Marathon is also a kick for spectators, so hotels tend to fill up ahead of it. The starter pistol fires in Blackheath; the home stretch is along Birdcage Walk near Buckingham Palace. If you want to run, apply by the previous October. www.virgin moneylondonmarathon.com. April 28, 2019.

Udderbelly Festival. Famously mounted in a giant inflatable purple cow's udder by the riverbank (really), this 410-seat offshoot of Edinburgh Fringe Festival's variety venue the Underbelly sells well over a million tickets. Dozens of acts range from comedy to musicals to circus, plus there's food, a beer garden, and other amusements. In 2017, it merged with the similar Wonderground festival to extend from 3 months to 5 months. www.udderbelly.co.uk, ☎ **0844/ 545-8282.** April to mid-July.

MAY

Regent's Park Open Air Theatre. Forget stuffy auditoriums. There's little shelter from sudden downpours, but in good weather the repertoire of high drama, musicals, and Shakespeare sparkles under a canopy of blue skies, towering trees, and natural beauty. www.openairtheatre.org, ☎ **0844/826-4242.** Mid-May to September.

Chelsea Flower Show. The Royal Horticultural Society, which calls itself a "leading gardening charity dedicated to advancing horticulture and promoting good gardening" (don't you just love the English?), mounts this esteemed show for 5 days on the grounds of the Royal Hospital in Chelsea. The plants, all raised by champion green thumbs, are sold to attendees on the final day, but sadly, foreigners aren't usually able to get their plants past Customs. Tickets go on sale in November for this lilypalooza, and they're snapped up quickly. The event is so celebrated that it is covered on nightly prime-time TV. Really. www. rhs.org.uk, ☎ **020/3176-5800.** Late May.

JUNE

Beating Retreat. Drum corps, pipes, and plenty of bugle calls: This anachronistic twilight ceremony, held for two evenings at Horse Guards Parade by St James's Park, involves the salute of the queen (or another member of the royal family) and the appearance of many red-clad marchers. Scholars trace its origins to 1554—so for tradition's sake, it's deeply meaningful. It's the nearest relative to the better-known Trooping the Colour, but without the crowds. Reserve ahead (£20–£45) in mid-December. www. householddivision.org.uk, ☎ **020/7839-5323.** Early June.

The Royal Academy Summer Exhibition. Artists have been in a frenzy to win entry to this blind competition for nearly 250 years.

SUMMER festivals

With many major music festivals taking over London's green spaces, summer is like one long Woodstock. Only the highlights:

- **May: All Points East.** Three days in Victoria Park. Acts in 2018 included Björk, Nick Cave, and LDC Soundsystem. www.allpointseastfestival.com.
- **Steel Yard.** Dance and trance under a gnarly metal superstructure. Finsbury Park. www.creamfields.com/steelyardlondon.
- **June: Field Day.** Alternative acts (Erykah Badu, Charlotte Gainsbourg, Mount Kimbie) over 2 days in Brockwell Park. www.fielddayfestivals.com.

- **Hampton Court Palace Festival.** High-end names (Lionel Richie, Van Morrison, Russell Watson, Tom Jones) in a temporary theater on palace grounds. www.hamptoncourtpalacefestival.com.
- **July: Lovebox.** A weekend in Gunnersby Park. Sunday is a virtual Pride festival. Past acts: Mark Ronson, Frank Ocean, and Goldfrapp. www.loveboxfestival.com.
- **New Look Wireless Festival.** Held alfresco in Finsbury Park for 3 days. Recent years: Chance the Rapper, DJ Khaled, The Weeknd. www.wirelessfestival.co.uk.

Paintings, sculpture, drawings, architecture—if you can dream it, you can enter it, and if you're one of the most talented, your piece is anointed as the best that year. The show is what the Royal Academy is known for, and although it's not envelope-pushing, it's a seminal event in British art culture and shouldn't be missed if you're in town. www.royalacademy.org.uk.

Trooping the Colour. Never mind that the queen was born in April. This is her birthday party (92 in 2018!), and as a present, she gets the same thing every year: soldiers with big hats. A sea of redcoats and cavalry swarm over Horse Guards Parade, 41 guns salute, and a flight of Royal Air Force jets slam through the sky overhead. The queen herself leads the charge, waving politely to her subjects before they lose themselves in a hearty display of marching band prowess. Try for grandstand seats (£35) instead of standing in the free-for-all along the route, where you'll only get a fast glimpse of passing royalty. Tickets are only sold in Jan and Feb. www.householddivision.org.uk/trooping-the-colour, ✆ 020/7414-2479. Mid-June.

Taste of London Festival. The city's top chefs and the region's finest farmers convene in Regent's Park for 5 days of belly-stuffing. https://london.tastefestivals.com, ✆ 087/1230-7132. Mid-June.

Pride London. A signature event on the world's LGBT calendar, in a good year London Pride can pull some 825,000 revelers, many of them heterosexual, with a buoyant roster of concerts and performances by famous names plus a parade (the U.K.'s largest) in the center of the City. The gay pride week, co-sponsored by the Mayor's office, also makes an excellent excuse for some blowout dance parties. www.prideinlondon.org, ✆ 0844/344-5428. Late June or early July.

Wimbledon Championships. Why watch on television yet again? Check p. 187 for how to be one of the 500,000 to witness it in person. www.wimbledon.org, ✆ 020/8944-1066. Late June to early July.

Greenwich and Docklands International Festival. An ambitious program of free theatrical and musical pieces, many of them developed by artists expressly for the spaces they're performed in. www.festival.org, ✆ 020/8305-1818. Late June and early July.

Meltdown. A compendium of hip prestige arts held at the Southbank Centre, curated in the past by such notables as Patti Smith, David Bowie, Robert Smith, and Yoko Ono.

JULY

BBC Promenade Concerts. The biggest classical music festival of the year, held primarily at the Royal Albert Hall, "the Proms" consists of orchestral concerts for every taste. Up to 1,350 standing places are available starting at £7.50. www.bbc.co.uk/proms, © 020/7589-8212. July to September.

The Lambeth Country Show. A free, old-fashioned farm show overtakes Brixton's Brockwell Park (for a single weekend, anyway) with farm animals, jam-making contests, a fun fair, tractor demonstrations, and Punch and Judy puppet shows. Very English stuff. Free. www.lambethcountryshow.co.uk, © 020/7926-7085.

AUGUST

London Triathlon. Some 11,000 participants cycle through the City from Westminster, sprint around the ExCeL center in Docklands, and swim in Royal Victoria Dock in this annual event. Sir Richard Branson attends. www.thelondontriathlon.co.uk, © 020/8233-5900. Early August.

Notting Hill Carnival. In August 1958, roving bands of white racists combed the slums of Notting Hill in search of Caribbean-owned businesses to destroy. Resulting community outrage and newly rediscovered cultural pride led to the formation of this festival, now Europe's largest street parade, attracting some 2 million people. It's a smorgasbord of cultures spanning the Caribbean, Eastern Europe, South America, and the Indian subcontinent. Sunday is kids' day, with scrubbed-down events and activities, but on Monday, the adults take over, costumes get skimpy, floats weave through small streets, and rowdy hordes celebrate into the wee hours. www.thelondonnottinghillcarnival.com. August Bank Holiday weekend.

Great British Beer Festival. Just like it sounds: More than 900 British ales and ciders are available to try at London Olympia—after all those tastings, you'll be relieved to learn the Tube is within easy reach. It runs 5 days. www.gbbf.org.uk. © 01727/798-440.

SEPTEMBER

The Great River Race. Always over too soon, the Race is the aquatic version of the London Marathon, with rowers vying to beat out 300 other vessels—Chinese dragon boats, Canadian canoes, Viking longboats, and even Hawaiian outriggers—on a morning jaunt upriver from the Docklands to Richmond. www.greatriverrace.co.uk, © 020/8398-8141. Saturday in mid-September.

Totally Thames. In conjunction with the Great River Race (above), nearly half a million souls attend London's largest free open-air arts festival, with more than 150 events. Southwark Bridge is closed for a giant feast, and there's a flotilla of working river boats, circus performers, and antique fireboats, tugs, and sailboats. Sunday sees the Night Carnival, a lavish procession of thousands of lantern-bearing musicians and dancers crawling along the water. Everything is topped off with barge-launched fireworks. www.totallythames.org, © 020/7928-8998. September.

Open House London. More than 800 buildings, all of them deemed important but normally closed to the public, yawn wide for free tours on a single, hotly anticipated weekend. Past participants have included the skyscraper headquarters of Lloyd's and Swiss Re (officially "30 St Mary Axe" but usually called "The Gherkin") and even No. 10 Downing St. The list of open buildings comes out in August. Some require timed tickets, but for most, the line forms at dawn. Open House also organizes year-round walking tours. www.openhouselondon.org.uk, © 020/7383-2131. Mid-September.

London Fashion Weekend. It's got nothing on its kin in New York or Milan, but here, pop-up shops from more than 100 designers are put on sale at deeply discounted prices in the hopes they'll build style buzz. www.londonfashionweekend.co.uk. Mid-September.

Dance Umbrella. For 4 decades, one of the world's best contemporary dance festivals, with plenty of standing-room seats for as little as £5. www.danceumbrella.co.uk. © 020/7257-9380. Peaks in late September.

10

PLANNING YOUR TRIP TO LONDON

London's Calendar of Events

Frieze Art Fair. More than 175 galleries vie for big money from collectors in a colossal 4-day tent show in Regent's Park. It has become influential in the contemporary art world. www.frieze.com. ✆ **020/3372-6111.** Early October.

Diwali. One advantage of visiting a multicultural city like London is that it affords you the chance to sample major international holidays in an English-speaking environment. One such treat is Diwali, the Indian "festival of light," when Trafalgar Square is transformed with lights, floating lanterns, massive models of the elephant god Ganesh, music, dance, and DJs. It's free. Mid- to late October.

BFI London Film Festival. An important stop on the cinema circuit, this event, sponsored by the British Film Institute, is geared toward media exposure, but there are plenty of tickets for the public, too. www.bfi.org.uk/lff, ✆ **020/7928-3232.** Mid-October.

NOVEMBER

Guy Fawkes Night. In 1605, silly old Guy Fawkes tried to assassinate James I and the entire Parliament by blowing them to smithereens in the Gunpowder Plot. Joke's on him: To this day, the Brits celebrate his failure by blowing up *him.* His effigy is thrown on bonfires across the country, fireworks displays rage in the autumn night sky, and more than a few tykes light their first sparklers in honor of the would-be assassin's gruesome execution. Although displays are scattered around town, including at Battersea Park and Alexandra Palace, get out of the city for the weekend nearest November 5, also called Bonfire Night—the countryside is perfumed with the woody aroma of burning leaves on this holiday. Mount Primrose Hill or Hampstead Heath for a view of the fireworks around the city. November 5.

Lord Mayor's Show. What sounds like the world's dullest public access program is actually a delightfully pompous procession, about 800 years old, involving some 140 charity floats and 6,000 participants to ostensibly show off the newly elected Lord Mayor to the queen or her representatives. The centerpiece is the preposterously carved and gilt Lord Mayor's Coach, built in 1757—a carriage so extravagant it makes Cinderella's ride look like a Toyota Corolla. That's a lot of hubbub for a city official whose role is essentially ceremonial; the Mayor of London (currently Boris Johnson) wields the true power. All that highfalutin' strutting is followed by a good old-fashioned fireworks show over the Thames between the Blackfriars and Waterloo bridges. www.lordmayorsshow.org. Second Saturday in November.

London Jazz Festival. Some 165 mid-November events attract around 60,000 music fans for 10 days. Many performances are free, and tickets are distributed by the venues. www.efglondonjazzfestival.org.uk, ✆ **020/7324-1880.** Mid-November.

Remembrance Sunday. Another chance to glimpse Her Royal Highness. She and the prime minister, as well as many royals, attend a ceremony at the Cenotaph, in the middle of Whitehall, to honor the war dead and wounded, of which Britain has borne more than its share. Those red flowers you'll see everywhere—red petals, black centers—are poppies, the symbol of remembrance in Britain. Sunday nearest November 11.

DECEMBER

Carols by Candlelight. Royal Albert Hall's annual evening of sing-along Christmas carols, readings from Dickens, and music by Handel, Bach, Mozart, and Corelli played by the Mozart Festival Orchestra—in period costume. www.royalalberthall.com, ✆ **020/7589-8212.** Late December.

New Year's Eve Fireworks. As Big Ben strikes midnight, London rings in the New Year with 12 minutes of fireworks over the Thames and the Eye. It's so crowded that in 2015, the city began limiting attendance to 110,000 and requiring tickets (£10). A few tickets can be booked via www.london.gov.uk/nye in mid-June, with the rest available in September.

[FastFACTS] LONDON

Accessible Travel London can't seem to strike the balance between preserving old buildings and making sure they're accessible to all. With the laudable exception of the Docklands Light Railway, only a few Tube stations have lifts, and those with plenty of escalators still require passengers to climb flights of stairs. Research your options at **Visit London** (www.visitlondon.com/access), **Transport for London** (www.tfl.gov.uk/accessibility; ✆ **0343/222-1234**), and **DisabledGo** (www.disabledgo.com). The website **UpDownLondon.com** keeps tabs on step-free access at Tube stations, including temporary maintenance obstacles.

Many London hotels, museums, restaurants, and sightseeing attractions have dedicated wheelchair access, all taxis and buses do, and persons with disabilities often get admission discounts. Generally speaking, the more expensive a hotel is, the more likely it is to be wheelchair accessible, but not always. The website for **Nationwide Disabled Access Register** (www.directenquiries.com) lists the accessibility features of a wide range of facilities, from attractions to car renters.

Blind or partially sighted travelers will find useful advice from the **Royal National Institute of Blind People** (www.rnib.org.uk; ✆ **0303/123-9999**). **Tourism for All** (www.tourismforall.org.uk; ✆ **084/5124-9971**) has accessibility information for older travelers as well as travelers with disabilities.

The British agency **Can Be Done** (www.canbedone.co.uk; ✆ **020/8907-2400**) runs tours adapted to travelers with mobility needs.

Area Codes The country telephone code for Great Britain is **44.** The area code for London is **020.** The full telephone number is usually 8 digits long. Businesses and homes in central London usually have numbers beginning with a **7;** those from farther out begin with an **8.** For more info, see "Telephones," p. 338.

ATMs/Banks See "Money," p. 335. *One quirk to note:* Retrieve your card immediately from ATM slots; many machines suck them in within 10 to 15 seconds, for security. Should that happen, you'll have to petition the bank to have it returned to you.

Business Hours Offices are generally open weekdays between 9 or 10am and 5 or 6pm. Some remain open a few hours longer on Thursdays and Fridays. Saturday hours for stores are the same; Sunday store hours are generally noon to 5 or 6pm. Banks are usually open from 9:30am to 4 or 5pm, with some larger branches open later on Thursdays or for a few hours on Saturday mornings.

Cellphones See "Mobile Phones," p. 334.

Credit Cards Credit cards are accepted nearly everywhere, but if you can, bring **Visa** or **Mastercard,** because **American Express** is accepted less widely. (If you try to use it at a place that doesn't accept it, you may be mistakenly told your card has a problem; don't panic.) Many credit card issuers levy an annoying international transaction fee on top of your purchase—many **American Express** cards have dropped that fee, as have **Capital One Venture** (www.capitalone.com; ✆ **800/695-5500**) and several options from **Chase** (www.chase.com). Try not to use credit cards to withdraw cash—you'll pay a currency exchange fee, and worse, you'll be charged interest from the moment your money leaves the slot.

It is now illegal for vendors to charge you a transaction fee to defray the cost of dealing with the card companies. Minimum purchases and clearly labeled service fees, however, remain legal.

Europeans use **"chip and PIN" cards** requiring a code number. Some vending machines won't accept swipe-only cards and may incorrectly inform you that you were declined. Most U.S. cards now come with such a chip, but if yours doesn't, ask your lender to send you one for free. If you do have a swipe-only card, inform clerks you're using a "Signature card," as they will usually have to scramble around for a pen (Europeans don't sign anymore). Restaurants will usually process your payment at your table wirelessly—the British consider it standard security practice not to let your card out of your sight and to check ID along with signature.

Customs Rules about what you can carry into Britain are standard but ever-shifting, so get the latest restrictions from **HM Revenue & Customs** (www.hmrc.gov.uk). Your own government is responsible for telling you what you can bring back home.

Doctors Ask your hotel first. Then try the G.P. (General Practitioner) finder at **www.nhs.uk**. North American members of the **International Association for Medical Assistance to Travelers** (IAMAT; www.iamat.org; 716/754-4883 in the U.S., or 416/652-0137 in Canada) can consult that organization for lists of local approved doctors. *Note:* U.S. and Canadian visitors who become ill while they're in London are eligible only for free *emergency* care. For other treatment, including follow-up care, you'll pay £60 to £150 just to see a physician.

Drinking Laws Legal drinking age is 18. Children 15 and younger are allowed in pubs if accompanied by a parent or guardian. Drinking on London's **public transport network** is forbidden; on-the-spot fines are issued to transgressors.

Electricity The current in Britain is 240 volts AC. Plugs have three squared pins. Foreign appliances operating on lower voltage (those from the U.S., Canada, and Australia use 110–120 volts AC) will require an adapter and possibly a voltage converter, although the range of capability will usually be printed on the plug. Many modern phone chargers and laptops can handle the stronger current with only an adapter. A few hotels provide North American–style outlets for a non-heating appliance such as a shaver, but don't count on one.

Embassies & Consulates In 2017, the **U.S. Embassy** moved from Grosvenor Square to an elaborate 4.9-acre complex in West London's Wandsworth district (Ponton Rd., SW8; https://uk.usembassy.gov; 020/7499-9000; Tube: Vauxhall). Standard hours are Monday to Friday 8:30am to 5:30pm. Most non-emergency inquiries require an appointment. You may bring tablets but not laptops. For passport information, call 877/487-2778 in the U.S.

The **High Commission of Canada**, 1 Trafalgar Sq., London W1 (www.canadainternational.gc.ca/united_kingdom-royaume_uni/index.aspx; 020/7004-6000; Tube: Charing Cross), handles passport and consular services for Canadians. Hours are Monday, Wednesday, and Friday 8 to 10:30am.

The **Australian High Commission** is at Australia House, Strand, London WC2 (www.uk.embassy.gov.au; 020/7379-4334; Tube: Temple). Hours are Monday to Friday 9am to noon.

The **New Zealand High Commission** is at New Zealand House, 80 Haymarket, London SW1 (www.nzembassy.com/uk; 020/7930-8422; Tube: Charing Cross or Piccadilly Circus). Hours are Monday to Friday 9am to 5pm.

The **Irish Embassy** is at 17 Grosvenor Place, London SW1 (www.embassyofireland.co.uk; 020/7235-2171; Tube: Hyde Park Corner). Hours are Monday to Friday 9:30am to 12:30pm and 2:30 to 4:30pm.

Emergencies The one-stop number for Britain is 999—that's for fire, police, and ambulances. It's free from any phone, even mobiles. Less urgent? Call 111.

Family Travel Attractions cater to the family market. The kingly treatment starts, at many places, with the so-named **Family Ticket,** which grants a reduced price for parents and kids entering together. For any length of stay, you can rent baby equipment from **Chelsea Baby Hire** (www.chelseababyhire.com; 07802/846-742). If you need babysitting, **Sitting Pretty Babysitters** (www.sittingprettybabysitters.com; 07971/083-207) will come to your hotel for a minimum of 3 or 4 hours, depending on the time of week; rates are around £10 an hour with a £6.50 booking fee and a £17.50 membership fee.

If you are a **divorced parent** traveling with your children, bring proof to the airport that you are entitled to take your kids out of the country.

Some resources for family-specific travel tips include the **Family Travel Network** (www.familytravel network.com) and **Travel with Your Kids** (www.travel withyourkids.com), which has a section just about London's finds. **The Family Travel Files** (www.thefamily travelfiles.com) lists tour operators and packagers geared to families, but its suggestions aren't always the most economical or efficient. *Time Out* (www. timeout.com/london) includes a section on kids' activities.

When it comes to **baby supplies,** pacifiers are called "dummies," diapers are "nappies," a crib is a "cot," and Band-Aids are "plasters."

Health Traveling to London doesn't pose specific health risks. Common drugs are generally available over the counter and in large supermarkets, although visitors should know the generic rather than brand names of any medicines they rely on. *Note:* The general-purpose painkiller known in North America as acetaminophen is called **paracetamol** in the U.K.

Pack **prescription medications** in carry-on luggage and in their original

containers, with pharmacy labels—otherwise they may not pass airport security. Also bring copies of your prescriptions, just in case. If you require **syringes,** always carry a signed medical prescription. Don't forget an extra pair of contact lenses or prescription glasses.

If you need the advice of a doctor or a nurse, the national health care system operates a free, 24-hr. hotline: **National Health Service Direct** (www.nhs.uk; ✆ **111**). Citizens of many European countries are entitled to free health care while in Britain (www. dh.gov.uk/travellers), but not everyone is. Non-EU citizens should carry health or travel insurance. Also see "Doctors," above.

Health Insurance U.K. nationals receive free medical treatment countrywide; visitors from overseas qualify only for free **emergency** care. **U.S. visitors** should note that most domestic health plans (including Medicare and Medicaid) do not provide coverage, and the ones that do often require you to pay for services upfront and file for reimbursement after you return home. You might want to buy international medical coverage from companies such as **United-Healthcare SafeTrip** (www. UHCsafetrip.com; ✆ **800/ 732-5309**) or **Travel Assistance International** (www.travelassistance.com; ✆ **800/821-2828**). **Canadians** should check with their provincial health plan offices

or call **Health Canada** (www.hc-sc.gc.ca; ✆ **613/ 957-2991**) to find out the extent of their coverage and what documentation and receipts to bring home if they are treated overseas. For **E.U. nationals** (and nationals of E.E.A. countries and Switzerland), reciprocal health agreements ensure they receive free medical care while in the U.K., but you must carry a valid **European Health Identity Card** (EHIC).

Hospitals In the U.K., the ER is usually called A&E, or Accident and Emergency. If your need is urgent, dial ✆ **999** (it's free no matter where your phone is registered) rather than risk going to a medical center that doesn't offer A&E. You can search **www.nhs.uk** for the nearest A&E, or go to the 24-hr., walk-in A&E departments at **University College London Hospital,** 235 Euston Rd., London NW1 (www.uclh.nhs.uk; ✆ **020/3456-7890;** Tube: Warren St.) or **St Thomas's Hospital,** Westminster Bridge Road, entrance on Lambeth Palace Road, London, SE1 (www.guys andstthomas.nhs.uk; ✆ **020/7188-7188;** Tube: Westminster or Waterloo). For less urgent needs, visit **Soho NHS Walk-In Centre** (1 Frith St., W1; www.clch. nhs.uk; ✆ **020/7534-6500;** Tube: Tottenham Court Rd.), which is open Monday through Friday 8am to 8pm and Saturday to Sunday 10am to 8pm.

Inoculations Unless you're arriving from an area

Innoculations

known to be suffering from an epidemic, inoculations or vaccinations are not required for entry into the U.K.

Insurance   You may want special coverage for **apartment stays,** especially if you've plunked down a deposit, and for any **valuables** you may bring with you; airlines are only required to pay up to $2,500 for lost luggage domestically, less for foreign travel. Compare policies at **InsureMyTrip.com** (✆ **800/487-4722**), or contact one of the following reputable companies: **Allianz** (www.allianztravelinsurance.com; ✆ **866/884-3556**); **CSA Travel Protection** (www.csatravelprotection.com; ✆ **877/243-4135,** or 240/330-1529); **Travel Guard International** (https://mvp.travelguard.com; ✆ **800/826-5248**); or **Travelex** (www.travelexinsurance.com; ✆ **800/228-9792**). Note that most insurers require you to purchase plans *before* you leave home.

Internet   Wi-Fi flows freely at pubs, cafes, museums, and nearly all hotels. Usually, you will have to fill in an email address to activate it, but often it's a data collection ploy and you can write dummy information. (See box on p. 324.) Virgin Media (www.virginmedia.com/wifi) provides Wi-Fi in many Tube stations but not between them. Visitors can buy passes for £2 (1 day), £5 (1 week), or £15 (1 month). See "Mobile Phones," below.

Laundry   Launderettes are not easy to find in central London anymore, and expensive hotels will only do laundry and dry cleaning if you're willing to shell out. Look into the app **Laundrapp,** which will pick up and drop off to your hotel for free. Prices start at £2 per article or £2.50 for 1kg (2.2 lb.).

Left Luggage   Useful if you're taking those cheap European flights with steep luggage fees, **Left Baggage** (www.left-baggage.com; ✆ **0800/077-4530**) has locations at Heathrow, Gatwick, and the big railway stations: It costs £12.50 per item per 24 hr. for up to a week, then £5 per item per day thereafter.

Legal Aid   If you find yourself in trouble abroad, contact your consulate or embassy (see "Embassies & Consulates," p. 332). It can advise you of your rights and provide a list of local attorneys (for which you'll have to pay if services are used), but they cannot interfere on your behalf in the English legal process. For questions about U.S. citizens who've been arrested abroad, telephone the **Citizens Emergency Center** of the Bureau of Consular Affairs in Washington, D.C. (✆ **202/501-4444,** or 888/407-4747).

LGBT Travelers   Gay and lesbian people have equality and marriage rights in England. Public displays of affection are barely noticed in the center of the city, although in the outer

suburbs couples should show more restraint. Gay bashings are rare enough to be newsworthy, but it's true that an element of society can, once full of ale, become belligerent. Particularly in parks at night, be aware of your surroundings and give wide berth to gaggles of drunken lads. This advice holds irrespective of your sexuality.

For nightlife planning, the best sources for information are **Boyz** (www.boyz.co.uk), which publishes a day-by-day schedule on its website, and the free **QX International** (www.qxmagazine.com). Both are distributed for free at many gay bars. Also see nightlife listings on p. 250.

Mail   An airmail letter or postcard to anywhere outside Europe costs £1.25 for up to 10g (⅓ oz.) and generally takes 5 to 7 working days to arrive. Within the E.U., letters or postcards under 20g (⅔ oz.) also cost £1.25.

Mobile Phones   Anytime you call a mobile phone in Britain, the fee will be higher than calling a land line, although there is no fee to *receive* a call or text.

Apart from renting a phone (not recommended to the casual visitor), many tourists simply enable their international **roaming** feature and buy a data plan from their provider. Depending on your contract, your allowance may be scanty and your provider may bleed you for extra data.

The other solution, if you have an unlocked phone that uses the GSM system, is to pop into any mobile phone shop or newsstand and buy a cheap **pay-as-you-talk** phone number from a mobile phone store. You pay about £5 for a SIM card, which you stick in your phone, and then you buy vouchers to load your new U.K. phone number with as much money as you think you'll use up (no refunds). That will give you a British number, which you can e-mail to everyone back home, that charges local rates (10p–40p per minute). Just call your provider before you leave home to "unlock" your phone (out-of-contract and last-generation phones are more likely to allow this), so that the British SIM card will function in it. That service is usually free. U.K. mobile providers with pay-as-you-talk deals, all comparable, include **Vodafone** (www.vodafone.com), **O₂** (www.o2.co.uk), **Lebara** (www.lebara.co.uk), **EE/T-Mobile** (www.ee.co.uk), and **Virgin Mobile** (www.virginmobile.com). Annoyingly, purchased SIMs come with automatic child content locks, which may block certain social sites. To remove the censorship, go to a mobile phone store run by your SIM provider to prove you're an adult. Bring your hotel's details—you must supply a U.K. address.

Even if your home mobile company won't permit you to unlock your phone, you can use its Wi-Fi features for Skype, FaceTime, WhatsApp, and on some phones, even texts and calling.

Money British pounds are divided into 100 pennies (p), the plural of which is called "pence." Coins come in 1p, 2p, 5p, 10p, 20p, 50p, £1, and £2 (the 2-pound coin is commonly called a "quid"). Notes come in £5, £10, £20, and £50. The government is amidst a redesign of its money. The new British pound (£1), a small, chunky, gold-colored coin with silver faces, looks round but is actually subtly 12-sided. The previous version, truly round and golden without shiny faces, was phased out in October 2017. Paper £5 notes were replaced with a polymer version in May 2017, and in mid-2018 the paper £10 is also going plastic. If someone tries to pass you a paper £5 or £10, request a new one or spend it immediately. (The £20 arrives in 2020.) If you find yourself holding outdated money and a local bank refuses to exchange it, go to the Bank of England on Threadneedle Street (Tube: Bank) to exchange it. Now and then, you'll receive notes printed by the Bank of Scotland; they're valid, but an increase in forgeries means some shops refuse them. Banks will exchange them.

In past years, the exchange rate has hovered in the vicinity of £1 = US$1.50, but it trended to about US$1.35 after the U.K. decided to leave the European Union in June 2016; consult a currency exchange website such as **www.oanda.com/currency/converter** or the Oanda or XE apps.

All prices (including at most B&Bs but not at all hotels) are listed including tax, so what you see is what you pay. No guesstimating required.

Every visitor should have several sources for money, but cash is still king. The simple solution is to pull cash from an ATM upon arrival; rates are the cheapest there. Before leaving home, warn your bank and your credit card issuers that you intend to travel internationally so that they don't place a stop on your account. You may also need to adjust your PIN, since English banks require 4-digit codes. (If you know your PIN as a word, memorize the numerical equivalent.) Most banks hit you with fees of a few pounds each time you withdraw cash, and your own bank may toss in a small fee of its own; gauge for yourself how much you feel comfortable withdrawing at a time to offset that fee. Also ask your bank if it has reciprocal agreements for free withdrawals anywhere. One institution that charges international usage fees below the industry standard is **Everbank** (www.everbank.com; ☎ 888/882-3837); another is **Charles Schwab** (www.schwab.com; ☎ 866/403-9000), which reimburses ATM fees.

Paying with **Apple Pay** on an iPhone is fast, but it

usually only works up to £30.

Traveler's checks are dead—most places decline them—but creditors have come up with **traveler's check cards,** also called **prepaid cards,** which are essentially debit cards loaded with however much money you choose to put on them. They work in ATMs, and should you lose one, you can get your cash back in a matter of hours. You can reload the card mid-trip by calling a number or visiting a website, although there may be fees of a few dollars for ATM transactions. Try **NetSpend** (www.netspend.com; ⓒ **866/387-7363**).

Changing cash is also on the outs. Old-fashioned cambios/bureau de change are few and far between, although you'll still find a few at the airport and around Leicester Square. If you must change money, better rates are offered by banks (open 9:30am–4pm).

Newspapers & Magazines London offers more publications than one would think a city of its size could support. The broadsheets, ordered from left to right, politically speaking, are the *Guardian,* the *Independent,* the *Daily Telegraph,* and the *Times.* On the Tube, *Metro* is free in the morning and *Evening Standard* is free in the afternoon. The salmon-colored *Financial Times* covers business. The tabloids are fluffier and more salacious: They include the *Sun,* the *Mirror, Daily Star,* the *Daily Mail,* and *Daily*

Express. Time Out publishes a free listing of events and entertainments.

Other popular magazines include the *Big Issue* (written and sold by homeless and formerly homeless people), *Radio Times* (TV listings and celebrity interviews), and *Hello!* and *OK!* (fawning celebrity spreads planted by publicity agents).

Packing For your wallet's sake, pack sparingly! It's not as easy as it used to be to wink your way through the weigh-in. **British Airways,** for example, grants coach passengers a puny 23kg (51 lb.); if you exceed that, you will be smacked with a flat fee of £25 per flight (and it charges you more if you wait to pay the fee until you get to the airport). Bags over 32kg (71 lb.) will be rejected outright. Some airlines, such as **Virgin Atlantic,** can be ruthless about making sure even your *carry-on* baggage weighs no more than 10kg (22 lb.). If you're taking multiple airlines, stick to the tightest restrictions of the lot. Many airlines (even the no-frills) discount for booking baggage at least 24 hours early, and charge more at the airport.

Pare toiletries to essentials. You're not going to the Congo—you will find staples like toothpaste, contact lens solution, and deodorant everywhere. Women should bring a minimum of make-up; the British don't tend to use very much themselves. Brits are also more likely to wear trousers than blue jeans. If you

plan to go clubbing, pack some fashionable duds—Londoners love to look natty.

You'll be most comfortable if you dress in clothing that layers well. Even in winter, London's air can be clammy, and dressing too warmly can become uncomfortable. No matter what the average temperature is (see weather box on p. 326), the air can grow cool after the sun sets; plan for that. A compact umbrella is wise year-round, as is an outer coat that repels water, since you never know when you're going to find yourself in one of those misty rains that make the British Isles so lush and green.

Don't bring illegal drugs (duh) or medical marijuana (duh), and also leave the pepper spray and mace at home; they're banned in the U.K.

Passports To enter the United Kingdom, all U.S. citizens, Canadians, Australians, New Zealanders, and South Africans must have a passport valid through their length of stay. No visa is required. A passport will allow you to stay in the country for up to 6 months. The immigration officer may also want to see proof of your intention to return to your point of origin (usually a round-trip ticket) and of visible means of support while you're in Britain (credit cards work). If you're planning to fly from the U.S. or Canada to the U.K. and then on to a country that requires a visa (India, for example), secure that visa before you arrive in Britain.

Pharmacies Every police station keeps a list of pharmacies (chemists) that are open 24 hr. Also try **Zafash,** a rare chemist that is open 24 hr., 233–235 Old Brompton Rd., SW5; www.zafash.co.uk; (📞 **020/7373-2798;** Tube: Earl's Court). For non-emergency health advice, call the NHS at 📞 **111.**

Police Dial 📞 **999,** or 112 if the matter is serious. London has two official police forces: the City of London police (www.cityoflondon.police.uk), whose remit covers the "Square Mile" and its 8,600 residents; and the Metropolitan Police ("the Met"), which covers the rest of the capital. Opening hours for all the Met's local police stations are listed at www.met.police.uk/local. In a non-emergency, you can contact your local police station by dialing 📞 **101.** Losses, thefts, and other criminal matters should be reported at the nearest police station immediately. You will be given a crime number, which your travel insurer will request if you make a claim against any losses.

Safety Crossing the street is the most perilous thing you'll do. Always look down to see which way traffic is flowing—the street will be painted "Look right" or "Look left" so you'll know. Also, a steady-lit green man on the crosswalk signal means it's safe, but when the green man flashes, do not begin crossing—it

means cars are about to gun it again.

Few places in London are unsafe. Neighborhoods that might be called sketchy are usually distant from the Tube lines, and they only feel tense after dark, when shops close. Simply be sensitive to who's around you and you'll do fine.

The biggest nuisance tourists might encounter—besides tipsy locals—is moped muggings. Each day, dozens of people are so absorbed in their smartphones that they don't notice the two-wheeled pickpockets zoom up, snatch their phone, and speed off. Simply be smart about how you use your phone and, of course, where you put your cash and what you leave sitting in the open.

London is always on the lookout for terrorists, and it has been since the days of IRA violence. Don't leave a bag unattended even for seconds or you may lose it.

Guns are banned in London—even on most police officers—so you don't often see the kind of violence taken for granted in the United States. Londoners cite knife crime as a problem, but the victims are almost always young men who themselves carry knives. Some male tourists have gotten fleeced at "hostess bars" in Soho. If you do suffer a lapse of judgment and accept the barker's invitation to go into one, understand that you might have cash exacted by

lunkheaded yobs with tattooed fingers.

Should you find yourself on the business end of the legal system, you can get advice and referrals to lawyers from **Legal Services Commission** (www.legalservices.gov.uk; 📞 **0300/200-2020**). Crime victims can receive volunteer legal guidance and emotional fortification from **Victim Support** (www.victimsupport.org.uk; 📞 **0808/168-9111**). In the event of a sexual assault, find help through the **Rape Crisis Federation** (www.rapecrisis.org.uk; rcewinfo@rapecrisis.org.uk; many caseworkers will only assist females).

Senior Travel Don't hide your age! Seniors in England—usually classified as those age 60 and over—are privy to all kinds of price breaks, from lower admission prices at museums to a third off rail tickets (to apply for the **Senior Railcard,** go to www.senior-railcard.co.uk). You may hear seniors referred to as OAPs, which stands for Old Age Pensioners, although that acronym is falling out of use—perhaps because it's rare to find a solvent pension fund anymore. Don't be offended if you're referred to as a "geezer"—in England, it's a compliment, meaning a fun-loving (if sometimes rowdy) bloke.

If you're over 50, you can join **AARP** (601 E St. NW, Washington, DC, 20049; www.aarp.org; 📞 **202/434-3525**) to wrangle discounts on hotels, airfare, and car rentals. Elderhostel's well-respected **Road Scholar** (www.roadscholar.org; ☏ **800/454-5768**) runs many classes and programs in London designed to delve into literature, history, the arts, and music. Packages last from a week to a month and include airfare, lodging, and meals.

Smoking Smoking is prohibited by law in any enclosed workplace, including museums, pubs, public transportation, and restaurants. If in doubt, ask permission.

Staying Fit PureGym (www.puregym.com) offers contract-free passes for 1 day, 3 days, or a week for as little as £12; it has facilities open 24 hr. in Piccadilly (Rex House, 4–12 Regent St., SW1; ☏ **845/835-6936;** Tube: Piccadilly Circus) and Holborn (Lacon House, 84 Theobalds Rd., WC1; ☏ **0845/835-6902;** Tube: Holborn). Additional locations are in Marylebone and Victoria, plus others.

Student Travel Have ID on hand, and always mention you're a student—it'll save you cash. Attractions gladly offer discounts of around 25 percent for full-time students. However, your high school or university ID may not cut it where clerks haven't heard of your school: Before leaving home, obtain a recognized ID such as the **International Student Identity Card** (ISIC; www.isic.org). Those 25 and under who are not in school can obtain an **International Youth Travel Card,** also through ISIC, which performs many of the same

tricks as a student discount card.

Before buying airline tickets, those 25 and under should consult a travel agency that specializes in the youth market and is versed in its available discounts: **STA Travel** (www.statravel.com; ☏ **800/781-4040**) is big.

Taxes Prices of all goods in the U.K. are quoted inclusive of taxes. Since 2011 the national value-added tax (**VAT**) has stood at 20 percent. This is included in all hotel and restaurant bills, and in the price of most items you purchase.

If you are permanently resident outside the E.U., VAT on goods can be refunded if you shop at stores that participate in the **Retail Export Scheme**—look for the window sticker or ask the staff. See p. 228 for details. Information about the scheme is also posted at www.hmrc.gov.uk/tax-on-shopping/taxfree-shopping.

Telephones When dialing a number in this book from abroad, precede it with your country's international prefix (in the U.S. and Canada, it's 011), add the U.K.'s country code (44) and drop the first zero in the number.

To make an **international call** from Britain, dial the international access code (**00**), then the country code, then the area code, and finally the local number. When calling from a mobile phone, dial the full number including area code.

Directory assistance is at www.bt.com or ☏ **118-500.** Local calls start with 020.

The main **toll-free** ("freephone") prefixes are 0800, 0808, and 0500. Numbers starting with 07 are usually for mobile phones and will be charged at a higher rate. Numbers starting with 09 are premium-rate calls that will usually be very expensive (around £1.50 per minute) and may not even work from abroad.

Many attractions, hotel companies, and services have changed their standard phone numbers to profit-generating ones that charge for every minute you call them. You often can't reach 0845, 0870, and 0871 numbers (charged at 10p a minute or less) from abroad, and when you can, you're charged more. Use the Web instead to get information.

The majority of London's **payphones** are gone. You can barely find a working one, let alone rely upon them.

Phonecards, though rarely used today, can be an economical method for both international and national calls. They are reusable until the total value has expired. Cards can be purchased from newsstands and post offices, and offer rates of a few pence per minute to most countries.

Hotels routinely add outrageous surcharges onto calls made from your room. Rather than dial directly using a hotel phone, use the Wi-Fi to make Internet calls.

Time London is generally 5 hours ahead of New York City and Toronto, 8 hours ahead of Los Angeles, 11 hours behind Auckland, and 9 hours behind Sydney. It is 1 hour behind western continental Europe. Greenwich Mean Time is London time.

Tipping **Waiters** should receive 10 to 15 percent of the bill unless service is already included—*always* check the menu or bill to see if service was already added. At **pubs**, tipping isn't customary unless you receive waiter service (not food drop-off). Fine **hotels** may levy a service charge, but at the finest ones, grease the staff with a pound here and there. Staff at B&Bs and family-run hotels don't expect tips. **Bartenders** and **chambermaids** need not be tipped. There's no need to tip **taxicab drivers** but most people round up to the next £1, although a 10 to 15 percent tip is becoming increasingly standard.

Toilets London doesn't have enough of them. Washrooms can be found at any free museum in this guide, any department store, any pub or busy restaurant (though it's polite to buy something), and at Piccadilly Circus and Bank Tube stations. Train stations may also have toilets; they're free at Charing Cross, Victoria, and London Bridge but may charge 50p elsewhere. On weekends, open-air *pissoirs* for men

are placed throughout the West End.

VAT See "Taxes," above.

Visas No E.U. nationals require a visa to visit the U.K. Visas are also not required for travelers from Australia, Canada, New Zealand, or the U.S. To be sure that hasn't changed, search "visa" at **www.gov.uk** long before your travel dates. The usual permitted stay is 90 days or fewer for tourists, although some nationalities are granted stays of up to 6 months. If you plan to work or study, though, or if you're traveling on a passport from another country, you'll need to obtain the correct paperwork.

Visitor Information Three official information units supported by British taxes are set up to help tourists, but only online: **Visit Britain** (www.visitbritain.com); **Visit England** (www.visitengland.com); and **Visit London** (www.visitlondon.com). Visit London possesses the biggest database and publishes a free app with offline maps called **London Official City Guide** and an app collecting upcoming happenings, **London Official Events Guide.** The only official information bureau with a public office is across the road from St Paul's Cathedral north of Millennium Bridge: The **City of London Information Centre** (St Paul's Churchyard; www.visitthecity.co.uk; ℂ 020/7332-1456) sells attraction tickets and Oyster

cards, runs tours, and supplies brochures and counsel for day trips throughout the country. It publishes walking tours, a free City Visitor Trail audio walking tour app, and children's discovery trail maps. Open hours are Monday to Saturday 9:30am to 5:30pm, Sunday 10am to 4pm.

Excellent independent sources for things to learn and things to do include **Londonist.com, London Calling.com, TimeOut.com/London, Townfish.com,** and the Twitter accounts Handpicked London (**@LDN**), **@LeCool_London,** and **@SkintLondon.**

Women Travelers First and foremost, lone women should avoid riding in **unlicensed London taxicabs,** especially at night. Flag down a black cab or call a minicab instead. The **Splitcab** app (www.splitcab.co.uk) allows women to find female-driven minicabs (and to share the cost with someone else going in the same direction). **Addison Lee** (www.addisonlee.com; ℂ **020/7407-9000**) has a huge, efficient fleet, and will text you the registration plate of your cab for added security. It has a free app for hailing rides.

A true club and not an agency, **Women Welcome Women Worldwide** (www.womenwelcomewomen.uk; ℂ **01494/46-54-41**) connects travelers worldwide and costs £37 a year to join, £27 a year to renew.

Index

See also Accommodations and
Restaurant indexes, below.

RESTAURANT INDEX

Map List

Photo Credits

Frommer's EasyGuide to London 2019, 6th Edition

Published by
FROMMER MEDIA LLC

ISBN 978-1-62887-422-8 (paper), 978-1-62887-423-5 (e-book)

Editorial Director: Pauline Frommer
Editor: David Low
Production Editor: Cheryl Lenser
Cartographer: Roberta Stockwell
Photo Editor: Meghan Lamb
Indexer: Cheryl Lenser
Cover Design: David Riedy

For information on our other products or services, see www.frommers.com.

Frommer Media LLC also publishes its books in a variety of electronic formats. Some content that appears in print may not be available in electronic formats.

Manufactured in the United States of America

5 4 3 2 1

ABOUT THE AUTHOR

Jason Cochran was twice awarded Guide Book of the Year by the Lowell Thomas Awards (Society of American Travel Writers) and once by the North American Travel Journalists Association. His voice has reached millions of travelers, from the mid-1990s, when he wrote one of the world's first travel blogs, to his familiarity as a commentator on CBS and for AOL, to his work today as editor-in-chief of Frommers.com and co-host of the Frommer's Travel Show on WABC. For this edition, he'd like to thank Martin Lowe, Joel Fram, Yhago Maia, Andre Beerman, Brian Fairbairn, Karl Eccleston, Hilary Bowsher, and Steve Bowsher.

ABOUT THE FROMMER TRAVEL GUIDES

For most of the past 50 years, Frommer's has been the leading series of travel guides in North America, accounting for as many as 24% of all guidebooks sold. I think I know why.

Though we hope our books are entertaining, we nevertheless deal with travel in a serious fashion. Our guidebooks have never looked on such journeys as a mere recreation, but as a far more important human function, a time of learning and introspection, an essential part of a civilized life. We stress the culture, lifestyle, history, and beliefs of the destinations we cover, and urge our readers to seek out people and new ideas as the chief rewards of travel.

We have never shied from controversy. We have, from the beginning, encouraged our authors to be intensely judgmental, critical—both pro and con—in their comments, and wholly independent. Our only clients are our readers, and we have triggered the ire of countless prominent sorts, from a tourist newspaper we called "practically worthless" (it unsuccessfully sued us) to the many rip-offs we've condemned.

And because we believe that travel should be available to everyone regardless of their incomes, we have always been cost-conscious at every level of expenditure. Though we have broadened our recommendations beyond the budget category, we insist that every lodging we include be sensibly priced. We use every form of media to assist our readers, and are particularly proud of our feisty daily website, the award-winning Frommers.com.

I have high hopes for the future of Frommer's. May these guidebooks, in all the years ahead, continue to reflect the joy of travel and the freedom that travel represents. May they always pursue a cost-conscious path, so that people of all incomes can enjoy the rewards of travel. And may they create, for both the traveler and the persons among whom we travel, a community of friends, where all human beings live in harmony and peace.

Arthur Frommer